Where to Watch Birds in

BEDFORDSHIRE, BERKSHIRE, BUCKINGHAMSHIRE, HERTFORDSHIRE & OXFORDSHIRE

Brian Clews, Andrew Heryet and Paul Trodd

CHRISTOPHER HELM
London

© 1987 Brian Clews, Andrew Heryet and Paul Trodd
Line drawings by Gary Claydon, Gavin Haig and Julian Smith
Christopher Helm (Publishers) Ltd, Imperial House
21–25 North Street, Bromley, Kent BR1 1SD

British Library Cataloguing in Publication Data

Clews, Brian
    Where to watch birds in Bedfordshire,
    Berkshire, Buckinghamshire, Hertfordshire
    and Oxfordshire.
    1. Bird watching—England—Midlands
    I. Title   II. Heryet, Andrew   III. Trodd,
    Paul
    598'.07'23445   QL690.G7

ISBN 0-7470-0401-3

The authors dedicate this book to the three ladies in our lives, without whose help, tolerance and understanding it may not have been produced. Hazel, Julie and Pat – thank you.

Printed and bound in Great Britain by
Biddles Ltd., Guildford and King's Lynn

CONTENTS

FOREWORD

The great modern increase in interest in birds is not confined to limited localities and certain seasons. As I wrote facetiously many years ago (in *Birdmanship*): 'No place is bad for birds, you know' – if observers are prepared to spend enough time waiting and watching. The counties covered by this book are not those which attract hordes of modern tally-hunters, now called twitchers, but all have excellent areas which repay regular visits at the seasons covered by the 'Calendar' entries. Most of them are very much affected by the activities of man and their best sites are often gravel pits and reservoirs.

The book has been carefully planned to suggest the places where up-to-date observations have yielded most results, and its primary use is to enable the reader, especially if a newcomer to the area, to build up a formidable list of species accurately observed. Having done this, one could try to settle to some particular piece of research which attracts, and for which the area is suitable. This will become meaningful if carried out with like-minded enthusiasts. Obvious projects are ringing, migration watches and studies of particular species, e.g. the area covered by this book contains several large Reed Warbler habitats which suggests that Cuckoo-watching may be profitable: there is still a great deal to be found out about this unique bird. The many urban areas in the counties covered by this book also suggest that winter feeding studies may be worth undertaking. But I suspect that the wetlands will prove irresistible to most readers and give them many hours of happy birdwatching.

Modern birdwatching, however, involves certain obligations: to get permission to visit private areas and to use such permission circumspectly, especially if a rarity turns up. The temptation to spread hot news is great, but the good name of what has become a great modern sport depends on keeping the rules.

Bruce Campbell

ACKNOWLEDGEMENTS

A work of this nature would be less complete but for the invaluable assistance of many people. In particular, the authors thank the many Wardens, Rangers and Park officials who aided our survey work. Numerous organisations have also been instrumental in our quest for details of sites, including all five County Councils, the County Recorders, the County Trusts, the RSPB, Forestry Commission and the Meteorological Office.

Of the many individuals who contributed, special thanks are due to Pat Burton for typing, Robin Dazley for a variety of support functions and to Bob Stockhausen for hours of proof reading and technical vetting.

Special thanks too go to Patricia Trodd for much typing and support for Paul (especially during a short but ill-timed spell of hospitalisation for him), to Julie Heryet, again for typing and moral support for Andrew, and to Hazel Poynter for extensive word processing instead of sunbathing.

The authors are also indebted to Mr Roger Wiggins for permission to use some of his research material.

The authors are particularly indebted to Dr Bruce Campbell for his valuable comments and advice, and for his Foreword to this book.

Illustrations

The authors are indebted to the three artists, Gary Claydon, Gavin Haig and Julian Smith for the line drawings created for this book. The drawings are distributed through the book at pertinent sites for each species, as listed below.

Ring Ouzels (*GC*)
Water Rail (*JS*)
Lady Amherst's Pheasants (*GC*)
Winter Thrushes (*GC*)
Kingfisher (*GH*)
Grey Partridge (*GH*)
Little Owl (*GC*)
Tree Pipit (*JS*)
Gull Roost (*JS*)
Smew (*JS*)
Lesser Spotted Woodpecker (*GC*)
Whitethroat (*GH*)
Sparrowhawk (*GC*)
Woodcock (*JS*)
Rook (*GH*)
Little Ringed Plover (*JS*)

Yellow Wagtail (*CH*)
Golden Plover (*CH*)
Wood Warbler (*JS*)
Hawfinch (*GC*)
Green Sandpipers (*GC*)
Common Tern (*GH*)
Willow Tit (*JS*)
Ruddy Duck (*GH*)
Wheatear (*GH*)
Grey Heron (*JS*)
Gadwall (*JS*)
Hen Harrier (*GH*)
Corn Bunting (*GC*)
Snipe (*JS*)
Skylark (*GC*)

INTRODUCTION

At first glance the five land-locked counties of Bedfordshire, Berkshire, Buckinghamshire, Hertfordshire and Oxfordshire would seem an unlikely area for birds. There are no moorlands or mountain ranges and no inviting estuaries, large tracts of wetland or seashore to attract birds. In addition the land area is subject to the pressures of increasing urbanisation brought about by industrial development, a rapidly growing population (already well over three million souls) and also by intensive agricultural practices. However, all is far from gloomy. The region is credited with some excellent ancient woodlands, fine river valleys with an array of habitats, some superb upland areas in the Chiltern Hills and Berkshire Downs, as well as many man-made lakes, reservoirs and pits. These features prove attractive to over 120 different species of breeding birds, and a similar number of species using the areas on passage or during the winter period. Birds are therefore very much a part of the region's life, giving any birdwatcher ample scope for pursuing this hobby.

In addition to the birds, the region also boasts a wealth of ornithological expertise. The British Trust for Ornithology (BTO) and the Bird Room of the Natural History Museum are both to be found at Tring, whilst at Oxford, the Alexander Library in the Edward Grey Institute for Field Ornithology is one of the finest collections of bird books in Britain. Europe's largest conservation organisation, the Royal Society for the Protection of Birds (RSPB) is based at Sandy in Bedfordshire and is responsible, among other things, for the management of over 100 nature reserves nationwide. At a more local level, there are many active RSPB member groups, whilst the younger birdwatcher is well catered for by The RSPBs junior section, The Young Ornithologists Club (YOC). All five counties have their Nature Conservation Trusts and many of their reserves are featured heavily in this book. The County Trusts really are the grass roots of local conservation, indeed without their valuable work much of the region's landscape and natural history heritage would have been lost. For a minimal membership fee, access is granted not only to regional reserves but also to most of the 1,300 nature reserves managed by the Trusts throughout Britain. Additionally the region has a large number of very active bird clubs and natural history societies with ornithological branches. These groups do much valuable work documenting the local avifauna, organising field trips and providing ample scope for learning and discussion. Today's birdwatchers are indeed fortunate in having this plethora of knowledge at their disposal. Do make full use of it, as this can only lead to a greater understanding and appreciation of the region's avifauna and habitats.

Habitat and Topography – some general points
While these five counties exhibit many similarities in the range of habitat, the composition of avifauna and the human influence, two geographical features common to each county influence the landscape and natural history most dramatically. Dominating the scene is the ridge of chalk running south-west to north-east. North of the Thames the chalk manifests itself in the Chiltern Hills and the steep, north-facing scarp,

overlooking the Vale of Aylesbury, contrasts markedly with the gentler dip slope that falls off gradually towards the lower and middle Thames Valley. Along the summit can be found remnants of the Beech forests of old (known locally as 'hangers'), productive feeding grounds for Brambling and Chaffinch during the winter. Where the tree cover is broken and the terrain too steep for the plough, some herb-rich pastures remain. These are the region's last surviving 'virgin' habitats and are most rewarding when grazed by sheep or rabbit, who crop the sward short, keeping the Hawthorn at bay. Skylark, pipits, buntings and Linnet haunt these sacred pastures and may be joined in winter by raptors such as Hen Harrier or Short-eared Owl. Where scrub has invaded the downland, warblers and finches breed in abundance and vast flocks of thrushes and Starlings swirl in to roost during the winter. Migration is also of note along the scarp, especially during the spring passage period.

South and west of the Thames, the Berkshire Downs, that also roll into neighbouring Oxfordshire, are different from the Chilterns in that they have far fewer Beech woods and an altogether much more open feel.

The second major influence upon the region is the River Thames and its many tributaries. Along these river valleys undisturbed wet meadows still exist, supporting an abundance of wildlife. The bank-side vegetation is often very lush and, with the feeding opportunities presented by the water, provide breeding sites for a wide range of species. Further feeding opportunities present themselves in the winter when flooding along parts of the river system is very much a feature of the region.

Along the valleys and elsewhere, marshes, reedswamp and water meadows are but a shadow of their former selves but still attract the typical riparian species. The more artificial water cress beds and sewage treatment works are readily exploited, providing ideal feeding grounds in the winter when all around is frozen over.

North of the Chilterns the surface geology is mainly one of clay with flints blending into limestone in the west. The scenery is dominated by 'prairies' of cereal and oil-seed rape with some hedgerow cover. Partridge and small numbers of summering Quail frequent these open plains. Avian interest is heightened where Oak woods are found and along river systems such as the Great Ouse that meanders across Buckinghamshire and Bedfordshire. A geographical feature that is scarce north of the Thames and can be found in the latter two counties is an outcrop of lower greensand. Heaths still survive along this predominantly conifer-clad ridge where a bird unique to the region, the Lady Amherst's Pheasant, finds safe refuge.

South and east of the Chilterns the picture is more varied as the ever-growing capital sprawls out into east Berkshire and Buckinghamshire and south Hertfordshire. Here reservoirs and refuse tips are both exploited by wintering wildfowl and gulls, along with the many flooded gravel pits along the valleys of the Colne, Lee and Thames. Further west the ancient hunting ground of Windsor Great Park is bordered to the south by fragmented Gorse-clad heaths. Woodland of the region varies from damp Oak/Hornbeam type in south-east Hertfordshire to dry coniferous woods in parts of Berkshire.

As can be seen, few parts of the region have escaped man's activities over the past 2,000 years. It is also true that there are now a greater variety of habitats than ever before, but the price to pay is the fragmentation of the classic bird-rich ecosystems such as ancient woodland and flood meadows. Ours is indeed an ever-changing landscape and it remains to be seen what the next 100 years has in store for the birdlife of Bedfordshire, Berkshire, Buckinghamshire, Hertfordshire and Oxfordshire.

County Recorders

Having visited a location, any records one has made can be very valuable in assessing the overall picture of birdlife in the region. Therefore, please pass on details of your sightings to the respective County Bird Recorder either immediately after your visit or at the end of each year. Records should ideally be presented in Voous classification order and accompanied, if possible, with a grid reference to facilitate easy processing. Indicate clearly any records which you feel should remain confidential and this will be respected.

Bedfordshire   Paul Trodd, 'White Garth', West Parade, Dunstable, Beds. LU6 1EN

Berkshire   Peter Standley, 'Siskins', 7, Llanvair Drive, South Ascot, Berks. SL5 9HS.

Buckinghamshire   John Marchant, 17, Church View, Long Marston, Tring, Herts. HP23 4QB.

Hertfordshire   Peter Walton, 'Twin Oaks', Rabley Heath, Welwyn, Herts. AL6 9UF.

Oxfordshire   John Brucker, 65, Yarnton Road, Kidlington, Oxford OX5 1AT.

Birdwatcher's Code of Conduct

1. The welfare of birds must come first.
2. Habitat must be protected.
3. Keep disturbance to birds and their habitat to a minimum.
4. When you find a rare bird think carefully about whom you should tell.
5. Do not harass rare migrants.
6. Abide by the bird protection laws at all times.
7. Respect the rights of landowners.
8. Respect the rights of other people in the countryside.
9. Make your records available to the local bird recorder.
10. Behave abroad as you would when birdwatching at home.

THE WEATHER

That weather affects the lives of birds probably needs not be stated and it is not within the scope of this book to consider the relationship between climate and the functioning of birds in any detail, as there is excellent reading available on this subject in books such as *Weather and Bird Behaviour* by Norman Elkins. However, it may be useful, in reviewing the weather pattern in the five counties concerned, to contemplate briefly why this aspect is so important to the success, or otherwise, of the resident and visiting species.

The two main day-to-day activities in a bird's life are eating and flying; indeed one is hardly possible without the other as birds need energy to fly and may well have to fly between food sources to achieve the necessary intake. The energy absorbed in flight is aggravated by such factors as wind and heat loss in rain or low temperatures. The availability of food, be it insects, grubs, seeds or vegetation, is governed by the amount of light, heat and moisture received by the food-bearing plants in the vicinity of the hungry bird. If extreme weather reduces the growth rate of plants or the cycle of insect productivity, many bird species come under pressure, with survival at stake. On the face of it, winters may be assumed to take more of a toll than bad summers, but that may not necessarily be the case. The third most important thing to any species after being able to move, and, therefore, to eat, is to procreate. Many species travel thousands of miles to summer in Britain in the hope of successful breeding, by which means their numbers may be significantly increased, to balance subsequent losses in any extreme winter encountered. In a good breeding season, such birds may produce typically eight to twelve young from each breeding pair.

Even allowing for the fact that not every summer visitor is mature enough to breed or achieves the finding of a mate (a point often overlooked by birdwatchers), the effect of a bad summer which reduces or even eradicates successful engendering can as much as halve the number of individuals which take off south again in autumn. On the other hand, provided the much hardier species which over-winter in Britain can find enough shelter and food for most of the time, they can withstand quite severe weather with possibly only a few per cent loss.

So, what of the weather in the area under consideration? Nationally, Britain's weather is normally warm and dry enough in summer to attract millions of breeding birds from the south, and warmer and drier in winter than many northern and eastern climes such that other species move in for Britannia's protection until spring. Being surrounded by the sea, which takes the chill off the air, contributes to this situation.

Inland locations are not subjected to tide-related sea breezes or the extremes of variability experienced on the coast. Geographical features such as the Thames Valley and the high ridges of the Chilterns and Downs, afford some protection from severe conditions but also create marginal differences in rain and cloud cover between such prominences and the area at large. Let us look at the various weather phenomena in turn. A recent period of five years has been assessed, and figures are shown in the appendix at the end of this chapter.

Appendix: *Weather conditions analysed over five years 1978 to 1982*

Annual Averages	Ave. Annual Rainfall mm	Ave. Daily Hours of Sun	Days of Frost	Highest Recorded Temp. °C	Ave. Highest Temp. °C	Lowest Recorded Temp. °C	Ave. Low Temp. °C
BEDS	736	3.91	70.6	29.7	28.2	−19.8	−12.4
BERKS	750	4.03	76.4	29.7	28.3	−18.5	−13.4
BUCKS	699	3.72	84.2	28.4	27.9	−21.2	−15.0
HERTS	748	3.93	64.8	29.4	28.6	−17.4	−11.9
OXON	753	4.02	68.4	30.4	28.8	−21.0	−14.8
AREA AVE.	737	3.92	73.0	29.5	28.3	−19.6	−13.5

Annual Averages	Days of Cloud			Days of Rain (0.2mm or more)	Days of Snow & Sleet	Days of Fog	Days of Hail	Days of Gales
	0 Oktas	Rest	8 Oktas					
BEDS	44	190	131	174	30	26	3	2
BERKS	51	194	120	180	23	26	4	4
BUCKS	49	198	118	159	23	15	3	1
HERTS	40	196	129	179	28	20	6	9
OXON	51	176	138	184	31	18	5	4
AREA AVE.	47	191	127	175	27	21	4	4

Rainfall

The region receives typically less than 50 per cent of the rain which falls in such areas as Wales and Ireland, and often only 25 per cent of that experienced in parts of Scotland. On the other hand, the five counties have been half-again as wet as Hampshire and Sussex over the last 30 years or so. August and September tend to be the wettest months and the average number of rainy days – over 0.01 in (0.2 mm) of rainfall in the day – has been around 175, with Oxon nearly always the wettest, with an average of 30 in (753 mm) per year, and Bucks the driest at 28 in (699 mm) per year. The highest rainfall recorded in a single day during the period assessed was 4 in (86 mm) in Beds on 14 August 1980. In terms of the extent of nest damage due to rain or high water levels therefore, the region seems to fare pretty well. On the other hand, a high proportion of passerine nest sites may be in the Chiltern woodlands and other such elevated sectors and it is a fact that rainfall is often significantly greater in higher areas than lower ones.

Sunshine

The mean number of hours of daily sun in the area is approximately 3.9 with Berks sunniest at 4.03 and Bucks the least so at 3.72. There is, needless to say, much seasonal variability as within any area of measurement, but generally durations of sunshine are high in the region, second only to the extreme south coast. Of course, extreme periods of sunny and dry weather can lead to drought and when such conditions pertained in 1976, the worst on record, much habitat was lost and huge numbers of birds died. It took some while before many of the species recovered. Some, such as the Dartford Warbler, possibly never will and the effects of that drought are still being felt in the region as evidenced by the large number of Beech and other trees which became split and are now falling.

Temperature

It has been suggested that temperatures in the atmosphere around the planet are rising due to an increase of carbon dioxide. There is nothing to suggest that the assessed region is affected by this situation any more or less than others. As a hilly region, the valleys will be colder than the hill-tops and, as a well populated area, temperatures in towns and cities may be as much as 0.5°C to 1°C higher than in the surrounding countryside. The highest temperature recorded in the region in the five years studied was 30.4°C in Oxfordshire, whilst the coldest was −21.2°C in Buckinghamshire. The county with the highest average warmth was also Oxon (28.8°C) with Bucks lowest at 28.9°C. The coldest county also was Bucks, averaging −15.1°C of lowest recorded temperatures over the period.

Wind

The region as a whole is much less windy than coastal areas and the prevailing wind is west or south-westerly with 47 per cent of the days in the year swept from this direction. The most normal wind speed is between 5 and 20 knots with, on average, 43 days per year of calm conditions. Oxon has more calm days than the other four counties. Damage to trees and nest sites occurs at windspeeds usually in excess of 30 knots, and there are only around three or four days in the average year that this transpires. Again this seems more likely in Oxon. Winds from the north tend to exist on around 40 days in the year, usually at less than 15 knots. Of course, it is the exception to the rule that brings in the rarities, especially during the two migration periods and Bedfordshire seems to experience more hours of wind above 30 knots than the other four counties, especially in October when 40 to 70 hours is typical. Oxfordshire seems to fare less well in this regard.

Cloud

Cloud cover is not a factor that affects birds particularly which is just as well because there are typically 130 days per year of full cloud cover (8 oktas) and only 45 clear days per annum on average. Oxon and Berks are marginally less cloudy than the other three counties.

Visibility

Again, other than during migration, visibility is not a major consideration for birds, only perhaps for birdwatchers. Visibility is generally lower in the five counties than it is in the north of England. This may seem surprising given the preponderance of industry in the north but then the effects of the Clean Air Act have probably been more noticeable in industrial regions than residential ones and, in any event, the prevailing winds referred to above possibly move industrial pollution still further north whilst blowing Europe's spent materials over the southern half of Britain. There are typically 200 days in the year when visibility is 13 miles (20 km) or more and 10 days when a gloomy 0.63 miles (1 km) or less is imposed. Generally, Oxon has the clearer air with Beds the most grimy.

Frost

Of all Britain's weather states, frost is potentially the most damaging to over-wintering birds and early spring breeders. Prolonged sub-zero temperatures can cause even the largest bodies of water to freeze over and push the energy requirements of birds to the limits and, regrettably, beyond. A sharp frost following rain can result in roosting birds becoming frozen to their perches and, if accompanied by snow, can prevent birds obtaining their own weight in food per day, as is necessary to survive.

On average the region suffers frost on 73 days in each year, with Bucks the most unfortunate at 84.2 days per annum. Herts is comparatively tropical, with 64.8 days in which frost is recorded.

Other Conditions

There are other weather features which occur, some of which affect birdlife more than others. For example, thunder is noted only on some 15 to 20 days of the average year and hail on 7 or 8. Snow and sleet on the other hand occurs, on average, 29.3 days of the year which is generally less than in many other regions but, if continuous for several days, can be nonetheless deadly to the winter species.

Summary

In general, therefore, it can be seen that the five counties covered by this book do not suffer the extremes or variabilities of many other parts of Britain. The more subtle effects, such as the vast reduction in hedgerow and woodland cover as protection against cold and wind may have been more noticeable in this rapidly developing part of Britain than elsewhere. On the other hand the dramatically increased number of inland waters in the area has doubtless contributed to improving shelter for seabirds forced inland during extreme coastal conditions. Of course, a five year period is a very small sample from which to draw many conclusions or to extrapolate any trends. In overall terms, the assessed period was relatively stable for the majority of weather phenomena, but there has perhaps been a tendency towards more extreme records in recent years, e.g. the wettest April, the windiest May, the coldest June and so on. However, during that period all five counties have experienced increases to the number of species recorded and so one may conclude that birds in the region have not suffered overly at the hands of the fascinating vagaries of the British climate.

HOW TO USE THIS BOOK

THE REGION

The region under discussion in this book consists of the counties of Bedfordshire, Berkshire, Buckinghamshire, Hertfordshire and Oxfordshire. Each of the five counties is discussed separately, in alphabetical order, as a complete section.

Each county is preceded with a county map with the relevant main sites plotted to give the reader a rough idea where the sites are in relation to main towns. Each main site has its own map in the map section and, in addition, a six figure grid reference for use in conjunction with the Ordnance Survey 1:50,000 series of maps. Main sites are described in alphabetical order; where further sites are discussed within a main site (for example, Colne Valley) subsidiary headings and maps are used to indicate the division.

At the end of each county section, additional sites are listed and grid references given. These are briefer accounts of how to get to them and what to expect when there.

Measurements
Road distances throughout are given in miles, with the kilometre conversion afterwards in parentheses; all other measurements in the book are stated in imperial first with metric in parentheses second. Conversions are approximate.

Habitat
A brief account of each main site's general features, habitats and topography, along with its size and status, if any (for example, Site of Special Scientific Interest (SSSI), Local Nature Reserve (LNR), etc.) is given. It may include a note of the other forms of wildlife present. Even the most blinkered birdwatcher would find it hard to ignore a riot of colourful wildflowers and their related butterflies in summer at certain Downland sites.

Access
Directions are given from the nearest main road, directing the reader to the relevant car park, lay-by or view-point. These directions should be used in conjunction with the related site map. The Ordnance Survey six figure grid reference used throughout will help the reader to pinpoint the site. (For anybody unsure of how to read these references, a simple guide is given on the inside back cover of any of the Ordnance Survey 1:50,000 series of maps.)

Details of the facilities that exist at the site are outlined as well as details of where to apply for information or, if necessary, a permit. (For further information see also the Useful Addresses section of this book.)

Railway stations are also mentioned if they are within reasonable walking distance of the site discussed.

Unless otherwise stated, it is important that birdwatchers remain on the permitted rights of way and also observe the Code of Conduct at all times. Failure to do so may jeopardise the opportunities that exist.

The best time of day to visit is included, and relates mainly to activities of the general public when they conflict with that of the birdwatcher. Generally speaking, the peak hours of bird activity are at dawn and dusk, although this is less applicable, for example, during the winter at a reservoir or gravel pit.

Species

This forms the main section of each site, where species most likely to be seen throughout a typical year are discussed in detail. A note or two may mention any past rarities that have occurred or what could be seen if observer coverage were to be intensified. Approximate numbers of birds are quoted as an average over the 5-year period from 1980 to 1985.

Birds however are fickle creatures, subject to the vagaries of weather, disturbance and habitat change; for these reasons a site that one year harbours a particular species may not be as good in subsequent years.

Calendar

This section forms a summary of events from the species account, allowing the reader a succinct point of reference as to what season or month a particular species can be expected. Some degree of overlap may occur at certain times of the year, as some species linger into the subsequent period.

THE SITES

The choice of sites for inclusion in this book was drawn up following discussion with many local birdwatchers, as well as the various conservation bodies active in the region since it was necessary to exclude any sites sensitive to additional disturbance by birders. Allowing for these criteria, the authors hope that in the course of their research, coupled with many years of local experience, that the information presented is accurate and that no glaring omissions have been made. Should any errors be noted, the authors would be pleased to hear of them.

Similarly, the authors would be pleased to hear from any observers who consider a site worthy of inclusion in future editions, bearing in mind the basic criteria already mentioned. Please address any correspondence to the publishers, Christopher Helm Publishers Limited, Imperial House, 21–25 North Street, Bromley, Kent BR1 1SD. Mark for the attention of Brian Clews (Berks & Bucks); Andrew Heryet (Oxon); and Paul Trodd (Beds & Herts).

GLOSSARY OF TERMS

In writing this book, the authors have attempted to minimise the use of technical terms but several have been utilised. The general meaning of these words or phrases is explained below. Several abbreviations are also expanded.

BBONT	Berkshire, Buckinghamshire & Oxfordshire Naturalists' Trust
BHWT	Bedfordshire & Huntingdonshire Wildlife Trust
Carr (or Carse)	Waterside scrub
Crepuscular	More likely found at dusk or perhaps dawn
Corvid	A member of the crow family (usually referring to Carrion Crow, Rook or Jackdaw)
Diurnal	Active during daylight (e.g. Little Owl)
Dabbling Duck	Surface feeding technique (e.g. Mallard)
Diving Duck	Species that feed on underwater vegetation or creatures (e.g. Tufted Duck)
Escarpment	Steep face of a ridge or plateau
FC	Forestry Commission
Fall	Arrival of large numbers of birds on migration, usually occasioned by weather conditions preventing onward progress
Feral	An introduced species (e.g. Canada Goose)
HMTNC	Hertfordshire & Middlesex Trust for Nature Conservation
Hirundine	One of the martins or the Swallow
Leaf Warbler	More correctly, Phylloscopus warblers (including such species as Willow Warbler, Chiffchaff and Wood Warbler)
NCC	Nature Conservancy Council
Nocturnal	Active during the hours of darkness
Passage	Referring to a bird on migration which may visit a location during its journey.
Passerine	A term used to describe any small bird encountered on land (as against seabirds, etc.)
Pelagic	A bird of the open sea
Phylloscopus	'Correct' term for Leaf Warbler (see above)
Raptor	Birds of prey which hunt in daylight (e.g. Kestrel or Sparrowhawk, but not including owls)
Redhead (or occasionally Brownhead)	Referring to female or juvenile Goosanders, Red-breasted Mergansers, Smew and Goldeneye
Reeling	A bird song resembling a fishing reel winding (e.g. Grasshopper Warbler)
Ringtail	Female or juvenile harriers (Hen or Montagu's)
Riparian	Inhabitant of river banks
'Roding'	Boundary territorial flight of Woodcock
RSPB	Royal Society for the Protection of Birds

RSPCA	Royal Society for the Prevention of Cruelty to Animals
Sawbill	Member of the family including Goosander, Red-breasted Merganser and Smew
SSSI	Site of Special Scientific Interest
Sylvia Warbler	Warblers of bushes and scrub (e.g. Whitethroat, Garden Warbler, Blackcap and Dartford Warbler)
TAVR	Territorial Army Volunteer Reserve
Thermal	A column of rising air caused by unequal heating of the land
Wader	Birds of estuaries, mud-flats and wet meadows, usually long-legged and long-billed (e.g. Redshank, Curlew)
Wild Swans/Geese	As against feral species, and excluding Mute Swan (e.g. Whooper Swan, Brent Geese)
Winter Thrushes	Fieldfares and Redwings, but also Mistle or Song Thrushes when flocked in winter.
Wreck	A fall of exhausted birds, due to exceptional storms. Occasionally results in arrivals of petrels and auks well inland

USEFUL ADDRESSES

National Associations

British Trust for Ornithology
Beech Grove
Tring, Hertfordshire
HP23 5NR

Forestry Commission (FC)
(Regional Office)
Upper Icknield Way, Aston Clinton
Aylesbury, Buckinghamshire
HP22 5NF

International Council for Bird
Preservation
219c Huntingdon Road
Cambridge, Cambridgeshire
CB3 0DL

Nature Conservancy Council (NCC)
Foxhold House, Crookham Common
Newbury, Berkshire
RG15 8EL

National Trust (NT)
(Regional Office)
Hughenden Manor
High Wycombe, Buckinghamshire
HP14 4LA

Ramblers Association
1/5 Wandsworth Road
London
SW8 2LJ

Royal Society for the Protection of
Birds (RSPB)
The Lodge
Sandy, Bedfordshire
SG19 2DL

County Associations
Bedfordshire

Bedfordshire & Huntingdon-
shire Wildlife Trust (BHWT)
Priory Country Park
Barkers Lane, Bedfordshire

Bedfordshire Natural History Society
Mr D. Kramer, Secretary
7 Little Head Lands
Putnoe, Bedfordshire
MK41 8JT

The Warden
Warden's Lodge, Priory Country Park
Barkers Lane, Bedfordshire

(There are RSPB groups at Bedford,
East Beds., and South Beds.)

Berkshire

Middle Thames Natural History Society
R.G. Peel
Framewood Lodge, Stoke Poges
Slough, Berkshire
SL2 4QR

Newbury District Ornithological Club
Mrs M. Tucker
Wood Close, Upper Woolhampton
Reading, Berkshire
RG7 5TG

(There are RSPB groups at East Berks.,
West Forest and Reading)

Thames Water Authority
The Amenity and Recreation Officer
Nugent House, Vastern Road
Reading, Berkshire
RG1 8DB

Buckinghamshire

Amersham and District Ornithological
Society
Mrs Joy Danter
Coniston, 141 The Drive
Rickmansworth, Buckinghamshire
WD3 4DJ

Buckinghamshire Bird Club
Jim Knight
319 Bath Road, Cippenham
Slough, Buckinghamshire
SL1 5PR

Chilterns Society
60 The Row, Lane End
High Wycombe, Buckinghamshire
HP14 3JR

Milton Keynes Natural History Society
Bradwell Field Centre, Old Bradwell
Milton Keynes

(There are RSPB groups at Aylesbury
and North Bucks.)

Hertfordshire

Cheshunt Natural History Society
Mrs J. Crew
26 St David's Drive
Broxbourne, Hertfordshire
EN10 7LS

Hertfordshire & Middlesex Trust for
Nature Conservation
Col P.E. Gerahty
Grebe House, St Michael's Street
St Albans, Hertfordshire
AL3 4SN

Hertfordshire Natural History Society
J. Melling
9 Devonshire Close
Stevenage, Hertfordshire
SG2 8RY

Lee Valley Park Authority
Myddletton House, Bulls Cross
Enfield, Middlesex
EN2 9HG

(There are RSPB groups at Hemel
Hempstead, Chorleywood,
Harpenden, Hertford, Hitchen/
Letchworth, Potters Bar, St Albans,
South-East Herts., Watford and
Welwyn Garden City.)

Welwyn and Hatfield District Council
The Campus
Welwyn Garden City
Hertfordshire

Oxfordshire

Amey Roadstone Corporation (ARC)
(Regional Office)
Dix Pit Complex, Stanton Harcourt
Oxfordshire

Banbury Ornithological Society
25 Main Road, Middleton Cheney
Banbury, Oxfordshire
OX17 2ND

Reading Ornithological Club
Mr T. Hasdell
18 Harcourt Close
Henley-on-Thames, Oxfordshire
RG9 1UZ

Berkshire, Buckinghamshire &
Oxfordshire Naturalists' Trust
(BBONT)
3 Church Cowley Road, Rose Hill
Oxford
OX4 3JR

Farmoor Reservoir
The Senior Warden
Farmoor
Oxford
OX2 9NS

Oxford Ornithological Society
Edward Grey Institute, Department of
Zoology
South Parks Road
Oxford
OX1 3PS

(There are RSPB groups at Oxford,
Henley and Vale of White Horse)

Bird and Wildlife Hospitals

Banbury Bird Hospital
Cliff and Joyce Christie
25 Main Road, Middleton Cheney, Nr
Banbury
Oxfordshire
OX17 2ND
(Telephone 0295-710665)

Berkshire Wildlife Rehabilitation Unit
Clive and June Palmer
8 Mill Lane
Padworth, Berkshire
RG7 4JU
(Telephone 0734-712781)

Bradwell Common Wildbird Hospital
Mr and Mrs V. Seaton
150 Bradwell Common Boulevard
Milton Keynes, Northamptonshire
MK13 8BE
(Telephone 0908-604198)

Newbury Wildlife Hospital
Louise and Yvonne Veness
The Cemetery Lodge
Newbury, Berkshire
RG14 7BU
(Telephone 0635-45009)

Royal Society for Prevention of Cruelty
to Animals (RSPCA)
Southridge Animal Centre
Packhorse Lane Ridge
Potters Bar, Hertfordshire
EN6 3LZ
(Telephone 0707-42153)

Wildlife Hospital Trust
Sue and Les Stocker
1 Pemberton Close
Aylesbury, Buckinghamshire
HP21 7NY
(Telephone 0296-29860)

Permits

Angling Manager
Leisure Sports Angling
Thorpe Park
Staines Road
Chertsey
Surrey
KT16 8PN

Summerleaze Gravel Co. Ltd
25 Ray Mill Road East
Maidenhead, Berkshire
SL6 829

BEDFORDSHIRE

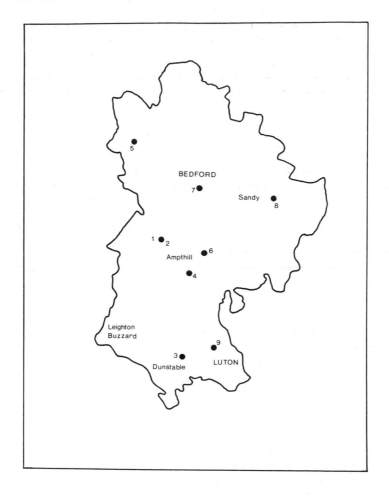

BEDFORD CLAY PITS & STEWARTBY LAKE

Maps 1 & 2/OS ref. TL 005 425

To the south of Bedford lies a series of pits, some worked some exhausted, formed by the excavation of Oxford clay by the London Brick Company. Together, these pits constitute the largest area of open water in the county and are of particular importance to wintering wildfowl.

Stewartby Lake is the largest of these flooded pits. As befits its status as a Country Park and its subsequent ease of access, it is treated as a main site. The remaining pits are discussed later in this section.

STEWARTBY LAKE

Habitat

Stewartby Lake itself covers 287 acres (116 ha) and the Country Park site 318 acres (128 ha). The water area is sub-leased to the Stewartby Water Sports Club by the county council and during the summer much disturbance takes place, with anything from water-skiers to power-boats careering across the lake. It is for this reason that an early morning visit is advisable, especially in April when migration is at its peak.

Initially brackish, the water has taken many years to establish an aquatic vegetation and in places is very deep. The margins vary from brick rubble in the north to marshy shallows in the south. A steep, wooded bank separates the lake from a small stream along the western edge and opposite an open grassy area leads down to a concrete slipway, providing somewhere for passage waders to stop-off. The man-made hillocks to the south are vegetated with rough grass, sedge and some scrub.

Access

Equidistant between Bedford and junction 13 of the M1 motorway, the lake is located 1 mile (1.5 km) north-east of the village of Marston Moretaine just off the A5140. A site car park is under construction but parking can be found in a lay-by on the main road; access is opposite, via a footbridge crossing the stream. Alternatively take the Stewartby road which runs along the northern boundary of the lake, parking near the entrance to the car breaker's yard, or travel further along the lane until arriving at the entrance to the Water Sports Club. Park in the pull-in just before and check the grass for waders and passerines, especially in the spring and autumn. A circular walk is marked out allowing access over the whole site.

Species

For most of the year Stewartby Lake seems incredibly mundane, with just the ubiquitous Coot breaking the monotony of the stark man-made landscape. Nevertheless some of the best birdwatching in the county can be experienced here, given the correct weather conditions.

When winter strikes with a vengeance, icing over the surrounding brick pits, Stewartby stays comparatively ice-free attracting a wide cross-section of wildfowl, sometimes in large numbers. Consequently during January or February if a cold spell is forecast be prepared for almost anything. Black-throated Diver have been recorded in these circumstances but are exceptionally rare. Great Crested Grebe numbers, usually about 30, rise to well over 100 with a chance of the scarce Red-necked Grebe in their midst. At times staying close to the bank on the south side, much persistent scanning is required to pick them out. Among the smaller grebes Dabchick can be seen all year, their numbers peaking into double figures during the winter, with a couple of pairs breeding amongst the small patches of reeds. Black-necked Grebe are very rare visitors, whether seen in winter or on autumn passage.

A flock of 100-plus Canada Geese frequent the fields toward Marston Moretaine; included in their ranks are the usual assortment of Barnacle and Greylag, most of dubious origin. A small herd of Bewick's Swan, dispersed from the Ouse Washes, sometimes delights the lucky watcher, but rarely stay more than a few hours. Cormorant seem to find the fishing much to their liking and can often be seen perched atop one of the many buoys drying their wings.

The commonest duck are Mallard, Tufted Duck and Pochard with small numbers of Teal and Gadwall scattered amongst them. During cold spells a noisy flock of whistling Wigeon can be expected commuting between the lake and nearby fields to graze. A flight of Pintail may come and go, the drakes resplendent in their breeding plumage and a few Ruddy Duck may be on show. Keeping well out in the middle sawbills arrive with Goosander sometimes numbering 20 to 30, the occasional party of Smew, mostly redheads, and rarer still Red-breasted Merganser. Goldeneye are present sporadically throughout the winter months but never in large numbers. Another duck frequently noted towards the end of the season is the Shelduck, usually found in pairs.

As dusk approaches a large gull roost assembles as birds return from a day spent foraging on nearby refuse tips. It consists mainly of Black-headed Gulls, with correspondingly lower numbers of the other common species; a wary eye should be kept open for the increasingly noted white-winged Glaucous Gull.

The scrub alongside the stream invariably attracts a few Goldcrest mingled in with the hyperactive tits. In the taller Alders, Siskin may appear, along with Redpoll. Where the path turns to lead out across the hillocks, a marshy patch sometimes holds a Water Rail. The rank tussocky growth has attracted Short-eared Owl on occasions to hunt voles, but a hovering Kestrel is more likely. Sparrowhawk are resident and are often encountered hunting near the stream, which is also good for Kingfisher as the steep banks provide ideal nest sites in the spring.

The first signs of spring are Chiffchaff calling energetically from the bushes along the lane, with Willow Warbler a little while later during the first week of April. The short turf near the Water Sports Club is perfect for a Wheatear and even more attractive to Yellow Wagtail. Counts of 50 have been made from the nearby lay-by in mid-April, as well as large numbers of Meadow Pipit and Pied Wagtail. Continental sub-species and races of Wagtail sometimes occur with Blue-headed and White Wagtail most likely to be found by the more diligent observer. The grassy bank and along to the jetty are the only areas suitable for passage waders and are best checked out as early as possible as disturbance is a problem later in the morning. Redshank are early arrivals from March onwards, noisily proclaiming their presence from any vantage point. Lapwing and Snipe are more sedate as they busily probe the wetter patches. Little Ringed Plover are regular in April with much bobbing and swaying to each other, signifying their courtship ritual is well under way. Careful scrutiny through a telescope will eliminate mistaking them for the similar Ringed Plover, who also pass through at this time of year.

Dunlin and Common Sandpiper are other regular visitors, the latter showing a preference for the brick rubble banks. Waders scarce to the county putting in an appearance have included Oystercatcher, Ruff, Sanderling, Whimbrel and Bar-tailed Godwit, but these really are the exceptions to the rule.

Out on the lake hirundines arrive; a trickle at first, building up to several hundred by the end of April, by which time the first Swift can be expected. Sadly over recent years Sand Martin have declined dramatically as a consequence of the Sahel drought. Common Scoter migrating across central England stop off briefly, always staying well out in the middle of the lake. Both passage periods seem to yield several small parties of these black sea-duck.

The end of April to the beginning of May is the best time of year for variety at Stewartby Lake. The chance to see quality waders is then at its peak, summer passerines arrive and, most exciting of all to the inland birdwatcher, now is the time of arrival of terns, sometimes in exceptionally high numbers. Common Tern are the most abundant, wheeling noisily overhead and plunge diving for small fish. The closely related Arctic Tern can also be expected en route to their northern breeding grounds; having wintered in the South Atlantic they make the longest migration trek of any bird. The stunningly elegant Black Tern can be seen over the lake in groups of up to 10, especially during periods of heavy rain. Unfortunately they do not stay for long, usually a couple of hours, before towering away out of sight. A scattering of Little Gull completes the spring seabird movement as the tempo relaxes with the approach of summer.

Scrub warblers busily rear their young amongst the thickets on the western perimeter, with Sedge and the odd Reed Warbler along the southern margin. Turtle and Collared Dove coo monotonously from the telephone wires along the lane and Cuckoo patrol overhead.

The autumn passage is less dynamic, with similar species to those in spring but in drabber, non-breeding plumages. Gale force westerlies during September is the time of year for an inland seabird 'wreck', with an outside chance of Leach's Petrel. If winds persist through the season the likelihood of a skua appearing increases and with it much debate as to its identity if it is a juvenile.

The only national rarity to have graced Stewartby was a White-winged Black Tern in August 1983.

Calendar

Resident Grey Heron, Dabchick, Great Crested Grebe, Mute Swan, Canada Goose, Mallard, Sparrowhawk, Kestrel, Moorhen, Coot, Collared Dove, Kingfisher, common tits and finches.

December–February Common grebes increase, chance of rare grebes, Cormorant, wild swans rarely, Wigeon scarce, Gadwall, Teal, Pintail occasional, Shoveler, Pochard, Tufted Duck, Goldeneye and sawbills sporadic, Ruddy Duck rare, gull roost, chance of Glaucous, Short-eared

Owl, Grey Wagtail, Goldcrest, Siskin, buntings and Water Rail.

March–May Shelduck March, Common Scoter, Hobby occasional, Little Ringed and Ringed Plover, Lapwing, Redshank, Snipe, Dunlin, Common Sandpiper, chance of rare waders, Little Gull, Common, Arctic and Black Tern, Turtle Dove, Cuckoo, Swift, hirundines, Yellow Wagtail, Meadow Pipit, Wheatear, common warblers.

June–July Waders return in July, otherwise quiet.

August–November Waders, terns, scoter, Meadow Pipit, Grey Wagtail in November, hirundines mass in September.

BEDFORD CLAY PITS

We now turn to the other pits which, with Stewartby Lake, form the site generally known as Bedford Clay Pits.

Access to the pits is often restricted. Most, however, can be viewed from nearby roads or existing footpaths.

Elstow Clay Pits (Map 2/OS ref. TL 045 456)
Situated 1 mile (1.5 km) south-west of Elstow and the proposed site for the dumping of low-level nuclear waste. A series of small pits and rough grassland with a large refuse tip that attracts many gulls during the winter; check thoroughly as Glaucous have been noted. A road at the southern end, west of the A6, affords views across the lake that usually holds small numbers of wintering duck.

Chimney Corner (Map 2/OS ref. TL 037 443)
A large irregular-shaped lake lying just north of Kempston Hardwick with a series of smaller shallow ones further north. The latter attract passage waders to the muddy edges and can be viewed from the lay-by west of the A418. A fishermans' car park on the south side provides a vantage point from which to scan the larger lake for wildfowl.

Vicarage Farm (Map 2/OS ref. TL 015 435)
Partially infilled but with some attractive habitat to the north for breeding waders, e.g. Redshank and Lapwing. No access but gateways give restricted viewing from the A5140 and the lanes running along the north and south perimeters.

Rookery Pit (Map 2/OS ref. TL 018 418)
Strictly private as it is still being worked. A footpath running parallel with the railway line to the west gives distant yet tantalising glimpses over parts of this huge site. Waders on passage with potential for the future.

Millbrook Pillinge (Map 2/OS ref. TL 006 413)
A small pit with an overlooking hide (suitable for wheelchairs) surrounding scrub and a small Poplar wood. Accessible only to members of the Bedfordshire & Huntingdonshire Wildlife Trust (BHWT) who should stay strictly on the footpath from Millbrook Station as shooting rights are let in the season. Good for common duck and the occasional oddity, usually disturbed from nearby Stewartby, such as

grebes or sawbills. Also Brambling and Tree Sparrow at Pheasant feeding stations during the winter.

Lidlington Pit (Map 2/OS ref. TL 000 401)

A tiny pit with small numbers of winter duck and Coot, will probably be infilled in the near future. View from lay-by.

Brogborough No. 1 (Map 2/OS ref. SP 978 395)

Roughly the same size as Stewartby but not as accessible. In winter large numbers of Pochard (about 500), Tufted Duck and Coot are present with sporadic visits by sawbills, rare grebes and the rarer diving ducks; e.g. Red-crested Pochard. Passage periods are good with terns, hirundines and Common Scoter. View from surrounding lay-bys.

Brogborough No. 2 (Map 2/OS ref. SP 968 400)

Scan from the bridge approaching North Common Farm for gulls and corvids on the refuse tip in winter; Glaucous appear fairly regularly. Some passage waders occur further north towards Marston Thrift.

BLOWS DOWNS   **Map 3/OS ref. TL 033 215**

Habitat

Sandwiched between Dunstable to the west and the M1 motorway to the east lies a 1.5 mile (2.5 km) long escarpment slope of the Chilterns known locally as Blows Downs. A maximum elevation of just under 650 ft (200 m) is attained, making this site one of the highest in the county. As its name implies, it is a windy area and the early morning observer is advised to wear warm windproof clothing. Some classic open downland still remains due to the combined grazing of rabbit and cattle. Contrasting with the short turf are several areas of mixed Hawthorn, Blackthorn and Elder scrub, a plantation of assorted deciduous and coniferous trees and a stand of mature Beech bordering the railway line to the north-east. A disused chalk quarry is of particular importance, along with the paddocks to the north-west.

Hare, Fox, Muntjac, Stoat and Badger are all resident and Slow Worm can often be encountered on warm summer days basking in the sheltered quarry bottom. The usual variety of plants typical of calcareous soil and their associated butterflies are found here too, especially along the steeper slopes.

Access

Turn off the M1 at junction 11 and take the A505 west toward Dunstable. At the first roundabout, turn left up Skimpot Road and park in the Ladbrokes Casino car park. Walk up to the railway line following a track under the bridge over a stile and onto the downs. If visiting early in the morning follow the barbed wire fence beside the cowshed to the top of the hill and then walk west. This way the sun is behind you and you are looking down at the birds. Keep to the top track, checking the scrub and downland regularly. When approaching the quarry creep up behind a clump of Hawthorn near the edge and peer over. Carry on until you clear the scrub and then head south-east to the plantations. Backtrack following the electricity grid lines toward the paddocks in the north-west. A footpath running parallel with the railway line will eventually bring you back to the bridge.

An alternative access point is from the A5, driving south from Dunstable town centre for 0.6 miles (1 km) and turning left up Halfmoon Lane. Park at the end of the road and continue on foot. For the plantations, take the Caddington Road east off the A5 and park by a gate half-way up the hill.

Public access is virtually unlimited across Blows Downs as it is designated common-land. All the migrants turn up here, so there is no need to venture into the private woods belonging to Zouches Farm.

Species

Although primarily a spring migration view-point, Blows Downs presents something of interest throughout the year. The most exciting period is the spring passage with Ring Ouzel and Black Redstart regularly appearing and, with increasing observer coverage, who knows what might turn up in the future!

In the winter months mixed flocks of Yellowhammer and Corn Bunting are found feeding amongst the straw around the cattle and horse sheds. A thorough search can often be rewarded with an odd Reed Bunting. The Beech stand in the north-east attracts large flocks of Chaffinch in hard weather to feed on the mast, along with small numbers of Brambling. Flocks of mixed tits, including Long-tailed, Marsh and Coal, forage ceaselessly amongst the scrub at this time of year, in a desperate effort to maintain their frail body weight. The most impressive spectacle of the year is in the winter of a common bird, the Starling, but nevertheless is well worth witnessing. About an hour before sunset they begin arriving, forming sub-roosts on the roof tops, television aerials and trees along the main A505 Luton to Dunstable road and adjacent side roads. Then in one huge swirling, garrulous mass they fly the short distance to the Hawthorn scrub on the downs and noisily roost up for the night. Other common species take advantage of this with House Sparrow, Collared Dove and thrushes roosting on the periphery. Sparrowhawk are occasionally noted taking any unwary bird.

Owls are reported intermittently from this site and no doubt a lucky watcher will one day find a roost of Long-eared Owl lurking amongst the Hawthorn.

Spring passage begins at the end of March with the arrival of Wheatear on the open downs and paddocks, their numbers building up in most years to over 30 by early April. However, they do not stay long, moving on quickly on clear nights. Black Redstart are next to arrive, occurring almost anywhere along the ridge until the end of April, with a special preference for the paddocks. Watch out for them on the barbed wire as they flick down to feed, exposing a shimmering orange tail. If a high pressure weather system predominates over Europe in early April, a fall of passerines can be expected with Blackcap, Chiffchaff and Willow Warbler leading the way. Stonechat are occasionally noted in the paddocks or along the fence bordering the railway line.

Throughout April, Ring Ouzel can be encountered anywhere along the ridge, the best spot consistently being the quarry. A word of warning should be mentioned here: do not enter the quarry from below! Instead approach stealthily from above (one regular birder even crawls the last five metres to the cliff edge) and the reward can be protracted views of a Ring Ouzel feeding in the quarry bottom. As many as eight have been recorded here at one time and some years the passage continues into May. By mid-April Redstart arrive; the males first in flashy breeding plumage. Careful checking in the sheltered hollows and gullies around mid-morning is the best time to see them. The distinct 'tsweep' flight call of Yellow Wagtail is heard as they briefly stop to feed amongst the livestock. The males are superb birds with lemon yellow underparts and constantly wagging tails. Tree Pipit also can be identified by their diagnostic 'teez' flight call, at once telling them apart from the more numerous Meadow Pipit, whose numbers on passage may reach 100 in a day. A few pairs of the former usually stay to breed, preferring the plantations, where song-flighting may be seen, the latter breeding on the more open downland around the quarry and the paddocks. Grasshopper Warbler also exploit the plantations, being most active at dawn and dusk when their 'reeling' song is at its height. Listen out also for Whitethroat 'scratching' away its characteristic song deep within the bramble patches. A few Garden Warbler and Lesser Whitethroat are

Ring Ouzels

usually noted near the quarry scrub; once again initial location is aided by song.

Towards the end of April, Whinchat are found on the wire fencing in the paddocks, occasionally flicking down to feed. Cuckoo and Turtle Dove begin to appear, the former staying on to parasitise Meadow Pipit, the latter racing north. As the middle of May approaches the passage slows down and all that can be expected is a trickle of the late-arriving Spotted Flycatcher, with perhaps the chance of a Nightingale. Some years the spring rush brings in a local rarity. Pied Flycatcher, Firecrest and Hobby are typical but should not be expected and are normally the reward of the local birdwatchers, who spend many hours on the hill in spring.

In the summer, an early morning visit is essential to avoid the disturbance of picnickers and walkers who flock here on warm days. Sparrowhawk are often seen hunting over the scrub, dashing after passerines to feed their hungry young. Kestrel are doing likewise, although their hunting technique is different, hovering in pursuit of small rodents. Following a heavy downpour don't be too surprised to find them out on the open downs pulling worms in a manner similar to a thrush! Summer is a busy time for warblers, many of them raising two broods. Their song is much subdued towards the end of the period as they fatten up in readiness for the long haul south.

The autumn passage is typically more extended and not as exciting as the spring. A trickle of Redstart, Wheatear, warblers and hirundines filter along the ridge, with Whinchat numbers peaking in late August in the paddocks. Spectacular flocks of Goldfinch are seen feeding on the abundant weed seeds, sometimes numbering several hundred. As October closes the first flocks of Redwing and Fieldfare arrive from the boreal forests, nervously gorging on the year's crop of Hawthorn berries. On clear nights Redwing can be seen in silhouette migrating in front of the moonlight, their identity betrayed by their distinctive 'steep' contact call.

Calendar

Resident Kestrel, Sparrowhawk, Red-legged and Grey Partridge, Mistle Thrush, Long-tailed Tit, Yellowhammer.

December–February Possible Long-eared and Short-eared Owl, Redwing, Fieldfare, Brambling, Corn Bunting, occasional Reed Bunting and a massive Starling roost.

March–May Late March to late April, Wheatear, Black Redstart, Ring Ouzel, Chiffchaff, Blackcap and occasional Stonechat. Throughout April, Meadow Pipit, Tree Pipit, Yellow Wagtail, Willow Warbler and Goldcrest. Mid-April to early May, Turtle Dove, Cuckoo, hirundines, Redstart, Whinchat, Grasshopper Warbler, Lesser Whitethroat, Garden Warbler and Spotted Flycatcher with occasional Nightingale. Waders overhead, Lapwing, Curlew and Golden Plover most likely. Stock Dove and Redpoll. Best chance of rarity in April, Pied Flycatcher, Firecrest and Hobby typifying.

June–July Breeding passerines, Skylark, Meadow and Tree Pipit, Willow Warbler, sylvia warblers, Grasshopper Warbler, finches and Yellowhammer.

August–November Passage migrants, large finch flocks form, winter thrushes arrive in October. Influx of Blackbirds from the Continent.

FLITWICK MOOR
Map 4/OS ref. TL 046 354

Habitat
Flitwick Moor is situated where the River Flit crosses an inlier of impermeable clay in the lower greensand ridge, forming, at 70 acres (28 ha) Bedfordshire's largest expanse of valley fen or carr. With the lowering of the water table and the river bed, the Moor has become much drier over recent years, although an attempt has been made to arrest the situation by controlling the underground springs with dams and sluices forming a mosaic of wet habitats. On the drier parts, Birch and Oak are the predominant tree species with Alder and Sallow growing in the wet more open areas, alongside sedge and reed. The Moor has a rich flora, especially in the surrounding wet meadows and an insect population which includes some nationally rare species of Sawfly.

Flitwick Moor is a relic example of a unique habitat in the region and is recognised so by its status as a SSSI.

Access
From Flitwick town centre take the road east towards Greenfield, after 0.5 mile (0.8 km) turn left into Maulden Road and head north for a further 0.5 mile (0.8 km) until you arrive at Folly Farm opposite a small industrial estate. Turn right alongside the farm and follow the unmetalled road to the car park. Walk along the main track into the wood until you reach the wooden bridge over the drain. Cross over the bridge and the most interesting part of the Moor, the reedswamp, is on both sides of the track. Carry on into the meadow following the River Flit right until another path takes you back into the wood, recrossing the drain. This will eventually lead back to Greenfield Road, or alternatively, double back through the wood to the car park.

The BHWT own or lease only parts of the Moor, so in order to prevent misunderstanding with landowners, birders should make sure they keep to the public footpaths.

Species
A visit to this site can be productive at any time of the year but, as with most woodland, springtime brings a peak of activity with the arrival of the summer migrants. Large flocks of Siskin and Redpoll are found throughout the wood during the winter, especially in the Alders along the river and marsh. Other agile finches reaping the seed harvest are Goldfinch and Greenfinch. The wet meadows bordering the River Flit are good for wintering Snipe and the occasional passing Grey Heron. The river itself usually harbours a couple of Grey Wagtail, smart little birds with a sharp flight call and yellow 'ringed' tail. They are mainly a winter visitor to the region from the northern moors, although a few pairs have stayed on in recent years to breed, mostly near old water mills where the water is more turbulent and to their liking. Teal and Mallard are typical dabbling ducks of the wetter parts of the meadows and reed fringed pools, a few pairs of the latter staying on to breed.

Towards the end of the winter, listen out for Water Rail, as they start to establish their territory. A crepuscular bird by nature, this is probably their only regular breeding site in the county. A good spot is the wooden bridge near the reedswamp in the north-east corner. A variety of squeals and grunts betray their presence, and with patience you should be able to glimpse them lurking amongst the dead reeds and sometimes even clambering into bushes! Another species most active at dawn and dusk from March to July is the Woodcock, whose distinctive 'roding' display flight can be seen or heard throughout the wood. Sometimes landing quite close by, their cryptic plumage enables them to blend into the leaf litter almost at once. Any observers getting protracted views should count themselves very lucky indeed.

Water Rail

With the onset of warmer weather, the summer migrants start arriving with, as always, Chiffchaff and Blackcap first. Willow Warbler are not far behind but do not breed in any great numbers, the wood being too wet for them. Sedge Warbler on the other hand are perfectly suited to this habitat and are soon getting up territories in the open marsh and river's edge, song-flighting vigorously from any vantage point. The closely related Reed Warbler arrives later and sticks strictly to the small reedbeds scattered throughout the Moor. They seldom leave cover, clinging to a stem and sidling with a quick jerky action to the top, from where the song is delivered. Arriving with the Reed Warbler is the Cuckoo who frequently parasitises the warbler and can sometimes be seen flapping amongst the reeds in an effort to locate the nest. The swamp loving Grasshopper Warbler is now only a sporadic visitor to the Moor; listen out for them 'reeling' at dawn and dusk. They are not as common as they once were because of the recent drying out and subsequent invasion of Birch scrub. Other warblers scattered through-out the site are Whitethroat in the hedgerows, Lesser Whitethroat in scrub and Garden Warbler in the wood. Yellow Wagtail can be found in the meadows on passage with the odd pair occasionally summering. Other common riparian species like Moorhen and Reed Bunting are present, and a pair of Kingfisher can usually be seen along the Flit, where suitable banks allow them to breed. In spring Willow Tit sing amongst the Birch, the many soft Elders offering good breeding sites as this tit excavates its own nest hole.

In summer the wood is alive with juvenile tits and Treecreepers as the season's broods are calling and feeding amongst the Oak and Birch. Good views are obtainable from any of the footpaths bisecting the wood. Woodpeckers are resident throughout the year, being represented by Lesser and Great Spotted, the former showing a preference for the waterside willows.

Birds of prey to be seen are Kestrel and Sparrowhawk in the daylight hours with Tawny Owl taking over at night. If visiting at dawn or dusk, check the posts along Maulden Road for Little Owl; by staying in the car a close approach is often allowed. The Barn Owl is much in decline in Bedfordshire, due mainly to loss of habitat and nest sites through intensive farming methods, but wet meadows are a favourite haunt so there is a slim chance of glimpsing this most beautiful of owls alongside the River Flit.

To summarise: Flitwick Moor is at its best around dawn on a fine May morning. Arrive an hour before sunrise and walk slowly through the wood stopping at the open marshes to listen for crepuscular specialities. Listen very carefully; because if any site in the county has the potential to turn up a rare crake then this is it.

Calendar

Resident Sparrowhawk, Kestrel, Water Rail, Moorhen, Tawny Owl, Little Owl (around Folly Farm), Kingfisher, Lesser Spotted and Great Spotted Woodpecker, Marsh and Willow Tit, Treecreeper, Redpoll and Jay.

December–February Grey Heron (occasional), Teal, Lapwing, Snipe, Woodcock (a pair or two stay on to breed), Grey Wagtail, Siskin and finches.

March–May Mallard, Turtle Dove, Cuckoo, Yellow Wagtail, Mistle Thrush, Grasshopper Warbler (occasional), Sedge and Reed Warbler, sylvia warblers, Chiffchaff, Willow Warbler, Reed Bunting.

June–July Breeding in full swing.

August–November Common passerines reach maximum numbers, warblers depart, tits start to flock together.

HARROLD & ODELL
COUNTRY PARK

Map 5/OS ref. SP 958 567

Habitat

Harrold and Odell are another of the Bedfordshire County Council's Country Park developments that have made use of exhausted gravel pits, similar to Priory Park. The habitat is much like the Bedford site although the island on the main lake is kept bare and stony at one end attracting some passage waders. The smaller water to the south is heavily fished and of little interest to the birdwatcher, unlike the nearby reedswamp and salix scrub which is a hive of activity the year round. The park also includes a 0.75 mile (1.2 km) stretch of riverbank and meadows alongside the Great Ouse, bordered with established willows and Alders. Management sympathetic to wildlife is soon to be operated under the guidance of a full-time Warden whose main task will be to keep the salix scrub from encroaching the reedswamp and to coppice suitable patches of willow.

Amphibians abound during springtime in the still waters and Grass Snake are regularly seen here and along the river. Mink are becoming an all too familiar sight throughout the Ouse Valley (despite a relentless trapping programme), and have completely replaced the indigenous Otter.

Access

Travelling from Bedford town centre north along the A6, turn left after 2.5 miles (4 km) towards Oakly. Follow the lane through to Harrold passing through the villages of Pavenham and Carlton. Just north of Carlton the road bridges the river and the entrance to the Country Park is a further 110 yds (100 m) on the right. Once inside the gate park alongside the newly constructed information centre where a blackboard should have the latest sightings chalked up. A footpath encircles the main lake with tracks branching off through the reedswamp and down to the river.

The information centre has a display room and classroom suitable for school parties; for details contact the Warden. A small group of ringing enthusiasts operate on site and if met will only be too pleased to explain the workings and purpose of their scientific studies.

Species

The focal point of interest to the birdwatcher, whatever time of year, is the island, as it affords refuge from human disturbance allowing the birds to rest in comparative safety. During the winter hundreds of feral Greylag and Canada Geese noisily congregate towards evening following daytime forays on surrounding farmland. Odd escapees, such as Barnacle and Bar-headed Goose can usually be found among them and sporadic records of genuinely wild geese like White-fronted and Pink-footed have been logged overhead. Out on the water variable numbers of duck are present with Mallard, Shoveler, Tufted Duck and Pochard most numerous. Smew and Goosander periodically occur in small numbers but rarely stay long. The early morning observer can often be rewarded with a flock of Wigeon grazing on the meadow or lakeside grass, at times numbering 300 strong. Goldeneye are present from late autumn to early spring along with a large pack of 300 to 400 Coot. The wet meadow attracts Snipe and Teal while the arboreal Siskin and Redpoll feed on cones situated atop the riverside Alders. Dusk sees the arrival of many Corn and Reed Bunting to roost among the reeds and osiers with occasionally a party of Bearded Tit joining the throng. Water Rail regularly winter and the secretive Bittern is sometimes encountered.

Spring commences with the arrival of Sand Martin over the water and Wheatear around the grassy edges. Parties of Redshank returning from their winter quarters on the east coast noisily proclaim their territorial rights with two or three pairs breeding. A pair or two of Ringed Plover breed just about annually on the island although most are just passage birds alongside a few Little Ringed Plover, Dunlin and Common Sandpiper. Periodically unusual coastal species such as Turnstone, Sanderling or Oystercatcher appear but can never be predicted and rarely stay long. Groups of terns pass through, mainly Common at first with Black Tern a little later in the season and once only a super rare Caspian Tern. Most passerines are less obvious visually although more so vocally, especially the warblers who drift north at night-time after feeding in the daylight hours among the salix scrub and patches of scattered timber. Small flocks of Yellow Wagtail haunt the open meadow beside the fishing lake along with an assortment of Pied Wagtail and Meadow Pipit, the latter frequently numbering 100 to 200. Check the alba Wagtails as White Wagtail regularly occur, the males most apparent sporting a sparkling grey back and rump.

Summer breeders include all the normal resident riparian species as well as a colony of 20 plus pairs of Reed Warbler among the phragmites and a few pairs of Yellow Wagtail in the surrounding fields. The ebullient Sedge Warbler ranges across the park nesting within any rank vegetation, whereas the more retiring Lesser Whitethroat prefers drier scrub thickets from which to utter its tuneless rattle. On the island a pair of Common Tern usually try their luck at nesting beside a motley selection of duck in eclipse plumage. The highlight of summer, particularly late summer, is the presence of a pair of Hobby who dash about at breakneck speed hunting hirundines and the larger flying insects. They breed in the open countryside surrounding the Ouse Valley which supports an abundance of likely prey on which to feed their young. When the hirundines mass in the osiers prior to migration the family group is in close attendance, weeding out any unwary birds.

A drawn-out wader passage sets in from late summer onwards with parties of Greenshank and the occasional Ruff enlivening proceedings. Curlew and Whimbrel may pass overhead calling but rarely settle. Common and Green Sandpiper scuttle around the margins and one or two marsh terns in dowdy autumn dress move through. Good numbers of sylvia warblers bounce into the ringers' mist nets, particularly Lesser Whitethroat, as well as Blackcap and Garden Warbler. Waterfowl increase in number with the chance of Black-necked Grebe or more unobtrusively a moulting Pintail; discernible at a distance from Mallard by a more attenuated profile. A party of Bewick's Swan is likely in late autumn as small numbers of Grey Wagtail take up station for the winter. Winter thrushes and Skylark abound on the open grass but quickly move south-west with the onset of harsher weather.

Calendar

Resident Great Crested Grebe and Dabchick, feral geese, Mute Swan, Tufted Duck, Mallard, Coot, Kestrel, Sparrowhawk, three woodpeckers occasionally visit, tits including Willow, Treecreeper, common finches and buntings.

December–February Bittern rare, chance of wild geese, Gadwall, Wigeon, Teal, Shoveler, Pochard, Goldeneye, Smew and Goosander occasionally, Water Rail, Coot, Snipe, winter thrushes, bunting roosts, Siskin in Alders, chance of Stonechat.

March–May Shelduck March, Sand Martin, Wheatear, small wader passage in April, Common Tern, Arctic and Black Tern rarer end April, wagtails, warblers and Meadow Pipit, Cuckoo; hirundines.

June–July Riparian breeders, Hobby, Swift, sylvia warblers end July–August, as well as returning waders, Kingfisher dispersed.

August–November Sandpipers, Greenshank, possible Ruff, Curlew or Whimbrel, Swallow roost September, Hobby, chance of Black-necked Grebe and Pintail, passage terns, Bewick's Swan November, Grey Wagtail, Skylark and Meadow Pipit, wagtails and winter thrushes.

MAULDEN WOODS   Map 6/OS ref. TL 070 390

Habitat

Maulden Woods, a part of Ampthill Forest, are a plantation type wood owned by the Forestry Commission. Varying stages of growth help to create some diversity of habitat, but little of the typical greensands woodland remains. Oak is the main deciduous tree with the most interesting stand growing alongside the lay-by. The pine plantations are almost impenetrable and of little use to birds apart from serving as good roosting sites in the winter. The young plantations are the most rewarding for the birdwatcher, forming an ever changing patchwork throughout the wood. Surrounding fields are always worthwhile checking, particularly on the southern perimeter where the edge of another wood can be overlooked.

This site has had well over 300 species of moths recorded within its boundaries so consequently during the summer months the local Moth Group is very active. Gathered around their mercury-vapour lamps, they make an eerie sight when encountered late at night.

Access

Maulden Wood is situated 1 mile (1.5 km) north of Clophill and to the west of the A6. Access is from a lay-by, where there is ample car parking space. The Forestry Commission have a nature trail marked out which takes you through all the different parts of the wood. As all the species can be seen from the tracks, there is no need to stray into the wood at all.

Species

Bedfordshire is the stronghold for Lady Amherst's Pheasant, with Maulden Wood being a particularly good place to see them. Introduced from China around 1900, they have spread out from their original release site at Woburn to colonise a number of the greensand woods. A resident species, they are more easily seen in the winter dashing across firebreaks and sometimes, with luck, feeding amongst the Oak litter. In spring, their grating call is heard from deep cover as the males set up territories. They remain elusive through the summer, keeping well into dense undergrowth.

All three species of woodpecker are represented, with the Great Spotted being the most common. Lesser Spotted are easier to see in the spring when they are displaying, favouring the more mature Oaks, where there is plenty of dead wood for them to drum on. Green Woodpecker are normally heard 'laughing' throughout the wood or seen bounding across clearings, a good spot being the field near the forester's cottage where they can often be seen leaping about in search of ants.

Small numbers of Hawfinch are resident, the lay-by stand being the likeliest area, although they can be found anywhere, even in the pines. Highly arboreal, Hawfinch will even nest in the flimsy upper canopy, and are sometimes noted picking up grit for their gizzards alongside the lay-by. Otherwise, their presence is usually betrayed by a distinctive 'tpik' flight call.

Resident raptors are Kestrel in the surrounding fields and Sparrow-

Lady Amherst's Pheasants

hawk in the wood, with Little Owl and Tawny Owl taking over the respective roles at nightfall.

Proceedings liven up considerably in the spring with the arrival of that powerful songster the Nightingale. Their numbers vary annually with a couple of pairs being about average, often frequenting the rank growth alongside the main track and the plantations, where there is plenty of cover. Another skulker, the Grasshopper Warbler, can be found here, prefering the damper area to the north of the main ride. A few pairs of Tree Pipit are scattered throughout the young plantations, song-flighting from any suitably exposed perch.

The main arrival of common warblers takes place from the middle of April, and the wood is soon alive with their song. This is a good time for a dawn chorus visit, when you could expect to see, but mostly hear, between 30 to 40 species in a couple of hours.

Woodcock and Redpoll are both typical birds associated with lower greensand woodland, their numbers increasing in the winter with the arrival of migrants. A few pairs of each stay on to breed, with Woodcock easily seen at dawn and dusk quartering the wood, performing their 'roding' display flight. Redpoll are much less predictable and are often seen flying in circles calling frantically, seemingly unable to decide exactly just where they are heading for!

All six species of tits are present along with the highly vocal Nuthatch and the not so obvious Treecreeper. The two 'black capped tits' are easier to identify this time of the year with the aid of their distinctive songs.

Those long distance migrants, the Turtle Dove and Cuckoo, are represented, the former breeding in small numbers, with just a couple of pairs of the latter. Spotted Flycatcher are the last to arrive but waste no time at all in setting up territories, and are well distributed throughout the Oak and along the woodland edge.

Bird song progressively tails off through the summer, and a visit on a warm afternoon can be very dull indeed, as everything keeps to cover, with adults feeding late broods and juveniles moulting.

Once the summer visitors have left by early autumn, the resident passerines have the wood to themselves and fatten up in preparation for the coming winter. Mixed flocks of tits and Goldcrests roam the wood in search of food, calling constantly to keep in touch.

Not the best wood in the region, but ease of access, coupled with a relatively small size makes it worth a visit during the spring for a good selection of common woodland birds, with a winter visit for Lady Amherst's Pheasant and the chance of Crossbill.

Calendar

Resident Kestrel, Sparrowhawk, Lady Amherst's Pheasant, Woodcock, Little Owl, Tawny Owl, Green Woodpecker, Great and Lesser Spotted Woodpecker, Mistle Thrush, Goldcrest, Willow Tit (scarce), Marsh Tit, Nuthatch, Treecreeper, Jay, Redpoll, Hawfinch.

December–February Lady Amherst's Pheasant easier to see, Crossbill occasionally, tit flocks.

March–May Mid-April for Cuckoo, Turtle Dove, Tree Pipit, Nightingale, Grasshopper Warbler, Garden Warbler, Blackcap, Chiffchaff, Willow Warbler, Whitethroat and, from mid-May, Spotted Flycatcher.

June–July Breeding passerines. If Nightjar ever return this is the best period, at dusk onwards.

August–November Flocks of small mixed passerines roam the wood.

PRIORY COUNTRY PARK   Map 7/OS ref. TL 070 492

Habitat

Despite its close proximity to Bedford town centre, Priory Park, formerly known as Barkers Lane gravel pit, regularly attracts a wide range of birds, complementing the general lure of wood and water. The main feature is an abandoned 62 acres (25 ha) gravel pit with sparsely vegetated margins and an island which unfortunately is overgrown and of little use to waders. Adjacent to the north-east corner of the lake are two smaller interconnecting lakes with much rank vegetation and dead timber, proving attractive to many forms of wildlife. A long hedgerow to the west borders a large open field with scattered trees and bushes. Elsewhere many clumps of sallow and other native trees have been planted with surrounding buffer zones of uncut grasses. Sweeping around the southern half of the main lake is the River Great Ouse with varying bank cover and many fine old willows along the towpath. Meadows to the south at Fenlake frequently flood to varying degrees attracting, in winter, numbers of gulls and ducks. Restricted views across a sewage works and adjoining farmland completes the array of habitats. In summer the smaller lakes harbour many forms of aquatic insect life among the marshy patches, while along the river sightings of Mink are becoming commonplace.

Access

Two access points are available, on opposite sides of the lake, with ample car parking facilities at both. For immediate access to the lake take the A428 east from St Neots town centre turning right after 1.25 miles (2 km) down the A418. Travel a further 0.5 mile (0.75 km) and turn left along Barkers Lane, between a garage and playing fields. Another 0.5 mile (0.75 km) and the entrance to the car park is on the right, over the New Cut bridge. Ahead in the large field is the Warden's Lodge, incorporating the new headquarters of the BHWT. Here can be found information sheets concerning nature trails and guided tours, a shop and toilet facilities. School parties and societies are catered for; anyone wishing further information should contact the Warden. (See Useful Addresses.)

For the southern entrance near the river, head along the A603 Sandy road from Bedford turning left after 2 miles (3 km) along Mill Lane, directly opposite Cardington Cross. Once in the car park a series of footbridges will eventually lead to the lake. Being a 'multi-recreational area' many different water sports and pastimes are practised, e.g. canoeing, fishing and sailboarding; making an early morning visit essential.

Species

This site's main virtue is its ability to offer a wide range of species at all times of the year, especially in springtime. Migrating birds seem to follow watercourses and the Great Ouse is no exception with the lake attracting passage waders for brief periods to rest. The lack of an exposed shingle spit or bar on the island means that most simply circle low over the water and then continue their journey. Nonetheless some do stop off on the large field and along the open footpath by the northern shore.

Winter wildfowl are most obvious on the main lake with varying numbers of Mallard, Pochard, Tufted Duck, Shoveler and Coot present throughout the season. Packs of noisy Wigeon come and go and a scattering of Gadwall are noted from late autumn until the new year. Small numbers of Goldeneye can be seen but sawbills are irregular with an occasional Red-breasted Merganser most likely on passage. Ruddy Duck, Pintail and Shelduck are just about annual, usually around the winter period; the former only recently having been recorded in the county. When the meadows across the river at Fenlake flood good numbers of Snipe (as many as 300 on occasions) probe for worms, with the odd Jack Snipe turning up, normally towards spring. Dabbling duck such as Mallard and Teal sift through the vegetable matter, while the opportunist Black-headed Gull pesters any Lapwing that are about. Similar conditions sometimes prevail between the two 'arms' of the river near the sewage works. The few breeding pairs of Great Crested Grebe and Dabchick are supplemented in winter swelling Great Crested to 50-plus individuals. Other grebes are scarce and mainly recorded on passage when once a Red-necked Grebe was noted, still partially in summer plumage. Grey Heron can be seen sentinel-like on the island the year round along with increasing numbers of Cormorant. The marshier parts of the smaller lake suit a secretive Water Rail and once a Great Grey Shrike hunted this area preying heavily on small passerines. The sewage works is worth checking from the gate for finches and buntings with a slim chance of Stonechat on calm days, using the fence as a vantage point.

Chiffchaff and Wheatear are usually the first spring migrants on land with Sand Martin over the water. Plovers are on the move now with Little Ringed settling around the stoney edges and occasional Grey or Golden overhead, along with other large waders such as Curlew or godwit. Into April and the tempo increases as Willow Warbler and Meadow Pipit move through in large numbers. In the early morning, attention centres on the large field near the lake as parties of wagtails arrive; the males in pristine breeding plumage. Several Blue-headed and White Wagtail are almost guaranteed among the commoner Yellow and Pied Wagtail. Thorough scrutiny of the pipit/wagtail flock is always challenging and sometimes rewarding with Water Pipit likely (and on one occasion the county's only occurrence of a superb male Grey-headed Wagtail).

Out on the lake terns start arriving; mostly Common with an occasional passage of Arctic and sporadically single Little or Sandwich Terns. Small groups of Black Tern tend to occur later on in the season particularly after heavy rainstorms. The highly oceanic Kittiwake and dainty tern-like Little Gull are noted annually; probably due to a more critical assessment of gulls by today's ultra-identification conscious birdwatchers.

While all this migrant activity is taking place the resident species are going about the business of mating and raising young. Now is a good time to hear Lesser Spotted Woodpecker drumming feebly from dead timber around the smaller lake, or calling from riverside willows. Kingfisher haunt the river along with Reed Bunting and Moorhen and a Willow Tit may be seen searching for a likely tree in which to excavate its own hole. Back on the lake hirundines swarm over the surface and Common Sandpiper flit around the margin. Cuckoo return along with

Reed Warbler and last to arrive are Spotted Flycatcher, who find safe refuge among the many ivy-covered trees.

Summer is a season of much disturbance by the public although an evening visit can be worthwhile as Hobby often dash in to hunt martins or dragonflies. Masses of Swift 'wheel' and 'tumble' in the sky overhead while riparian breeders busily feed their fledglings. A trickle of returning waders in late summer, such as Green Sandpiper and Greenshank, leads into a more protracted passage period with similar species to spring, though never as dynamic. A few Whinchat pass through as several Grey Wagtail are seen along the river or canoe course. As the year turns full circle a flock of Bewick's Swan sometimes overshoot their normal wintering site further north on the Ouse Washes, delighting the fortunate observer.

Calendar

Resident Great Crested Grebe, Dabchick, Mute Swan, Mallard, Kingfisher, Lesser Spotted Woodpecker, Long-tailed and Willow Tit, finches and buntings.

December–February Common grebes increase, Cormorant, feral geese, Wigeon, Gadwall early winter, Teal Fenlake, Pintail and sawbills scarce, Shoveler, Tufted Duck, Goldeneye, Pochard, Water Rail, Lapwing and Snipe on wet meadows, occasional Jack Snipe, Stonechat, Goldcrest, winter thrushes.

March–May Possible Shelduck, common passage waders (mostly overhead), Little Gull, Kittiwake, Common, Arctic (from April), Black Tern (May), hirundines, pipits and wagtails highlight of season. Wheatear and Chiffchaff from end March. Common warblers, Cuckoo, Reed Warbler and Spotted Flycatcher in May. Chance of local rarity, e.g. Pied Flycatcher or Black Redstart.

June–July Breeding riparian species, sometimes Common Tern, hunting Hobby, Swift, returning waders end July.

August–November Sandpipers, terns, wagtails, pipits, Whinchat in August, warblers depart, Grey Wagtail, wildfowl increase in November, chance of wild swans.

THE LODGE

Map 8/OS ref. TL 188 478

Habitat

The headquarters of the RSPB are situated in what is Bedfordshire's finest example of lower heath to have survived the ravages of the twentieth century. The site has been managed to allow a good selection of both animal and plant life to prosper and is justifiably rated a SSSI.

A part of Sandy Warren, this 104 acre (42 ha) reserve's most precious asset is its relic heathland. Here, heather is allowed to flourish alongside fine small grasses and bracken, although the latter is controlled to prevent it smothering the entire heath. The woodlands vary from areas of native Oak, Birch and Scots Pine to several small conifer plantations. The more formal gardens in front of the house abound with exotic trees and shrubs, making ideal roost sites in the winter. A small bird garden can be viewed from an adjoining Nature Discovery Room and is a valuable teaching aid for the many school parties that visit The Lodge every year.

Water is a scarce commodity on heathland so the construction of a 1 acre (0.4 ha) lake added an important new element to the reserve's habitats. A second much smaller pond has been excavated in a nearby wooded valley, both being overlooked by hides.

Among the mammals are a variety of rodents including the unusual Yellow-necked Mouse and two colonies of Long-eared Bat. Through the summer months be prepared for Common Lizard sunbathing on the heath, and, by the car park, many butterflies attracted to the Buddleia. The lake holds a small number of the recently introduced Natterjack Toad.

Access

The Lodge lies 1.5 miles (2.5 km) south-east of the village of Sandy on the B1042 Sandy to Cambridge road. Approaching from the village, turn right at the reserve signpost following the road to the car park and reception centre. Three well marked nature trails are laid out, one with an accessible hide which is suitable for disabled visitors. There is also a picnic area, a shop and toilets.

The reserve is open all year, 9.00 a.m. until 5.00 p.m. on weekdays and 10.00 a.m. until 5.00 p.m. at weekends. On Sundays and Bank Holidays it is only open to members of the RSPB and BHWT and their guests. A Warden is on site all year round.

Species

Resident passerines abound at The Lodge making it an ideal site for the beginner to learn the basics of bird identification. All the woodland tits are here including the tricky Marsh and Willow Tit. A good pair of ears is vital for separating them as they ceaselessly move through cover, rarely allowing protracted views. The plantations and other scattered conifers attract good numbers of Coal Tit and Goldcrest, both birds typically associated with the lower greensand ridge. Occasionally in winter Crossbill occur, usually in small parties but more regularly Siskin and Redpoll are noted, sometimes drinking at Jacks Pond. At this time of year the available cover is exploited at dusk with finches and thrushes

Winter Thrushes

streaming in to roost in thick evergreen shrubs such as rhododendron; while Meadow Pipit and Yellow-hammer prefer ground cover on the heath.

Spring is an ideal time for watching woodpeckers, as all three species are at their most vocal. Green can often be seen bounding across the heath or calling furiously from Scots Pine, while the two Spotted Woodpeckers 'drum' from dead timber. Many nest boxes are strategically positioned around the reserve and, in the breeding season, the majority are tenanted by Blue and Great Tit as well as Nuthatch, who characteristically plaster mud around the entrance hole as they would a natural cavity. The thin call of Treecreeper is commonly heard as it spirals, mouse-like, up a tree trunk, extracting insects from the bark with its fine bill.

Our familiar songsters are soon joined by summer visiting warblers and the woodlands are quickly alive with their song. Blackcap and Garden Warbler are present in good numbers wherever a canopy exists while Lesser Whitethroat and Whitethroat can be found amongst scrub around the heath and in adjoining farmland hedgerows. Chiffchaff and Willow Warbler are numerous, the latter more so, but Wood Warbler are only recorded as a scarce passage migrant. Firecrest, currently enjoying a range expansion, must be regarded as a potential coloniser as a pair recently bred successfully. Out on the heath Tree Pipit arrive, quickly song-flighting from isolated pines while Redpoll chatter overhead in search of nest sites high up in conifers. At dusk Woodcock display over the treetops and Tawny Owl can be heard. Cuckoo parasitise common woodland birds such as Dunnock and Robin and are often misidentified as Sparrowhawk, who regularly hunt over the woods. Spotted Flycatcher is the last migrant to arrive but is easy to see in the garden sallying forth after flying insects.

The lake merits attention during the summer as birds come down to drink, especially pigeons and doves. A passing Grey Heron may be present or even a Kingfisher. More likely are pairs of breeding Moorhen and Mallard leading their obedient offspring in search of food. In late summer, if there is exposed mud a migrating Green Sandpiper or Snipe might drop in to feed, while hirundines hawk low over the water for insects.

As the summer passerines leave and tits flock together, finches feed on the abundant weed seeds. Hawfinch favour mixed woodlands along the lower greensand outcrop, but being a shy bird is rarely encountered with any regularity. With autumn well under way the first winter thrushes arrive, sometimes feeding on the lawn, but most passing overhead. Great Grey Shrike have wintered in the past ranging over Biggleswade Common and along the old railway line. Irregularly raptors are noted from late autumn to spring with Buzzard, Merlin and Hen Harrier most frequent. Flocks of Chaffinch are joined by small numbers of Brambling in search of food among the leaf litter, their numbers varying annually.

The Lodge is best in spring when the full flavour of a greensand wooded heath can be appreciated, with perhaps a winter visit for finches and the chance of Crossbill. The likelihood of a rarity is remote, but an impressive number of species of raptor have been recorded flying over, including Osprey, Honey Buzzard and Marsh Harrier.

Calendar

Resident Grey Heron occasional visitor, Mallard, Sparrowhawk, Kestrel, partridges on farmland, Moorhen, Woodcock, Stock Dove, Tawny Owl, Kingfisher occasional, Green and Spotted Woodpeckers, Jackdaw, Jay, tits, Nuthatch, Treecreeper, Mistle Thrush, Goldcrest, finches including Redpoll, Yellowhammer, Tree Sparrow scarce, Hawfinch rare.

December–February Roosting passerines at dusk, tit flocks, occasional winter raptors and Great Grey Shrike, Siskin and Brambling, winter thrushes. Crossbill occasionally.

March–May Common warblers, chance of Hobby, passing Wood Warbler. Tree Pipit, Cuckoo, Turtle Dove, Swallow, Firecrest (in future?). Occasional chat or Wheatear on farmland, Spotted Flycatcher mid-May.

June–July Breeding passerines, possible Dabchick on lake.

August–November Snipe and Green Sandpiper on lake if muddy. Masses of juvenile tits, warblers and finches. Pied Flycatcher occasionally.

WARDEN & GALLEY HILLS

Map 9/OS ref. TL 091 261

Habitat

Situated on the northern outskirts of Luton, Warden and Galley Hills, the former rising to 640 ft (195 m), have still managed to retain some of their downland mystique. As the hills are no longer sheep-grazed, Hawthorn scrub dominates the scarp slope with patches of Dogwood here and there. 'Scrub-bashing' by local conservation groups has opened it up in places and here a typical calcareous flora can be found. The eastern dip-slope is arable land and of limited interest. The South Bedfordshire Golf Course to the west adds to the variety of habitats with clumps of trees and open fairways. North of the old Icknield Way the scene is open farmland with a small Forestry Commission stand of conifers tucked in by Galley Hill.

Brown Hare can be seen in abundance on hill and field alike and it is not unusual to see 10 to 20 performing on the open 'prairie' towards the A6.

Access

Head north out of Luton along the A6 turning right after 2 miles (3 km) down Warden Hill Road. Park at the top of the road in a small pull-in near the entrance to Cardinal Newman School. Access onto the hills is unrestricted with many well trodden tracks criss-crossing the site. A couple of footpaths bisect fairways on the golf course so beware of low flying golf balls!

An alternative route to Galley Hill is to carry on north along the A6 to the Streatley Crossroads and turn right towards Hexton. Drive for 1.25 miles (2 km) and park near an old farm track on the right. This runs south toward the plantation crossing the Icknield Way near Galley Hill.

For a more adventurous hike the ancient Britons' road can be followed north-east across the county boundary with Hertfordshire to Deacon Hill south of Pegsdon.

Species

The Hills are indeed desolate looking in the dead of winter when most bird activity is centred around the golf links and out in the fields adjoining New Farm. Here coveys of both Grey and Red-legged Partridge can be seen scratching about in the winter barley or oil-seed rape, with flocks of 200 to 300 Woodpigeon. A scattering of the smaller, more compact Stock Dove can also be found, along with the inevitable Collared Dove. Large flocks of Lapwing feed undisturbed except when harried by passing Black-headed Gulls. Corn Bunting are resident, with groups of 20 to 30 noted in winter. They usually form part of a larger mixed flock of Yellowhammer, Greenfinch, Linnet and the occasional Reed Bunting. The latter have recently taken to breeding away from wetland sites and a pair or two sometimes remain in the fields behind Galley Hill. Sparrow and finch flocks, often seen along farm tracks, should be checked out for Tree Sparrow. A high pitched 'chip' call immediately identifies this much overlooked and declining species.

Raptors are often reported along the whole range of hills from Luton to Pirton, usually by lone observers, and no doubt with increased coverage many more would be found. The resident Kestrel and Sparrowhawk are sometimes joined in winter by a ringtailed Harrier or a Buzzard, with odd sightings of Goshawk or Peregrine probably relating to escaped falconers' birds (but who knows!). Little Owl hunt the golf course and farmland while Tawny are more common further north around wooded Hexton. 'Eared Owls' visit fairly regularly with Short-eared most likley to be seen in late afternoon hunting over the thinner scrub adjacent to the fairways on Galley Hill.

Migrants pass along the ridge in spring making this site potentially as exciting as Blows Downs. Although more difficult to work, persistent watchers should be rewarded with small numbers of Wheatear on the fairways and Black Redstart and Ring Ouzel on the hill-tops. The usual passage of warblers occurs with many Willow Warbler and a few Whitethroat staying to breed. Variable numbers of Meadow and Tree Pipit can be expected; the former regularly breeding, the latter sporadically. Quail are irregular visitors in late spring to the surrounding fields of barley, when their presence is betrayed by a distinctive and highly ventriloquial, trisyllabic whistle.

The summer period is busy for breeding passerines such as Skylark, pipits, buntings and finches. Being close to a large town walkers swarm onto the hills on warm summer days making a birdwatching visit inadvisable.

Autumn passage is typical of most along the Chiltern Hills from the August build up of warblers, to November winter thrushes. Rain and mist during October can bring with it a fall of common migrants such as Meadow Pipit and Goldcrest.

Warden Hill, and particularly the downs running north-east to Pirton, are under-watched, thus presenting the pioneering birder in search of pastures new a real challenge. Although the terrain is, for the most part, a seemingly uncompromising arable desert with a few beleaguered virgin hill-tops, a sense of remoteness still remains. Wild enough perhaps to attract a trip of migrant Dotterel or a prospecting Stone Curlew.

Calendar

Resident Sparrowhawk, Kestrel, Red-legged and Grey Partridge, Tawny and Little Owl, Skylark, Tree Sparrow, common finches, Corn Bunting, Yellowhammer, Reed Bunting occasional, Long-tailed Tit.

December–February Possible winter raptors, eared Owls, Lapwing pigeon and dove flocks.

March–May Wheatear, possible Black Redstart and Ring Ouzel, Meadow and Tree Pipit, Cuckoo, Willow Warbler, Whitethroat, chance of waders overhead, hirundines.

June–July Quail late May early June (irregular), breeding passerines.

August–November Sylvia warblers and Whinchat in August, pipits, Goldcrest, winter thrushes October–November.

ADDITIONAL SITES

Ampthill Park (OS ref. TL 027 385) & Coopers Hill (OS ref. TL 027 377)

A large municipal public park on the greensand ridge with open fields, scattered timber and mixed woodland to the east alongside the A418 Ampthill to Bedford road. Ample car parking with good access and many footpaths. Visit early morning.

A good cross-section of resident passerines including three wood-peckers, six tits and Hawfinch. In spring Wood Warbler and Firecrest have been noted on passage; good numbers of breeding leaf and scrub warblers in the summer as well as Spotted Flycatcher.

Cross south over the A418 Woburn road for Coopers Hill. This site, also known as The Firs, is a SSSI and 30 acres (12 ha) in area. It is one of the best remaining heaths on the greensands and was declared a Local Nature Reserve by Bedfordshire County Council in 1980.

Barton Hills (OS ref. TL 090 300)

A classic piece of sheep-grazed chalk downland east of Barton-le-Clay on the A6 and a National Nature Reserve. Roadside pull-ins give minimal parking along the B655 where public footpaths lead south onto the hills.

Typical downland species breed such as Lapwing, pipits, Skylark, Linnet and buntings. Spring brings Wheatear, Ring Ouzel, warblers and Turtle Dove; check at dusk for waders calling overhead. Very under-watched; spring passage could be similar to Blows Downs. Winter raptors likely.

Blunham Gravel Pit (OS ref. TL 159 511)

An old pit in the Ivel Valley just north of Sandy. Park along the A1 northbound at TL 163 509 and follow the track to the lake.

A collection of pinioned wildfowl (Whooper Swan, Goldeneye and Ruddy Duck) attract small numbers of genuine wild winter ducks; Ferruginous have been recorded. Check any passerine flocks on market-garden fields. A good place to find a national rarity as the offices of *British Birds* journal are nearby!

Charle Wood (OS ref. SP 930 329)

A mixed Oak, Chestnut and conifer wood owned by the Bedford Estates. Park by the county boundary roadsign and keep strictly to the marked public footpath as the wood is heavily keepered.

Lady Amherst's Pheasants are the main attraction, winter being the best time to see them. The usual resident woodland species occur, with Woodcock and Grasshopper Warbler vocalising in summer.

Dunstable Downs (OS ref. TL 005 195)

The highest point in the county, 794 ft (242 m) with an impressive view across the farmland of Beds and Bucks. A National Trust holding with much scrub and some sheep-grazed slopes near Whipsnade Zoo. Plenty of parking off the B4541. Hang-gliding and conventional gliding attracts hordes of people at weekends and public holidays; avoid these times!

The usual downland pipits, Skylark and buntings are present with a passage of Wheatear and Ouzel; check the Wallaby enclosure at Bison Hill for the latter two. Winter brings large numbers of passerines to roost, including a sizeable collection of Magpies. Corvids are attracted to offal at a nearby pig farm and 'eared' owls are often noted.

This site is notoriously difficult to explore and is not for the faint of heart. However birds are there and one dogged observer proved so by recently recording a Subalpine Warbler!

Felmersham Gravel Pits (OS ref. SP 991 583)

A chain of old pits covering 52 acres (21 ha) of the Ouse Valley between the villages of Felmersham and Sharnbrook in north Beds. Owned by the BHWT and a SSSI this site is more of interest to the botanist. Park in the small reserve car park by the lane.

Typical riparian birds abound with good numbers of warblers in the summer. Bittern occur fairly regularly during the winter and the county's first Purple Heron was recorded here. A likely site for colonisation by Cetti's Warbler in the future.

Home Wood (OS ref. TL 140 463)

A predominantly coniferous wood owned by the Forestry Commission. Park carefully along the lane from Northill and keep to the way-marked tracks.

The usual woodland species with occasional Nightingale and particularly good numbers of Grasshopper Warbler.

Marston Thrift (OS ref. SP 972 415)

An excellent ancient Ash and Oak wood on clay with the southern 13 acres (5 ha) managed by the County Trust. Turn off the A5140 at the sign to Wood End, parking in the small reserve car park at the end of the lane.

Visit in spring and early summer for all six species of tits and three woodpeckers. Warblers and Nightingale in the coppiced area.

Odell Great Wood (OS ref. SP 960 590)

A large damp heavily gamekeepered Oak wood. Approach along bridlepath from Odell village. Avoid visiting during the shooting season, especially on Saturdays.

A good cross-section of deciduous woodland birds including Nightingale and Woodcock. Wintering Buzzard have been noted. An ideal site to visit in conjunction with nearby Harrold and Odell Country Park.

Pegsdon Hills (OS ref. TL 120 295)

Classic chalk downland around Deacon Hill contrasts with the more intensively farmed area around Pegsdon Common Farm. For Deacon Hill park near the public house and explore the downs from footpaths and bridleway. The farmland north can be worked from a car or ideally a bicycle.

A high density of breeding pipits and Skylark on the sheep walks with scrub warblers in the Hawthorn. In winter chance of a raptor; Hen Harrier and Short-eared Owl most likely. During spring the bean fields are worth checking for a chance of Curlew or even more remotely Stone Curlew or Dotterel.

Radwell Gravel Pits (OS ref. TL 015 575)

Some parts still being worked but most of the southern pits are flooded. Approach down a narrow lane from Radwell village and park near the entrance to the works. The pits are private but a public footpath bisects the site affording views over the water and along the river.

Waders and terns pause a while on passage. Formerly a good site for breeding Sand Martin. Check the fields for wagtails and chats in spring and autumn. Chance of Hobby in summer.

Rowney Warren (OS ref. TL 120 405)

A Forestry Commission nature trail passes through some 1.25 miles (2 km) of conifers and greensand heath. Good public access and parking along the A600 Bedford to Shefford road.

A minimal selection of greensand species with much disturbance from the public.

Stockgrove Country Park (OS ref. SP 920 290)

A Bedfordshire County Council property 2.5 miles (4 km) north of Leighton Buzzard. Good access with ample parking and toilets.

A superb primary Oak wood (SSSI) supports an abundance of woodland birds with high densities of Nuthatch and Treecreeper. Three woodpeckers bred as well as tits, warblers and a few Redstart. The open heath areas are good for finches.

Kings Wood to the north is worth a visit as it is less disturbed. Cross the lane opposite the car park and follow the footpath past the style.

Wavendon Heath (OS ref. SP 925 340)

A Bedford Estates property of mainly coniferous woodland with Oak and Birch to the south. Take the lane west off the A5130 towards the golf course and park in the sandy car park near the county boundary.

Resident greensand birds include Green Woodpecker, Woodcock, Stock Dove and possibly Long-eared Owl. Summer brings breeding Tree Pipit and Redstart with sporadic records of Nightjar.

Woburn Park (OS ref. SP 960 330)

The grounds of Woburn Abbey consist of a wide range of man-made habitats with mixed woodland and open deerpark combining with lakes and streams to form an area that is rich in species. Access is restricted and an entrance fee is payable.

The Rhododendron-fringed lakes harbour Mandarin Duck and Goosander occur on the open water during winter. The parkland is good for Jackdaw, Nuthatch and woodpeckers. Most of the woods are out of bounds but Buzzard are often seen drifting over in the colder months.

BERKSHIRE

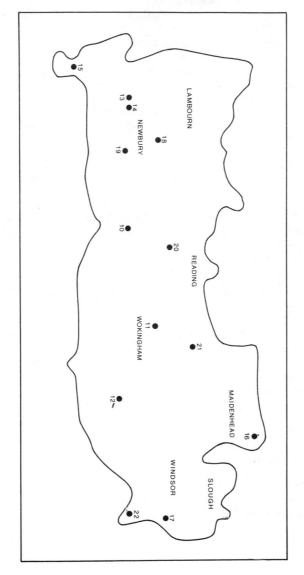

BURGHFIELD & PADWORTH COMMONS

Map 10/OS ref. SU 635 653

Habitat

Encompassed by Padworth, Ufton Nervet, Burghfield and Mortimer is an area of common-land and woods of varying maturity covering some 750 acres (300 ha). Many of the plantations have been felled in recent years and younger plantations have succeeded them. These range from areas of marsh scrub, as in the case of Padworth Common, through 6.5 ft (2 m) high conifer compartments, such as at Ufton Court, to more established stands in the vicinity of Four Houses Corner. Much of the timber management is carried out by the Englefield Estate and whereas the majority of the area is by no means of 'reserve' status the resulting habitat is a valuable haven to many species of bird. There is in fact a small conservation area near Ufton Court where other creatures as diverse as Glow-worms and Roe Deer can be found. South of this area is a region of deciduous woodland and a small enclosed pool and, on the Hampshire border, there is a significant parcel of land reclaimed from mineral excavations and left covered in gravel after levelling. Padworth Common itself has been established by Newbury District Council and, save for a small stand of Scots Pine, is entirely open with emerging Birch and shrubbery. The boundary of the Common with Hampshire is a mature Gorse hedgerow which provides a dense nesting area for several species.

Access

The general area is 4 miles (6.5 km) south of Theale and the nearest main road connections are junctions 11 and 12 of the M4. Other than popular off-road parking in the Burghfield Common area, there are no 'official' car parking areas. However there are several places along the lanes serving the area where one might safely leave a vehicle. Stratfield Mortimer hosts the most adjacent mainline railway station. Pedestrian access is reasonably good over much of the area, although permitted access to parts of the Englefield Estate is restricted to one or two public footpaths and main tracks.

Species

How fortunate are the birdwatchers among the local population to have the nearby gravel pits of Theale and Burghfield at which to while away the winter weekends and the woods and commons even more immediately available in which to stroll in summer, for this is when the subject area is at its best. Whilst the winter scene is by no means dull with the woodland flocks of foraging tits and finches, and the farmland gatherings of winter thrushes and corvids, it is the warmer months, heralded by the spring passage, that provides the impetus to the species count for the area. The territorial behaviour of Tawny Owls in January and the first broods of Long-tailed Tits by early April are events of the past by the time the summer visitors start to pass through and, although there is the prospect of seeing Crossbills in the more mature conifers at almost any time of the year, this likelihood may well be enhanced during migration. The edges of the more mature conifer stands could well tempt Redstarts to make a brief stop over whilst Whinchat can be seen in the open scrub areas nearby, during April. Wandering Barn or Short-eared Owls are seen in the general area from time to time, but the Little Owl is resident in the Ufton sector, and probably elsewhere too. Green and Great Spotted Woodpeckers also frequent the same region and whereas occasional sightings of Lesser Spotted Woodpeckers are a possibility, there may be too little deciduous woodland here to entice them to tarry.

By late April the avian scene for the next few weeks is set. With possible encounters with Nightingale in the Padworth area and the occasional Nightjars that may have strayed across the Hampshire border, a definite summer flavour is taken on. Whitethroats are fairly common though one may sometimes only be aware of their presence by their scolding 'tchack' call from dense bushes or Gorse if the observer becomes unwittingly close to a nest. Linnets are found pretty much over the whole area and Garden Warblers frequent the Burghfield and Ufton regions. Warm summer days are made all the more cheerier with peals of Willow Warbler's song, usually delivered from the top of a small Birch or conifer but the denser and more mature woodland patches will need to be visited to locate Chiffchaff and Blackcap. Coal Tit, Long-tailed Tit and Goldcrest breed in the more thickly planted soft wood stands of 19 ft (6 m) height or more. Woodcock have been seen 'roding', but the status of this bird in the locality is uncertain.

If one bird in particular enhances the summer setting however it is the Tree Pipit. Having arrived in April, and probably seen many others passing on, small numbers of these extrovert songsters stay on. They may well be found near Ufton or Burghfield and even more regularly on Padworth Common where treetops and power lines alternate as song perches. Every birdwatcher has a favourite songster. For many this may well be the Nightingale. However, whereas this species delivers its melody from the depths of bushes, usually lurking unseen, the Tree Pipit has a proclivity for delivering its lyrics during a prolonged and elaborate song-flight. Not for this bird the shyness of the Nightingale and if one is fortunate enough to come across several Pipits displaying in this manner at the same time it can provide a memorable occasion. Yet possibly even greater pleasure might be derived from a chance meeting with Woodlark which are reported in the general area from time to time.

The gravel-strewn infill between mature conifer compartments near Four Houses Corner can also be interesting. Often resembling a barren waste there are occasions when several Pied Wagtails can be seen feeding on the ground and hirundines will hawk over the area for insects, sometimes accompanied by Swifts. Conditions here could also suit Little Ringed Plover, a species which, over the years, has expropriated an increasingly wide range of habitats. Another bird which can be expected almost anywhere in the district is the Cuckoo. The small woodland pool near Padworth will usually host Moorhen and one or two Little Grebe, but any strange 'bird' calls in early spring at the pool side will be frogs calling. The high-pitched contact calls of Spotted Flycatcher in the overhanging trees however, will be real enough.

These sights and sounds are of course curtailed in autumn and for a while the area may be rather quiet, the deciduous woodlands being only slightly more active than the coniferous compartments. Gradually groups of Redpolls build up in numbers, 20 or so being typical, and

Siskins appear. The marshy conditions on and around Padworth Common become favourable for wintering Snipe and Lapwing, and it would be worth looking out for Golden Plover beyond the Gorse hedge. Ironically the woodland loses its foliage at a time when there is less to be seen, and so the local birdwatchers revert to the gravel pits for another season. For a somewhat unusual mixture of habitat within the county, the Commons are almost certainly under-watched and merit greater attention.

Calendar

Resident Little Grebe, occasional Sparrowhawk, Kestrel, Grey Partridge, Pheasant, Lapwing, Snipe, probably Woodcock, Collared Dove, Tawny and Little Owl, Skylark, possibility of Woodlark, Meadow Pipit, Pied Wagtail, Goldcrest, common tits, Nuthatch and Treecreeper. Linnet, chance of irregular Crossbill.

December–February Possibility of occasional Golden Plover, and Snipe, Tawny Owls courting, numbers of Rooks and Jackdaws increase in adjacent fields, winter thrushes at woodland edge, mixed tit flocks in evergreen sectors, Siskin and Redpoll in deciduous woodland.

March–May Early breeding species ensconsed, more summer warblers on site by late April, as with Cuckoo. Nightingale and Tree Pipit by early May followed by Spotted Flycatcher.

June–July Main breeding period for many species, chance of churring Nightjar or reeling of Grasshopper Warbler.

August–November Passage activity not too evident, but winter thrushes may have arrived before the end of November. Possibility of overwintering Chiffchaff or Blackcap.

DINTON PASTURES &
LAVELL'S LAKE

Map 11/OS ref. SU 780 725

Habitat

Dinton Pastures Country Park was established by Wokingham District Council in 1979 following extensive mineral extraction on the site. This had resulted in seven lakes in an area of some 250 acres (100 ha), half of this being water, between the River Loddon and the Emm Brook. After an initial programme of intensive landscaping, these lakes were established for a variety of purposes. The main expanse of water, Black Swan Lake, is the only one on which sailing, canoeing and boardsailing is permitted. It has two islands which some species use for breeding. Anglers use White Swan Lake, the second largest, which is well stocked with Carp, Roach, Tench, Rudd and Pike. Sandford Lake was established as a wildlife area and possesses gravel pits, shallows and small islands suited to gulls and waders, which can be viewed from a small hide. The remaining, smaller pools are in rather quieter corners of the Park and are more marshy, tree-lined and secluded. Floating rafts have been installed on Sandford Lake to enhance tern nesting possibilities. Wader scrapes are also being constructed. There are quite large areas of scrub and old meadowland which support a wide range of wild flowers, including the Loddon Lily. A golf course provides an area of open grassland, and there are stretches of established hedgerow at various points around the Park.

More recently an adjacent area, Lavell's Lake has been nominated as a conservation area and the Friends of Lavell's Lake have constructed footpaths, hides and wader scrapes on this 40 acre (16 ha) site which already possessed mature reed stands.

Access

The site is north-east of Wokingham and the main entrance is off the B3030, Davies Street, approximately 200 yds (180 m) north of the bridge over the A329(M). By road, the area is served by the M4 (junction 10), taking the A329(M) towards Reading, the A329 to Wokingham, and turning left onto the B3030. Alternatively, from the A4 at Twyford, travel south on the A321, turning right to the B3030 at Hurst.

The main car park at the site holds some 70 vehicles but overflow parking is available in the angler's car park. There is a pedestrian access to the pastures at two locations near Sandford Mill to the north and over the Loddon footbridge near Tufty's corner to the south-west.

The nearest railway station is at Winnersh approximately 0.6 miles (1 km) from the main entrance. The Park Centre comprises an information office, Warden's and administrative facility, lecture rooms, study rooms, toilets and a small refreshment area. The Park management run a programme of sports and educational activities throughout the year, including birdwatching, but also natural history subjects, mammal study, photography, conservation and many others. Access to the only hide on Sandford Lake is unrestricted and the same will apply to the two hides being provided on Lavell's Lake.

Species

Since regular records of sightings at Dinton were commenced, the total species count has risen to over 165 and whilst many may only make irregular appearances, the combination of lakes and mature trees and hedgerows guarantees a good variety at any time. A day at the Park in April can yield as many as 80 species. As with all such locations, the waters are most active in winter, the bushes and vegetation in summer. At the beginning of the year, waterfowl numbers build up on all of the main lakes and Dinton Pastures may be unusual in having Gadwall outnumbering Mallard and even Tufted Duck. Up to 150 of this delicately marked duck have been counted, still tending to move around in pairs rather than as a flock, and in hard weather, following Mute Swan closely, no doubt picking up the scraps of weed the Swans bring to the surface. The Swans themselves often number in the high eighties, partly because the local Swan Rescue Service release treated birds in the Park for their recuperation.

Rafts of Pochard accumulate, particularly on White Swan and Sandford Lakes whilst similar numbers of Wigeon occur on Black Swan Lake. Small numbers of Shoveler and Goldeneye can be seen throughout January and February, but March sees the build-up of Canada Goose flocks which, along with Common Gulls, have learned to come to the bank to feed on bread, providing excellent opportunities for photography. Another of Dinton's specialities, the Egyptian Goose, is also likely to join in these feeding forays, its plumage pattern regarded as exotic by some, as faintly amusing by others.

The southern island on Black Swan Lake is usually guarded by anything up to 25 Cormorant, perched like black sentinels on a large dead elm tree in the middle, sometimes accompanied by Heron. Elsewhere in the Park, Mungell's Pond and the River Loddon are worth checking for Little Grebe and the occasional Water Rail. Whilst near the Loddon, a scan of the Alders along the bank will usually be rewarded at this time of year by large flocks of Siskin, occasionally interspersed with small numbers of Redpoll and followed by groups of Goldfinch, especially at Mortimer's Meadows and the weir above Heron's Water. Pied and Grey Wagtail can usually be seen in the vicinity of the sports club buildings, or near Tufty's Corner whilst Kingfisher can be expected almost anywhere on the site but particularly on Emm Brook and the islands on Black Swan Lake.

Lavell's Lake has yet to establish itself after recent landscaping work, but the wader scrape is likely to prove very successful and Golden Plover can be expected amongst large flocks of Lapwing in the meadows beyond. With Smew, Pintail, Ruddy Duck, Goosander, Snipe, and Woodcock all recorded, together with rare appearances of Bewick's and Whooper Swan, a winter visit will never be wasted.

As spring advances, the flocks of winter thrushes and Teal give way to passage migrants. Wheatear and Yellow Wagtail pass through regularly, usually seen on or near the golf course. Common and Green Sandpiper may well be seen from the Sandford Lake hide and, when water levels are low, around the sandy banks of the two Swan Lakes. Whilst uncommon, Water Pipit and Tree Pipit have occurred and both species of godwit have made appearances. Curlew and Whimbrel have passed through on occasions and, amongst the Common Tern which stay on, Sandwich Tern and Little Gull are regarded as rare visitors. Whinchat can be located at this time, perhaps along Emm Brook on fence posts or exposed vegetation. Large numbers of hirundines pass through on their way to the many other Thames-side gravel workings in the area.

As the frenetic activity of the spring passage abates, Dinton becomes the domain of those species which have stayed on to join the resident birds for procreation. Around 50 species are known to breed here. Amongst the more notable records are the first Gadwall to breed in Berkshire, and the Common Tern which nest on Sandford Lake alongside the Little Ringed Plover. The resident pair of Egyptian Geese usually produce one brood of young and recently the local Kestrel pair have also raised young. By midsummer, the majority of visiting warbler species have nested, the Sedge and Reed Warblers near the car park, the Whitethroat, Blackcap and Willow Warbler near Mungell's Pond. Bullfinch and Reed Bunting breed around Middle Marsh and Stock Dove near Lavell's Lake. Both Green and Great Spotted Woodpecker breed occasionally, the Lesser Spotted species, although sometimes seen in the Park, apparently nesting elsewhere.

Kingfisher

By late summer, the creche of Canada goslings are chaperoned around by elected mothers, the remaining adult birds having moved off elsewhere to reduce the pressure on available food. The young Little Grebes on Mungell's Pond will also be well advanced and, if they are having a good year, the Great Crested Grebe second broods will be well on the way. The nest box scheme has proven very successful but attempts to attract Sand Martins to artificial nest holes in suitable sandy banks have, to date, failed. The Kingfisher on the other hand needs little encouragement to multiply within the confines of the Park. Amongst the non-breeding visitors that may be seen would be Hobby and Sparrow-hawk. On rare occasions Garganey have stopped over briefly. Grasshopper Warblers have not bred here for some time but occasionally delight the fortunate ear with their reeling notes. Chiffchaff call out their name in the small bushes between Mungell's Pond and Tufty's Corner. The Nightingale is an uncommon, but nonetheless welcome visitor, as is the Nuthatch. With the approach of autumn, the inevitable pull of the south takes its effect on the summer visitors, their places taken by others who pay a brief visit during their own journeys. Green and Wood Sandpiper may be encountered at this time as may Greenshank and, on the smaller side, Coal Tit. As the seasonal cycle completes itself, the more usual winter birds may be joined occasionally by Red-legged and Grey Partridge, Meadow Pipit and Corn Bunting to the south of the site, Dunlin on Sandford Lake and Brambling amongst the small flocks of finches that build up. One coud reasonably expect to see Goosander from time to time, usually the female of the species, and Short-eared Owl has been recorded on a few occasions. Tree Sparrows sometimes frequent the car park, providing something of a treat when discovered amongst the more numerous House Sparrows.

Thus, Dinton Pastures, after just a few years, has become one of the foremost birdwatching sites in the County and the continued management programme, combined with development pressures elsewhere which tends to concentrate birds into the few remaining untouched habitats, is likely to ensure that its record will improve still further.

Calendar

Resident Common wildfowl, Great Crested Grebe, Little Grebe, Heron, Cormorant, Egyptian Geese, Stock Dove, Skylark, Pied and Grey Wagtails, Kingfisher, Kestrel, Green Woodpecker, Reed Bunting, Bullfinch, Goldcrest.

December–February Pochard, Wigeon, Gadwall, Shoveler, other ducks in larger numbers, Siskin and Redpoll, small groups of Yellowhammer, some winter thrushes, numerous Mute Swan, increased gull numbers, occasional Goldeneye and sawbills, occasional groups of Dunnock, Tree Sparrow.

March–May Passage migrants, including Wheatear and Yellow Wagtail, summer warblers arrive led by Willow Warbler and Chiffchaff, with Sedge Warblers, Common and Lesser Whitethroat soon after. Common Sandpiper, possibility of Hobby.

June–July Breeding period, Kestrel, Sparrowhawk and Cuckoo very active. Canada Goose creche formed, Egyptian goslings in evidence, Common Tern nesting, many nest boxes in use. Hirundines hawking over pools in large numbers.

August–November Late breeding Great Crested Grebe still on the nest, large number of juveniles of many species, hirundines gathering for departure, winter thrushes arriving, Goldfinch and Linnet flocking.

ENGLEMERE POND   Map 12/OS ref. SU 905 687

Habitat
This rather small site was acquired by Bracknell District Council in 1977 from the Crown Estate and comprises 65 acres (26 ha) of mixed woodland surrounding a reed-edged pool which is classified as a SSSI. The tree-line to the north, and adjacent to the golf driving range, is essentially deciduous with numerous Silver Birches but with some conifers in the area of the timber yard. South of the pond the woodland comprises mainly Scots Pine, dense in places but generally quite open with an area of heathland near the railway line, which although small, contains three species of heather.

Nestling in the middle of the woodland is Englemere Pond, approximately 25 acres (10 ha) in size and extensively reeded on three sides. In fact the site boasts the largest reedbed in east Berkshire. The edge of the water nearest the car park has a small area of Alder carr. Fishing is exercised, although restricted to permit holders. A board-walk extends out across the water from the northern perimeter as a means of enlarging the fishable area.

Access
Englemere Pond is 546 yds (500 m) south of the A329 mid-way between Bracknell and Ascot. A small car park, housing up to 15 vehicles, is entered from the Swinley Road (B3017). There are pedestrian entrances near the railway bridge and on either side of the timber yard. A number of tracks are available to explore the wooded areas and it is possible to walk all around the pond, although the eastern boundary path is usually very boggy, requiring suitable footware and an intrepid nature. When walking in the north-western sector, it is wise to beware of wayward golf balls from the adjoining driving range.

Species
A walk around Englemere can be of interest to the birdwatcher at any time of year, although spring and summer time are best. The winter scene is dominated by small flocks of various tits, Goldcrests and Treecreepers moving through the conifer stands in the south, occasionally joined by one or two Reed Buntings who forsake the pool now and again. The deciduous woods north of the pond exhibit a similar spectacle but in this location it is mixed finch flocks that predominate, often including Redpoll and Siskin. These trees are adjacent to the open driving range affording suitable roosts for small numbers of Redwing and Mistle Thrushes, but Fieldfares only occur infrequently. Groups of Long-tailed Tits are particularly active even after some of their number have paired off and commenced nesting in March. As spring approaches the resident Great Spotted Woodpeckers begin hammering out their courtship intentions, both male and female participating, and Green Woodpecker may be seen on the golfing fairway or the deciduous stand, having been perhaps a little less obvious during the winter months. Tawny Owls may not be resident in these woods but are often encountered, particularly at this time of year when they become a little more vociferous. Throughout this period the pond will not have been

too busy save for daily visits of up to 100 Black-headed Gulls that move in to bathe having spent the morning on the local rubbish tip. However the resident Water Rails will by now be preparing their own nest, being more likely heard than seen.

The pond edge, particularly the western carr and the southern tree-line, hosts Goldcrest throughout the year and by early March the courtship routine of the Willow Tit can be observed, commencing with a high-pitched Nightjar-like 'churring' from the female whilst the male excitedly flits from branch to branch above her uttering single piercing notes in response. An early morning visit may be rewarded with a sight of an overnight Heron or an occasional Pochard, but the water is not especially inspiring until the summer months when the chattering of breeding Reed Warblers is conducted by the metronome calls of Chiffchaffs in the bank-side trees. The slightly different chattering of the Sedge Warblers should also be listened for, the cream-coloured supercilium being the give-away to this species if seen. At the height of summer the reedbed becomes an important roost for many House Martins, wagtails and the occasional Swallow. Pied Wagtails have been known to nest in the timber yard which also provides a haven for Wrens and Robins to rear their offspring.

In some years, Sparrowhawks decide to breed in Englemere Wood and the arrivals and departures of the parent birds can wreak havoc to the idyllic scene below. However, the raptors seem quite content to carry out the majority of their hunting on neighbouring farmland and predation to other resident nesting species is likely to be low. In fact small breeding passerines are more likely to be harassed by the local Jays than by the Sparrowhawks. As summer draws to a close numerous juveniles of a variety of species swell the woodland population. Speckled offspring of Reed Buntings may be seen waiting for their final feed on the anglers' board-walk looking not unlike the winter plumage that will shortly adorn the adult male. There may even be the opportunity of seeing a young Cuckoo being urged on its way by its unsuspecting Reed Warbler foster parents and large numbers of immature Blue and Long-tailed Tits will be active in both types of woodland present, unaware that a pitifully small number of them will survive to maturity. The second broods of noisy Nuthatches will also be readily located.

The autumn passage is difficult to monitor in this small and compact site, but is not likely to be a significant event. Over-wintering Crossbills may well be seen and there is always the prospect of a Firecrest sampling the delights of the evergreen sector. The tall trees on all sides of the pool do not help to attract flocks of roosting ducks and geese and this situation is likely to pertain until the time of any felling planned in the vicinity of the lake. However occasional Shoveler and Gadwall may be seen in small numbers. As the nights draw in and the foliage falls from the Oaks and Birch in the northern area, it will certainly be worth keeping an eye open for an occasional Lesser Spotted Woodpecker as they move around a number of small tree-scapes in the area.

Despite being a somewhat diminutive locale, there is every prospect of seeing a reasonably wide range of woodland birds with the added flavour afforded by the reed-lined pond, and serves well as a reminder of the probable scene over a much greater area before the vast Windsor Forest was interfered with by man, and the conifers were added.

Calendar

Resident Mallard, Sparrowhawk, Water Rail, Moorhen, Blue Tit, Great Tit, Willow Tit, Long-tailed Tit, Coal Tit, Goldcrest, Reed Bunting, Chaffinch, Bullfinch, Greenfinch, Nuthatch, Treecreeper, Pied Wagtail, Great Spotted Woodpecker, Green Woodpecker.

December–February Redpoll, Siskin, Crossbill (occasionally), winter thrushes, Black-headed Gull, Shoveler, occasional Jackdaw, infrequent Lesser Spotted Woodpecker.

March–May Chiffchaff, occasional Blackcap, Garden Warbler, possible Cuckoo, Willow Warblers on passage.

June–July Possible Spotted Flycatcher, occasional sightings of Hobby on the periphery, hirundines in good numbers.

August–November Small passage movement, gathering of mixed feeding flocks of finches and tits.

FREEMEN'S MARSH   Map 13/OS ref. SU 334 687

Habitat

The area consists of some 100 acres (40 ha) of marsh, west of Hungerford mostly registered as common land, but some in private hands. The 1.25 miles (2 km) stretch of land runs alongside the Kennet and Avon Canal and also hosts the meandering River Dun. The carse forms rough grazing and includes reedbeds, small groups of bushes, some established trees, including willow and Alder, and more recently planted Poplars and other species. The area has a mainly open aspect and fishing is a popular pastime, particularly on the canal.

The northern perimeter is tree-lined, though not densely so and beyond lies the vast arable Hopgrass Fields. To the south of the area is the main railway line beyond which is also arable land. The marsh is well served with footpaths and footbridges across the canal, river, ditches and streams. Some parts can be exceptionally boggy during spells of wet weather.

The site is of botanical interest and in a ten-year study of the fauna and flora of the marsh, R.G. Frankum and M. Frankum recorded over 300 species of trees, shrubs, grasses, sedge, rush, flowers and herbs, many of them uncommon in the region. The railway embankment harbours Cowslips in spring and various chalk land species. At other times Stoat may be seen hunting along the river bank.

Access

The site is 3 miles (5 km) south of junction 14 on the M4 and may be approached on foot along the canal footpath out of Hungerford Town; cross at the swing bridge (which is known locally as Church Bridge) opposite the church. However, parking in the town can often be difficult and the alternative would be to travel west from Hungerford along the A4 for approximately 1 mile (1.5 km) at which point a large lay-by will be found, suitable for accommodating some 30 vehicles, adjacent to a small fruit farm. From this point, access to the marsh is via Ford Gate. One is free to wander over the non-private sections of the marsh, but there is a footpath route around much of the perimeter which usefully serves a circumnavigation of the area if preferred. The canal may be crossed at any one of the three locks or via Church Bridge. In any event it may prove worthwhile exiting at Ford Gate during a visit to view the large fields north of the marsh in anticipation of flock activity, especially in autumn and winter.

Species

During the ten year study referred to, 132 bird species were recorded on the marsh and adjacent fields. The canal has good numbers of Mute Swan, particularly in autumn when herds of 30 or more can be found. Smaller groups occupy the streams which run through the grazing area, the males securing territory with much hissing and posturing. The Little Grebe is also numerous with several breeding pairs, and Heron are common. There is no reason why Kingfisher should not be expected, and Dipper have been recorded on occasions. Water Rail have regrettably not bred here for many years, but they are regular winter visitors, the best chance of seeing this shy bird being early morning when all is frozen. Teal are a regular winter visitor in small numbers, amongst much larger numbers of Mallard, Tufted Duck and Coot. However, the area is not renowned for over-wintering duck species.

The most common raptor is the Kestrel, which breeds nearby, whilst Sparrowhawk, though a less frequent visitor, can be seen circling the western edge of the marsh occasionally. The affect of this over the heavily populated Hopgrass Fields in autumn can be quite dramatic with large numbers of Lapwing, Black-headed Gull, Skylark and Meadow Pipit put to flight. Passage sightings of Hobby are also made fairly regularly, and there is always the possibility of Buzzard soaring over from nearby Walbury Hill. Of the birds with their feet more firmly on the ground, Grey Partridge and Pheasant are regularly found, especially during periods of scant cover in the adjacent arable areas. Then their guttural croaks and squawks can be heard almost anywhere on the marsh. Quite often during winter months Golden Plover may be spotted amongst the Lapwing whilst the only other regular wader is the Snipe, which has used the marsh as a breeding ground in the past. Jack Snipe visit occasionally in winter and other common waders make sporadic visits on passage. Whilst gulls do not often alight on the marsh itself, several of the common species will be seen over-flying at the beginning and end of short winter days.

Owls are uncommon on the marsh particularly since 1 February 1986 when the 'local' Barn Owl was hit by a train south of Marsh Lock. Woodpeckers also are not seen regularly due to the lack of mature trees and the Lesser Spotted variety has not nested for many years, since the death of the majority of the Elm trees. Numbers of hirundine vary from year to year, but quite sizeable roosts occur in the reedbeds. With relatively few trees on the marsh, sightings of Nuthatch and Treecreeper are considered a bonus.

The resident thrushes all nest regularly, and in the early part of winter, before the relatively few Hawthorn bushes have been stripped, winter thrushes are numerous. Of the warblers, Willow, Reed and Sedge will usually be encountered in summer and Lesser Whitethroat may be more regularly seen than the Common Whitethroat.

Blackcap and Chiffchaff also breed in the area. The Grasshopper Warbler on the other hand is becoming more scarce at the location. Spotted Flycatcher can be expected, particularly in the vicinity of the church and at Bottomers Heyes. Both Pied and Grey Wagtail breed on the marsh, but the Yellow Wagtail is usually only seen on passage.

Most members of the finch family including Siskin are quite common, gathering in large mixed flocks in autumn. The Redpoll and Brambling are scarcer, whereas Corn Bunting are frequently seen (or heard). During a good summer, the Cuckoo may have a busy time. The male will alight upon a prominent perch calling loudly, its long wings almost touching beneath its tail with each call, as if in a self-congratulatory applause. The female meanwhile will be more obscured, watching for anxiously disturbed nesting birds during her short visit to Britain.

The marsh therefore attracts a wide variety of species and, given the prospect of occasional visits of such birds as Wryneck, Red-backed Shrike, Goldeneye and Garganey, all of which have been recorded over the years, it is a site well worth a regular visit.

Calendar

Resident Mute Swan, Little Grebe, Tufted Duck, Kestrel, Sparrowhawk, Skylark, Snipe, Great Spotted Woodpecker, Reed Bunting, Pied Wagtail.

December–February Water Rail (occasional), Black-headed Gull, Herring Gull, Jack Snipe (occasional), Meadow Pipit, winter thrushes, Siskin, sometimes accompanied by Redpoll.

March–May Common warblers, Spotted Flycatcher, Grey and Yellow Wagtails, Turtle Dove (occasional), Cuckoo.

June–July Rather quiet during breeding period, much disturbance from visitors.

August–November Flocks of Swallows, House Martins and Sand Martins preparing for migration, early Redwing and Fieldfare, small numbers of winter visiting duck arrive, mixed flocks of finches build up.

HUNGERFORD COMMON Map 14/OS ref. SU 345 680

Habitat

The Common is a small area, perhaps some 125 acres (50 ha) of dry pasture edged with mixed woodland to the south-east and the linear waterways of the Kennet and Avon Canal and the River Kennet running parallel with each other to the north.

Along the water system is a trout farm near the Down Gate, a lock near the Dun Mill entrance, and a small sewage farm on the Kintbury side. Just north of the river, east of the sewage farm, is a dense thicket of willows and Hawthorn. The Common itself is interspersed with mature trees and gently sloping grassland and, despite free access for vehicular traffic, can be a most tranquil place at times. With picturesque views of Inkpen Hill in the south, one can readily forget the hustle and bustle of Hungerford town which abuts the Common. A small Beech wood at Deadman's Corner obscures an old worked-out chalk pit, now also overgrown with trees, and a favourite hiding place for Red-legged Partridge. Botanically the site is also of interest and, as with Freemen's Marsh, a great deal of study work was undertaken by R.G. and M. Frankum during the 1970s and early 1980s. The reports published following this work at the two sites are detailed in the Bibliography of this book.

Access

As may be expected, the Common lies alongside Hungerford, south of the A4, and east of the A338. The nearest motorway interconnection is junction 14 of the M4, 4 miles (6 km) to the north, and the nearest mainline railway station is within 110 yds (100 m) of the town-gate entrance. Vehicular access is at four points: Down Gate near the town, Dun Mill (Denford Gate) to the north, Kintbury Gate to the east and, from the south, Inkpen Gate. To avoid the town, the Dun Mill entrance from the A4 may be preferred but expect to meet cattle on any of the roads once the grids have been crossed. Parking is available throughout the area but the Trustees appreciate drivers not pulling more than a few feet off the road, in order to contain erosion of grassland.

Species

Although not a bird sanctuary in the true sense, the simple fact that both the Common and the waterways are maintained as such, has given stability to the variety of birds attracted to this site. Probably any new records, or increased sightings of unusual birds, are the product of dedicated observation over long periods rather than any change in the habitat. The combination of water and common-land ensures worthwhile visits at almost any time of year. In winter, the trout farm is a good place to start in the hope of Water Rail and Grey Wagtail. The many Herons which used to congregate here have long since been successfully deterred, but the odd one or two might be seen. Dabchicks will be more in evidence on the canal than at other times of the year and a flock of Golden Plover may be seen occasionally wheeling over the fields north of the A4. Large flocks of Siskin can be found moving between the water-side trees and the main plantation, occasionally with one or two

Redpoll among their numbers. On the Common, Fieldfare and Redwing are abundant, especially on Elder bushes alongside the plantation, and the hedgerow beyond Deadmans Corner will often accommodate groups of Yellowhammer. Meadow Pipits abound, either on the grassed areas to the east or the farmland in the south-west.

The spring passage is fairly evident with regular sightings of Wheatear and less regular visits by Whinchat and Redstart. Nightingale can be heard in the thicket north of the canal from April and one or two are likely to stay on. Near the sewage farm, House Martins and Swallows are seen early on and, if one has luck on one's side, a Grasshopper Warbler may also show up. Another regular migrant in recent years has been the Hobby and Buzzards fly over infrequently, perhaps from the heady heights of Inkpen Hill. By mid-May many of these species have moved on and Hungerford's breeding season gets underway. Not that all species which summer here actually nest. Yellow Wagtails are certainly in evidence but not proven to have bred and Linnets, whilst regularly seen, also appear to prefer nesting elsewhere, perhaps in more dense vegetation which is sparse on the Common. In the coniferous and deciduous plantation alongside the eastern boundary of the site however, several species make good use of the summer months. Goldcrest are much in evidence, their young sometimes calling from the small Holly bushes at the edge of the tree-line and Marsh Tits can be heard calling from within the woodland. Long-tailed and Coal Tits will be found in the plantation and the willow scrub beyond the river. This latter site is also occupied by Blackcap, Garden Warbler, occasional Chiffchaff and numerous Willow Warblers.

Woodpeckers are often encountered. Green Woodpeckers can be seen flying over the more open areas whilst the Great Spotted Woodpecker will be heard making its familiar 'tchak' call from within the plantation, hopefully just prior to flying across to one of the exposed trees on the Common, where better views are possible. The third woodpecker species, the Lesser Spotted is also present, though perhaps not on a full-time basis and in any case is more easily seen during winter months when the leaves have fallen. Nuthatches and Treecreepers are also well-established and the unassuming Dunnock is always on hand to serenade all and sundry. Owls are not seen or heard regularly, though a Short-eared Owl might flick through on autumn passage and Woodcock, though in the area, cannot be guaranteed to entertain every evening. This information may avoid a wasted evening visit.

Through August and September, the numbers of Swallows and House Martins dwindle and the obvious juvenile plumages of Pied and Grey Wagtails become apparent at the sewage farm. Any Turtle Doves that were in the area will have commenced their long journey back and the Cuckoo that made infrequent visits to the Common will already have completed their return trip. Groups of gulls will assemble overhead each evening having spent the day on nearby farmland and significant flocks of Lapwing will accumulate north of the A4. For a while the Common is rather quiet, awaiting the return of winter thrushes and pipits and the waterways, now devoid of occasional Common Sandpipers, become a less congested hunting ground for the resident Kingfisher. The area around the chalk pit reveals the success of breeding amongst Grey and Red-legged Partridge and also the colony of Chukars which are probably bred for hunting purposes on the adjacent estate. Sparrowhawks, no

Grey Partridge

longer with young to feed, become less prominent whereas corvids group in good numbers, and the seasons have come full circle.

Calendar

Resident Little Grebe, Heron, Mallard, Tufted Duck, Canada Goose, Mute Swan, Sparrowhawk, Kestrel, Red-legged and Grey Partridge, occasional Chukar. Pheasant, Moorhen and Coot. Lapwing, occasional Woodcock, Stock Dove and Woodpigeon. Collared Doves infrequent. All three woodpeckers, Kingfisher, and all common corvids; six tits, Nuthatch and Treecreeper. Mistle Thrush numerous. Blackcap and Chiffchaff have over-wintered quite often recently. Goldcrest, Dunnock, Pied and Grey Wagtails and the common finches. Occasional Yellowhammer.

December–February Small numbers of Teal, Gadwall and Pochard. Water Rails regular, Snipe less so. Golden Plover on adjacent sites. Mixed gulls over-flying daily. Corvid numbers increase, Fieldfare and Redwing in reasonable quantities. Meadow Pipits, numerous Siskin, occasional Redpoll. Bramblings scarce.

March–May Hobby, Wheatear and Turtle Dove on passage. Cuckoo and hirundines arrive early April. Occasional Skylark. Nightingales, one or two of which stay over. Sedge and Willow Warblers regular visitors but Reed and Grasshopper Warblers scarce. Blackcap, Garden Warblers, but few Whitethroat and Lesser Whitethroat. Chiffchaff, Spotted Fly-catcher, occasional Yellow Wagtail.

June–July Not especially active but the site is pleasant enough to make up for that. Occasional Common Sandpiper.

August–November Summer visitors gradually disperse by September. Chance of Hobby or Buzzard on the move. Winter thrushes and Meadow Pipits arrive by October.

INKPEN & WALBURY
HILLS
Map 15/OS ref. SU 370 620

Habitat
Other than to partake of the magnificent views of the Downs in summer or to experience the ferocity of winter gales, the birdwatcher may possibly only visit this site during periods of migration.

At 975 ft (297 m) Walbury Hill is the highest point in Berkshire; an ideal place to get on top of one's birdwatching. Inkpen Hill is grassed on both its steep and gentler slopes, whereas Walbury has a more arable flavour with stony fields on either side of the ridge. The southern slope is used for grazing but possesses scattered Gorse and Hawthorn shrubbery. A small conifer compartment complements a dense Hawthorn thicket, with a horshoe-shaped line of mature Beech trees and passage birds can be seen passing over the roadway between them. The north-facing slope of Walbury is also partly tree-covered, affording good shelter for wandering birds. Hang-gliding is a popular pastime but this does not appear to disturb the birdlife in the area.

Access
The Hills overlook a mosaic of country lanes which interlace the lowlands between the A343 running south from Newbury and the A338 running south from Hungerford. An Ordnance Survey map will be necessary to extricate oneself from this maze of picturesque roadways and to arrive at either of the two car parks situated on the top of the escarpment. These two parking spots are joined by a track but this is not always capable of taking a vehicle due to depth of mud or reduced ground clearance when tractors have made regular use of the link during periods of heavy conditions. One is free to walk the ridge itself and footpaths lead to various adjacent locations, including Combe Wood 0.6 miles (1 km) to the south.

Species
The opening comments of this chapter are not intended to suggest that there are no resident birds on the Hills, particularly as this is one site in the county where Buzzards can be expected in any month of the year. From Inkpen Hill one can poach a view of Wiltshire's Jackdaws which often gather in huge numbers, though even in such large flocks one can observe pair-bonding by early April. The stoney fields around Walbury are regularly visited by Pheasant and Grey Partridge and passerines such as Corn Bunting, Yellowhammer and Meadow Pipits. The grassy slopes and boundary fence-posts are often occupied by Linnets or occasional Goldfinches and Skylarks provide a musical accompaniment to this airy place. The opportunity often presents itself to view Kestrels, and sometimes Sparrowhawks, from above as they traverse the slopes at a lower elevation; in fact, on a good 'raptor day' one might be fortunate enough to see both of these species and the previously mentioned Buzzards. The scrub and woodland areas attract many Greenfinches and the more common tits. Magpies are very much at home on the field margins of the various small copses.

66

When birds are on the move in spring, and to a lesser extent in autumn, the ridge is the sort of environment that appeals to those in need of rest or food. One of the earliest visitors is the Wheatear, usually seen on the grassed southern slope of Inkpen Hill but not often in more than ones or twos at a time.

Another regular short term guest is the Ring Ouzel which, like the Wheatear, will soon push on towards the Midlands or beyond to establish a breeding territory. Both Redstart and Black Redstart can be expected, the low bushes and hedgerows probably being the best places to look.

The Stonechat is another colourful bird one might hope to come across but, if it is a female, one would be advised to check carefully as there is always the possibility of Whinchat also passing through at this time. Larger birds too will be present on occasions with Hen Harrier observed in small numbers in most years, and the Hobby, as well as being found on passage, can be seen from time to time throughout the summer. Rough-legged Buzzard is another possibility, differing from the more common Buzzard in having a much paler underwing colouring and a noticeable black band at the tip of the tail. On the much smaller side the Merlin, as always, is more difficult to spot and one will in any case have to await the autumn passage and winter period to see this dashing bird of prey.

Owls too can be quite prominent up here, particularly between October and April when the resident Little Owls on the Hills and the Tawny Owls of Combe Wood are joined sporadically by Short-eared and Barn Owls. In March, just prior to the main incoming movement, Fieldfares and Redwings can be seen gathered in flocks of 200 or more of each species south of Walbury Hill. Chaffinches flock in similar numbers in this area, making the singling out of Brambling all the more difficult, but persistence will often be rewarded. For most of the other migrating passerines however one will have to spend some time either in Combe Wood or the scrub and thicket areas of Walbury where many of the common warblers are likely to be found and where particularly good fortune may grant the sighting of a Pied Flycatcher heading for Wales. A stroll over the undulating terrain of the Hills, and through Combe Wood can be invigorating in April or October, to say the least, but the opportunity to see species which are otherwise not common in Berkshire should not be ignored.

Calendar

Resident Sparrowhawk, Buzzard, Kestrel, Grey Partridge, Pheasant. Woodcock and Tawny Owl at Combe Wood. Little Owl in the arable areas. Green and Great Spotted Woodpeckers. Common tits and finches. Large numbers of Jackdaws.

December–February Meadow Pipits, Yellowhammers and Skylarks numerous. Short-eared Owl, Brambling, possibility of Merlin. Flocks of Woodpigeon.

March–May Possibility of Hen Harrier and Barn Owl. Large flocks of winter thrushes and Chaffinches. Wheatear, Ring Ouzel and Turtle Dove on passage. Redstart and Black Redstart also moving through with common warblers. Likelihood of Tree Pipits.

June–July Several species breeding in Combe Wood and in surrounding arable farmland, good chance of Hobby. Occasional Cuckoo.

August–November Stonechat, Whinchat, Meadow Pipits. Winter thrushes arrive in November. Prospect of Merlin.

NORTH COOKHAM   Map 16/OS ref. SU 888 865

Habitat

There are many pleasant areas of Berkshire through which to walk and Cookham, although exhibiting a somewhat arable flavour, encompasses a varied habitat as it follows the River Thames by way of lowland marsh, chalk hills and mixed woodland, and as such provides interest for the birdwatcher. Cockmarsh comprises some 200 acres (80 ha) of National Trust land which is used for grazing for much of the year, and is suited to ground nesting birds and waders. Parts of the marsh are flooded during the wetter periods of winter and indeed a small number of pools are present throughout the year. Nearby Winter Hill rises steeply to some 390 ft (120 m) above sea level and the chalky slopes suffer a little from erosion, but there is a liberal covering of Hawthorn and scrub. Further west is a series of deciduous woodlands, including Quarry Wood, High Wood and Fultness Wood, which slope sharply downwards to the streams and meadows of Bisham below.

Access

Because of the Thames which bounds most of the walk to the north, and the lack of parking facilities on the A404 and Quarry Road, all access by car has to be along the southern parts of the walk. The National Trust car park at Cookham Moor caters for 30 vehicles and is approached through the picturesque village of Cookham from the A4094 Maidenhead-Bourne End Road (the only toilets in the vicinity are at this junction). There are also parking spaces along Winter Hill Road and room for a small number of vehicles near the entrances to Quarry Wood. Most of the other lanes are too narrow to permit parking. A useful footpath map of the whole area is available from the Ramblers Association. (See Useful Addresses.)

(In the following text for this section, path numbers from the Ramblers Association map have been used. They also appear on the North Cookham map.)

Species

A convenient starting point would be the National Trust car park on Cookham Moor. Take footpath 39, cross the field towards the river; in summer look for Yellow Wagtails on the way. The river is reached adjacent to the sailing club and there will most likely be Great Crested Grebe and possibly Kingfisher to accompany the mandatory Mallard and Coot. In summer, Common Tern may be seen whilst winter can result in small numbers of Pochard loafing against the far bank. Heron find the river too busy to occupy its banks, but single birds may well be seen flying over, particularly at dusk when they emerge from numerous tributaries in search of a roosting point.

In dry weather it is worth following the river bank on path 60 and then picking up one of the paths across Cockmarsh. In very wet spells it is preferable to use the linking path to the golf course, joining path 36, as this crosses the marsh on firmer ground. The copse near the railway bridge is popular for Goldcrest and Bullfinch and occasionally Whinchat, which favour the fence alongside the ditch. Follow the tree-line to the marsh, looking for Mistle Thrushes and Little Owls.

Having reached the marsh itself one should expect to see Lapwing, particularly in winter when quite large numbers will share the open space with 200 or more Canada Geese and sizeable mixed flocks of winter thrushes. Occasionally Snipe will be encountered though only in small numbers and Greenshank are a common bird of passage. In summer, both Lapwing and Redshank will breed here if conditions are favourable. Choosing between the steep incline of path 57 or the steadier climbing route of path 58, one soon reaches the top of Winter Hill which will produce Linnet and Yellowhammer at most times and Whitethroat, Willow Warbler and Chiffchaff in summer. Blackcap breed among the bushes along the slope and, in addition to Collared Dove, a reasonable amount of good fortune should ensure the sight of Turtle Doves though their soft purring may be the first indication of their presence. From the 'peak' of Winter Hill, it is fascinating to watch hirundines and Swifts from above as they make maximum use of the air currents fashioned by the slopes. House Martins proliferate more so than Swallows and the continuous movement of these birds hawking frenetically for insects can make it difficult to pick out other species present.

Soon, Dial Close is reached. To the right hand side of the main entrance is footpath number 4, which heads off towards the wood, avoiding the narrow and sometimes busy lane. This route passes through quite dense woodland, but one will see, or hear, Green Woodpecker 'yaffling' and, in summer, Chiffchaff singing. Countless Wrens will disclose the observer's presence to every other species in the area in typical fashion. It is also a favourite courting place for Greater Spotted Woodpecker, the males vying for the attentions of indifferent females with much head bobbing and chattering. This path exits at Quarry Wood, which comprises mainly Beech, Oak, Sycamore, some Silver Birch and Rowan and approximately 5 per cent conifer. This is fairly open woodland and therefore attracts all three species of woodpeckers, particularly in the higher reaches on the southern boundary. The tit family is also well represented with numerous Blue and Great Tit and with smaller numbers of Long-tailed, Coal and Willow. One may take the steep (very steep) path 3 down towards the lower reaches, or follow the somewhat zig-zag road which is rather less adventuresome. At the bottom, the footpath follows a small stream, parallel to the A404, and along the water's edge Pied Wagtail should be seen, together with Jay and Little Owl which make occasional use of the bank-side trees.

Once at the bottom, the return route is again the subject of choice, there being gentle sloping paths numbered 10 and 12, via Fultness Wood, or the direct but much more challenging path 11 which ascends rapidly the edge of the private Inkydown Wood. This latter route to the top has the advantage of following a line of paddocks which is likely to enhance the variety of species seen. A small colony of Jackdaws should be found en route and, with moderate good fortune, Sparrowhawk will be seen, sometimes dashing through the wood at low level with an uncanny ability to avoid collisions. Passing through High Wood, especially in mid-summer, one should see Goldcrest, Willow and Long-tailed Tit, often in mixed family groups feeding together. It is quite possible to find oneself suddenly amidst several dozen fledgelings of

Little Owl

these species, together with the Blue Tits and Wrens. It is also interesting to keep a count of the number of Wren territories discovered in these woods which seem to have quite a large population. Blackcap, Kestrel and Treecreeper also breed in this location. In winter quite large flocks of finches, including Siskin, busy themselves in the tree-tops. Re-entering Quarry Wood along Dry Lane (path 12), it is worth looking out again for woodpecker as this is the area where all three species might be seen, and Nuthatch also breed here. In addition one might see, or more usually hear a Tawny Owl. Having emerged from Dry Lane, footpath 3 may well be worth exploration as it bisects one of the more open but bracken-covered areas, where a variety of warblers and finches may be seen.

At this point one may retrace one's steps over the out-going journey, or follow Winter Hill Road back as far as the hill itself, remaining on the road and heading for paths 29 and 33. On the way it is worth a look on the larger lawns along the lane as they often play host to small numbers of Grey Partridge. The paths mentioned direct walkers across the golf course, and one first becomes a target for golfers to your right and, 100 yds (92 m) further on, from your left. Watch out for Skylark, Meadow Pipit, wagtails and Swallow. Kestrel and Green Woodpecker are not infrequent visitors to the links, the latter making itself very unpopular on the greens. Where path 33 crosses the railway line, check over the parapets to the single track below in the hopes of seeing Linnet, Corn Bunting or again, Kestrel which often gives an eye-level display of its hovering techniques. At the next junction of the paths it is worth turning left as this leads, within some 100 yds (92 m), to the local sewage plant. All three wagtails can be seen here in numbers approaching 100 in autumn, and in the warmer months House Martin, Sand Martin, Swallow and Swift will hawk within inches of a quiet observer. It is also another location to find Grey Partridge and Whinchat. Turning back on the path will return you to the car park, via a narrow ditch inhabited by many Bank Voles.

It is clear that several hours can be consumed in following the route outlined, but the scenery and variety of species will warrant return visits to enable more time to be spent in particular areas of the walk.

Calendar

Resident Kestrel, Sparrowhawk, Lapwing, Great Crested Grebe, Heron, Kingfisher, Pied Wagtail, Grey Wagtail, Mute Swan, all three woodpeckers, Willow Tit, Skylark, Yellowhammer, Corn Bunting, Goldcrest, Tawny Owl.

December–February Pochard, Tufted Duck, Snipe, winter thrushes, Meadow Pipits. Large Starling flocks, Siskin, occasional Redpoll and Teal. Over-wintering Chiffchaff.

March–May Whinchat, Cuckoo, hirundines, Blackcap, Willow Warbler, both species of Spotted Woodpecker. Wheatear and Greenshank on passage.

June–July Whitethroat, Yellow Wagtail, Redshank (usually one pair only), Spotted Flycatcher. Common Terns over the Thames, Turtle Dove.

August–November Family groups of Canada Geese, House Martins and numerous wagtails into October. Redwing and Fieldfare (often exceeding 200 of each species), large numbers of Black-headed and Common Gull on flyway to London reservoirs.

QUEEN MOTHER
RESERVOIR

Map 17/OS ref. TQ 005 770

Habitat

Queen Mother Reservoir is a totally artificial, steep-sided body of water, 350 acres (140 ha) in size with concrete walls and no marginal vegetation. The water is very deep and this, together with its enormous size, ensures it does not freeze over even during the most insistent of frosts. The outer banks which form the retaining walls are grassed on the outside and grazed by sheep. Immediately to the south is a much smaller and shallower pit formed from gravel workings, which often hosts interesting species, particularly during sailing days when birds are 'evicted' from the reservoir. A small stream surrounds the site. The reservoir is managed by Thames Water who publish a leaflet on the birdwatching facilities at a number of other reservoirs in the district. (See Useful Addresses.)

Access

The site is immediately south of the M4 at junction 5 and the only entrance is half-way along the Colnbrook-to-Horton road. There is an enormous parking area at 'ground' level but one is free to ascend the ramp and park in the vicinity of the sailing club centre at water level. Public access to the perimeter wall is restricted to the general area of the clubhouse which represents perhaps only 10 per cent of the periphery. A telescope is therefore essential to scan the surface on this enormous area. The small gravel pit mentioned can be seen from a gateway on the B376, although vehicles must not be left unattended there because of contractor access needs. Alternatively a footpath runs along the western edge of the water and, provided the most exposed parts of the bank are avoided, minimum disruption should be caused to the birds.

Species

It has to be said that a summer visit to the reservoir is likely to be less than productive. True, the grassy banks will be occupied with many Crows, Jackdaws and Skylarks and a Kingfisher will often brighten the scene as it dashes along the stream, but the main expanse of water is not usually too inspiring. The pool near Sunnymeads station can be fairly busy with a variety of common duck together with breeding Mute Swan and Canada Geese. Common Terns drop in (literally) from time-to-time and House Martins are present in small numbers. It is however, during the depths of winter and times of passage that this site comes into its own.

Perhaps one of the more regular and most noticeable features of the reservoir is the enormous roost which is formed, just prior to dusk, by one of the west London gull colonies. During the last hour of daylight, thousands of Black-headed, Common and Herring Gulls can be seen silhouetted against the setting sun as they stream in from locations up to 15 miles away, past the stark outlines of Windsor Castle, to descend noisily and argumentatively before alighting on the ever-reducing area of free water in the centre of the lake. Many pass over to stay instead at

Wraysbury reservoir, or one of the other nearby waters. On windy nights the raft of gulls is slowly blown across the surface and there is constant movement as birds at the rear take off and reposition themselves at the front. Usually, Great Black-backs are amongst the throng which, by early morning, will have dispersed for another day. Further spectacle is afforded by other common species, with Tufted Duck often numbering up to 1,000 and Coot exhibiting a similar proclivity for gregariousness. Gadwall also spend the winter here with upwards of 100 to be seen. Teal seem to prefer nearby Staines reservoir for their largest grouping, but there will usually be a few at Queen Mother.

The sheer quantity of Tufted Duck, combined with the surface area of the lake, makes the identifying of Scaup a particularly challenging pastime but this bird does visit the site regularly so perseverance is the order of the day. Great Crested Grebe may also number up to 100 but it is the more scarce grebes that steal attention away from their larger relative. Red-necked and Black-necked Grebes are regular visitors in ones or twos and Slavonian Grebe spend a few days here occasionally. Cormorants are regular visitors but it is as well to look twice at any distant bird 'dismissed' as this species as all three divers are possibilities during December to February. There have been occasions when Black-throated and Great Northern Divers have been seen together on the lake in the past. Shags have appeared here also, just to make the task more difficult still.

Winter ducks are well represented with Long-tailed Duck beginning to visit regularly, good numbers of Shoveler and Pochard and both Common and Velvet Scoters turning up almost annually. The Eider Duck too is far from unknown here. Goldeneye and Smew on the other hand, though occasionally present, seem to prefer Wraysbury gravel pits. Meanwhile, the small gravel pit near the railway station is likely to tempt several Goosanders (usually red-heads) and increased numbers of Canada Geese. Red-breasted Mergansers may be found there but the third sawbill, the Smew, seems to be seen in ever-reducing numbers of late. Back on the reservoir, bad weather may well cause some less regular species to turn up, such as Ruddy Duck. Guillemot and Little Auk have been recorded and any of the skuas may pass through. Nor is all the interest upon the water itself. The grassed surrounds of the lake attract tremendous numbers of Meadow Pipits and occasional Green Woodpeckers. Kestrels hover hopefully and Merlin often frequent the area. Of the more unusual passerines, Snow Buntings, and even Lapland Buntings, have been seen on the gravel path and sloping concrete walls.

The spring passage usually involves spectacular numbers of Swifts and any of the usual terns can be expected, the Black Tern perhaps looking the most attractive. Too soon the summer months arrive and we must patiently wait September's end when the reservoir becomes more lively again. A visit here on the way to, or from, Wraysbury gravel pits is thoroughly recommended.

Calendar

Resident (Including the gravel pit). Little Grebe, Great Crested Grebe, Cormorant, Mute Swan, Canada Geese, occasional Shelduck, Mallard, Tufted Duck, Kestrel, Black-headed Gull, Kingfisher, Green Woodpecker, Jackdaw, Reed Bunting.

December–February Most active period. Spectacular gull roosts, large numbers of Tufted Duck and other common winter ducks. Possibility of all three divers and five grebes, Shag, scoters, Scaup, all three sawbills Ruddy Duck, Eider and Long-tailed Duck. Prospect of Merlin. Bewick's Swans have visited gravel pit where in any case occasional Grey Plover, Dunlin and Redshank may be found. Heavy weather may produce wrecks of auks such as Guillemot and Little Auk. Many Meadow Pipits. Possibility of Black Redstart, and look out for Snow Buntings.

March–May Much of the December–February scene overflows to March but will gradually become enhanced with spring movement. Ringed Plovers and Common Terns on the gravel pit. Possibility of skuas, occasional Kittiwakes and Black Terns on the reservoir. Large numbers of Swifts by April. Worth checking ground level car park in case Wheatear, Whinchat or any of the three wagtails are passing through.

June–July The quiet period.

August–November Gradual build up to winter scene. Winter ducks arriving from end of September by which time passage terns will have gone through. Meadow Pipits flock around the reservoir. Possibility of Common Sandpiper on the gravel pit.

SNELSMORE COMMON   Map 18/OS ref. SU 460 708

Habitat

Comprising some 250 acres (100 ha), Snelsmore Common represents the largest tract of heathland remaining in Berkshire. In fact it accounts for one sixth of the total of this sort of habitat in the county. Some of the heath has been overtaken by woodland, mainly deciduous to the west, but more coniferous in the east. The boundary between heathland and woodland is fashioned by advancing Birch scrub which is controlled by voluntary conservation groups who are attempting to increase the area of heather. Habitat variety is enhanced by valley bog with its particular flora, including Bog Bean, Bog Asphodel and sundew. The site is excellent for butterflies, including White Admiral and Purple Emperor. Lizards and Grass Snakes are common, and Adders are prevalent in some years. Mammal species on the Common include Fox, Badger, Stoat, Weasel and occasional deer. Frogs and Newts too are plentiful in the various pools that have been formed.

Access

The Common lies to the west of the B4494 Newbury to Wantage road, approximately 1.25 miles (2 km) north of Donnington. The area is reached from junction 13 of the M4 or via the A4 which runs through Newbury. There are ample parking facilities and toilets are available at the main entrance. Although not a rural common as such, the owners of the land permit visitors to roam freely over the site. However, it is obviously preferable to utilise the many footpaths and tracks that exist to avoid unnecessary damage to plants. A bridleway has been nominated around the periphery which, in wet weather, can be difficult to traverse but in summer provides a useful track for circumnavigation of the Common.

Species

The presence of both deciduous and coniferous areas of woodland has no doubt enhanced the species list for the site which, for completely open heathland, might otherwise be much shorter. In winter, the Common serves up a fairly typical menu of species. Conglomerations of Blue, Coal and Long-tailed Tits in consortium with Goldcrest will be found near the car park. The main group consists of foraging Song Thrushes and Robins, with occasional Redwings, in addition to many active Nuthatches, Treecreepers and Great Spotted Woodpeckers with occasional Tawny Owls. Lesser Spotted Woodpecker may be found, as will small numbers of Siskin and Redpoll. Away from the woodland, the open heath attracts Meadow Pipits and small groups of Yellowhammer, but whereas conditions might be suitable, an observer of a Stonechat on this site would most likely get his initials in the local club's annual report.

If nothing else, winter visitors will have whetted the appetite for the warmer months ahead when the Common provides nesting facilities for many species. Bullfinches and Greenfinches are frequently encountered; Goldfinches less so. Linnets are regular occupiers of the heather where Whitethroats can also be expected. Willow Warblers seem to occupy every small Silver Birch, their trailing song laconically punctuated by the less numerous Chiffchaffs. The edges of the open valley bogs and heather beds are the likely places to find the Tree Pipit. Four or five pairs of this speckled bird are usually found here, observed either in full song-flight with pink legs dangling, or moving about low down amongst marginal leaf-litter. In the wooded area, all three woodpeckers can be seen, the two spotted species utilising existing holes in dead Silver Birch trees as their most popular nesting site. The Willow Tits however, if they breed on the Common, are likely to be more active and excavate a new nest hole each year. Cuckoos exploit the area, though look closely as the resident Sparrowhawk is even more likely to show up and one will need to check for its less direct flight and slower wing beat. Further identification problems can occur on the occasions that a Hobby decides to pay Snelsmore a visit, but regrettably these are few and far between.

Of the speciality birds, Nightingales seem not to find favour with the Common all that often and conditions are perhaps not ideal for Redstart However, an evening visit between May and July could well be rewarded with the 'churring' of Nightjars. Numbers have never been high here and recently even fewer have turned up, but the prospect certainly remains. In any event, whilst waiting perchance in vain, 'roding' Woodcock are another possibility, and if one is particularly fortunate, a Barn Owl might be seen, especially during the passage periods. It is perhaps in the deciduous woodland, however, where better fortune might be bestowed upon the speciality-hunter for this is the domain of the local Wood Warblers. Never numerous, this most attractive bird nonetheless appears quite regularly at Snelsmore in the areas of less dense, but canopied woodland. One's attention might first be drawn by its song. The introductory notes are reminiscent of a Blackbird's alarm call, though higher pitched and less frantic. This part of the song is quite

Tree Pipit

often delivered on the wing as it flutters weakly between favourite perches. The final trill, somewhat Wren-like, is however always pronounced from the perch, primarily because the effect is created by vigorous vibrations of body, wings and tail alike, a feat which, if performed in flight, would almost certainly guarantee a forced landing. In song, the bird can be very confiding, but if the single note alarm call is detected it is advisable to withdraw as the maximum success of any breeding which is going on must be assured for this scarce, but striking visitor.

Spotted Flycatchers are not recorded as often as one might expect and Garden Warblers will probably take some finding. Blackcaps are however relatively common, breeding in the understory of the deciduous woodland. During the autumn passage it will be difficult to separate those birds which had over-summered here from their relatives which may make fleeting visits during their return from northern breeding grounds. Nonetheless it seems all too soon that the slightly less ebullient species take charge of this pleasant and important piece of the county for another winter.

Calendar

Resident Sparrowhawk, Kestrel, Pheasant, Woodcock, Stock Dove, occasional Collared Dove, Tawny Owl, Green, Great Spotted and Lesser Spotted Woodpeckers. Dunnock, Song Thrush, Mistle Thrush, Goldcrest. Willow, Marsh, Long-tailed, Blue, Great and Coal Tits, Nuthatch, Treecreeper, occasional Jackdaw, common finches, Yellowhammer.

December–February Small mixed feeding flocks of tits and Chaffinches, some Redwing, but few Fieldfares. Groups of Siskin and Redpoll.

March–May Arrival of breeding species, possibility of passage Hobby and Nightingale.

June–July Breeding in progress. Singing Wood Warbler, Tree Pipit and 'roding' Woodcock. Chance of Nightjar (probably non-breeding birds).

August–November Migration builds up during August and early September, though Willow Warblers may still be found almost to October. Winter thrushes arrive in November.

THATCHAM MOOR   Map 19/OS ref. SU 511 667

Habitat

Straddling the A4, Thatcham rests in the umbrella of sprawling Newbury 2 miles (3.2 km) away, and is a little east of where the River Lambourn drains the Downs into the River Kennet. At Thatcham Moors, the River Kennet and the Kennet and Avon canal combine with moorland and woods, well served with footpaths, to provide a varied habitat for birds. The local authority has extended the footpath scheme and created a small reserve area adjacent to the sewage works, itself an attraction to several species. Pits formed by earlier gravel workings have been filled with water and have been landscaped to the benefit of birds and anglers alike. The fishing rights are shared by the Newbury Angling Association (NAA) and the Thatcham Angling Association (TAA) who have carried out extensive management and tree planting. To the south of the railway line are other NAA pools with good access for non-members to skirt the lakes. Further south is the canal and river complex, beyond which are the trout fishing lakes, again created from previous mineral extraction.

Still further south lies Bowdown Woods, a 50 acre (20 ha) wood comprising mixed deciduous trees and a large number of woodland plant species, recently purchased by the Berkshire, Buckinghamshire & Oxfordshire Naturalists' Trust (BBONT). With the adjacent Chamber-house Wood and Baynes Reserve, Bowdown forms a SSSI and BBONT hope in due course to achieve nature reserve status for this area. The wood slopes down into the Kennet Valley and a matrix of small streams passes through the woodland glades, supporting Alder at these levels, in contrast to the Oak, Hazel, Birch and Rowan, plus some Cherry trees, on the higher reaches. Deer can be found in these woods together with a reasonable cross-section of woodland birds. The area between the woods and waterways is taken up by the meadows, pastures and arable fields belonging to Lower Farm. The adjacent Baynes Reserve is also of significant interest but is only accessible to BBONT members; at least one good reason for joining that organisation.

Access

Thatcham can be approached going west along the A4 from junction 12 of the M4 or, from junction 13 via Newbury on the A34. Running parallel to, and south of, the A4 through the town is Lower Way and there are three accesses to the subject area along this road. Prince Hold Road, the most westerly, is an unmade track which can hold a few vehicles, but the official council car park, with capacity for more than 20 vehicles, is on the right at the bottom of another track almost opposite Heron Way. Alternatively 500 yds (450 m) further east on Lower Way is a third track, opposite the local nursery school, at the end of which is parking for 20 or so cars at Jubilee Lake. If it is intended to walk the whole area referred to, including Bowdown Wood, this is as good a starting place as any.

Bowdown Wood itself has parking facilities. Taking the A34 south from Newbury, turn left at the island at the end of the dual carriageway and follow this road through Bury's Bank. Passing the golf course on the left, there is a track, also on the left, which leads to Lower Farm, the trout pool, and the wood. The car park is some 550 yds (500 m) along this track. BBONT members wishing to visit the Baynes Reserve should continue along Bury's Bank Road to another track on the left down which a small car park will be found past Beggars Roost.

Species

It may be useful with this extensive site to propose a route for a walk which will take in most of the area concerned. Assuming a start to the walk from Jubilee Lake car park, set off towards Long Lake. A high hedge of Hawthorn and Willow extends around the east end of Long Lake and attracts Whitethroat in summer and Yellowhammers and Bullfinch all year, in addition to more common hedgerow species. The lake itself is always likely to contain Great Crested Grebe which breed here so look out for the elaborate courtship routine in January and February. The maturing reeds at both ends provide cover for Coot and Moorhen. The only other species this lake may attract are Mute Swan and small numbers of Black-headed Gull. The southern edge of this lake is lined with small pollarded Willows and some reeds and a small ditch runs alongside the pathway. Beyond the ditch, and extending to the railway line some 55 yds (50 m) away is a large bed of Yellow Iris, nettles, docks and thistles, covered in pink Field Bindweed in summer. This patch is often host to Goldfinch, Linnet, Greenfinch, warblers and Reed Bunting, the latter usually on a prominent perch flicking its tail provocatively, or dashing out and hovering over the water fleetingly to take an insect in mid-air.

At the other end of the lake, the path turns right and then immediately left again to skirt a new pool being created, and to the north of the path the Alders and Willows Lakes. The first is relatively small and not particularly lively but the other lake is larger and has a small gravel island near the centre which may attract waders. In addition to Great Crested Grebe there will be Mute Swan from autumn and Cormorant are beginning to show interest in this pool. Its diameter is great enough to tempt large numbers of gull in winter in addition to 100 or more Pochard who spend most of the cold days loafing after nocturnal feeding.

At the junction of footpaths, turn left towards the railway line, which has a permitted crossing at this point. (The line carries high-speed 125s so a good rule would be that, if a train is seen, no matter at what apparent distance, *wait* until it has passed *before* crossing.)

The new pools beyond the railway line are already gaining reeds and attracting warblers and occasional Water Rail. Great Crested and Little Grebe frequent and breed in these pools and Canada Goose is fairly common. Blackcap, Chiffchaff and occasional Lesser Whitethroat in summer are replaced by mixed flocks of tits and finches in winter. There are small islands on the main pools, often attracting Black-headed Gull. Cetti's and Grasshopper Warblers have been recorded in the perimeter shrubs and vegetation, but are more likely to be heard than seen.

The path leads to the bank of the canal at the point of a disused lock. There are quite extensive reed patches along this stretch and a cautious approach plus a few patient minutes spent here will usually be rewarded with good views of one or two Kingfishers. Dabchick favour this area too small groups of five or so will gather in winter, diving in unison for weed. Turning right to follow the canal bank, watch out for Cuckoo in summer and Kestrel and Sparrowhawk all year round. After one or two hundred yards the opposite bank opens up somewhat to the meadowland in which another pool resides, well stocked with trout. The area attracts many Coot but these can be outnumbered by Pochard in winter. Occasionally there are Redshank and other waders at the water's edge and large flocks of Lapwing on the surrounding farmland. It may well be worth looking for Golden Plover in winter although the best place for this bird is yet to come. Following the bank still further, the point is reached where the railway passes over the canal.

Use the small swing bridge to cross the canal and the small footbridge opposite to cross the gravel chute, taking the footpath which approaches the railway embankment. There are plans to build a new lane under the tracks to avoid the hazards of the present pedestrian crossing. The lane on the other side of the tracks leads to Lower Farm. At this point there is a good view of the race course and, on non-racing days, there may well be sizeable flocks of Lapwing and Carrion Crow. In winter, these will be joined by 200 or more Golden Plover, their almost crescent-shaped wings contrasting with those of their black and white cousins. Fieldfare and Redwing can be expected at this time of the year and Skylark and Meadow Pipit will almost certainly be seen.

Approaching the farm buildings it is worth looking out for Pied and Grey Wagtail. Collared Dove are often present as are, in summer, Swallow, House Martin and a few Sand Martin. In September, several hundred of these hirundines will be seen gathering on the wires and trees near the farm. The trout pool is now to the left and worth scanning for waders. The lane is bordered with thistles and small hedges and Yellowhammer, Corn Bunting and Goldfinch can be expected whilst a small ditch to one side of the lane has attracted Sedge Warblers on occasions. The golf course is next encountered and Mistle Thrush and Pied Wagtail might be seen and, on dry days, possibly a Green Woodpecker searching for ants. A little further on is Bowdown Wood.

At the entrance to the wood is a notice-board indicating the routes of paths through the area. It is an interesting woodland, more open than most and contains a wide variety of plants so it is worth taking a suitable guide book. All three woodpeckers are present and there are numerous Wren, Robin and Dunnock territories. Nuthatch and Tree-creeper may be few in number but should be locatable. Along the right-hand footpath a small and rudimentary shelter has been con-structed from which tits, Goldcrest and finches may be watched in relative comfort or, in early morning, possibly Roe and Muntjac Deer. Be prepared for mosquitoes, especially at evening time if waiting for Nightingale, Tawny Owl or Woodcock. Butterfly species include Purple Emperor, Purple Hairstreak and Grayling. The adjacent Baynes Reserve has produced regular sightings of Tree Pipit.

Retracing one's footsteps over the farm lane, railway track and canal, rejoin the original footpath under the railway bridge. Continuing north, over the western edge of the marsh, may reveal Heron and mixed gull flocks from a small pit on the left which has recently been landscaped. Cross the small footbridge at the far side of the marsh (observing the missing plank in the middle) and turn right to the sewage works. Several species may be seen here, often in large flocks, especially House Sparrow and Starling. Grey Wagtail frequents this area too, until the local Sparrowhawk puts everything to flight. Further along this path is the Newbury District Council Reserve car park which abuts a number of small pools on which Dabchick and Reed Warbler breed. The over-head power cables are favourite roosting places for purring Turtle Dove. Beyond the car park are Willows and Alders Lakes again and the return path to the Jubilee car park. Before putting the binoculars in the boot, if little fishing is going on, it is worth looking out for Kingfisher on this bank. They can be quite confiding.

Although much of the water is fairly recent habitat it is becoming more and more eutrophic and it will always be worth looking for migration visitors at the appropriate time of year. Lesser Black-backed Gull and Common Tern are frequently seen and Black Tern has been sighted. Wintering duck species include Gadwall, Pochard, and Teal with occasional Shoveler, Goldeneye and sawbills. Typical of such sites, almost anything might turn up at Thatcham Moor and previous records include Curlew, Ringed and Little Plover, even Oystercatcher, Osprey and Bittern. American Wigeon have been a recent addition. No doubt the 'list' for the area will increase with further observation in the future.

Calendar

Resident Little Grebe, Grey Heron, Mute Swan, Canada Goose, Kestrel, Sparrowhawk, Grey Partridge, Lapwing, Woodcock, Collared Dove, Tawny and Little Owl, Kingfisher, all three woodpeckers, Skylark, mixed corvids, Treecreeper, Linnet, Reed Bunting, Corn Bunting, Yellowhammer. Pied and Grey Wagtails, occasional Barn Owl.

December–February Bewick's Swan (occasional), Gadwall, Teal, Shoveler, Pochard, Goldeneye (occasional), Smew, Water Rail, good numbers of Golden Plover, Snipe, sizeable flocks of mixed gulls, Meadow Pipit, winter thrushes, Siskin and Brambling, over-wintering Chiffchaff. Chance of rarer waders and waterfowl.

March–May Turtle Dove, common warblers, Whinchat, Cuckoo, Common Sandpiper.

June–July Occasional Ringed and Little Ringed Plover, Common Tern, Swift, hirundines, occasional Yellow Wagtail. Reed and Sedge Warbler, Nightingale. Chance of Cetti's Warbler.

August–November Canada Geese start flocking, winter duck arrive, many on passage, final broods of Great Crested Grebes, passage waders, large flocks of gull, especially Black-headed and Herring, hirundines massing for migration and winter thrushes arrive. Mixed flocks of finches gather from September. Irregular visits of Stonechat.

Gull Roost

THEALE GRAVEL PITS   Map 20/OS ref. SU 676 703

Habitat

This well known site consists of a series of gravel pits, of varying sizes, most of the waters being fished regularly. Many are used for sailing and waterskiing; however, there are some quiet corners where waterfowl and waders are given a chance to exist with less disturbance. In total, the complex includes some 125 acres (50 ha) of water surface, but this is changing continuously as extensive mineral extraction works continue. Some of the diggings are being refilled with rubbish with eventual agricultural use planned. During this back-fill activity, enormous numbers of gulls and corvids swarm over the site. (To assist the reader in relating the text to the associated map, letter references are used in the following paragraphs.)

The two pools north of Smallmead Road (A and B) are not particularly productive, and are heavily fished. Further north is a major excavation which has been left unfilled for some time and is often used by ducks and waders. However, infilling is a prospect for this veritable crater. The Pingewood pools each side of Kirtons Farm (C and D) are becoming well grown with vegetation but the eastern one of the pair is used for water sports. The larger areas of water around Searls Farm Lane are the best for birds in this sector, pools F and H being the most productive.

Knight's Farm is also straddled by lakes. Pool E is not easily seen from the road but I and J can be scanned from several locations, the latter having areas of shorter grass suitable for loafing. Either side of Field Farm Road are more recent workings, the gravel patch to the north being best. Wellman's Water (L) is another excellent site with a sizeable island in the centre. The lake south of the motorway (M) is by far the largest and is used by a busy sailing club and tends only to have notable birdlife on islands near the south shore. Two more pools, N and O, near Sheffield Bottom can be very productive, one having extensive islands and gravel bars and being kept free of angling and water sports. The lakes north of the motorway are often know as Burghfield Gravel Pits.

Access

The general area lies either side of the M4 motorway between junctions 11 and 12. Few of the pools have specific access or parking facilities, save for permit holders of the various angling associations or sailing clubs. However, most of the lakes can be viewed from adjacent roadsides. Most of the lanes are too narrow and twisting but the associated map indicates the more suitable places to leave a vehicle.

The area may be approached from the Southcote district of Reading, or via Theale with access from the first road on the left on the A4 south of junction 12, or via Three Mile Close off the A33 south of junction 11.

Many of the waters are very deep and there is much gravel machinery around the whole area. Birdwatchers are therefore encouraged to remain outside the sites to observe. This in any case reduces disturbance and can result in close views.

Species

Needless to say most of the birds one might expect to see in such an area are waterfowl, waders and gulls, and by far the best time to visit the site is September to May. Prolonged frosts in winter produce interesting situations with ducks and gulls concentrating on the pools that retain open water. These tend to be H, L, and M, although the last mentioned does not have an especially good record for birds. Kirtons Farm can be good for gulls and if Mediterranean Gull begins making regular visits, after several sightings in the county in recent years, this may well be one of the places where careful scanning of Black-headed Gulls may pay dividends. The Searls Farm pools seem to be favoured by Pochard and Shovelers and is one area where occasional small numbers of Smew can be anticipated. It is also a good spot for Kingfishers. The frosty scene at Wellmans Water is likely to be dominated by 50 or more Cormorants on the main island but if the water is more open, there will be many Mute Swans, and reasonable numbers of Gadwall, Mallard and Teal. Wigeon are not seen in large numbers, probably due to lack of grazing facilities round most of the ponds. Scaup is certainly a possibility, so it is advisable to look at each and every one of the numerous Tufted Duck. Coot too are plentiful, but nothing like the numbers that accumulate on lake O, the southernmost pool in the complex where Teal will occasionally reach three figure numbers. More luck however, is required to spot the one or two Jack Snipe in the area most years, though everywhere the air is constantly full of gulls, presenting a neck-aching challenge to pick out rarer species.

Theale Pits are very much a place to be during passage periods. Ringed Plovers are noted from early in the year, the later arrivals staying on to breed, as do Little Ringed Plovers. Redshank, which can be seen in most months of the year, are more numerous in spring but Greenshank, seen at Theale and Pingewood in most years, are more obvious during autumn migration. Golden Plover, often at Moatlands or Pingewood in small numbers, move out in March, the few Grey Plovers seen in the same area already having left. Ruff, seen in both directions of movement at the south of the site, need practice to discern from Redshank at a distance but the occasional Whimbrel which passes through poses no such problem. Snipe will be moving around everywhere, Kirton Farm perhaps being as good a place as any to find them. Some of the Canada Geese which will have wintered at lake L move to lake I for breeding and, although past records do not suggest that winter visiting geese utilise these pits regularly, this pool may be one of the more likely to attract them. Sanderlings start appearing from April, bringing with them the problem of separation from Dunlins, a species which is usually around the Theale area all year.

March and April will witness the return of hirundines and occasionally a spectacular fall of around 1,000 House Martins can occur over these waters. The spring passage is also the more notable of the two for gulls and terns. Little Gull is found almost annually. Common Terns are quite numerous but it becomes difficult by May to know which ones are staying to breed at Lake L, and which ones are going on. Little Tern, with their buoyant flight, are very pleasing to the eye and the Black Tern, occasionally found in twos and threes can frustrate as one patiently waits, in vain of course, to see them plunge into the water as they swoop downwards to scoop up insects above the surface. Common Sandpipers now start popping up all over the place, at lakes L and O in particular. Breeding is soon underway with Little Ringed Plover and Common Terns on the island on Moatlands and both Grey and Red-legged Partridges around the periphery. Collared Doves, which can attain numbers of 50 or more near this lake in winter, disperse to a variety of breeding sites and this is also one of the better places to find Turtle Doves in summer. Other breeding species at this location include Reed Bunting, and Lesser Whitethroat. There is a sizeable Sand Martin colony at the south of the general site in most summers, but this situation is always subject to the state of excavation works.

By late summer, the earlier return migrants such as Green Sandpiper begin to put in an appearance. Greenshanks are also perhaps seen more often at this time of year. By the time the nights are drawing in the overall scene is taken over by increasing numbers of gulls which sometimes accumulate in such numbers that some of the smaller pools look almost totally white at dusk. Corvids, dominated by Jackdaws, accumulate at several locations in tremendous flocks and groups of Tree Sparrows get together to while away the winter months in each other's company. The size of the rafts of Coot reveals the success of another breeding season and the few Goldeneye and Goosander that regard Theale as their winter quarters gradually arrive, and the 'numbers' game is well under way for another year. With the prospect of Bewick's Swans, Red-necked and Black-necked Grebes making their infrequent visitations, these pits, interesting at any time, beckon even more strongly to the many birdwatchers who brave the ravages of winter to ensure nothing is missed.

Calendar

Resident Great Crested and Little Grebe, Cormorant (most months), Grey Heron, Mute Swan, Canada Goose (and one regular feral Barnacle Goose), Mallard, Shoveler (small numbers), Tufted Duck (some breed), Kestrel, occasional Sparrowhawk, Red-legged and Grey Partridge, Pheasant, Water Rail, Moorhen, Coot, Dunlin and Redshank (most months). Black-headed Gull, Herring Gull, Snipe. Great Spotted Woodpecker, Pied and Grey Wagtail, Dunnock, common tits and finches.

December–February Chance of rare grebes, occasional Bewick's Swan, large rafts of Coot, Tufted Duck, Pochard and Mallard. Fewer Wigeon, Shoveler and Teal. Occasional Pintail and scarce Scaup. Goldeneye, and sawbills not usually numerous. Huge gull flocks. Chance of Jack Snipe, Golden Plover.

March–May Much wader activity. Redshank, Greenshank, Green and Common Sandpipers. Occasional Knot and Sanderling. Good tern movement, including Little and Black Terns. Possible Little Gull.

June–July Common Tern, Ringed and Little Ringed Plover nesting on islands. Sand Martin colony of up to 100 pairs in some years. Greenfinches flocking by end July.

August–November Autumn passage commences by early August. Chance of Whimbrel and Little Stint. Greenshank regular, as is Green Sandpiper. Gull colonies well established by November. Winter thrushes and ducks moving in. Possible Common Scoter. Flocks of 20 plus Tree Sparrows. Whinchat likely.

TWYFORD GRAVEL PITS   Map 21/OS ref. SU 785 755

Habitat
The site comprises a series of worked-out gravel pits in picturesque surrounds, rich in mature trees and vegetation but few reeds at present. The first lake to be restored was the northern lake adjacent to Twyford Mill (which changed purpose from silk to flour during the last 150 years). This lake possesses a number of small islands which offer sanctuary to breeding birds. South of the railway line are several more lakes, the largest one as yet with only sparse vegetation but with a substantial island at its centre. Further south still is another sizeable pool, bisected by a private track, and the recipient of many young trees recently planted by the gravel company. Most of the waters are fished and to this end have been well stocked with such species as Chub, Barbel, Tench and Bream. The River Loddon embellishes the scene as it passes through the site via the mill-race and provides even more 'footage' for the angler. There is no significant flora but the shrub layer is quite dense in places. Sand and gravel are still being extracted to the south-east of the site and this area is well-liked by martins and certain waders.

Access
The Mill and its lakes are to the south of the A3032 between Twyford and Charvil, the nearest main road being the A4, 0.6 miles (1 km) to the north. Some 250 acres (100 ha) of water are accessed by a number of public footpaths and anglers' tracks, though some of the fishermen's walkways are only available to permit holders.

A public car park, with room for some 30 cards and including toilet facilities, is available on the Twyford side of the railway bridge. Additional parking is available off Park Lane (anglers' car park) near the railway and further along the lane beyond the ford where space is available for 12 cars. The nearest railway station is Twyford only 270 yds (250 m) away from the Mill.

Species
In common with other habitats of this nature, birds of the water predominate in winter, those of the scrub and hedgerow being more numerous in summer. Prolonged freezing affects most of the lakes but usually only the smallest become totally iced over. Lake A is home to many Coot and Tufted Duck, with a few Pochard sleeping most of the day away. There is a small sand spit to the north of this lake, viewable from the footpath in the north-west and this will often have Heron, Snipe and Redshank, with Green and Common Sandpipers also present during migration periods. The adjacent meadow floods quite often in winter and can be another location to find Snipe, together with Lapwing and Meadow Pipit. Lake B is possibly more productive as this is where the main groups of Pochard, Wigeon and Tufted Duck seem to congregate, in so doing attracting varying numbers of Teal, Gadwall and Shoveler. Pintail occasionally show on this water but Goldeneye are not especially regular. The small islands host Canada Geese and Teal, who disdainfully ignore the protestations of Black-headed and equally numerous

Common Gulls. The surrounding bushes are worth checking for Reed Buntings and over-wintering Chiffchaffs but the resident Kingfishers usually make themselves quite evident. Another species frequently encountered, particularly around the periphery of Lake A, is the Little Grebe, which can occasionally outnumber the Great Crested Grebe.

Beyond the arches of the railway bridge, which accommodate Kestrels and Pied Wagtails, lies another group of lakes. Those that flank the Loddon are not especially well blessed with winter visitors but Lake C is beginning to attract large numbers of gulls, including Herring Gull and occasional Lesser Black-backed Gulls. In addition it can be a more reliable lake for Goldeneye and Goosander, a fine male of this latter species occasionally blessing the pool with its presence.

Being slightly larger, and a little less disturbed, there is reason to hope that even more scarce species will make use of this pool. The gravel process plant to the south of this lake is a regular haunt of both Pied and Grey Wagtails and the small woodland opposite usually contains a group of busy Siskins. The small paddock further on is a good place to pick up Brambling among the Chaffinches. Lakes D and E seem to attract most of the Gadwall, often with up to 25 pairs *in situ* and twice that number of Wigeon. Teal can also be found here but the lack of a protective loafing island possibly deters larger numbers from accumulating. Cormorant seem happier on this pool though, and most of Twyford's Mute Swans find their way to this particular water for much of their over-winter stay.

The spring passage is signalled by occasional Greenshanks which arrive at a time of dwindling numbers of waterfowl. Lake B would probably be the most likely one that rarer gulls might visit briefly whilst Lake C, being more open, would be favoured by Black Terns. The north-west corner of Lake A, with its submerged vegetation, would be well worth checking for Gargeney later in the migration season. By the time the summer visitors have settled, Lake A will have Sedge Warblers and Reed Buntings nesting around its edges. The bushes around Lake A will have been taken over by Willow Warblers and Whitethroats with occasional Lesser Whitethroat. Bullfinches also breed regularly and most of the other common finches will be seen. On the main island, Redshanks may well attempt to raise young, but the petulant pair of Common Terns (there are rarely more) usually only hold territory and do not nest. The resident Kestrels may be forgiven for thinking otherwise, however, considering the unmerciful treatment they receive if they venture too close. Lake C is favoured by Canada Geese as a breeding ground whilst the surrounding hedgerows are occupied by Blackcaps, Reed Buntings and Linnets. When passing beneath the railway to reach this lake in summer, it is worth waiting with eager ear as a Redstart is in prospect in the vicinity of the embankment itself and the stand of young conifers running parallel with it. Look out also for the occasional Yellow Wagtail on the grassy banks of Lake C.

The two southern-most lakes, D and E, have yet to reach full maturity but Great Crested Grebes breed on the edges of the water whilst Whitethroats can be found in the surrounding shrubbery, occasionally elevating themselves to the overhead power lines. These same cables, as is often the case with the small-capacity low-level power lines, are popular perches for many birds who use them during temporary disturbance from the hedgerow by passing pedestrians and cyclists. Greenfinch, Woodpigeon, Kestrel, Swallows, Sand Martins and Turtle

Doves can all be seen regularly on the cable route by the gravel plant. Further along this road is the site of continued workings and the adjacent footpaths can provide views of nesting Sand Martins, numerous Lapwing and occasional Little Ringed Plovers. Green and Great Spotted Woodpeckers are also found in this corner. With any luck this excavation will be restored with even more of an avian flavour than the present lakes, with shallows, wave-proof lagoons, reedbeds and tern-islands. One can but hope. In the meantime the Twyford site is already one of character, probably best visited during December to February and April to June.

Calendar

Resident Great Crested and Little Grebe, occasional Heron, Mute Swan, Canada Goose, Mallard, Tufted Duck, occasional Sparrowhawk. Kestrel, Moorhen, Coot, Lapwing, Black-headed Gull, Stock Doves, Wood-pigeon, Collared Dove, occasional Tawny and Little Owls. Kingfisher, Green and Great Spotted Woodpeckers, Grey and Pied Wagtails, Jay. Possible Chiffchaff. Long-tailed Tit, Treecreeper, Bullfinch, Greenfinch, Goldfinch, Linnet, Reed Bunting, occasional Yellowhammer.

December–February Several Cormorant, good numbers of Gadwall, Wigeon, Teal and Shoveler. Prospect of Pintail and occasional Shelduck. Numerous Pochard. Goldeneye and Goosander regular in small numbers, Smew less frequent. Water Rail sometimes reported, Snipe frequently seen. Large rafts of mixed gulls. Possibility of Stonechat. Winter thrushes in small numbers. Probability of Brambling. Small parties of Siskins. Possible Egyptian Goose.

March–May Always the chance of scarcer grebes on passage and waders such as Common and Green Sandpiper, Greenshank, Ringed Plover and Ruff also passing through. Gulls dispersed by April. Cuckoo and early warblers in position by mid-April, Sand Martin and Swallow even earlier. Any Spotted Flycatcher seen is probably passing through, as is the case with Yellow Wagtails.

June–July Redshank and Common Tern holding territory. Sedge Warbler and many other species breeding. Look for Redstart.

August–November Main departure period for summer visitors, primarily in September, though House Martins may be still seen in October. Possibility of Whinchat, in addition to some wader movements.

Smew

WRAYSBURY
GRAVEL PITS

Habitat

Following extensive mineral extraction over many years, a number of gravel pits between Windsor and Staines have been filled with water, resulting in a total area of 450 acres (180 ha) being made available for water sports and nature conservation. The lakes form part of the southern-most sector of the Colne Valley Park, a major scheme originated in the 1960s by a number of county and borough councils to improve and conserve the remnants of the Metropolitan Green Belt in a region extending over the 14 miles (23 km) from Rickmansworth to the Thames. Whereas much of the Park area is being restored to agricultural usage, most of the Wraysbury development has been water-based, providing some 10 miles (16 km) of bankside fishing and large sailing and power-boat recreation facilities. Part of the complex forms one of only two nature reserves in the whole Park scheme.

The northern part of this site is a wetland habitat of a rural nature situated between the Thames and the Colne Brook. Adjacent arable areas give this section a distinct country environment. Streams with established reeded banks and mature trees interlace an area which has undergone extensive management in the form of tree-planting. This section is quite rich in plant species and attracts good numbers of butterflies. Heathrow's incessant activity does not seem to disturb the birdlife.

(Letter references are used in the following paragraphs to relate the text to the map.) Lake A known locally as Kingsmead, is used for angling and is also a fish farm, but has some uninterrupted corners favoured by birds, including some areas suited to waders. A footpath crosses the lake at its most narrow point via a bridge. Lake B (known locally as Wraysbury 1), was similarly formed but is used for fishing and boating, particularly at weekends. Nonetheless it offers some suitable roosting and breeding facilities, especially for the less timid species. Lake C (Wraysbury 2), the nature reserve nominated by the Regional Park Authority, is bounded by built-up areas, a busy road and the local railway line and is regularly fished. However, the numerous islands and small bays formed by its somewhat 'random' shaping has made it very suitable for waterfowl. There are areas of mature trees, scrub, untended grassland and a small amount of mineral extraction continues. Much of the bank is steep-sided and unsuitable for waders.

Lake D is almost exclusively used for sailing on a regular basis and little habitat management has been carried out. Lake E, Heron Lake, is a somewhat exposed area but, to date, it has been left out of the 'recreation' plan and its shallower areas and reed-lined sections afford reasonable wildfowl facilities.

The River Colne runs alongside the lake, with mature trees over much of its length, and good numbers of established bushes interspersed along the land between these two waters. Lake F has been designed for power-boating and water skiing but when these activities are not being pursued the pool attracts birds despite the continuous noise of the adjacent motorway. Several other smaller lakes exist at this end of the site but are of no particular significance. Further excavations have commenced recently opposite the railway station but the details of future restoration plans have not yet been finalised.

Access
The site is situated in an area well served by road and rail services. Wraysbury station is central to the site, with connections to Waterloo. By road, the pits are south of junction 5 on the M4 and reached via the B470/B376. Alternatively, one may exit the M25 at junction 13 and travel west on the B376. Parking is difficult in all sections of the site, the main car park being at The Green with a capacity for approximately 60 vehicles. A further 20 spaces exist in the station car park but are naturally often utilised by commuters. At the Horton end, there is limited parking available in Park Lane near the access to the public footpath.

To some extent, public access to the pits is restricted. The Horton-Wraysbury footpath, although often a little overgrown, passes through the more rural areas and affords good views over much of the Kingsmead waters and follows the route of Colne Brook for some of its length. Another short footpath known as the Worple Footpath passes beside the northern extremity of Lake C, the nature reserve and a third footpath runs south from the railway line to Hythe End between the River Colne and Heron Lake. On the other hand much of the water can be seen from various parts of the B376 or from the football pitch near The Green.

However, far better access is available to holders of a permit which, for much of the area, is available from Leisure Sports (see Useful Addresses), which facilitates use of three private car parks at Douglas Lane, Wraysbury Club and adjacent to the village school. Although some footpaths and viewing points are on the 'wrong' side of the water from the point of view of sun glare, there are plenty of observation positions suited to normal light situations.

Species
The site supports a good variety of species, including most of the waterfowl one might expect of such a wetland area and many of the smaller waterside and hedgerow birds. The Kingsmead waters are notable for large numbers of Great Crested Grebe and also Heron, with 20 or more often encountered. The western edge has some shallows which attract Snipe, Common Sandpiper and occasional Redshank. Shelduck can also be quite numerous in this area, particularly in the region of the railway line although numbers reduce in autumn when adults fly to Heligoland for their annual moult. The reeded section of the Colne Brook attract several warbler species in summer including Reed and Sedge whilst the nearby scrub hosts Willow Warbler, Chiffchaff, Whitethroat and Blackcap. Reed Bunting can be fairly common on this stretch. In winter sizeable flocks of mixed finches feed on the arable plots, but rarely far from a tree-line. Kestrel can be seen regularly all year, Hobby occasionally in summer distinguished by its more dashing and purposeful flight. Kingfisher make regular use of the Brook, although a flash of blue is all that might be seen through overhanging bushes, accompanied by a high-pitched Starling-type 'Tzeep'. In the vicinity of the dog kennels to the north at Horton, Spotted Flycatcher is always a possibility in summer, at which time large numbers of House

Martin accumulate over the water, and it is quite a challenge singling out the Sand Martins amongst them.

On non-sailing days, Lake B can often host quite large numbers of dabbling and diving ducks, with Mallard, Gadwall and Tufted Duck all year and Teal and Wigeon in autumn. Smew and Goldeneye in small numbers are also fairly common at the turn of the year together with occasional Pintail and Shoveler. On sailing days, most of these birds depart either for Lake C or for nearby Wraysbury reservoir. However, sailing rarely occupies the whole lake outside of peak summer recreation periods and numerous small bays may still hold some duck and occasional waders such as Snipe and Common Sandpiper. It is always therefore worth looking at this lake, even for non-permit holders who will only have views from the B376 or part of the footpath at Douglas Lane. The two resident grebes can be seen at any time and Water Rail has been recorded, but an early start will be necessary to find one. In summer, hirundine numbers may be less than at Kingsmead but Common Tern can be expected particularly late in the season when family groups move in from adjacent breeding sites. In winter, small flocks of Siskin, with occasional Redpoll, forage among the lake-side Alders.

Lake C is arguably the most productive water in the complex. Although a lot of the bank is extensively fished, Little and Great Crested Grebe find places to breed, often into October, and as many as 50 or more of the latter species can be seen towards the end of the year. Coot, Moorhen and Canada Goose do well here also, their winter numbers swelled by visitors from outside. The Canada flock occasionally conceal one or two Barnacle Geese. Black-headed and Common Gulls are always plentiful, usually roosting on the fish farm cages in the centre of the lake and sometimes joined by Herring and Lesser Black-back Gull, particularly during periods of disturbance on nearby reservoirs. The gulls often have to share these cage perches with Heron and Cormorant. A sizeable raft of Tufted Duck, Pochard and Shoveler builds up toward the end of the day for roosting but probably the most rewarding sights are afforded by several thousand Jackdaw, their early morning dispersal being a spectacle in its own right. Regular winter visitors include Smew (usually red-heads), Goldeneye, Goosander and Teal whilst less regular visits may be made by Shelduck and Ruddy Duck. Slavonian and Black-necked Grebe have been seen by a lucky few as have Red and Black-throated Divers.

Long-tailed Ducks, characterised by the large proportion of time spent underwater trying to sate their specialised diet, have over-wintered previously and Short-eared Owls have passed through.

In summer, although affording few breeding facilities, Common Tern will be seen, Arctic and Sandwich Terns having also been known to visit If very dry weather results in a falling water level, Snipe, Redshank, Greenshank and occasional Ruff are possibilities but otherwise waders are not likely to be seen frequently on this particular lake. One bird that will be seen at almost any time however is the Kingfisher which breeds in the vicinity and the lake appears able to support several birds, all of which seem particularly confiding, often flying low over the water between small islands and the bank in front of observers. Sometimes views are close enough to detect the red lower mandible of the female. Of the smaller birds. Reed Bunting, Bullfinch, Linnet and Goldcrest are regular residents whilst most of the more common warblers occur in summer, particularly in the scrub region between Lake C and Lake E, where Green Woodpeckers breed. The area of farmland to the west of the station supports finches and winter thrushes, Kestrel and Tawny Owl. The tree clearing in preparation for the next mineral extractions may however affect these species.

Heron Lake is home to large numbers of Coot and Gadwall. Mute Swan breed in the reedbed to the south-east of the lake whilst Goosander and Goldeneye are likely in winter. It may seem that Goldeneye males are usually greatly outnumbered by females but of course, the juveniles of both sexes resemble the female in first winter plumage. They can be discerned from the adult by the lack of yellow on the bill. Juvenile males can often be detected from occasional sky-points of the bill as a precursor to a dive. But it is the magnificent adult male that is the main prize, particularly just prior to migration when his courting display may be observed during which the head is thrown back almost violently onto the mantle for a second or so. Whether he manages to stay with his selected mate all the way to the breeding grounds is uncertain. The small pool to the north-west will often have female Smews in winter and Little Grebe all year. The tree-line abounding the Colne and the footpath is favoured by resident Treecreepers and Great Spotted Woodpeckers, Blackcap and Chiffchaff in summer and flocks of up to 100 Fieldfares in winter, when small numbers of Siskin may also be encountered. The adjacent Wraysbury reservoir is an important gull roost and large numbers will be seen over the gravel pits on their way to and from the reservoir.

A circular walk from Horton to Hythe End via the footpaths, and returning along the B376 will result in a good number of species at any time of the year, and as the site becomes more regularly watched, the list of rarities is certain to grow.

Calendar

Resident Great Crested and Little Grebe, Heron, Mallard, Tufted Duck, Coot, Moorhen, some Pochard, Reed Bunting, Yellowhammer, Wren, Robin, common species of tit, Linnet, Kingfisher, Canada Goose, Kestrel, Jackdaw.

December–February Wigeon, Gadwall, more Pochard, Teal, Cormorant, increased numbers of grebes, occasional Black-necked and Slavonian Grebes, irregular Pintail and Long-tailed Ducks, gull roost with even larger numbers overhead. Occasional Snipe and Redshank, regular Smew and Goldeneye, occasional Goosander, Siskin.

March–May Reed and Sedge Warblers, sylvia warblers, Spotted Fly-catcher, Swift and hirundines.

June–July Cuckoo, Turtle Dove, riparian species breeding.

August–November Canada Geese flocks, large numbers of House Martins and Swallows August and September, passage waders, Fieldfare and Redwings begin to arrive in November.

ADDITIONAL SITES

Ashley Hill Forest (OS ref. SU 830 810)

Ashley is some 200 acres (80 ha) in size and comprises a significant mixed deciduous section, with conifer compartments, all surrounded by arable land. Access is either on the A4 at SU 829 802 where up to ten cars may park, or SU 832 805 where there is room for three vehicles on the A404. The site is managed by the Forestry Commission. The mixture of woodlands permits a comparison of the favoured habitats of a number of species of bird. The conifer stands will be utilised by many of the tit family for food, particularly the Coal Tit with its slightly longer bill. However, Blue and Great Tits will probably nest only in the adjacent deciduous wood. Blackcaps and Garden Warblers rarely stray into the conifers but Siskins can be found in both. Woodcock is a possibility and the two spotted woodpeckers should be found. Chiffchaff is another regular visitor, especially in the area of the picnic facility half-way down the western side. Conditions in the softwood area are ideal for Long-eared Owl but the status of this bird here is uncertain. Little Owl is a regular resident however. Yellowhammer and Reed Bunting frequent the edge of the woodland and the adjacent farmland is taken over by large number of Chaffinches, Jackdaws and Collared Doves in winter. There is always the possibility of wandering Crossbills but the woodland has now grown too mature for two previous occupants; the Nightjar and Tree Pipit.

Bray Gravel Pit (OS ref. SU 911 785)

The pit is to the north of the A308 Maidenhead-to-Windsor road, along which one or two gateways afford the best views over the majority of the water. The eastern end of the lake can be seen from the next lane going north past the sailing club towards Monkey Island. The 50 acre (20 ha) lake is quite deep in places but possesses a number of shallower bays suited to dabbling ducks and Little Grebes. In winter the deeper water hosts diving ducks such as Tufted Duck and Pochard. Goldeneye are occasional visitors and a Red-crested Pochard once spent a few hours on the site. The area between the main road and the south bank is grassed and often contains many Crows, Woodpigeon, Lapwing and Canada Geese. This bank is also probably the most likely along which to find waders, particularly in spring. Unfortunately, sailboarding is a popular summertime pursuit on the pit and this level of disturbance may well prevent the site becoming anything more than of average interest to the birdwatcher.

Brimpton Gravel Pit (OS ref. SU 571 654)

Lying alongside the road from Woolhampton to Brimpton, south of the A4, is a small gravel pit which, over the years, has had quite a remarkable record of guest appearances. The site comprises two pools. One is a rather featureless round basin which is nonetheless found quite acceptable by common resident waterfowl. The other pool is larger, more complex in shape and with maturing reeds and sallows in the north. This same portion is quite marshy, extending away from the water's edge. In summer, Reed and Sedge Warblers, Mute Swan and

93

Dabchick will be found breeding and enormous flocks of House Martins and Swifts, with some Sand Martins and Swallows, wheel over the surface of the water. To some extent the site may be past its best from the point of view of short-stay visitors and birds of passage due to the improved access and pedestrian facilities around the lake now that mineral extraction work has ceased. Some 100 species have been recorded over the years including Osprey, Hen Harrier, Merlin and Barn Owl. Hobby and Short-eared Owls remain possibilities. Redshank, Ringed and Little Ringed Plovers have bred there and may continue to do so. The five commoner terns all occur and Mandarin and Garganey have been noted. Waders which have used the water's edge include Curlew, Jack Snipe, Grey Plover, Curlew Sandpiper and Turnstone, but increased disturbance may affect this record. Best visited mid-week, early morning there is parking inside the site found by turning up the small track north-west of the point where all three roads intersect.

Bucklebury Common (OS ref. SU 555 692)

This site, and parts of the adjacent Upper Common, are similar in nature to Snelsmore Common and this is reflected in the species richness of the area. The two locations are to the north of the road between Cold Ash and Chapel Row and car parking facilities are provided on either side of this road at the eastern site. Resident birds include Tawny and Little Owls, Green and Great Spotted Woodpeckers (with occasional Lesser Spotted Woodpecker), Woodcock and the common tits and finches. Redstarts and Whinchat are passage visitors but species which can be found in summer include Tree Pipit and Lesser Whitethroat, Nightingale and Wood Warbler produce regular sightings and Spotted Flycatchers breed quite frequently. Kestrel and Sparrowhawk are readily seen, but seeing Hobby requires some good fortune. However, some lucky birdwatchers have been able to report Osprey and, in winter, Merlin. It is also in winter that good numbers of Chaffinch, often in excess of 100 are present. Linnets also group together, at this time of year often in close association with Greenfinch and it is well worth double-checking small clusters of House Sparrows; they may actually be Tree Sparrows. Hawfinch has occurred but cannot be guaranteed. Bullfinches are plentiful in the scrub areas. A worthwhile site at any time, but probably best in May.

California Country Park (OS ref. SU 786 649)

Lying to the east of Arborfield Garrison is an area of mixed woodland, nowadays nominated as a Country Park, with permitted caravanning. It can therefore be a 'popular' area in summer, but is much quieter for the remainder of the year. There is ample car parking within the site itself. Small areas of bog and heathland lend variety to the Park, but the large pool in the centre is not particularly productive for birdwatchers. A good general range of woodland birds exists including all 3 woodpeckers, the common tits, finches and numerous Jays. Stock Doves and Collared Doves are common, and occasionally Jackdaw roost. Winter visitors include small flocks of Redwing, Siskin (Redpoll take a little more finding) and occasionally Brambling near the pool. Summer birds are the Blackcap, Chiffchaff and the occasional Willow Warbler. One or two small areas are suitable for Wood Warbler, but the status of this species here is uncertain. Adjacent arable fields are excellent for gulls, Mistle Thrushes, Fieldfares and mixed corvids in winter. Goldcrests are always numerous. The Bog area and the stream-sides are of botanical interest.

Child Beale Wildlife Trust (OS ref. SU 620 780)

Situated at the A329 Pangbourne to Oxford road, this Thames-side site is the headquarters of the World Pheasant Association and contains a collection of wildfowl, pheasants and owls in a parkland setting including several lakes. Whilst not everyone is in favour of collections, they can afford the opportunity for birdwatching beginners to become familiar with more unusual visitors to British shores such as Red-breasted Goose, Garganey, and Pink-footed Goose. There are over 120 species in the collection spread over 100 acre (40 ha) site, but the overhanging Beechwoods to the west and the widening Thames in the east have also created an attractive habitat for wild birds. Over 134 such species have been recorded here since the sanctuary was created, including Bittern, Mandarin, Osprey and Peregrine Falcon, Wryneck, Barn Owl and Hawfinch. Of course, one will not see such species on every visit but the centre is of educational value to the younger birdwatcher (although an entrance fee is levied).

Crowthorne Woods (OS ref. SU 856 648)

Part of the original Windsor Forest, and managed by the Forestry Commission, Crowthorne Wood is some 220 acres (90 ha) of essentially coniferous woodland abutted by similar Crown Estate habitat to the north and the heathlands belonging to the Royal Military Academy to the south-east. Parking is available at Caesar's Camp on the B3430 or at several small entrance bays along the A3095. A reasonable variety of woodland birds can be found including Green and Great Spotted Woodpecker, the six common tits, Nuthatches and Treecreepers. Winter birds include Siskin and increased numbers of Redpolls plus occasional Crossbills. In fact the Rare Birds Committee is considering reports of a small group of Parrot Crossbills that once visited. The woodland edge near the heath attracts Woodcock and Sparrowhawk and this side of the wood is also better for summer warblers. Owls are not common, Tawny being the most usual but conditions are suitable for the Long-eared species. Tree Pipits are fairly regular although much of the woodland is becoming somewhat mature for this rather particular passerine.

Finchampstead Ridges (OS ref. SU 813 636)

The National Trust manage two sites which straddle the B3348 between Finchampstead and Crowthorne. In total they comprise some 60 acres (24 ha) of heath and woodland with a blend of Oak, Birch, Chestnut and Scots Pine at each of the two locations. Density varies somewhat and in places conditions are suitable for Wood Warbler, and they oblige with annual appearances. The area south of the road slopes down to a boggy region at the lowest point, passing through many Robin territories and, in summer, families of Willow Tits and Treecreeper are much in evidence. A small pool in the south-east is home to a family of Moorhen and Chiffchaff entertain these rails from waterside song-posts. Jays are prevalent at both sites. The other woodland surrounds a car park which can accommodate some 50 vehicles. Great Spotted Woodpecker breed in this larger wood which also attracts breeding Garden Warbler and Nuthatch. This wood too has a pond, much larger than its neighbours, and Mallard, Moorhen, Canada Geese and Dabchick are regularly found. In Winter, Siskin and Redpoll frequent the sites readily, as Birch and conifers are their favourite meal-tables. Crossbills are a possibility, perhaps popping in on their way between Crowthorne Woods and the Bramshill plantation. Overall, the site may be a little small to be noteworthy, but it is a pleasant spot to visit from April to September.

Maidenhead Thicket (OS ref. SU 855 807)

The Thicket comprises 175 acres (70 ha) of dense Hawthorn, Blackthorn and other shrubbery in the east and mature mixed deciduous woodland to the west. It is situated astride the A423(T) road to Henley and is managed by the National Trust. Parking is in Pinkneys Drive where there is room for 25 vehicles. A very good site for general woodland birds, the dense portion being attractive to all six tits and Great Spotted Woodpeckers all year round, and Blackcap, Garden Warbler and Chiffchaff in summer. Lesser Whitethroats are regular passage visitors to this sector, that used to be a regular haunt for Nightingales which again may nowadays only be encountered on passage. The more open and mature woodland on the other side of the road hosts all three woodpeckers and occasional Tawny Owl. Treecreepers are quite abundant and Collared Doves roost in small numbers in winter. Sparrowhawk occasionally dash through the undergrowth on hunting sorties. Spotted Flycatchers are not regular but Turtle Doves will be seen most years. The mammal life of the Thicket includes Foxes and occasional Muntjac Deer, and several species of bats are prolific in summer.

Northerams Wood (OS ref. SU 856 682)

A small mixed deciduous woodland on the A3095 Bracknell-to-Crowthorne road. At only 7.5 acres (3 ha), it does not take long to explore but with varied coppice and mature stands of Oak, Hazel, Sycamore and Sweet Chestnut, a surprising range of bird species can be found, albeit rarely anything especially exciting. Parking on the main road is difficult but driving into the Great Hollands Estate south of the site and turning right, there is parking in Wroxton Road. Most of the common resident woodland birds can be expected and summer visitors include Blackcap and Garden Warbler. The site is also good for butterflies at this time of year. Occasional Siskins in winter.

Summerleaze Gravel Pit (OS ref. SU 895 827)

A sizeable pit to the north-east of Maidenhead with several planted islands for breeding ducks and geese. There are also some flat gravel spits both used by Common Terns and Little Ringed Plovers for breeding, and a gravel-filled floating raft provided by the local RSPB group. In winter the water is very busy with mixed gull roosts of several hundreds (with occasional rarities), and significant numbers of Coot, Tufted Duck and Canada Geese. Quite a few Pochard over-winter and there are always small numbers of Goldeneye and Wigeon, occasional Ruddy Duck, Goosander and Smew. Shelduck and Pintail occur and several Teal are usually present. Winter and passage waders include Greenshank, Ruff, Redshank, Snipe, Dunlin and Common Sandpiper and occasional Ringed Plover. In summer all three wagtails are regulars, Kingfishers are resident and Sand Martins breed occasionally in the area. Surrounded by farmland, Corn Bunting, Yellowhammer and Little Owl are frequently encountered and Meadow Pipits are numerous in winter. Small pools on the periphery of the main lake have regularly hosted passage Garganey in recent years. Best visited in the period October to May. Access is restricted to all but permit holders who have applied to the local Summerleaze Gravel Company. (See Useful Addresses.) However reasonable views over most of the lake are possible from the public footpath running to the west of the pool except in the mornings when sunshine may be a problem.

The Downs (OS ref. SU 430 800)

Needless to say the Downs cover an enormous area of north-west Berkshire and extend into the Vale of White Horse in Oxfordshire. The scene is typical with vast tracts of rolling pasture and stoney arable fields, in an almost tree-less landscape. One of the highest spots is the Devil's Punchbowl south-west of Wantage and some of the steeper rises exist at Thurle Down near Streatley which is also one of the few wooded peaks in the area. One of the ways of exploring this erstwhile barren terrain is to walk The Ridgeway which runs along the North of the Downs. The species of birds encountered typifies the surroundings with many birds of the fields such as Crows and Rooks, Skylarks and Meadow Pipits, Pheasants and Grey Partridges and, in winter, some Fieldfares. The Downs are the only remaining area of the county where one might chance across a Stone Curlew, which has a tenuous and threatened grip. Small numbers still attempt to breed, with uncertain success. One may stand a better chance of seeing them during the spring passage. The Quail is another bird fussy about its habitat and that may also be expected in small numbers, around Compton and Thurle and over in the Lambourn Downs.

The vast open prairie-like field system also appeals to Britain's larger raptors. The Compton and Blewbury area seems the most productive and both Hen Harrier and Marsh Harrier have been recorded in most years. Buzzards are a more regular visitor and are happy to explore the Lambourn area too but the Rough-legged Buzzard is far more infrequent in showing up. Hobby are a possibility. Short-eared Owls put in regular appearances at the Thurle end, where Barn Owl is a scarcer prospect. The River Lambourn, in the south-west corner of the Downs, provides a more varied habitat in which Snipe and Kingfisher thrive. In winter, Brambling are a likely find, though never numerous and the Great Grey Shrike has been a notable December bird in some years. Wheatears could be found almost anywhere in one's and two's during April and May.

In summary, a huge area which one could spend a lifetime becoming familiar with. There is the possibility of some really good species being found but only through regular and detailed prospecting.

Windsor Great Park (OS ref. SU 962 723)

At some 4,800 acres (2,000 ha), the Great Park is aptly named. Stretching away from the Royal Castle, the Park comprises deciduous woodlands of Oak, Beech and Hornbeam, open deer parkland, farmland, and three bodies of water, including Virginia Water which, at 2 miles (3 km) from end to end, is by far the largest and rests partially in Surrey. Vehicles are not permitted in the Park but there is ample parking on the A332 to the west and several car parks at Blacknest Gate, Virginia Water in the south, and Bishops Gate in the east. Fees are charged at some of these parking places. The farmland attracts species which typify such habitat, including winter flocks of mixed corvids, with Jackdaw often the most numerous. Green Woodpecker frequents the open parkland whilst both other woodpecker species can be found throughout the woodlands and near 'The Village' at the centre of the Park. Smiths Lawn, the polo grounds, attract passage Wheatears and the surrounding birch scrub will host the first Chiffchaffs and Willow Warblers. The more open woodlands contain many hole-nesting birds including Stock Doves and Willow Tits. Also, although in decreasing numbers of late, Hawfinches occur.

Great Meadow Pond is not available to the public but its resident flock of Canada Geese, together with the local group of Barnacle and Bar-headed Geese, will be seen flying in to roost at dusk. Another evening spectacle is provided when the small colony of Mandarin Duck, which breed successfully here, move to adjacent waters to spend the night, their high-pitched call seeming somewhat inappropriate for a bird of this size. An even more awesome sight at the end of winter days are the clouds of many thousands of Starlings that sometimes gather at the Park, wheeling in harmony against chequered skies. With the main areas of water containing Cormorant, Dabchick and Gadwall in winter, and most of the common summering species in the wooded areas, a visit at most times of the year can be worthwhile. Mid-week days between October and July might be best, but allow plenty of time.

It is a long time since Long-eared Owls bred here regularly and the Park will doubtless see many more changes, but the site could be ideal for introducing Lady Amherst's or Golden Pheasant, and the nearby flock of Ring-necked Parakeets at Runnymede may, in due course, establish a colony at the Park.

Wood End (OS ref. SU 935 702)

A pleasant walk through farmland and private parkland with a sizeable lake in the centre. Parking is near the entrance, off the lane between Cheapside and Ascot; a footpath runs north along the private drive. Approximately 109 yds (100 m) along, another footpath leads off left into a small woodland and emerges near the lake. The path follows a tree-lined lane to Wood End from where one may retrace one's steps or follow the B383 to the northern end of the original footpath and drive and complete a circular walk to the starting point. The woodland is inhabited by Great Spotted Woodpeckers and Redpolls whilst the trees to the west of the lake form a substantial Jackdaw roost. The water is also a significant roost for winter gulls and usually has good numbers of Pochard and Great Crested Grebe during this season. Sawbills are a reasonable prospect. The farmland areas are favoured by Grey Partridge, Goldfinch and winter thrushes and a pair of Sparrowhawks are resident. Reasonable activity at most times of the year. A further, smaller lake in Silwood Park, 400 yds (360 m) south of the starting point, often has large numbers of Mandarin, particularly in winter.

BUCKINGHAMSHIRE

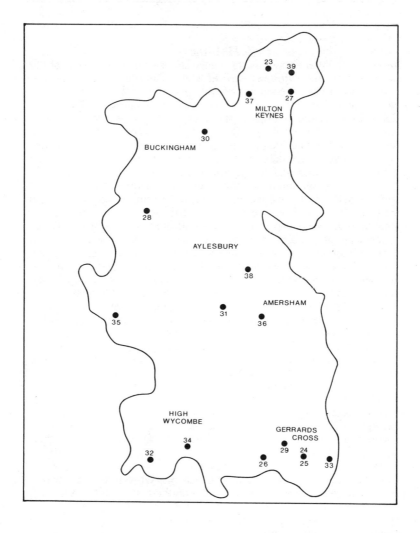

23
39
37
27
MILTON
KEYNES
30
BUCKINGHAM
28
AYLESBURY
38
31
AMERSHAM
36
35
HIGH
WYCOMBE
GERRARDS
CROSS
34
29
24
32
26
25
33

ARC WILDFOWL CENTRE

Map 23/OS ref. SP 840 430

Habitat

This reserve, also known as the Great Linford Reserve, is one of the many mineral extraction sites in the Milton Keynes area, but has the distinction of having been specifically restored as a sanctuary and a study centre. The research establishment is managed by The Game Conservancy Council on behalf of the Amey Roadstone gravel company and has a full-time staff of biologists and a conservation officer. The research programme includes the study of alternative techniques for creating reserve habitats from completed gravel workings, giving guidance on ecological development planning and investigating the influence of restoration and management activity on wildfowl breeding success rates. Interactive feeding habits of fish and waterfowl are also studied. The site itself comprises a 100 acre (40 ha) gravel pit, structured and landscaped to maximise its attractiveness to wildfowl.

The main lake has been developed with many shallow 'fingers' and islands to optimise the shore-line and to create suitable breeding areas. Loafing and grazing areas are included and a variety of plants have been added. It is intended to establish a reedbed which could add substantially to the number of birds known to frequent the site.

Over 70 species of moth and 14 butterfly species have been recorded. The waters are well-stocked with a variety of fish, including Pike, but fishing rights are reserved. The perimeter moat deters many species of mammal from wandering onto the reserve, but Mink have managed to establish themselves. The River Great Ouse meanders close to the site and an area of farmland and pasture is immediately adjacent. The nearby Haversham Lake to the west, though larger, is less productive, with little bankside vegetation. To the east, Redhouse Lake and Vicarage Spinney Lake also provide refuge for many species, but these lakes are extensively fished and sailed and access is more restricted. However, occasional sightings of grebes of the more scarce species are possible.

Access

Great Linford Reserve is on the road between Wolverton and Newport Pagnell, access to the site being on the northern side of this road, just east of the Black Horse public house. The nearest main road interconnections are to the east, junction 14 on the M1 via the V10 at Milton Keynes (where most roads are numbered this way) and, to the west, the A5 at Stony Stratford. Having turned into the complex, Blackhorse Lake will be seen to the right and this is used for sailboarding. The track on the left leads to the Centre itself which has a car park for some 20 vehicles, including space for a coach. The main building contains laboratories and a lecture room extremely well equipped to give audio/visual presentations to audiences of around 50. Toilet facilities are available inside the building which was erected in 1980.

Access to the refuge and its two hides is strictly by permit, available from the Centre. (See Useful Addresses.) Visitors are encouraged to attend the reserve between August and the end of February as the breeding sanctuary is closed during the period March to end of July. Small parties, particularly school groups, are welcome (with one month notice), again, provided the breeding season is avoided. For those without permits, reasonable views over much of the lake are available from the lane which runs between the lake itself and the river.

Species

The expertise employed in the development of the sanctuary in the 15 years since its creation is not only evidenced by the variety of habitats provided, but also by the 170 or so species that have been recorded. A fair number of these are resident and in addition to the expected Little and Great Crested Grebe, there is a thriving flock of Greylag Geese which was introduced when the site was formed. Several hundred share their time between Linford, Haversham and Stony Stratford Nature Reserve. A small number of Shelduck stay close to the site throughout the year. Water Rail have also remained faithful though more usually heard than seen. The surrounding farmland hosts Pheasant, both species of partridge and Lapwing, and also attracts Little and Tawny Owls whilst the Great Ouse flowing around the perimeter guarantees regular sightings of Kingfisher. All three woodpeckers are recorded, particularly the Green species which favours the waterfowl loafing areas. Skylarks and Pied Wagtails are prominent at most times, but Meadow Pipits require a little more finding. The tit family is well represented and both Nuthatch and Treecreeper should be discovered without too much trouble. One species that is a pleasure to discover quite frequently is the Tree Sparrow which, like most of the birds referred to above, breed quite regularly at the Centre.

The winter scene is, of course, dominated by waterfowl and waders. From the hides one will see up to 100 Teal, 600 Wigeon and 50 or so Pochard, usually accompanied by several Shovelers and a few pairs of Gadwall. Tufted Ducks are numerous, but it is worth looking carefully at them as Scaup have put in occasional appearances. Similarly Coots should be scrutinised to ensure one does not overlook a Common or Velvet Scoter on one of their rare visits. The hides provide an excellent opportunity to watch sawbills at close quarters and whilst most of the visiting Smew and Goosander are females or juveniles, the magnificent males of these two species will sometimes brighten up the surroundings. Goldeneye are another regular addition, so watch for the male's display towards the end of the winter period. The whole of this watery setting is frequently graced with Bewick's Swans amongst the more numerous Mute Swans. Meanwhile the edges of the pool are also quite active. The grassy banks may well be occupied by White-fronted or even Pink-footed Geese whilst the taller grasses and reedbeds have become more regular haunts for one or two Bitterns in recent years. Redshank and Snipe provide the most usual wader sightings during this season with less frequent reports of Jack Snipe, but at passage times Greenshank, Green and Common Sandpipers, together with Curlew, can be anticipated and fortunate observers may chance to see Turnstone, Dunlin and Sanderling on their way through. The even luckier birdwatcher will stand an outside chance of spotting a Whimbrel, one of the godwits or even the challenge of identifying a Little Stint.

As the backdrop of winter gulls fades away other, more obvious migrants pay brief visits, such as Black and Arctic Terns. Little Terns are observed infrequently, but Common Terns, in small numbers, usually stop over, though to date have failed to breed. The same cannot be said of Ringed and Little Ringed Plovers which both breed successfully, their favourite sites sometimes bedecked with Yellow or Grey Wagtails. The adjacent reedbeds revel in a maelstrom of Sedge, Reed and Willow Warblers, Whitethroats and Reed Buntings, whilst the scrub and bushes between the beds provide song-posts for Chiffchaff, Blackcap and Garden Warblers. All of this is just too much for the local Cuckoos who can be seen during May and June moving around the reserve selecting nests of unsuspecting passerines to parasitise. Spoilt for choice with so many waters in the area, Swifts and hirundines are not always common here though this appears not to deter the Hobby from making the odd visit, but certainly with nothing like the regularity of the resident Kestrel and Sparrowhawk. The shrubbery around the site has advanced to a stage which is attracting Linnets, Redpolls and Bullfinches, and Greenfinches now breed regularly. The number of woodland species is likely to increase on the site as the recently planted trees mature (although Woodcock are already seen from time to time).

As mentioned above, much of the reserve is closed during the peak breeding season and so it is important to contact the Conservation Officer before making any visits at this time. These restrictions are however removed for permit holders in time for the autumn passage when many of the migrants seen earlier in April return, together with occasional Oystercatchers. Wheatears, suspected of breeding here in the past, also move through with flocks of hirundines which summered further north. Short-eared Owls present themselves for irregular viewing and at least one Osprey usually pops in enticed by the success of the site's fisheries activity. Merlin too can be seen on occasions. It seems only too soon that flocks of Redwing, mingling with Fieldfares in abundance, signal the shortening days ahead. Corn Buntings noticeably quieten, their janglings taken over by squeaking Siskins and screaming gulls. It can be difficult to fit in a visit to all the wetland sites of Milton Keynes in a single day, but if a choice has to be made, the ARC Wildfowl Centre would compete with Willen at the head of the list and, with the added comfort of the hides, could well come out on top.

Calendar

Resident Little and Great Crested Grebe, Heron, Canada and Greylag Goose, Mute Swan, occasional Shelduck. Mallard, Tufted Duck, Sparrowhawk, Kestrel, Red-legged and Grey Partridge, Pheasant, Water Rail, Moorhen, Coot, Lapwing, Redshank, Black-headed Gull, Stock and Collared Doves. Little Owl, Tawny Owl, Kingfisher, all three woodpeckers, Skylark, Pied Wagtail, Dunnock, Wren, all the common thrushes, and the six common tits. Yellowhammer and Reed Bunting, common finches including occasional Redpoll. Tree Sparrow, Magpie, Jackdaw and Crow.

December–February Cormorant, occasional Bittern, chance of White-fronted and Pink-footed Geese. Bewick's Swan, occasional Whooper, Teal, Gadwall, Wigeon, Shoveler, Pochard, Tufted Duck. Possibility of Pintail and Ruddy Duck and rare visits of Scaup, plus Common and Velvet Scoter, Goldeneye, Smew and Goosander all regulars. Possibility of Merlin. Occasional Golden Plover, Woodcock, Snipe and Jack Snipe. Lesser and Greater Black-backed Gulls. Herring Gulls and occasional

Common Gull. Meadow Pipit, Grey Wagtail, Siskin, occasional Brambling.

March–May Occasional Garganey, Osprey and Buzzard. Passage waders include Greenshank, Common and Green Sandpipers and Curlew. Less frequently Turnstone, Sanderling and Ruff. Possibility of Curlew, Sandpiper and Dunlin. Black Tern, Arctic Tern and Wheatear passing through, whilst Common Tern stay on. Common warblers arrive with Swifts and hirundines. Cuckoo arrive before Turtle Doves. Occasional Spotted Flycatchers.

June–July Many species breeding including Ringed and Little Ringed Plover, Redshank, Tufted Duck and Water Rail. Most of the common warblers and buntings nesting in reedbeds and surrounding vegetation.

August–November Some continued breeding in good summers with both passerines and Great Crested Grebe. Hirundines present until late October. Passage possibilities include Osprey and un-common waders. Winter thrushes and gull flocks build up from November.

BLACK PARK & LANGLEY PARK

Maps 24 and 25/OS ref. TQ 010 825

Habitat

These two adjacent locations were once part of the Langley Marish Estate, but were purchased by Buckinghamshire County Council in the 1940s and are now classified as Country Parks. They are still regarded as being in the Green Belt and as such form the western extremity of the vast Colne Valley Park which stretches from Staines to Rickmansworth.

Black Park covers 550 acres (220 ha) and got this name around 1880 from its extensive plantations of black-barked Corsican Pine. This species still covers some 30 per cent of the planted area, but nowadays there exists a greater variety of trees, with Larch and Scots Pine in the conifer stands, in subtle diffusion with deciduous woods which cover about half of the estate with Oak, Beech, Sweet Chestnut, Hemlock, Birch and a few Mountain Ash. Large areas were replanted after the Second World War and were thinned 20 years later, with more deciduous plantations than previously.

Different habitat again exists at the Five Points Crossroads where, during the drought of 1976 nearly 50 acres were lost to fire. This area has been sparsely planted with conifers but in the meantime has reverted to scrub, Heather, Gorse and Broom, providing a lower vegetation level than anywhere else in the Park, and which may be retained by the management. It is however a shame to see the effect of the 1976 drought on the mature Beech trees in adjacent stands.

The lake itself is some 12.5 acres (5 ha) in area and, for many years, was quite deep over most of its expanse. Recent work however has created a shallow section in which small islands have been provided to attract waterfowl. The eroded bank is being restored by diverting footpaths and this has already proven successful, as has been a nest box scheme, both on the islands and in several of the woods. The Park represents some 15 per cent of the public woodland in the county and the management programme is imaginative with conservation a high priority.

Langley Park is classified as parkland, rather than woodland, although a proportion of its 135 acres (55 ha) is committed to mature Oak stands. At the centre of the Park is the Ashlar-faced Langley Mansion which has recently been converted to offices, but the grounds have been maintained and include a small lake, a significant arboretum with some 40 species of tree, and a large expanse of Rhododendrons and Azaleas. The remainder is open grassland with a small farmed area and adjacent orchards.

The management programme, apart from maintaining the extensive formal gardens, is one of clearing birch encroachment and replenishing the areas of Oak.

Access

The two parks straddle the A412 between Uxbridge and Slough and the nearest trunk road connections are junction 1 on the M40 and junction 5 on the M4. The nearest main line station is at Slough.

Access to Black Park is along Black Park Road, turning into the car park which has space for some 400 vehicles and is surrounded with picnic sites. Beyond the lake are refreshment and first-aid facilities, toilets, changing huts and the Ranger's office. Special note should be made on arrival of any information on closing times. The Park has a peripheral footpath and the many accessible tracks through the woods are indicated on the map as solid lines. There is an organised nature trail, details of which are contained in the Trail Guide available at the Park. The area north of the lake is a small marsh and, until construction of a board-walk is completed, wellingtons are recommended if this area and along the main footpath by the side of the Pinewood Film Studios are to be explored. About 20 car parking spaces are available in Fulmer Common Road.

Access to Langley Park is from Billet Lane turning into the car park which can accommodate 100 or so vehicles. (Again, it is important to note locking-up time to avoid a long walk to the Ranger's house to get a key.) Toilet facilities are provided between the formal gardens and the open area. The Park itself has a clearly arranged path scheme and the private area surrounding the mansion has public footpaths around the periphery. Several pedestrian entrances are available.

Species

Birdwatchers have a propensity for avoiding 'formal' parklands in favour of wilder countryside, mainly on the grounds of too little habitat variety and too many people. Whereas Black Park can be a very popular place for picnics and walking it is relatively easy to find times when one can practically have the wood to oneself and at such times it is an ideal site for beginners to become familiar with a wide range of bird species. Winter is a good time to start whilst there is little vegetation in the shrub areas or on the trees. Discovering all three species of woodpecker, particularly in Strawberry Wood, can be satisfying, whilst Nuthatch and Treecreeper are also easier to locate at this time. Roving groups of Goldcrests, Long-tailed Tits, Blue Tit and Willow Tit are especially prominent as are the boisterous Jays and Magpies. Small parties of Redpolls can be found throughout the Park and, at the periphery, Redwings and Grey Partridge can be regularly seen. The car park can be a good place to find Bramblings, the male still looking magnificent even in his winter plumage. An evening visit could well be rewarded with Tawny Owl whilst an early morning visit would be necessary if one wished to find any of the Woodcock that are occasionally put up from the bracken-strewn conifer stands east of the lake by inquisitive dogs. This same compartment is one of the more usual sites to find the group of Crossbills that often frequent the wood, although usual sightings are as silhouettes against a grey sky and one will need to take care not to get over-excited by small numbers of Greenfinch which can be encountered in the same area. The pool at this time of year is not likely to be too productive. The adjacent heronry was abandoned some 15 years ago and although the first visitors of the day may occasionally find a Heron which has spent the night there, it is the more obvious Canada Geese that occupy most of the overnight roosts.

Meanwhile, the winter scene at Langley Park is slightly different, the more open parkland and less enclosed pool attracting some additional species. Little Owl in particular is far more abundant than in Black Park, often seen bounding along the main avenues of trees alongside the access roads in full daylight. The pool, though smaller and more prone to freezing over than its neighbours is generally better populated, with Pochard, a few Shoveler and the occasional Wigeon usually present. A pair or two of Gadwall might well be passing through and Teal could be present but their somewhat more timid nature may well determine that they stay but for a brief period. One may come across a wandering Grey Wagtail near the pond but Pied Wagtails are far more likely, either at the pool-side or in the grounds of the mansion. Gulls are also more numerous here though usually restricted to Common and Black-headed species. Redwings are joined by slate-headed Fieldfares in and around the orchard to the east of the Park and close scrutiny often reveals considerable size differential between individual Fieldfares. These winter thrushes may also be found at the formal garden area which is often visited by a few Brambling. The woods, being generally less mature than Black Park in many places, possess fewer birds but the list of species is similar including all three woodpeckers. The farmland in the meantime attracts the usual flocks of corvids, gulls and Lapwings. These mixed feeding scenes are interesting to observe as individuals of different species harry each other petulantly, yet there must be advantage in foraging together in this way as they mix so readily. They are often joined by large numbers of Starlings just before nightfall, first wheeling casually into the general area and then finally descending to the ground rapidly, almost violently, like heavy rain.

As winter loosens its frosty grip on Langley Park, the gulls move off and the winter ducks bequeath the pool to breeding Mute Swans. Sightings of Meadow Pipits diminish, and Reed Buntings set up their own nesting territories. Small flocks of Yellowhammer disperse in pairs as the spring passage unwraps its annual surprises. A pair or two of Gadwall may stop over and Pintail have been noted. The area of the arboretum has produced Pied Flycatcher at this time of year and once the migration flood gates are fully open, Chiffchaff, Willow Warbler and Blackcap are soon in evidence. Many Blackbirds and Song Thrushes will have paired up, again the formal gardens being a good place to watch their bond-forming arguments, carried out under the doleful eyes of numerous Collared Doves. The first Nuthatch broods will be piping amongst the deciduous parts of the woods while less discernible calls of countless other young birds seem to emanate from every bush and tree-hole. There will usually be two or three pairs of Spotted Flycatcher breeding near the mansion outbuildings and it can be quite amusing watching the nearly matured young making their first attempts at catching their own food. However, perfection is quickly established. Those of the Little Owls that have chosen to breed will be even more active during the day than usual but the more menacing Sparrowhawk, often seen hunting over the open rides, has a greater effect on the woodland community when it puts in an appearance.

Black Park will also be changing its scenery and, perhaps being more recognised as an amenity than Langley Park, numbers of visitors will be increasing and the pool is utilised for paddling and boating, becoming almost devoid of birds save for the few breeding Coot and Mallard at the reserve end of the lake. After much ceremony in the spring, when intending partners call to each other with a cry resembling rusty gate hinges, Jays will be eagerly producing their progeny. In fact so prolific has this handsome bird become on the site in past years that control of numbers has been necessary. Here again, family groups of Nuthatch make themselves most obvious and the majority of the 170 or so nest boxes provided will have been utilised by something, even if it is Wood Mice. Towards the end of May the first Starling broods begin to colonise again, fashioning feeding parties of between 100 and 200, chiefly in the Oak trees near the main car park. Kestrels also breed on the site and on rare occasions can be seen posturing with Sparrowhawks for hunting rights.

Without doubt, however, the single most important sector of Black Park in summer from the birdwatcher's point of view is the area around Five Point Crossroads, the scene of earlier devastation by fire following intense drought. Now, a decade on, the area has attained a dense covering of mature Heather, Gorse and Broom, interspersed with young conifers up to 5 ft (1.7 m) high and emerging Birch scrub. The overall size of the affected area is large enough to have created a useable habitat for a number of heathland species. A warm summer's morning, ideally at 6.30 a.m. or so, is the best time to visit this corner of the Park. Stepping out into the sunshine from the wooded approaches, one is first likely to be greeted with the plaintive calls of Willow Warblers and the equally distinctive sound of Yellowhammers. Several pairs of Linnets will be busily collecting food in the bushes and trees, pausing only occasionally for song before disappearing into a dense nest site. A small number of Reed Buntings have found this to be a suitable breeding area and several pairs of Bullfinch also indulge. Garden Warblers also afford ample opportunity for the birder to familiarise the sight and sound of this drab-looking but cheerful bird in comparison with the similar sounding Blackcap. Green Woodpeckers move between the few mature trees that survived the ravages of the fire. These same trees, mainly Oaks, are used as song-posts by two birds that very much specialise in this sort of terrain; the Tree Pipit and the Whitethroat. Some five or six pairs of each are usually present and it is interesting to compare the song-flights of these airborne serenaders.

The Tree Pipit will usually start from a low perch and will climb silently to its selected altitude. The descent is then slow and graceful, wings fluttering, tail spread and slightly erect and the head arched upwards. Throughout this delightful 'parachute drop' the bird utters a vigorous fluting song, ending in a repetitive flourish as it alights on an oft-used perch. The Whitethroat on the other hand may commence from a loftier branch from which it will go into a more arched descent, with a variety of rapid falls and occasional hoverings, ending in a dashing dive into cover. Its song is not as melodious as that of its aerial partner and is punctuated with harsh chatterings. Long-tailed Tits also inhabit this new plantation, building their domed nests in Gorse bushes. Much less regularly, but doubtless with even greater pleasure, one might be fortunate enough to come across a Grasshopper Warbler reeling from within the denser vegetation. Surrounded by these ornithological delights one may well overlook the Muntjac Deer that occasionally stroll out of the plantation onto the pathways.

Small though it may be this section of the estate is of great significance given that there is little similar habitat for quite some distance. A sympathetic management could be in a position to retain the status of this compartment, perhaps by using it as a nursery plantation, transferring the young trees to other locations on a short-term rotational basis. In the meantime these Parks will continue to offer good opportunities to study a wide range of woodland bird species.

Calendar

Resident Mute Swan, Mallard, Tufted Duck, Sparrowhawk, Kestrel, Grey Partridge, Pheasant, Snipe, Woodcock, Woodpigeon, Stock Dove, Collared Dove, Little Owl, Tawny Owl, all three woodpeckers, Skylark, Meadow Pipit, Pied Wagtail, common corvids, Goldcrest, Marsh Tit, Willow Tit, Nuthatch, Treecreeper, Bullfinch, Goldfinch, Linnet, Redpoll, Crossbill, Reed Bunting, Yellowhammer.

December–February Occasional Little Grebe and Wigeon. Teal, Shoveler, Pochard. Red-legged Partridge irregular, large flocks of Lapwing with possibility of Golden Plover in small numbers. Most of the more common gulls in small numbers. Occasional Grey Wagtail, numerous Redwing and Fieldfares. Mixed flocks of feeding tits and Goldcrest. Possibility of Tree Sparrow and Brambling. Siskins and groups of Redpoll.

March–May Winter thrushes and mixed feeding flocks persist through March. Passage birds include Wheatear, Whinchat and prospect of Pied Flycatcher and Redstart. Cuckoo and early passage warblers by early April. Prospect of migrant Turtle Doves in May by which time Tree Pipit, and the common Sylvia and leaf warblers have arrived. Spotted Flycatchers by mid-May.

June–July Breeding residents and summer visitors, nest boxes in use for second broods of several species.

August–November Adult Cuckoos depart in August; third brood for some species in good summers. October passage not particularly marked. Winter thrushes return and gull numbers increase in November.

Lesser Spotted Woodpecker

BURNHAM BEECHES   Map 26/OS ref. SU 950 850

Habitat

As the name implies, this site is mainly Beech woodland, extending over an area exceeding 500 acres (200 ha) and represents 14 per cent of the county's wooded public area. The wood once stretched from Taplow to Burnham and as far as the Thames, and some of the Beech specimens are between 600 and 800 years old. There are many other species of tree on the site, some areas comprising open stands of mature Oak and Beech, with little secondary undergrowth, whilst others consist of younger Oaks interspersed with Birch and Holly. There are sizeable areas of scrub and bracken and also small conifer plantations. The site encompasses Burnham Common, with open grassland and heathland, together with numerous bushes and bramble. Rhododendron is fairly common, particularly in the north-western sector, where moss-covered mounds and a more prolific herbaceous layer exists. There are marked undulations throughout the woods which enhance the atmosphere.

This sub-boreal Grade 2 wood is managed by the Corporation of London who have, since 1879, provided several roads and pathways. Whilst many of the ancient trees are left untouched other than pruning for safety reasons, management policy for younger trees follows a felling programme of approximately 80-year cycles. There is evidence of the earlier pollarding of Beech for charcoal. There are two rather insignificant pools in the southern sector. White Helleborine and Birds Nest Orchid are just two of the woodland flowers that can be found. Grey Squirrel have colonised the woods for a long time and Fox can be seen around the periphery.

To the north of Burnham Beeches is the 400 acres (160 ha) Egypt Wood, different in habitat to the Beeches and in private ownership. Nonetheless it almost doubles the size of the woodland area and therefore has an important overall effect on birdlife. There are two public footpaths through this additional area, which is believed to have got its name from an early gypsy encampment. Alternate stands of Larch, Birch and evergreen specimens lend character to the scenery. As a result of being a much quieter area, Muntjac Deer can be seen regularly.

Access

Burnham Beeches is north of Slough and on the western side of the A355, which runs between junction 2 of the M40 and junction 6 of the M4. There are several points of entry from the A355 itself and also from Hawthorn Lane and Pumpkin Hill to the south, and Park Lane to the west. There is a small network of metalled roads through the wood, a number of them joining at Victory Cross near the centre, where the main car park and refreshment area is located. Subsidiary car parks and other pull-offs combine to accommodate up to 1,500 cars (an indication of how busy it can get at this popular site). Toilets have been provided at the southern end of Lord Mayor's Drive. Egypt Wood is not so well blessed for parking with one or two places near Abbey Park Farm or in Egypt Lane on the opposite side. The nearest mainline railway station is at Slough which is served from Paddington.

Species

It is often said that woodland in wintertime is less than inspiring for birdwatchers. Perhaps on a dull, wet and windy day there are more exciting places to visit but a clear frosty morning in January can portray a wood in all its avian glory almost as well as on a warm spring day. There may be fewer species but the resident birds, having less competition during winter, range further and are quite active. There is too, of course, the added advantage in deciduous woods that the absence of dense foliage at this time of year makes observation all the easier, and what better time is there to practise one's skill of identification by sound? The winter orchestra is somewhat less confusing but nonetheless challenging, as courting calls and territorial outbursts start early in the year.

Previous work has established that typical bird density in artificially planted conifer woods is 6 per hectare whilst mixed natural woodland can attract as many as 40. Parts of Burnham Beeches come well into the latter category, the mixed feeding flocks of tits and Goldcrests in winter giving way in summer to family groups of the same species but added to by Nuthatch fledglings clamouring noisily for morsels of food from their parents. Much quieter, but equally delightful to watch, are Spotted Flycatchers hunting in characteristic fashion for insects to feed their four or five young, a high pitched squeak being all that may be expected. Jackdaws, raucous and rowdy in their year's-end gatherings split up to raise young in the larger trees, often contesting potential sites with Mistle Thrush which have similar intentions. The striking colours of the male Bullfinch may prove difficult to find when the woods are in full foliage, and the same is certainly true of the Great and Lesser Spotted Woodpeckers, but in winter they are much more readily observed.

The scrub around Crabtree Heath, and the bushes on East Burnham Common are likely areas for Blackcap and a singing male can be quite captivating. However, as the Garden Warbler is far from rare in this vicinity, and has a song remarkably similar to the Blackcap, it is worth the time gaining a view of the songster to be absolutely sure. That other woodland specialist, the Wood Warbler, appears to prefer Oak and Birch woods elsewhere in the country but in the south of England is more often found in mixed deciduous woodlands like Burnham Beeches, particularly where there is little well-developed secondary undergrowth. Whilst a sighting of this leaf-warbler cannot be guaranteed, the upper canopy may well be worth careful examination in the more open sections.

As with any reasonably large expanse of trees, Burnham Beeches is a refuge for Woodpigeon, Collared Dove and also Stock Dove, and quite large numbers roost in the area. The size of the woods also makes it an ideal location for owls and whilst it is many years since the Long-eared species nested on this site, the more common Tawny Owl will certainly frequent this sort of woodland. When young are to be fed one is more likely to see them during daylight than at any other season, especially in Egypt Wood but ordinarily they are not diurnal and one will need to await the oncoming of dusk to catch a glimpse of this bird. From December however, the hoarse hooting of the male and the shrill 'kuvit' of the female can be heard as territorial battles are enacted. As the young stay with the parents for several weeks after fledging, late summer and autumn may be the best time to see these owls.

Beechwoods produce leaf-litter in prodigious quantities, anything up to 3.9 tons (4,000 kg) per hectare in a year, and this furnishes ground foraging birds with good feeding, particularly during the colder months when the leaves shelter insects and maintain soil warmth and moistness. Blackbird, Song Thrush and Robin can be heard searching noisily and occasionally Green Woodpecker, or Yaffingale as it is sometimes called, may also join in this feeding technique. Chaffinch flocks should be scrutinised for occasional Brambling. Meanwhile in the northern parts of Egypt Woods, flocks of 20 or so Redpolls will be moving amongst the Silver Birches. In early spring, the wood is filled with tapping sounds as woodpeckers search for food, Nuthatches hammer open small nuts, Great Tits tap inquisitively and, if one is lucky, a Willow Tit may be found excavating a nest hole, thereby providing one of the more distinct ways of discerning this species from neighbouring Marsh Tits.

Some 150 years ago, Honey Buzzards nested in these woods; those days are gone but the special atmosphere of woodland birdwatching is still readily available on this site in any season.

Calendar

Resident All three woodpeckers, Nuthatch, Treecreeper, Jays, Kestrel, Sparrowhawk, Tawny Owl, Goldcrest, Willow Tit.

December–February Siskin, Redpoll, winter thrushes, Starling flocks, small groups of Bullfinches, occasional Brambling, flocks of mixed tits, Pheasant, Grey Partridge, Woodcock.

March–May Turtle Dove, Garden Warbler, Chiffchaff, Blackcap, Whitethroat, Cuckoo, Spotted Flycatcher, possible Wood Warbler on passage.

June–July Quieter period with breeding in progress for numerous species. Raptors particularly busy.

August–November Passage migrants move through with departing warblers. Resident bird numbers greatly enhanced, large numbers of Starlings begin to gather.

CALDECOTTE LAKES   Map 27/OS ref. SP 893 355

Habitat

The lakes at Caldecotte have resulted from one of the many mineral extraction projects in the Milton Keynes area. Originally a single large lake, the recent construction of road H10 across the centre has transformed the site into two small ponds. Ironically this may improve the site as time goes on, by virtue of the extra length of bank fashioned by the causeway and the extensive planting programme undertaken along the new road. The reduced area of open water may also minimise bank erosion through wave action. On the whole, the site presents a rather bare appearance with little vegetation around either lake and much of the shore-line is fairly steeply banked or edged with large rocks. However, each pool contains islands with some vegetation suitable for breeding species. The western edges resemble sloping grassed parkland where the River Ouzel has been diverted through a new channel, whereas the eastern extremity is essentially farmland with some mature hedges and trees. There is ample opportunity to create marginal reedbeds, nesting rafts and improved wader scrapes. Nonetheless the site already has an excellent record for bird species as we shall see.

Access

Caldecotte is located in the semi-rural aspect of south-east Milton Keynes and the lake occupies the area in-between the A5 trunk road and Brickhill Street (V10). The nearest main road junction is number 14 of the M1, 3 miles (4.8 km) to the north, bridged by the A5130 and A421 from that junction. The nearest railway station is at Brickhill, 0.25 miles (400 m) to the south. No formal access has been arranged, but limited parking is available in Walton Road and a footpath extends from this road to the eastern edge of the southern lake. The northern lake can be approached, again from Walton Road. Both lakes can be viewed from the new road which passes between the two waters. One of the best wader sections is the eastern bay of the south pool and this is best approached from behind the small line of bushes there to avoid early dispersal of one's quarry.

Species

Not possessing major breeding facilities, Caldecotte is probably more renowned for its winter and passage visitors. Numbers of ever-present Dabchicks build-up to around 20 by late autumn whilst their equally attractive relative, the Great Crested Grebe, may be twice as numerous for a while. As numbers of Redwing and Fieldfare increase in late October, eventually to reach treble figures, Greenshanks show up and both Green and Common Sandpipers can be expected. As the last Whinchats and Wheatears pass through, enormous numbers of gulls adopt the lake as a roost with several thousand Black-headed and a few Lesser Black-backed gulls dominating the evening scene. On the other hand, in line with other pools in the area, Common Gulls tend not to live up to their name. Ruff and Dunlin will be noted on passage and reasonable numbers of Snipe occur. Meadow Pipits will be found in double figures and groups of 50 or so Goldfinch chatter along the hedgerows. Tree Sparrows, one bird that does breed on the site, also flock together at this time of year. Waterfowl have also adopted these lakes as winter quarters and gregarious species such as Pochard, Wigeon, Tufted Duck and Shoveler amass, occasionally moving from one pool to another. The 'Milton' Greylags do not yet give Caldecotte a fair proportion of their attention, but this is made up for by 200 or 300 Canada Geese favouring this location from time to time.

This, then, is a fairly common scene for such a site. However it is the less common species which are putting in appearances, more frequently in recent years, that add spice to Caldecotte's erstwhile drabness. During the autumn passage, Black-necked Grebe has been seen, sometimes loitering for several days and, on at least one occasion, shared the site with a Slavonian Grebe, permitting rare opportunities for comparing these rather similar birds. Remnants of breeding plumage will of course make this easier than later in the year. Common Scoters and Scaup pass through whereas Ruddy Duck are beginning to be seen in most months. An even greater prize has been Black-throated Diver, a surprisingly confiding bird when it turns up on inland waters outside of the breeding season. Numbers of Goosander can be quite high as winter progresses, but Red-breasted Mergansers are recorded fairly often so it is worth checking all 'redheads' carefully for neck markings. If in doubt, one can only hope a male turns up to ease the task. Waders also make their mark here. Golden Plover is a possibility and Knot has been noted. Most of the usual terns can be expected up to October and the Little Gull, with its somewhat tern-like flight, has appeared. In addition, Iceland Gull and Pomarine Skua have been recorded. Whilst many of these more scarce species will only be paying quick visits, Short-eared Owls seem to have taken quite a shine to Caldecotte with one or two likely to be seen throughout the winter months, more usually at dusk, 'loping' moth-like on long wings over the open grassed area to the west of the lakes or the farmland sector. That other diurnal specialist, the Little Owl, can also be quite noticeable throughout the same period, again in the region of the farm.

The spring passage is equally interesting with March likely to see early movements of Greenshank and Green Sandpiper whilst Common, Black and Arctic Terns will be seen in April. Whimbrel and both of the godwits are possibilities and, with Curlew breeding in the vicinity, there is always the chance of seeing one or more on occasions. Wheatears are another irregular visitor. Look for them on the open scrub area east of the southern pool or on the grassy banks on the opposite side (although the length of this grass will gradually deter them from this particular locale). The early warblers coming back may well cross with the late Bramblings and winter thrushes on their way out. Quite large numbers of Redwing might accumulate in the Oak trees along Walton Road murmuring to each other Starling-fashion in pre-migration conference. All three common wagtails will be found and White Wagtails, possibly more common in this country than reports suggest, have also been spotted. The rocky banks are a difficult terrain to scan over, but worth the effort for the chance of picking out Dunlin or Turnstone which can be seen up until mid-May. At the present time, the site may be to some extent under-watched. With the avian Mecca of Willen so adjacent it seems unlikely that at least some of the rarer birds so often reported there do not utilise Caldecotte on some occasions. Clearly the site has tremendous potential and, if left undisturbed to mature, or better still aided by active management for birds, would become an excellent location.

Calendar

Resident Great Crested and Little Grebe, Canada Goose, Mallard, Tufted Duck, Sparrowhawk, Kestrel, Grey Partridge (occasional Red-legged), Pheasant, Moorhen, Coot, Snipe, Black-headed Gull, Stock Dove, Collared Dove, Little Owl, Kingfisher, all three woodpeckers occur, Grey and Pied Wagtail, Greenfinch, Goldfinch, occasional Redpoll, Reed Bunting in small numbers, Yellowhammers.

December–February Chance of rarer grebes, occasional Cormorant, visits from local Greylag flocks, Gadwall and occasional Pintail. Numerous Wigeon, Pochard and Tufted Ducks, but only small numbers of Teal. Goldeneye, occasional Common Scoter, all three sawbills are likely, and prospect of Ruddy Duck. Some of the winter waders, e.g. Golden Plover. Short-eared Owl, groups of Meadow Pipits, winter thrushes, over-wintering Chiffchaff. Good numbers of Goldfinch and Siskin (sometimes mixed), occasional Brambling. Spectacular gull roosts. Look out for occasional rarities amongst them.

March–May Size of winter duck rafts reduce, winter thrushes flock before departure, sawbills passing through from more southerly waters, passage waders such as Whimbrel, Black-tailed Godwit, Ruff, Curlew, Greenshank, Green and Common Sandpiper (particularly on rocky parts of shore-line). Little Gull, Black, Common and Arctic Terns, hirundines (though not especially numerous), Yellow Wagtails, Whitethroat, Chiffchaff and other warblers passing through in April (not many stay). Chance of Hobby.

June–July A fairly quiet period. Occasional Cuckoo. Common waterfowl breeding, along with Tree Sparrow. Occasional Corn Bunting. Prospect of Hobby. Lapwing and Redshank on exposed mud-banks. Few first-summer Black-headed Gulls wheel around. Occasional non-breeding Common Terns.

August–November Start of reverse migration. Possible Whinchat. Redpolls and Goldfinches form into flocks. Gull numbers increase dramatically.

CALVERT JUBILEE Map 28/OS ref. SP 683 250

Habitat

Calvert Jubilee is a nature reserve of some 95 acres (38 ha) managed by BBONT on a 14-year lease from the London Brick Company by whom it was previously used as a clay pit. The resulting lake is some 50 acres (20 ha) in area and, being very deep at the centre, acts as a refuge for numerous species of waterfowl. The northern area of the reserve was used as a municipal refuse dump (and still is by some unthinking members of the public) but is now covered with fine-grained clay. This soil supports relatively little plant life but specialist grasses and mosses are present and some Bee and Common Spotted Orchid thrive along with Cowslips. There are extensive patches of dense and thorny scrub making ideal nesting and roosting sites. Many of these bushes can be looked down upon from the raised embankment formed by a disused railway line in the north-east. There is a narrow strip of land around the remainder of the lake with further scrub, areas of open tall grass favoured by Green Woodpeckers, and a row of substantial trees to the south.

Rabbits are the most obvious of the resident mammals although Weasels can be found in the Hawthorn surrounds. Foxes are common and will bask in the open if not disturbed. Normally however the chief indication of their presence is the rancid smell of their scent trails. A few nest boxes, including a Kestrel box, have been erected. The adjacent Grebe Lake is used solely for sailing and waterfowl seem to realise this as it seldom has any birds on it whatsoever. The tranquillity of the site can be regularly interrupted by low-flying jet fighters on their way to the nearby airbase at Upper Heyford.

Access

The Calvert Jubilee Nature Reserve is situated 1.5 miles (2 km) north of Edgcott along the road to Gawcott. The nearest main road is the A41(T) between Aylesbury and Bicester, to the south. There are no public transport facilities. A small car park for three vehicles is at the main entrance to the west, opposite Grebe Lake. The site has a single hide, well positioned and with good facilities for the disabled.

A peripheral footpath exists although this involves 'clambering' a fairly steep bank by the old railway bridge, and removing a lift-off fence on the bank opposite the hide to facilitate a full circumnavigation. However, the lack of cover to the east and south of the lake causes great disturbance to the waterfowl if walked and it is preferable to explore only the thicket area in the north and utilise the hide for lake viewing. There is no hide on the eastern bank but, if one is caught in a shower, the old bridge affords shelter, provided one prepares for the surprise of the clattering of departing Stock Doves which use the structure as a roost and for nesting.

The site should not be confused with the much smaller Jubilee Lake 0.6 miles (1 km) further to the north.

Species

'The Jubilee' is most noted for its waterfowl and, whilst it may be that it hardly revels in records of rarities, it is an excellent site to study the more common species. The winter scene is primarily of rafts of Coot and Pochard, occasionally several hundred of both species, the Pochard spending most of the daylight hours loafing in the sheltered southern bay. Wigeon in some numbers arrive a little later and usually depart a little earlier than the Pochard, but will be more active for the birdwatcher whilst they are present. Goldeneye, more often females or juveniles than males, can be seen in one's or two's and the same applies to Goosanders, but these two specialist diving ducks often only stay for a day or so (possible scarcity of food being a deterrent). Tufted Ducks also populate the lake at this time and a couple of pairs usually stay on into the summer and attempt to breed. Great Crested Grebes are numerous, the late local breeding of a few pairs, together with wandering migrants resulting in a wide range of plumages in the groups of this most streamlined of diving birds.

By late March most of these birds have forsaken the Jubilee and the prospect of seeing Slavonian or Black-necked Grebe on their fleeting visits will have passed for another season. However it is at this time that one will be most likely to see Garganey on their passage route and also Water Rail. Water Rail may in fact be a resident species, but, once the vegetation has fully restored itself to summer lushness, the chances of seeing this elusive bird becomes more remote. The most promising spot to scrutinise is the overhanging vegetation on the bank opposite the hide to the right of several old tree stumps sticking out of the water. The birds' movements are slow and determined and several seconds observation at each point, working slowly along the water-line, is the only way to guarantee success, but such patience will be well rewarded if that slender bright red bill can be seen contrasting with a wary slate grey head and neck. Ironically, they are more difficult to see in this locality if the sun is shining directly on the bank opposite.

By April, flocks of Meadow Pipits and Pied Wagtails will be paying short-stay visits on the open ground in the north and the last of the winter thrushes will have left the Hawthorn bushes which are soon colonised by Bullfinch, Goldfinch, Linnets and Whitethroats. The open grass areas are favoured by local Green Woodpeckers, and occasionally Skylarks, whilst Pheasants breed in the denser undergrowth at the base of the Hawthorn thicket, though with doubtful success given the proximity of the resident Fox. Another passage visitor, usually in early May, is the Black Tern which can be seen swooping low over the water for insects, rather than diving for fish.

Although the terrain is not ideal, leaf warblers such as Willow and Chiffchaff can be found on the reserve but the almost total absence of reeds at present (the establishment of a bed is planned) eliminates much likelihood of encountering any of the reed warbler family. However, the site is beginning to be suitable for Cetti's Warbler and it may only be a question of time before one can expect regular sightings here. First recorded in the county 20 years ago, it has long since been removed from the British list of rare birds as it is more regularly seen nowadays. Its piercing 'too-ee' call is unmistakable but if only seen it might be easily taken for a Nightingale, a bird which can be seen in this locale, usually in the north-west corner. Not all the breeding activity is restricted to the scrub area by any means. At the waterside, Little Grebe, Coot, Mallard and Great Crested Grebe will be raising young. Nesting rafts were provided by the London Brick Company at one stage and may

Whitethroat

be replaced again later to encourage other species to promulgate their numbers. It is not certain whether the Kingfishers, which are seen regularly over the lake, actually breed in the banks here or merely use the pool for catching prey whilst nesting in the streams nearby, which are fed by the Padbury Brook.

As autumn advances, waterfowl numbers gradually increase, initially by flocks of wandering male and non-breeding Canada Geese, spurned by the females busy with their successful broods elsewhere in the county; and subsequently by migrant Teal and the previously-mentioned over-wintering ducks. The last of the warblers desert the scrub area and southward-moving martins and Swallows swoop over the water building up reserves. The relatively high position of the hide affords an excellent opportunity to examine the Swallows, hopefully for evidence of a Red-rumped species amongst the flock and for practising the discernment of House Martin from Sand Martin. The small secondary pools should be checked for passing Snipe and other waders, although a cautious approach is essential to avoid unintended dispersal from this secluded spot. By November the Hawthorn hedges and other berry-bearing bushes attract large numbers of Redwing and small groups of Mistle Thrushes. The tall poplars host large roosts of Woodpigeon and a few Jackdaws. But it is in the depths of the winter months that Calvert Jubilee becomes most heavily populated for, at that time, in addition to the substantial numbers of over-wintering waterfowl, enormous flocks of gulls use the lake as a nighttime roost. Just before dark, hundreds of Black-headed, Common and Herring Gull rain in against the backcloth of the white steamy smoke belching into a cold blackening sky from the brickwork's many chimneys. Small numbers of Greater and Lesser Black-backed Gulls are also present.

For this spectacle alone, the site is probably best visited from December to February, but if variety is of greater interest, the period April to June might be preferable. The refuge is a quiet place, it often being possible to spend many a pleasant hour with the whole site to oneself. Provided the readers of this book do not flock there all at the same time, it may stay that way.

Calendar

Resident Great Crested and Little Grebes, Grey Heron, Canada Goose, Mallard, Tufted Duck, Kestrel, Water Rail, Moorhen, Coot, Stock Dove,

Tawny Owl, Kingfisher, Green Woodpecker, Pied Wagtail, Dunnock, Willow Tit, Reed Bunting, Bullfinch.

December–February Possible rare grebes, Gadwall, Wigeon, Teal, Shoveler, Pochard, occasional Scaup, Goldeneye and Goosander in small numbers, Black-headed, Common and Herring Gulls all in large numbers, some Greater and Lesser Black-backed gulls, Meadow Pipit, Redwing, Fieldfare, groups of Yellowhammer.

March–May Gull numbers dwindle whilst those of winter ducks fluctuate with passage flocks, possibility of several Garganey passing through. Chiffchaff, Willow Warbler and Blackcap usually well established by mid-April, followed by Whitethroat and Nightingale by the end of the month. Cuckoo, Turtle Dove and passage terns by early May, together with hirundines. Kestrel breeding.

June–July Main breeding period, chiefly for passerine species, chance of Hobby pursuing hirundines. Occasional non-breeding Common Tern over the water.

August–November Adult warblers depart late-August to early-September, leaving juveniles for a while longer, occasional passage terns before winter thrushes arrive. Waterfowl return from mid-November.

CHURCH WOOD   Map 29/OS ref. SU 972 872

Habitat

Church Wood is a deciduous woodland of some 34 acres (13 ha) consisting of mature Oak and Beech with Ash, Alder, Birch and Hazel interspersed widely over the area. In fact no species of tree is particularly dominant and there are also conifer stands and a small group of impressive Wellingtonias. It is the only RSPB reserve in the county and local members' groups carry out coppicing and clearing on a voluntary basis to encourage improved secondary growth. The more open areas are covered in a variety of grasses and bracken, encouraged by a number of streams which flow down the gently sloping ground on which the wood resides. Generally, the woodland is more dense in the northern sector than elsewhere and there are numerous bramble patches.

Botanically, some 200 species of plant have been identified and certain of these attract numerous butterflies in summer, including Purple Hairstreak, White Admiral and Common Blue. Foxes make regular use of the wood and Muntjac Deer can still be seen regularly in the early morning. A substantial nest box scheme is operated, including owl boxes. The site is surrounded by pastureland and small meadows and the tree line of the edge of the wood forms a sanctuary for birds of the fields between bouts of feeding. The private woodland which abuts Church Wood to the east approximately doubles the overall size of the tree-scape.

Access

Church Wood lies between the small village of Hedgerley and the more dominating Gerrards Cross, protection from encroachment of the latter area afforded by the M40 motorway nearby. Other than by means of a lengthy walk the woods can only really be reached by car. The nearest main road routes would include junction 2 of the M40, from which the first road on the left along the southerly A355 reaches the village at the second turning on the right. Alternatively, the B416 from Gerrards Cross to Stoke Poges can be used to approach Hedgerley from the south via other local roads. On arrival, parking is a problem. There may be space for one or two vehicles along the lane leading to the wood but cars left beyond the white-topped post on the left will incur the wrath of the local landowner wishing to gain access to his fields. Limited parking is possible at one or two places in the village. The main entrance is along the lane south of the church but there is also a stile along the bridleway to the north of the church. A good footpath scheme has been provided in the wood with coloured marker posts to assist visitors new to the reserve. The paths essentially follow the perimeter but there are tracks through the centre of the site.

Species

This compact woodland attracts a surprising variety of birds and can be a delightful place to visit at any time of the year. In winter time, with the trees bare and undergrowth less dense, a slow stroll will be rewarded by close views of all the common tits, including Marsh Tits, as they feed

119

with Goldcrests and Treecreepers, especially along Leafy Trail and Endless Walk. The dried off bracken in this area is also where one might be lucky enough to see Woodcock. Although this bird is most active at dawn or dusk, it will roam unobtrusively amongst the undergrowth during the daytime if there is no obvious disturbance. Furthermore, this southern sector, being adjacent to farmland, is favoured by both Tawny and Little Owl, the former more usually heard than seen during the day whilst the latter may well be spotted bounding along the tree-line.

One can anticipate seeing all three species of woodpecker and Stock Dove might readily be dismissed as Woodpigeon if not checked carefully. The middle of the wood often attracts parties of Redpoll, joined by a few Siskin, feeding fervently on the Silver Birch seeds. Usually seen only in silhouette, it is worth trying to position oneself in such a way that an evergreen tree or large bole is immediately behind the feeding group, so as to appreciate the delicate markings of the Redpoll and the varying degrees of pink on the chests of the males. Occasionally, after an extensive bout of feeding, the mixed flock will descend to the ground to forage in the leaf-litter for fallen seeds, often attracting tits to the feast. Towards the end of February, Nuthatches become more vociferous and other resident species, including Tree Sparrow, become territorial.

Early spring brings about enhanced numbers of species as passage and summer resident warblers arrive and the more open areas resound with the songs of Blackcap, Chiffchaff and Willow Warbler. A little later they are joined by Spotted Flycatchers and Turtle Doves, the latter often seen sharing the power line perch with a Kestrel, totally unconcerned. This circumstance is far less likely to obtain however when the local Sparrowhawk puts in an appearance.

By summertime many of these species, together with Garden Warblers, are quietly breeding and during this time the more open feeding areas such as Endless Walk and the open ride beneath the pylon route may be the most productive birdwatching location. As autumn

Sparrowhawk

approaches, the enlarged population prefers the protection afforded by the denser foliage around Brock's Trail for the main feeding forays, as many of them build up fat reserves for their imminent migration, shortly leaving the expiring vegetation to the resident birds. This exclusive ownership lasts just a few weeks before over-wintering finches return to complete the cycle.

This small area thus provides an ideal opportunity to monitor the seasonality of birdlife in mixed woodland, and whilst a dawn visit during the main build-up to the visitors' breeding period can be exhilarating, the chorus of the resident population can be nonetheless rewarding at sun-up in early April.

Calendar

Resident Woodcock, Sparrowhawk, Marsh Tit, Willow Tit, Tree Sparrow, Nuthatch, Treecreeper, Stock Dove, Tawny Owl, Green Woodpecker, Great and Lesser Spotted Woodpecker, Bullfinch.

December–February Redpoll, Siskin, other mixed finches and also mixed feeding parties of tits, Goldcrests and Treecreepers. Roosting Jackdaws and Woodpigeon.

March–May Willow Warbler, Chiffchaff, Blackcap, Garden Warbler. Worth looking for Firecrest on passage.

June–July Turtle Dove. Spotted Flycatcher, Swallows over adjacent pastures. Many passerine species breeding. (Please overcome the temptation to look in the nest boxes which have been mounted at unusually low levels.)

August–November Passage birds, finch flocks including Redpoll and Siskin. Tawny Owl more active.

FOXCOTE & HYDELANE WATERS

Map 30/OS ref. SP 720 355

Habitat

Foxcote Reservoir was formed by the Anglian Water Authority in the 1950s by flooding a 60 acre (24 ha) field. In 1963 BBONT made an arrangement with the Authority, and this was formalised in 1971 by the granting of a 21-year licence. The reserve, now a SSSI, comprises the lake itself and a narrow strip of grazing land around the periphery, partly planted with Willow and Alder. Some bankside has been fenced off to encourage waterside vegetation as a means of establishing breeding areas which were originally few and far between on the site. To the north of the pool is a small deciduous wood in private ownership and the tree-line abuts the water's edge. At times of low water a certain amount of exposed mud can attract waders. Floating islands have been provided on occasions to act as a sanctuary in an otherwise somewhat exposed area, subjected to fishing at certain times of year, during which many of the wildfowl vacate the location for one of the other waters in the vicinity. The surrounding area is generally arable in nature.

Hydelane Lake is a little smaller than Foxcote Reservoir but is more interestingly shaped with many bays and inlets and quite mature vegetation. A small area of woodland lends variety to the species likely to be seen. Anglers use the water regularly and there are fewer fishing restrictions than on the reservoir. An inflatable breakwater has been installed at the western end to prevent erosion in rough weather. To the south of this water is a BBONT reserve which encompasses the narrow strip of land between the public footpath and the lake. This was once part of the Buckingham Canal and was obtained by the Naturalists' Trust in 1972 to protect aquatic fauna in the remnant pools of the canal. It is bounded by ancient hedgerows and mature willows.

Access

Foxcote Reservoir lies 1 mile (1.6 km) north of the A422 Buckingham to Old Stratford road on the lane between Maids Moreton and Leckhampstead. Direct access to the refuge is restricted by permits, issued by BBONT, which allow the use of the hide to the south of the site. However, most of the water can be seen from the roadway just east of the dam and the whole lake can be viewed from the public footpath to Foxcote Wood which traverses the eastern bank at some 164 yds (150 m) distance. As a result of this distance a telescope will prove useful. Due to sun reflections, morning or early afternoon are the best times to view. Nominated parking spaces are not available but there are one or two places where one might leave vehicles in the lane.

Hydelane Lake is south of the A422 and some of the water can be seen from this road. There is a car park at the southern-most tip of the lake which is approached via a rough track from the main road. The entrance will be found on the left and the gate should be kept closed at all times. There is a public footpath which follows the southern bank, passing through the BBONT reserve, and this is accessed from the car park at a gate just beyond the Anglian Water Authority pumping station.

Species

Due to the relative lack of cover, few species breed at Foxcote and for much of the summertime the lake is owned by Coots, Mallards and Mute Swans, with Sand Martins buzzing around their heads. What surrounding vegetation there is attracts Reed Buntings and Goldfinches and the hedges along the track to the hide provide nesting sites for Garden Warblers and Chaffinches. It is in winter that Foxcote gains prominence with large numbers of waterfowl, peaking in January. Several hundred Mallard at this time would ordinarily make Gadwall-spotting a challenge but for some reason the Gadwall is one species rarely found at this location and so one has the choice of not bothering to check or to scan in detail in the hope of being one of the lucky ones to record it here. Wigeon are also difficult to predict because, although numbers remain fairly consistent at most of the surrounding waters, at Foxcote they fluctuate wildly, sometimes up to 150, sometimes none. Pochard on the other hand are plentiful in most of the winter months as are the more numerous Tufted Duck. A few Shoveler are usually present and Goldeneye call in occasionally. One species that seems to prefer Foxcote to adjacent lakes is the Goosander with up to 30 present as the spring passage nears. Strangely, the neighbouring lake at Hydelane rarely receives this sawbill but will host greater numbers of Canada Geese and Great Crested Grebe. This latter body of water is also quite a regular venue at which small numbers of both Bewick's and Whooper Swans spend the winter, allowing an ideal opportunity to practise separating these two magnificent creatures. Little Grebes reside at Hydelane but it's back to Foxcote for anyone hoping for a glimpse of rarer Black-necked or Red-necked Grebes.

The spring passage coincides with reducing gull roosts but the limited areas suitable for waders, other than the sloping wall along the south bank of Foxcote, may mean that seabird movements are the more obvious aspects of migration. On the other hand Common Sandpipers have learned to use the fishermen's dug-out steps at Hydelane and one or two of them will occasionally be put up, whereupon they may well alight on the inflatable bund, bobbing in typical fashion. The same perch is also popular with Common Terns, one or two pairs of which usually stay on at each of the two lakes. Keep a look out for other passage terns and possible Shelduck. Pied, Grey and occasional Yellow Wagtails prefer Foxcote, again using the sloping wall near the road.

Of the resident species of Hydelane, the Kingfisher is one of the more precocious and can be seen on branches overhanging the water at almost any point. A number of Reed Buntings favour the barbed wire fence around the anglers' car park from which the males issue their territorial song. The bushes here, too, often have a Corn Bunting or two singing from the upper branches. As summer advances, the small BBONT reserve along the old canal walk comes into its best, gloriously wild throughout its length beneath a canopy of Hawthorn and willows. Here, Blackcap, Willow Warblers and Garden Warblers can be found, but previous records of Bittern are unlikely to be repeated. Water Rail on the other hand find the dense reedbed most acceptable. (If a walk along this old canal is intended in high summer it is advisable to wear long trousers as the undergrowth, including nettles and thistles, often engulfs the footpaths.) At the eastern end of this footpath is a new footbridge across the canal and this leads into a small lake-side Poplar wood favoured by Great Spotted Woodpeckers and Treecreepers. The pool at this end is one of the nesting sites for the several pairs of Great Crested Grebe which breed at Hydelane.

Another species which breeds around the periphery of the lake is Sedge Warbler but by September it is the birds of the water that take over once again. Scaup can be found on Foxcote at this time and it is worth scanning the reservoir's edge for Greenshank. One should not get too excited though at seeing a couple of Snow Geese here as they are more than likely to be a well-known pair of escapees. At Hydelane it will be November before waterfowl numbers start to build up again and by December groups of Golden Plover can be seen in the meadows south of the old Canal, sometimes towered over by two or three Herons. In recent years, greater numbers of skuas have been recorded at inland waters, either because more are making such sorties or simply that more birdwatchers are recognising them and, more importantly, reporting them to their club or county recorder. Whilst it is not asserted that Foxcote and Hydelane have any particular magnetism for such species, indeed they may both be a little on the small size, it will always be worth looking again at 'immature gulls', especially if one of them is seen pursuing other gulls in piratical fashion, or causing general disturbance. A bird that is more likely to have this effect though is the resident Sparrowhawk.

In summary, whilst access might to some extent be limited, neither water should be overlooked by birdwatchers who find themselves in the locality, especially between October and May.

Calendar

Resident Great Crested and Little Grebe, Heron, Mute Swan, Canada Geese, Mallard, Sparrowhawk, Grey Partridge, Water Rail, Moorhen and Coot, Little Owl, Green and Great Spotted Woodpecker, Pied and Grey Wagtails, Dunnock, Treecreeper, Yellowhammer, Reed and Corn Buntings.

December–February Prospect of Red and Black-necked Grebe at Foxcote. Cormorant, large flocks of Canada Geese. Look for occasional Greylag or Barnacle Goose. Shelduck, Wigeon, Teal and Pochard, with some Shoveler and occasional Pintail or Gadwall. Many Tufted Duck and sometimes hundreds of Mallard on Foxcote. Goldeneye and Ruddy Duck on infrequent visits but Goosanders plentiful. Good numbers of mixed gulls (mainly Black-headed, Common and Herring). Golden Plover, Lapwing, Meadow Pipit.

March–May Gull roosts persist, even more Goosanders may be seen, up to end of March. Dunlin, Greenshank and Common Sandpiper on passage. Swallow and House Martin early April, Swifts a little later. Sedge and Garden Warblers arrive, after Willow Warblers and Blackcap.

June–July Some breeding, mainly Great Crested and Little Grebe, Coot, Moorhen, Kingfisher, Sedge Warbler and Reed Bunting. Small numbers of Common Tern and Common Sandpiper in the area. Some potential wader movement.

August–November Hirundine numbers increase, often after Swifts have already left. Gulls become more prominent and early winter duck arrivals commence. A few winter thrushes might be found.

GRANGELANDS &
PULPIT HILL   Map 31/OS ref. SP 827 049

Habitat

Occupying part of the Chiltern ridge, this 50 acre (20 ha) site comprises ancient chalk downland and Beech woodland. The National Trust wooded area, known as Pulpit Hill, is 800 ft (248 m) high and, in addition to Beech, many White-beams are present, representing the natural succession to the Rose, Hawthorn and Elder scrub evident on the slopes of Grangelands below. Unfortunately, these slopes had to be ploughed during the Second World War and are only slowly restoring themselves to their previous status. Juniper is another feature of the area, which was created a SSSI in 1972. The surrounding grassland is being encouraged by scrub control and a wide range of plants and butterflies can be found. The wood itself is not particularly dense and includes small areas of coniferous trees. A new plantation is being established to the north-west.

Part of the associated area was once a rifle range which has been left gradually to emulate Grangelands, both of these areas being reserved for BBONT members. The wood however has full public access. To the north of the site lies the well-known Box-wood belonging to the Chequers Estate, much of which is also a BBONT reserve.

Access

The Pulpit Hill car park is approximately 0.6 miles (1 km) to the east of the A4010 Princes Risborough to Aylesbury road, along the lane from Askett to Great Missenden. The car park accommodates only some 12 to 15 vehicles. There are several footpaths and tracks through both the woodland and downland sectors, some of these meeting the Ridgeway footpath to the north.

Species

The birds of Grangelands and Pulpit Hill are perhaps typical of those encountered on the grassy slopes and wooded peaks of the Chiltern escarpment. A winter's visit will reveal most activity on the woodland edge and the areas of scrub. Mistle Thrushes will ferry between the open feeding areas and the protection of the tree-line, often accompanied by small numbers of Fieldfare and Redwing. Fair numbers of Chaffinch, with occasional Bramblings among them, may be found on the wider pathways and parties of Yellowhammers will be working the Hawthorn bushes on the slopes. Green Woodpeckers will be seen foraging on the grassy banks before 'yaffling' their way back to the wood and Kestrels can be expected hovering over any of the downland areas. The conifer compartments, particularly the one at the base of the hill, will host flocks of Siskin and Redpolls, especially where Silver Birch is present and the Goldcrests amongst the mixed feeding flocks in the main woodland should be examined carefully as there is always the prospect of a Firecrest or two paying a visit from neighbouring, and more traditional sites.

Where the site abuts farmland to the west, numerous Meadow Pipits will be seen and the same area may produce Stonechat at this time of year. Mixed corvids on these fields can accumulate in quite dramatic numbers and the Rooks in particular may be seen collecting acorns from caches prepared when food was more plentiful. On the periphery of Pulpit Wood, Marsh Tits can be found busily removing tufts from teasels and taking them to a nearby branch for a vigorous attack upon them to extract edible elements. Within the wood itself Long-tailed and Coal Tits stick together in protective groups in their search for a meagre meal, ever watchful for the resident Tawny Owls who are quite garrulous at this time of year.

The advent of spring brings the annual movement of migratory birds and, as with any reasonably high point, the possibility of a variety of passage birds stopping off briefly. Any 'Blackbird' seen at this point in time should be checked to ensure it is not a Ring Ouzel, easily recognised when face-on by its white crescent-shaped bib, but more difficult to discern from other angles of observation. Of the larger birds moving around at this time of year, the Short-eared Owl may occur for the fortunate observer, hunting over the chalkland slopes briefly, whilst occasional glimpses skyward could well be rewarded by the sight of a Buzzard passing overhead. The first sounds of summer birds are, as may be expected, generated by the Chiffchaff, one or two of which may well have over-wintered in the general area, and by late March the Yellowhammers are singing about their 'little bit of bread and no cheese' accompanied occasionally by Corn Buntings issuing their territorial jangling. A little later, Common Whitethroats will be seen (or more probably heard) and it will be difficult to determine passage birds from those intent on staying. The Lesser Whitethroat is a less regular visitor as is the case with the Tree Pipit, but Blackcap and Willow Warblers abound in the scattered bushes of Grangelands and those of the Ridgeway Path at the top of the slope. As the general movement of birds becomes less frantic, the late arrivals such as Spotted Flycatcher and, occasionally Turtle Doves, settle down for their summer residence. Cuckoos, which will have arrived up to a month earlier will be quite active looking for the nests of unsuspecting Dunnocks, particularly to the north of the site from which, at one or two vantage points, impressive views of the lowland Vale of Aylesbury can be seen stretching away into the distance. Sparrowhawks on the other hand may be seen at any point on the site either soaring high above Grangelands or charging through the wood itself.

The early summer flora of Grangelands can be quite a spectacle and a pleasant time can be had sitting on the top of the slope looking at birds from above against a backdrop of yellow Cowslips and Primroses. Equally colourful are the Bullfinches which breed on the site although once again, at the height of summer with the foliage most dense, it will be the somewhat mournful single note call that will betray its presence. In the woodland, Nuthatch, Treecreeper and Great Spotted Woodpecker breed, but the Pheasants which roam the forest floor sifting through tree-litter are probably disturbed too often to make breeding attempts worthwhile. The same disturbance probably deters Woodcock from using the site particularly often but the area of bracken-filled and less dense woodland to the north is the most likely place to see them, at the appropriate time of day of course. The ubiquitous Blue and Great Tits colonise open and enclosed areas alike whereas Goldfinch and Linnet are likely only to be found on the slopes of Grangelands. The Swifts and hirundines over these slopes may well attract a Hobby to the area. Whilst not likely to be a regular visitor, sightings of this sickle-winged raptor have increased in the region in recent years.

Before winter visitors rejoin the resident species there is a brief period during which the crop of juveniles that have survived thus far swell the numbers of birds noticeably. Tawny Owls become a little more prominent, often active during the day and adult passerines which have struggled through the breeding spell can forget marauding Jays, Magpies and squirrels for another season. This part of the year challenges springtime for being the best time to visit Grangelands and Pulpit Hill. A dull, wet winter's day should be avoided but a crisp, sunny morning during a cold snap can provide a good start to the day for a birdwatcher on his way to Weston Turville or Tring reservoirs.

Calendar

Resident Kestrel, Sparrowhawk, Pheasant, possibility of Woodcock. Stock Doves, Collared Dove, Tawny Owl, Green and Great Spotted Woodpeckers, with visits from roaming Lesser Spotted species. Skylark, occasional Pied Wagtail, common corvids, Goldcrests, infrequent Stonechat, the six common tits, Nuthatch and Treecreeper. Possibility of Hawfinch, Goldfinch, Linnet, Redpoll, Reed Bunting, and Yellowhammer.

December–February Large flocks of Woodpigeon, Meadow Pipits more evident and other birds of the field in greater numbers. Redwing and Fieldfare, Siskin and additional Redpolls.

March–May Occasional Buzzard. Cuckoo, Swift, passage Tree Pipit. Sand Martin and Swallow, occasional Yellow Wagtail, Garden Warbler and Blackcap following Willow Warbler and Chiffchaff. Whitethroat regular, Lesser Whitethroat less so. Chance of passage Wood Warbler. Wheatear may make short visits to Grangelands whilst moving through, and always a chance of Whinchat in the vicinity of the Ridgeway, where Corn Bunting may also become more evident.

June–July Spotted Flycatchers well ensconsed. Likelihood of Turtle Dove, though not guaranteed. Reasonable chance of Hobby, especially in the evening as the season advances when insects give way to hirundines as the staple diet.

August–November Warblers gradually disappear, though one or two Chiffchaff may stay over. Any Cuckoo sighted likely to be juvenile, parents long since departed.

HOMEFIELD WOOD   Map 32/OS ref. SU 815 866

Habitat

Homefield Wood nestles amongst Buckinghamshire's southern-most undulations of the Chiltern Hills in arable surroundings at a point where this chalkland ridge stoops rapidly down into the Thames Valley. The wood is part of the Chiltern Forest and consists of 250 acres (100 ha) of mixed Forestry Commission woodland. It is a fairly 'young' wood with the majority of trees less than 50 years old. At first glance the wood appears essentially coniferous and indeed many of the stands are well blessed with a wide range of primitive evergreens including Scots Pine and Douglas Fir, together with Corsican Pine, European and Japanese Larch. The scene is enhanced by small numbers of Noble Fir, Western Hemlock and Lawson Cypress. However, almost one third of the total area is covered with broadleaved species, primarily Beech, but also Silver Birch and a few Oak. This is not immediately apparent due to the imaginative way the species are mixed in the various stands. Holywick Wood is perhaps the least dense of the three main sectors, whilst Heath Wood rises to 390 ft (120 m) and is the highest sector.

A small area of chalkland meadow of botanical interest to the east of the site is managed by BBONT. Butterflies abound in summer, including such species as Marbled White, Dark Green Fritillary and White Admiral. From the point of view of birds, it is perhaps best visited in spring and summer.

The rides and fire breaks provide grazing for Muntjac Deer which can be seen regularly, or heard barking from the denser parts of the wood. Roe Deer occur occasionally, perhaps encouraged by the fact that sporting rights are reserved.

Access

Homefield Wood is 2 miles (3.2 km) west of Marlow and is best approached from the lane between Bockmer End and Lower Woodend, where the main entrance facilitates the parking of four or five cars. Little other parking is possible. Several pedestrian access points exist around the perimeter, particularly to the south and west. There are many wide tracks through the woods and a number of more intimate pathways that penetrate most of the woodland. After rain, the calcareous soil makes conditions under foot quite difficult, but few of the main tracks are on particularly steep slopes. Some of the paths are numbered at various points on the sides of prominent trees.

Species

Many of the blocks of trees in Homefield Wood are quite dense, precluding birds such as woodpeckers and Nuthatch, but even the more tightly packed areas provide a territory for various tits including the Willow Tit whose presence is more usually revealed by its striking call. Goldcrest also are at home in the confines of the close knit stands, usually searching for food at the height where the brown lower bracts of conifers meet the greener growth of the upper tree. In winter small mixed hunting groups of Coal Tits, Blue Tits and the two species mentioned above move amongst the evergreens. Where the trees are more thinly spread, such as in Holywick Wood, these groups are joined by Long-tailed Tits, and occasionally Treecreepers, and these areas do attract woodpeckers. The shorter days of the year are dominated by argumentative Jays and Magpies and the hoarse protestations of Pheasants as they browse amongst the pine needles. Cold winter nights carry the calls of Tawny Owls as they visit Homefield and other nearby copses. Little Owl can be seen along the tree-line abutting the fields of Woodend Farm and rattling Mistle Thrushes patrol the same area. Parties of Yellowhammer decorate the barren hedgerows which radiate from the northern extremities, whilst Siskin and Redpoll feast on the Silver Birch which are scattered throughout the wood.

But it is perhaps in the warmer months that this woodland really comes alive.

The resident species referred to are joined by various summer visitors, temporarily at first as passage warblers move north through the area. By late spring the flower-edged rides and tracks echo to the songs of Chiffchaff, Willow Warbler and Blackcap, birds which seem not to mind the relative lack of significant understory. The absence of such secondary growth does however mean that Whitethroat and Garden Warbler are less likely to be seen. Any Robin-like movement seen at this time of the year will be worth verifying as there is always the possibility of Redstart passing through, their chestnut tails quite distinctive even in the darker parts of the wood which they seem to favour.

A warm summer's day will tempt clouds of insects into the pine-scented air to be eagerly consumed by hordes of Swifts whilst an occasional Swallow will hawk the wider pathways. Spotted Flycatchers favour the more open areas such as the Beech stand near Homefield Hall to the south and the mixed Beech and Oak areas at the centre of the main wood. Breeding Blackbirds and Mistle Thrushes are harassed by voracious Jays, but this strikingly coloured corvid is in turn an easy indicator for Sparrowhawks to follow to the Jay's nest and the ensuing battle is a noisy and vicious affair. However, the end is usually the same with the Sparrowhawk the victor, flying off to its own nearby site complete with prey. Bullfinches too may be much in evidence at this stage, the lifetime pairs having moved away from the small winter groups to fashion their own breeding territory especially in the

Woodcock

coniferous areas to the north of Heath Wood where the gamekeeper has his Pheasantry. From this point it is worth looking out across the fields to the north for the Corn Bunting which may by now be in evidence by song if not by sight, and as night approaches, a 'roding' Woodcock may be encountered on its lap of honour.

Homefield Wood is not an especially large area and does not possess the bird density of more open deciduous woodland; however, it does have its own character and offers a tranquillity not often found in this busy part of the county.

Calendar

Resident Jay, Magpie, Willow Tit, Coal Tit, Pheasant, Green and Great Spotted Woodpecker, Nuthatch, Treecreeper, Goldcrest, Sparrowhawk, Tawny Owl, Little Owl, Bullfinch.

December–February Siskin, Redpoll, Yellowhammer, roosting Woodpigeon and Jackdaw.

March–May Willow Warbler, Chiffchaff, Blackcap, chance of Redstart.

June–July Spotted Flycatcher, Swift, Corn Bunting in surrounding fields, occasional Cuckoo and Woodcock.

August–November Large numbers of young Pheasants wander through Holywick Wood, mixed flocks of tits and Goldcrests.

LITTLE BRITAIN
COUNTRY PARK

Map 33/OS ref. TQ 050 810

Habitat

This rather grandiose title will eventually be appended to an area which currently hardly warrants the status. Between Denham and Rickmansworth is a major wetland area following the line of the Colne Valley through picturesque countryside. South of Denham however, the Colne meanders through a region of industrial estates, abandoned factories, derelict buildings and overgrown wastelands. Many of the streamside businesses are scrapyards and there is a somewhat unkempt air about the place. If there was such a SSSI category as 'eyesore' much of the area might qualify. Surrounded by busy roads, motorways and the sounds of Heathrow's growing pains it is perhaps surprising that any self-respecting bird would inhabit such a site. However, it is clear that birds are far less discriminating than we humans and a surprising range of species can be found at various points around the Park.

There are three main elements to this site. South of the Grand Union Canal are two pits, one of which is fished by the Metropolitan Police and is surrounded by mature bushes and shrubbery. Adjacent is an abandoned factory estate where most of the buildings have been demolished and the remaining area has been taken over by scrub and mature Buddleia which attract many butterflies in late summer. North of the canal is a large lake, Farloe's Lake, restored for angling and yachting. The owners have gone to great lengths in their conservation programme with the creation of many small tree-covered islands and an extensive planting scheme. On one side of the lake is a small but dense Hawthorn thicket and a sizeable nettle-bed, whilst on the other is a sewage works. Further north is the private parkland of Huntsmoor Park and Little Britain lake itself, a small lake with established vegetation and which is popular for walking and fishing.

Still further north is Woodland's Park Lake, much utilised for back-filling during the construction of the M25 motorway and still being extensively worked. Again, the pastimes of angling and yachting are pursued but whereas much of the area described so far is scheduled to become a Country Park this lake will be reduced in size in the interests of agriculture. The River Colne and the Grand Union Canal provide a consistent theme in an otherwise somewhat random habitat.

Access

The site lies to the west of the A408 West Drayton to Uxbridge road. The nearest main road connections are junction 4 of the M4. Woodland's Park Lake can be accessed from the A4007 (where a small number of riverside parking spaces exist) just before crossing the bridge in a westerly direction. A few parking places also exist on the B470 near Huntsmoor Park and there is always room along the lane south of the Park. The most convenient places however, are around the edge of Little Britain Lake which is accessed via Packet Boat Lane from the A408. From this location one may make a circumnavigation of the lake, at the western side discovering a narrow footpath between the pond and the Colne River, which forms the county boundary at this point. A small footbridge over the river at the end of Packet Boat Lane enables one to cross to the Farloe's Lake side and although both lakes here are private, good views are available through the chain link fence (although extensive tree planting along some of this sector may make this less easy in years to come). Further along this lane one may take the public footpath through Huntsmoor Park with its mature Limes, Sweet Chestnuts and Copper Beeches. The path next becomes quite a picturesque stream-side route albeit via slightly overgrown vegetation in places. This path exits on the B470 just north of a small weir and a circular walk can be completed via the canal-side lane which in turn re-joins Packet Boat Lane. Alternatively one might continue past Farloe's Lake to the fisherman's entrance which has been extended to a new footpath on the eastern side of the M25, alongside a footbridge which spans the motorway. Do not cross the bridge but continue past the sewage works to the canal, taking the towpath in an easterly direction to the next canal bridge. At this bridge one might take the north-going path back to Packet Boat Lane via its somewhat wild and un-managed nature, pausing perhaps to explore the thicket and Nettle-beds on top of the eastern embankment. On the other hand those with no eye at all for aesthetics may decide to delay savouring these delights by first exploring the path south of the canal bridge which, by way of dense shrubbery, affords fleeting glimpses of the anglers' pools and, subject to a little scrambling up the bank, facilitates viewing the vista of an area of post-industrial wilderness favoured by warblers in summer. From this high bank, views over the lake are enhanced, which does not necessarily improve the likelihood of seeing anything exceptional, of course.

Although there are parking facilities at Woodland's Park Lake, a problem exists with the footpath which used to extend to the B470. Motorway construction has severed this pedestrian link and one can only walk as far as the yacht-club and then retrace one's steps, should a visit be considered worthwhile. Except during the very driest parts of the year it should be assumed that most of the footpaths will be extremely muddy. For those willing to pay a train-fare to explore this, in places, 'forgotten' area, the nearest railway points are Uxbridge (main line and underground) or Yiewsley (main line only).

Species

As one might gather from the opening remarks, this is no site for the aspiring rarity-hunter, although Merlin and Ferruginous Duck have been recorded here. But for those who find delight in discovering a surprisingly wide range of more common birds in somewhat unusual surroundings, at least one visit should be made, before the Country Park planners get their hands on it and 'tidy it up'. Little Britain Lake is an obvious place to start. In winter, when it is not completely frozen over, it hosts small numbers of Common and Black-headed Gulls, with occasional visits by Herring and Lesser Black-backed. The resident Mallards, Coots, and Moorhen and Great Crested Grebes are joined by Dabchicks, particularly on the adjacent Colne and, amongst a few Pochard and Tufted Ducks, small numbers of Smew and Goldeneye. Although these two species tend to move on after only short visits they do offer perhaps unusually close viewing due to the small size of the pool. Kingfishers can be seen more often perhaps at this time of year, usually on branches overhanging the canal by the scrapyard, ignoring totally the work going on there, or along the river, beyond which a small number of Heron can be seen from time to time roosting in a large Scots Pine. The trees around, and in the vicinity of the pond, are inhabited by Nuthatch, Treecreepers, all the common finches and tits (with the exception of Marsh Tits) and all three woodpeckers. Redwing and Fieldfare are common and Siskin can be expected in the riverside trees.

In summer the scene is one of striped-head Grebes, red-faced Cootlets and many breeding passerines who are aided and abetted in this preoccupation by visiting Chiffchaff and Blackcaps. All three wagtails can be expected and both Kestrel and Sparrowhawk breed in Huntsmoor Park, where Little Owl is occasionally heard. Farloe's Lake at this time of year has even larger numbers of breeding Great Crested Grebe. Being larger and less disturbed than Little Britain, Farloes' Canada Goose creches are a common site and Sedge Warblers also breed there. In winter however, these physical features seem to have less influence and winter duck and gull numbers are not especially high. The adjacent sewage works attract a few Meadow Pipit amongst the winter Starling throng but is at its best in summer when Pied and Grey Wagtails, together with Swallows and House Martins, swell the numbers. Water Rail, seen here infrequently in winter, might possibly breed but this is uncertain.

The other two pools beyond the canal can be viewed more easily in winter when vegetation is at its thinnest. Again duck and gull numbers are seldom dramatic but the prospect of scarcer grebe species are higher here, especially Black-necked Grebes which explore the area a little before eventually settling on the large reservoirs nearby. The spring passage entices Black Terns on occasions and in summer one or two pairs of Common Terns frequent the pool but breeding facilities are poor for this bird, perhaps something that could be addressed during the future establishment of Country Park status in the area. Reed Warblers and buntings breed in peripheral vegetation. The scrub-land on the eastern side of the footpath in this sector is the domain of Woodpigeon, Collared Dove and resident finches in winter, with the possibility of Black Redstart near the remaining but crumbling factory buildings. In summer however it can be surprising perhaps to find Whitethroat, Blackcap, Garden Warbler and Sedge Warblers, their song providing an orchestral backing to dancing butterflies, tempo maintained by the rhythmic purring of one or two pairs of Turtle Doves. Bullfinches, Linnets and Greenfinches nest here and it is likely that Pied Wagtails do too. The other wild area just north of the canal has its summer visitors; Whitethroats again but also Garden Warblers which, together with Chiffchaff, prefer the small thicket and riverside shrubbery. The return path to Little Britain Lake is a regular haunt for Goldcrest and Long-tailed Tits and another feature is a large elongated island in the middle of the river whose banks are worth scanning in winter for Water Rail and upon which the many mature trees host Great Spotted Woodpeckers, Nuthatches and Mistle Thrushes all year.

Woodland's Park Lake once had a reasonably good record for birds but recent work has changed all that. Further excavations, followed by extensive and on-going back-fill work has left the scene practically featureless with no protective or breeding islands on the water, a tree-line that only extends for part of the periphery and little emerging vegetation. This is reflected in the avian scene with few waterfowl and only occasional sightings of Common Tern in summer. The land reclamation area south of the water can be of interest during the nesting season with Ringed Plover and Little Ringed Plover likely to be encountered, together with breeding Linnets and Reed Buntings. As development work progresses, even these species may find it difficult to sustain their presence, at least until any future conservation work is completed. However, considering the area as a whole it can be seen that an unexpected range of species can be found amongst the ramshackle and desolate surroundings. If there is one speciality of the area it is the Ring-necked Parakeet and one can only hope that the picnic sites, camping grounds and other planned 'improvements' do not destroy entirely the wastelands that this bird, and many of those mentioned above, thrive on.

Calendar

Resident Little and Great Crested Grebe, Heron, Canada Goose, Mallard, Tufted Duck, Sparrowhawk, Kestrel, Moorhen, Coot, Woodpigeon, Collared Dove, Stock Dove, Little Owl, Kingfisher, all three woodpeckers, Grey and Pied Wagtails, Jay, Goldcrest, Willow Tit, Long-tailed Tit, Nuthatch, Treecreeper, occasional Tree Sparrow, Bullfinch, Greenfinch, Goldfinch, Linnet, Reed Bunting, Yellowhammer. Occasional sightings of Ring-necked Parakeets.

December–February Black-necked Grebe, Cormorant, Water Rail, Gadwall, occasional Pintail, Wigeon, Teal, Shoveler, infrequent Shelduck, Pochard, Goldeneye (usually redheads), possibility of Goosander. Smew (mainly red-headed females or juveniles), common gull varieties, Meadow Pipit, occasional Black Redstart, Redwing, Fieldfare, Siskin, occasional Redpoll.

March–May Common Sandpiper, passage Black Tern. Swift, Swallow, House Martin, Yellow Wagtail, Sedge Warbler, Reed Warbler, Garden Warbler, Blackcap, Whitethroat, Willow Warbler, Chiffchaff.

June–July Turtle Doves more in evidence, possibility of Ringed and Little Ringed Plover.

August–November Passage terns over all lakes in August and early September, hirundines mass occasionally over the two southern pools later in September, winter thrushes arrive in November.

LITTLE MARLOW
GRAVEL PIT

Map 34/OS ref. SU 876 876

Habitat

Still being worked for minerals in one or two places, this 50 acre (20 ha) Thames-side site has been, and continues to be restored as, a sallow-lined lake. The lack of peripheral vegetation is compensated for by a small overgrown island used for nesting by waterfowl. An area of exposed sand in shallow water is favoured by gulls and waders, whilst perching birds are accommodated by stands of Beech and Poplar on the approach road and an avenue of Oak and Hawthorne which leads to the river. Adjacent waters host a variety of sports leaving the subject site free of disturbance save for anglers. Alongside the gravel pit is a sewage works, edged by plots of grasses, Willow Herb and Nettle, which adds variety to the range of bird species which can be expected. A small stream runs parallel to the northern bank, and the land in between is to be excavated in the next phase. It is also known as Spade Oak.

Access

The gravel pits are to the south of the A4155 road between Bourne End and Marlow, the nearest main road being the A404 which joins the M40 at junction 4. Access is via the public footpath which runs along the western edge of the lake; park in Church Road and walk past The Cottage on the right. Access to the lakeside itself requires a permit from the local angling association but adequate views are available from this footpath, which runs between the lake and the sewage works. One may cross the railway line at the end of the path and follow the Thames eastwards to another crossing at Coldmoorholme Lane, passing the anglers' car park before taking the westerly footpath which rejoins the original route at Church Road. Views from the eastern side of the lake are made difficult by evening sunshine.

It is planned to build a public footbridge over the Thames in the Temple area and eventually therefore access by foot will be possible from Cockmarsh on the Berkshire side. Avoid parking under the mature trees near the church in winter evenings as a significant Starling roost may readily transform the colour-scheme of the car.

Species

As with most inland water areas, the gravel pit is probably more productive for the winter birdwatcher, but the surrounding woodland and sewage works are also very active in mid-year and therefore a visit in any season is worthwhile.

The year starts with large flocks of Starlings attracted by the shelter and food source offered by the sewage treatment works. Their noisy chorus is occasionally silenced by a resident Sparrowhawk soaring overhead, and the Starlings swirl silently in open squadrons or simply cower in adjacent tree-tops. They may even be outnumbered by substantial flocks of Black-headed and Common Gulls which ply constantly between the sludge tanks and the exposed sand flat on the gravel pit. Small numbers of Herring Gull and occasional Lesser

135

Black-back Gulls may be detected in the throng. Even after searching frosts the lake does not become completely frozen over, and waders may visit the shallow area, Snipe being the most usual with sometimes a few Dunlin. Winter ducks include Gadwall and Teal, but more numerous will be Pochard and Tufted Duck. Smew and Goldeneye put in irregular appearances. On the other hand, one will often see Cormorant on the submerged tree-frames. Heron will be seen quite often but the still sparse cover usually results in a prompt but elegant departure. Not so however with the resident Kingfishers which can be surprisingly confiding and easier to see at this time of year. Flocks of up to 70 Meadow Pipit and small numbers of Redpoll feed on the scrub area around the sewage works.

The gulls, and most of the Starlings disperse with the onset of spring and the small woodlands, previously occupied by mixed feeding parties of tits, Goldcrest and Treecreeper, are soon colonised by Blackcap and Chiffchaff and, quite often, Willow Warbler too. The lake will be more empty but passage waders such as Oystercatcher, Little Stint, Green and Common Sandpiper may be seen along with the more regular Redshank. The resident Reed Buntings will be seeking out nesting places as early Swallows arrive and, by the time Common Terns and Spotted Flycatchers have appeared, many species will already be breeding. By early summer the first creche of Canada Geese can be seen being escorted around the lake whilst parent ganders and non-breeding geese graze in the meadows beyond the railway line. One or two pairs of Mute Swan grace the water, and Water Rail occupy the northern bank. Little Ringed Plover will also have attempted breeding. The courtship routine of these small waders is quite elaborate. Following much high-speed pursuit along the ground, usually a few feet apart, the female eventually stops and the male slowly sidles up to her alternately stamping one foot and then the other prior to a brief encounter.

The sewage works meanwhile will have been taken over by Yellow Wagtails, Goldfinch and Sedge Warblers and occasionally Skylarks are attracted to the quieter corners of the site. Lesser Whitethroats also nest in the confines of the works, they and their neighbours quickly seeking cover when one of the local Kestrels works its way along the railway embankment. Linnets and occasional Corn Buntings occupy the southern hedgerow throughout the summer. After mild winters, numerous Wrens will be defending quite small territories, usually in hedgerows, their tiny delicately woven domed nest in a small crevice amongst ivy containing six or more young. Following severe winters, far fewer will have survived to breed but those that do may subsequently rear up to a dozen young, all crammed into the same sized nest.

Many of the larger houses around Marlow are of earlier vintage and their traditional eaves attract nesting House Martins. With young to feed there is constant aerial activity over the sewage beds as hundreds of these white-rumped acrobats hawk for insects. Despite the recent demise of the Sand Martin in its over-wintering quarters, small numbers may be picked out as they skim over the water, but there are no suitable nesting sites in the immediate vicinity.

The autumn passage tends to be less dramatic than that of spring but it is always worthwhile checking the lake's shallows for Ringed and Little Ringed Plover and occasional Ruff before this area of the pool becomes the domain of Lapwing and wintering gulls once more. With the numbers of the various breeding species swelled by offspring, augmented by the southerly movement of others, it is a very busy time for the local birdwatcher. Arctic Terns may join more numerous Common Terns on their way through and fleeting visits from Black Terns should not be discounted. There follows a short period of relative calm before Shovelers lead the winter ducks back and the contact calls of Fieldfares and Redwings can be heard once again amongst the clamouring of mixed finch flocks in perimeter hedges. The lengthening nights are preceded by the roosting rituals of dozens of Woodpigeon, occasionally accompanied by the calls of Tawny Owls.

Little Marlow Gravel Pit may not be a prominent site for rarities and following prolonged freezing the duck population may migrate to other waters, but it affords an excellent opportunity to see a wide variety of more usual species. One local birdwatcher has already amassed a record of over 160 species on the site over several years and when the restoration work is complete and has matured, the area may then realise its full potential.

Calendar

Resident Great Crested and Little Grebe, Water Rail, Cormorant (most months), Tufted Duck, Mallard, Coot, Moorhen, Kestrel, Sparrowhawk, Lapwing, Snipe, Heron, Stock Dove, Kingfisher, Great Spotted Woodpecker, Pied Wagtail, Reed Bunting, Meadow Pipit, Linnet.

December–February Mute Swans (numbers vary year-to-year), Canada Geese more numerous and alternate with nearby Summerleaze pits, over-wintering dabbling ducks such as Gadwall, Teal and a few Wigeon and Shoveler, diving ducks such as Pochard and on rare occasions Scaup. Smew and Goldeneye infrequent. Occasional Dunlin. Large gull roost. Redpoll.

March–May Hobby on passage, Wheatear on adjacent meadow, occasional Whinchat. Common Sandpiper and other wader species. Arctic and Common Terns in April, with Sylvia warblers returning. Possible Pied Flycatcher passing through. Cuckoo arrives early April. Barn Owl has been noted.

June–July Large numbers of hirundines, Spotted Flycatcher, occasional Turtle Dove.

August–November Mixed groups of juvenile wagtails, late broods of Great Crested Grebe, many House Martin leave by early October, some stay on until end of the month. Starling roost builds up, winter thrushes and ducks start to arrive. Occasional Stonechat.

SHABBINGTON & WATERPERRY WOODS
Map 35/OS ref. SP 620 110

Habitat
These two woods form part of the Bernwood Forest Nature Reserve and are managed by the Forestry Commission. Shabbington Wood is by far the larger of the two at 717 acres (287 ha) and is also more meandering in character. The majority of stands are between 25 and 50 years of age and the most numerous of the species is Norwegian Spruce which covers some 100 acres. Shabbington actually comprises several woods, Oakley Wood being perhaps inappropriately named as most of its area is planted with Norwegian Spruce mono-culture. However there is a substantial area of Oak and Birch to the north. The Shabbington sector to the east has many mixed stands with Oaks variously paired with Spruce, Lawson Cypress, Red Cedar, and, in a 5 acre (2 ha) area in the north, with Beech. York Wood possesses similar mixed stands but in addition there are plantations of younger trees, especially Western Hemlock, Sweet Chestnut and a few Grand Firs. Hell Coppice is, in the main, densely planted Norwegian Spruce but this species is mixed with Ash and Oak in places.

On the other side of the road to the south lies Waterperry Wood which has a total area of 340 acres (136 ha) and is a little different to Shabbington in character in that all the stands are mixed and that it is generally more densely planted. Oak and Norwegian Spruce is the most common mix, but Clearsall has a sizeable area of Birch and Oak, whilst Hursthill has a 9 acre (3.5 ha) plot of Birch, and a new plantation of Spruce and Oak at shrub level only. However the size of this plot is unlikely to attract any specialist birds. Polecat End has a variety of small plots with Scots Pine, Lawson Cypress, Western Hemlock and some miscellaneous mixed deciduous trees. Drunkard's Corner has a large area of Oak and Birch but also a significant 20 acre (8 ha) sector which consists of a veritable patchwork of small 1 acre (0.4 ha) plots of such species as Scots Pine, Grand Fir, Hybrid Larch, Corsican Pine and deciduous scrub. This particular section is classified as a SSSI. Elsewhere in the woods are a number of small glades and clearings which add variety to the general scene.

Adjacent to the two woodland areas is a small BBONT reserve, Bernwood Meadows, which is well-known for its plant species, including 23 grasses, and its ancient hedgerows.

Of the mammal species one is likely to encounter, the Grey Squirrel is by far the most numerous. Small groups of half a dozen or more Fallow Deer range throughout both woodlands but particularly in Waterperry. Muntjac Deer will also be seen occasionally. Both woods, and the BBONT reserve referred to are particularly renowned for their butterfly populations, the open rides and meadows speckled with fluttering colour as large numbers of a variety of species wander from plant to plant.

Access
The site is north-east of Oxford, near the village of Holton. The car park

at Shabbington Woods is on the road between Boarstall and Stanton St John and has room for some 20 vehicles. Beware of the one-way approach road system. There is no car park for Waterperry Wood but there is a small lay-by for a single car just beyond the Forestry Commission entrance track. Parking in the Forestry Commission entrances to both woods is deterred to ensure rapid access of fire appliances if needed at any time. The BBONT reserve has a small car park for only three vehicles but is only open at weekends. (The entrance to this car park is quite near a dangerous 'S' bend and caution should be exercised.)

The system of pathways in Shabbington is quite extensive and, like all managed woodland, subject to change. The map for this site indicates the main tracks only and many of the offshoot tracks only go to the woodland boundary. There is no perimeter path. If it is intended to explore as far as the eastern extremity it should be noted that this involves a round trip of over 1.3 miles (2 km).

The path layout at Waterperry Wood is somewhat more straightforward and essentially on a square grid arrangement. Once again there is no perimeter track as such although some lateral paths do join adjacent parallel tracks at the periphery. However the full character of the wood cannot be fully appreciated without exploring some of these sidepaths, especially in the south-east and north-east where there are quite open deciduous stands. There is no access into the SSSI in the south-west.

Due to the movement of heavy forestry machinery and permitted horse-riding, the main tracks in particular can be very muddy at any time of the year.

Species

Woodland management is similar to long-term farming. Crops are grown and eventually harvested, annually on farmland but only after many years in the case of timber. Accordingly the habitat change in woodland is gradual and bird species move in and out of the tree-scape over the decades that the trees take to mature. Then, almost overnight, the entire habitat will have disappeared after felling. The effect of this on birdlife varies from wood to wood. If a small woodland is completelly felled in one go the effect could be dramatic. If however only small portions are felled at one time the effect will be less noticeable. On the other hand, constant felling and planting work will cause disturbance to birds in adjacent stands. Size of woodland is therefore as important as management technique and the area encompassed by these neighbouring woods is adequate to ensure plenty of undisturbed land at any one time. This helps to maintain a stable community of bird species and the mixed nature of the tree types which exist here also maximises the range of varieties of birds present.

Like many woods of any nature, Shabbington and Waterperry have less bird activity in winter. The numerous conifer stands attract flocks of Treecreepers, Goldcrests, Blue, Long-tailed and Great Tits up to 50 or more in number. However such large feeding parties range fairly widely through the wood and one can go some time before chancing across them. Redpolls are found especially where the conifer compartments are edged with mature Birch, upon which Siskin may also be seen. Coal Tits are common, particularly near or on Larch trees and, in the less dense evergreens, Great Spotted Woodpeckers can be found. Pheasant, together with many Blackbirds and Song Thrushes, rummage amongst the field layer looking for prey which is seeking protection from the cold weather in the leaf- and needle-litter. The prospect of finding Crossbills must not be overstated but equally should not be ignored. Their likely presence is often related to the three or four year cycle in which the fructification of the Norway Spruce is regulated and there are far more acres of Spruce in Shabbington than Waterperry. The rides of both woodlands are occupied by numerous Jays and Magpies, and some of the Goldfinches that stay to over-winter will be found in perimeter trees.

The deciduous and mixed stands exhibit several additional species, the hole nesting varieties being more free to roam outside the breeding season. Nuthatches are fairly abundant and all three woodpeckers are present. Treecreepers and Willow Tits are abundant and, wherever Birch or Alder is present, Siskin and Redpoll again are likely to be in situ. Ubiquitous Wrens and Chaffinches are probably the most vocal at this time, apart that is from the Jackdaws that also spend much time in the woods. Bullfinches too will be found, perhaps two or three pairs together, and Linnets should be looked for. It will also be worth keeping an eye open for Tree Sparrows but Stock Doves will be much easier to discover. Mistle Thrushes and Redwings are usually located around the woodland edge. The most productive tracts of this deciduous nature are to be found in the northern parts of Shabbington and in Clearsall and Polecat End at Waterperry. At times they can be readily found by following the calls of the Tawny Owls which frequent these sectors.

It is these same deciduous elements that see most activity in summer, many of the species mentioned staying to breed but joined by Willow Warblers, Chiffchaff, Blackcap and Garden Warblers. A few Whitethroats can be expected and Spotted Flycatchers should be seen. The extent to which other woodland specialities visit these sites is however dependent upon the felling and replanting programme. Tree Pipits and Nightjars of course prefer fairly extensive areas of recently planted conifers, interspersed with heather and small Birches. At the present time there are perhaps too few such sections in these woods to attract either species on a regular basis. There is one such patch on the eastern side of the Waterperry main path and odd clearings in Shabbington but it may be some years before any major felling, followed by a period of 'rehabilitation', creates the right environment for these two birds. In terms of species richness therefore, the two woods fare quite well and a visit would rarely be in vain. A winter visit guarantees little competition with other people but even in summer the place does not get crowded. The most popular pursuit apart from walking and horse-riding, is butterfly spotting and with several of the fritillaries, blues and skippers in residence during the warmer months, it is advisable to go equipped with an appropriate guide book.

Calendar

Resident Sparrowhawk, Kestrel, Pheasant, Woodcock, Stock Dove, Woodpigeon, Collared Dove, Little Owl, Tawny Owl, Green, Great and Lesser Spotted Woodpecker, Dunnock, Goldcrest, Robin, Blackbird, Song and Mistle Thrush, Long-tailed, Coal, Great, Blue, Marsh and Willow Tits, Nuthatch, Treecreeper, Yellowhammer.

December–February Mixed feeding flocks, Redwings, possibility of Crossbills, Occasional Fieldfares.

March–May Winter thrushes depart in March. Early breeding of some residents in April, as summer warblers arrive. Chance of singing Nightingale. Listen for hammering of woodpeckers.

June–July Blackcap, Willow Warbler, Chiffchaff and Garden Warbler breeding. Occasional Cuckoo and Turtle Dove.

August–November A quiet period though numbers increased by successful breeding. Warblers left by September, winter thrushes arrive in November.

SHARDELOES

Habitat

Shardeloes House stands in its grounds of 250 acres (100 ha) consisting of arable and pasture farmland, open parkland and mixed woodland. The house looks out over a significant lake which has engulfed numerous bushes and small trees, thus providing many nesting opportunities for waterfowl. The lake also has islands affording a roosting and breeding haven for geese and ducks. The tree scape in the immediate vicinity of the house is mainly one of mature deciduous trees including Oak and Lime whilst the wood to the south-west is chiefly coniferous. In the area of Mop End, and surrounding an electrical sub-station, are more open areas recently created which have begun succession to Birch and Hawthorn scrub. This somewhat heath-like scene has been augmented by a small arboretum adjacent to a maturing stand of Larch.

Access

Shardeloes House and estate lies 1.5 miles (2.5 km) west of Amersham along the A413 to Great Missenden and Aylesbury. A small lay-by outside the lodge gates accommodates approximately ten cars though vehicles are not permitted inside the grounds. For a short visit the most favourable footpath is the one that runs along the south bank of the lake which returns to the A413 0.6 miles (1 km) from the car park. However, the main road is not too inspiring from a birder's point of view so retracing one's footsteps is preferable.

A longer walk is possible by way of the footpath to Mop End with a return route down the sloping pathway on the western side and following the lakeside path to the main entrance. This entails a round trip of some 3 miles (4.8 km) but is likely to be worth it, as the path skirts both conifer and mixed woodland and also emerging scrubland in the vicinity of the electricity sub-station. Alternatively one may pull off the A404 at Beamond End to approach the estate from the higher ground and perhaps visit the adjacent Penn Wood.

The nearest main line railway station is at Amersham which is also served by the Metropolitan Line of the London Underground.

Species

If the owner of this estate were to keep a record of his 'garden' birds, a most impressive chronicle it would be. Birds of one species or another are active throughout the year, each day commencing with morning assembly in the rookery adjacent to the main house. Jackdaws share this roost and readily augment this noisy awakening although in the months of winter the gathered ensemble are soon off to the arable fields for a day of feeding. These fields will often attract large flocks of Meadow Pipit and Skylark offering the opportunity of comparing the markings and behaviour of these two farmland birds. The Pipits will probably be more numerous and will be noted as a slightly smaller and more stream-lined bird and will usually be the more active of the two whilst the chunkier Skylark can be detected by its small crest (although this is absent in juveniles of the species), and its Starling-like wings. Other birds of the winter field such as Pheasant, Grey Partridge, Lapwing and Black-headed Gulls are much in evidence whilst the rolling lawns and pastures will accommodate Mistle Thrushes and Fieldfare in good numbers. The grassy banks of the lake feature Pied Wagtails stepping daintily between noisy Canada Geese and other feral relatives such as Greylag and occasional Barnacle Goose. Sparrowhawk is frequently encountered, especially in the Mop End sector.

The water itself at this time of year provides an important refuge for many common waterfowl and perhaps most prominent are the parties of whinnying Dabchick, some of whom lurk amongst the submerged roots of shrubbery whilst others are content with open water. The more substantial islands in the pool provide loafing areas for geese, Mallard and, less frequently, Gadwall. Snipe will also take up this locale in the event of inclement conditions affecting their more usual territory. Shoveler pay irregular visits at this time of year, though not in large enough numbers to show off their tandem feeding technique to the observer. Nor is the water area large enough to attract particularly large numbers of gull regularly but Kingfishers on the other hand can be expected, and Reed Buntings often roost around the pool in some numbers. The woodland sectors can be rather quiet at this time of year though sizeable flocks of Fieldfare and Redwing can be found near Mop End, which is also a likely spot for Little Owl. The conifer stands hold small mixed feeding groups of tits and Goldcrests and is an area of protection for a large flock of Linnets which often roam the surrounding district. Look out also for smaller numbers of Tree Sparrows which might pop up anywhere on the estate.

The spring passage is much in evidence with Wheatear likely to be found at Mop End or even on the cricket pitch which they will share with Pied, and early Yellow Wagtails. Shortly after this the first Sand Martins will stop over fleetingly near the lake which is also the first place the Chiffchaff may be heard. Brambling, not being a regular winter resident here, may well be seen in March or April as small parties move northwards with the newly-arrived summer species. The fence line adjacent to the lake is worth checking for Whinchat during April. It can be rewarding to be at the lakeside at dusk during this time as groups of Canada Geese, intent on overnight accommodation, arrive from surrounding areas, their noisy approach drowning out the calls of Tawny Owls near the main house and the more staccato utterances of overflying Snipe and the occasional Woodcock. However, daylight is necessary to see if a Common Sandpiper or two happens to be paying a visit on the main island.

By early May, the breeding period already well underway for resident birds, the visiting migrants will also succumb to this seasonal urge and the lakeside is probably the area where this activity is most obvious. Coots and Moorhen and possibly Dabchick, will be feeding young on the water whilst Reed Buntings forage on behalf of their young amongst the reeds which, though not extensive, have tempted Reed Warblers in the past. In the meantime there is continuous aerial activity as Swallows and House Martins hawk for insects to the cackling accompaniment of unruly Rooks. Predatory Crows cause more disturbance than do the Kestrels which breed on the site. The tree-line and gardens of the lodge can produce singing Blackcap whilst the less intruded area of Mop End may well be favoured by the attractive Tree Pipit, whose slightly sibilant song can be thoughtlessly interrupted by the strident protests of Mistle

143

Thrushes protecting their nests from marauding Jays and Magpies.

Probably the most interesting breeding successes in the general area of south Buckinghamshire however are those of the Barn Owl, a pair of which having produced offspring in recent years not too far away. Although a totally wild pair, their success has almost certainly been helped by the release scheme organised by D. Lewis who has nursed numerous sick and injured owls to health and re-introduced over 30 pairs into the region. The establishment of adjacent territories by these birds not only results in more regular sightings of this magnificent bird but possibly galvanises the few remaining wild pairs in the district into 'competitive' breeding. Barn Owls will hunt for one or two hours after daybreak so an early rising is necessary for the aspiring observer. As the season advances and the young become larger and more demanding there is a better chance of seeing the adult pair hunting together in ghostly silence if their hunting territory extends to Shardeloes.

Towards the end of summer, visitations from two other specialities of nearby waters are quite possible, whilst not frequent. Ruddy Duck may be found in ones or twos, possibly non-breeding birds from Weston Turville not welcomed by their busier colleagues, and the occasional Mandarin might pay a short visit from one of the breeding grounds in Berkshire. This perching duck may have the edge over the stiff-tailed Ruddy Duck in the plumage stakes, at least as far as the males are concerned, but both are striking additions to the Shardeloes scene when present.

The advance of colder damper weather brings about the gradual departure of migrant birds to their winter quarters. The Garden Warblers vacate the woodland at Mop End leaving its periphery free to increasing numbers of roosting Corn Buntings whilst the reeded area of the lake becomes almost devoid of passerines for a while. Several hundred House Martins gather into early October, their own departure followed by short visits of other parties of their kind moving down from more northern climes. By late October or early November, the Meadow Pipits will have installed themselves once more and the last of the Yellow Wagtails and Common Sandpipers will have passed through. The chance of a glimpse of roaming Crossbills in the conifer compartment is enhanced slightly and early Siskins return. Any Redpoll that may have stayed during the summer, though unlikely to have bred, will be joined by several others and the resulting group seems to move between various small woodlands in the area throughout the ensuing winter months. Woodpigeon assemble in enormous numbers, doubtless to the consternation of the landowner.

Thus it can be seen that something avian is happening continuously at Shardeloes albeit not always on a grand scale, and therefore a visit at any time can be fulfilling. Perhaps on balance April/May and October/November are best.

Calendar

Resident Little Grebe, Mute Swan, Canada Goose, Mallard, Tufted Duck, Kestrel, visiting Sparrowhawk, Pheasant, Coot, Moorhen, Little Owl, Tawny Owl, Barn Owl in the area, Green and Great Spotted Woodpeckers, Skylark, Pied Wagtail, Dunnock, all six tits, Nuthatch and Treecreeper, Goldfinch, Yellowhammer, Corn Bunting, Reed Bunting, Rook, Jackdaw.

December–February Great Crested Grebe in small numbers, winter Gulls also in small flocks, occasional Shelduck and Wigeon, Teal and Shoveler, possibility of Goldeneye but not likely to stay due to proximity of footpath, Grey Partridge more prominent, Water Rail on occasions, Snipe, Meadow Pipit, Grey Wagtail.

March–May Possible Hobby and Buzzard, though scarce, might be seen overhead. Cuckoo, Swallows and House Martins, Yellow Wagtail on passage, Reed and Sylvia warblers in small numbers. Occasional Spotted Flycatcher, Whinchat and Wheatear. Tree Pipits.

June–July Breeding passerines, some on second brood, Turtle Dove, Swift.

August–November Common Sandpiper on passage, larger numbers of hirundines around the lake prior to departure, Redwing and Fieldfare arrive, Woodpigeon and Stock Dove numbers increase.

Rook

STONY STRATFORD
NATURE RESERVE

Map 37/OS ref. SP 786 413

Habitat

The site was excavated for gravel some years ago and the Milton Keynes Development Corporation decided to refill it specifically to create a wet-meadow environment with a number of lakes, mostly shallow, together with a series of islands, gravel bars and loafing areas. The site is both mown and grazed and much tree planting has been undertaken by the borough council. Phragmites reedbeds have been established and regular maintenance work is carried out to keep the gravel islands in the most suitable state.

Access

The reserve is 0.6 miles (1 km) east of Old Stratford and is best reached on the old road to Bletchley, which runs parallel to, and south of, the A5 trunk road. Approximately 250 yds (230 m) east of the junction with the A422 is a large lay-by suitable for several cars. Alternatively there is a small lane, next on the left-hand side, a further 100 yds (92 m) on along which will be found a small car park. Pedestrian access is either from this car park or at the western end of the reserve alongside the River Great Ouse. A pathway is routed around the west, north and eastern edges of the site but the southern boundary can only be accessed by permit from BBONT. However, views from the old Bletchley Road are usually more than adequate. A hide is available to visitors, halfway along the northern path.

Species

Before excavations were carried out, Redshank bred on the flood meadow that existed. Since the refilling exercise these birds, and many others, have returned to the site on a regular basis. The graded muddy shores of the pools are ideal for waders all year and in addition to Snipe and Ringed Plovers, Green Sandpiper and Common Sandpiper are regular visitors. The Snipe often reach double figures in winter and it is well worth a careful look at each one in case a Jack Snipe is amongst them, as a few of these birds are seen frequently in the locality at this time of year. Occasional Dunlin can be expected and almost any other common wader might pass through. Water Rail certainly over-winter and may be resident. The flooded fields to the north of the pools are usually inundated with Lapwing and Starlings in winter and one should look out for the odd Golden Plover that could just be in their midst. Little Ringed Plovers too are beginning to be regulars here from springtime and autumn, times when a Greenshank or two are possible, or even an Oystercatcher. Ruff and Curlew Sandpiper are other prospects. The road along the south of the site is the best place to look, the bushes which obscure the view being easily avoided from the high-banked pavement.

This same roadway, or the public hide to the north, are good places to observe winter waterfowl and, in between the occasional comings and going of Grey Heron, there are usually small numbers of Teal, Pochard, Tufted Duck and Wigeon. Shovelers cannot be guaranteed and sawbills

Little Ringed Plover

only seem to make irregular visits. There is usually a small herd of Mute Swans and these should of course be scrutinised for the outside chance of a Bewick's or Whooper though they may only stay one day. Great Crested Grebe numbers fluctuate rather and Dabchicks are not always seen, the Great Ouse possibly being a better place for them. Whilst checking the river for this delightful grebe, there is a likelihood of coming across a Kingfisher, which will occasionally make a sortie onto the reserve itself. There are always Pied Wagtails on the reserve and the same can probably be said of the Reed Bunting, but the numbers and variety of wagtails increase dramatically in the passage periods. Up to 50 or more Pied Wagtails, with six or seven Grey Wagtails, can be seen in the vicinity of the 'gravel pile' in April, or indeed anywhere along the water's edge. Maybe as many as 30 Yellow Wagtails might pass through at one time. The rarer wagtails, such as the splendid grey-backed White Wagtail, are fairly regular, and the striking Blue-headed Wagtail has been suspected here.

Geese are also well represented at Stony Stratford, usually in the form of 100 or 200 Canada Geese or by appearances of the 'local' Snow Geese and Barnacle Goose. However, conditions are often ideal for any other regular winter geese to visit. Brent Goose has been recorded. Shelduck are occasional visitors but the more scarce Pintail, and the passage Garganey, should not be expected with any regularity. Of the hunting birds, Sparrowhawk is perhaps the only regular patron but Short-eared Owl has been noted. Great Spotted Woodpeckers make occasional use of the more mature trees in the south and Green Woodpeckers, plentiful in the northern parts of the county, may also be seen, possibly on the grass in the adjacent parkland. Gulls are not specially prominent here, usually represented by Black-headed and Common Gulls. A reported sighting of a Ring-billed Gull however is of significance and is being considered by the Rare Birds Committee.

On the smaller side again, Siskins are often seen around the periphery and Stonechat can show up in the wet-meadows area where numerous

Meadow Pipits and a few Skylark will be found. Ring-necked Parakeet have stopped over. The spring passage may well bring Black Redstart and Wheatear. As the reedbed develops, other species may well become even more regular breeders than at present and any activity of Reed or Sedge Warblers should be viewed from the hide. Best visited in winter or passage periods, and far from a waste of time in summer, this small but dynamic site owes its success to the foresight of the Milton Keynes Development Corporation, the generosity of the local borough council and the tenacity and dedication of the Warden. These joint efforts have produced a remarkably successful reserve that can only improve with maturity.

Calendar

Resident Little and Great Crested Grebe, Grey Heron, Mute Swan, feral Snow Goose and Barnacle Goose on occasions. Canada Geese numerous, Shelduck infrequent. Mallard, Tufted Duck, Sparrowhawk, Kestrel, Water Rail (possibly), Moorhen, Coot, Lapwing, Snipe, Redshank, Black-headed Gull, Kingfisher, Great Spotted Woodpecker occasionally. Grey and Pied Wagtail, Dunnock, Crow and Rook. Reed Bunting plentiful.

December–February More Great Crested Grebe for a time, occasional Whooper Swan, Brent Goose possible, Canada Goose number 200 plus, small numbers of Wigeon, Teal, Shoveler and Pochard. Chance of Pintail, and Ruddy Duck. Possibility of occasional Golden Plover, Curlew Sandpiper, Dunlin and Jack Snipe. Snipe numbers up to 50. Ring-necked Parakeet (but not regular), possibility of Short-eared Owl.

March–May Some resident species paired and breeding at the commencement of this period. Redshank holding territory. Passage waders such as Oystercatcher, Ringed and Little Ringed Plover, Ruff, Greenshank, Green and Common Sandpiper. Common Tern, and plenty of wagtail activity. Possibility of Stonechat, before common warblers arrive.

June–July A little quiet. Breeding in process, possibility of Cuckoo. Early returning waders end of July.

August–November Return passage in full swing, almost anything might turn up.

WESTON TURVILLE   Map 38/OS ref. SP 863 096

Habitat
The reservoir at Weston Turville is a 10 acre (4 ha) lake owned by the British Waterways Board, used for angling and sailing, but with extensive reedbeds on three sides. On the southern side, the surrounding area comprises marshy undergrowth, dense shrubbery and established hedges whilst to the north is a small area of woodland with a variety of deciduous trees and Hawthorn bushes. The site is encompassed by farmland and as such the variety of habitat that results is reflected in the range of bird species likely to be seen. The land immediately adjacent to the water's edge is managed by BBONT on behalf of the water board. Shooting rights are reserved and management entails keeping the marsh area from becoming overgrown and containing the reedbed from encroaching into the sailing area. The bank to the north-east is raised and totally exposed but affords a good observation point from which to view the water. The site was classified a SSSI in 1976.

Access
Weston Turville Reservoir lies just north of the A413 between Aylesbury and Wendover. There is a large lay-by in World's End Lane which can accommodate up to 30 vehicles and the main entrance is at the southern end of this lay-by. There is a permitted footpath around the western and northern edge but the southern bankside is only accessible to BBONT members and is in any case in need of some restoration. A public footpath skirts the southern tree-line and another passes to the north-east.

Species
Although not a large area of water, the reservoir nonetheless provides the traditional haven for over-wintering waterfowl and as such is probably best visited in the winter months. At this time of year, whilst numbers are not normally high, such species as Great Crested Grebe, Shoveler, Pochard and occasional Gadwall will be found amongst Coot, Tufted Duck and Mallard. The exposed western shore, often fished, usually causes most of the birds to collect near the reedbed at the far end and when sailing is also taking place, those that remain often retreat well into the reedbed itself. These twin disturbances are likely to mean that, other than in mid-week, numbers of waterfowl will not often be high. Nonetheless, the location of the lake is such that a variety of visiting species may be expected. Heron may be found, mainly in the early morning but occasionally as darkness falls a lone bird, or sometimes several, may glide in out of the gloom, resembling huge fruit bats, and circle for a while before alighting at a chosen roosting spot. Small numbers of Canada Geese also use the reservoir overnight but their aerial approach is altogether more clamouring. Another resident, the Little Grebe, is more readily seen at this time of year, venturing further from the reeds than in the breeding season, often in small groups. Although perhaps more attracted to the larger waters of the nearby Tring complex, both Smew and Goosander may well be seen at

Weston, usually the 'redhead' of the species in both cases.

The first passage of the year brings increased numbers of winter ducks for a short period but as quantities begin to dwindle, Shelduck may call in for a few days, and Garganey has also been recorded. Of the non-water specialists, Chiffchaff and Reed Warblers, both of whom breed on the site, will usually be the first to arrive but whilst they stay on, wandering Short-earted Owls merely pass through. Great Grey Shrike have been noted. The mixed flocks of Lapwing and Black-headed Gulls which gather in adjacent fields during winter begin to disperse and the small number of 'resident' Ruddy Ducks make fewer visits to other waters nearby and prepare for breeding with much head-bobbing and tails erect. March winds cause the water to become quite choppy because of the lack of shelter on one side, but, because of the position of the sun, the exposed bank is probably the best place from which to view the entire site.

The surrounding tree-line only caters for occasional small parties of Redpoll and Siskin to accompany the resident tits, Greenfinch and Chaffinch, and there are a few Bullfinches to be found but, by April, Great Spotted Woodpeckers have selected their nest site, leaving the Starlings to fight over the numerous tree-holes remaining. By mid-summer, the reedbed is vibrant with chattering Reed and Sedge Warblers and as such is a major attraction to Cuckoos who can be seen perched in prominent lakeside trees scanning for a suitable guest house for their eggs. Their woodpecker-like feet are especially adapted for working through dense reedbeds with two toes forward and two back. Despite this predation however, the warblers do succeed in raising young of their own. Another predator particularly active at this time of year is the resident Sparrowhawk, the male in particular making several sorties a day to collect the necessary morsels for the much larger female to feed to her brood. Throughout the warmest months hirundines, often in huge numbers, billow over the water, accompanied by many Swifts which, as evening advances, can be seen soaring upwards higher and higher until out of sight, spending the night on the wing. Another welcome visitor in summer is the Common Tern. There are no nesting facilities here for this bird but non-breeding individuals often use Weston as one of their feeding sites and pairs that have raised young at other locations sometimes bring their offspring to this reservoir for a short while before leaving for migration. Maybe BBONT will provide a gravel-filled raft and some perching posts sometime in the future to make this elegant tern a more regular visitor.

Being a small site, the autumn passage may not be too evident, perhaps sometimes only in fluctuating numbers of common waterfowl, but one may be fortunate to see Whinchat on the fence-line of the adjacent meadow or the occasional Buzzard soaring overhead. Of the local summer visitors, the House Martins are probably the last to depart, leaving the reedbed as a regular roost for Pied Wagtails. The site can be very quiet in March, but a visit at almost any other time of year can be rewarding, particularly if a non-sailing mid-week day can be selected.

Calendar

Resident Great Crested and Little Grebe, Coot, Moorhen, Mallard, Tufted Duck, Ruddy Duck, Reed Bunting, Yellowhammer, Green and Great Spotted Woodpeckers, Sparrowhawk, Jay, Magpie, Dunnock, Tree-creeper, Long-tailed Tit, Marsh Tit, Pied Wagtail.

December–February Larger numbers of resident waterfowl. Small groups of Pochard and Shoveler, occasional Goldeneye and Wigeon and good chance of Pintail. Numerous gulls, worth checking flocks of common species for rarities such as Mediterranean or Little Gull. Short visits by Scaup always possible.

March–May Can be a 'temperamental' site in March once over-wintering waterfowl have left. Busier in April and May. Few passage waders but a general northerly and easterly movement of ducks through the area. Garganey a good possibility in April. Chiffchaff early April (if not in fact over-wintered). Willow Warbler two weeks later, followed by Reed and Sedge Warblers. Possible Arctic Tern.

June–July Cuckoo active, hirundines in fluctuating numbers. Chance of Hobby. Occasional Turtle Dove. Common Tern.

August–November Reedbed very active in August. Swallows and House Martin numbers swell as September heralds autumn. Juvenile Great Crested Grebes still to be seen.

WILLEN LAKE

Map 39/OS ref. SP 878 404

Habitat

If one did not know better, Willen might be described as another water-filled gravel pit on which a great deal of sailing takes place and round the edge of which many people are walking every day. Just what it is that makes this location one of the foremost inland birdwatching sites in the country is difficult to identify. True, it was one of the first lakes to be created out of the birth of the new Milton Keynes and has had over ten years to establish itself and it does have a large island in the centre of the northern basin with a well prepared mud scrape. However, the periphery is almost devoid of cover and observers risk disturbance to surface-feeding flocks. Fortunately, the sailing is restricted to the southern basin, but even there enormous numbers of birds occur. The surrounding area is open grassed parkland with plots of gradually maturing shrubbery. Some trees on the north shore are quite established now and a few reeds are growing in places. A high grassed bank passes through the centre of the site, except at the point where the two pools meet at a small weir, and this bank is ominously in line, and level with, a road which currently terminates near the lake. One can only hope that it stays that way.

Access

The lake is immediately adjacent to junction 14 of the M1 and is approached initially on the A509 to Milton Keynes, but turning north along V10 (Brickhill Street) to the second car park on the right, where space for 30 or so cars will be found.

Alternatively, from H4 (Dansteed Way) in the north, take the third turning on the right down Millington Gate, crossing the large roundabout and turning right into Willen Road. At the end of this road is another small car park and some picnic facilities. A footpath runs all the way round the outside of the two lakes but it is likely to be the north lake that is worth viewing in particular. The best view of the wader scrape is from the area in the vicinity of the weir between the two bodies of water. A telescope is advisable in view of the distance to the island, which is over 110 yds (100 m).

Species

It would be easier to write about the birds which have not yet been recorded at Willen, as there have been nearly 200 species seen since accurate records were kept. This may have been in the past due to the size and position of the lake, although Linford and Caldecotte are adjacent and equal in water area. However, it is most likely the good sized wader scrape, somewhat remote from interference, combined with the fact that it is probably one of the most-watched sites in the county, so very little escapes notice. Whatever the reason there always seems to be something of interest. Most of the resident species are not especially unusual with Canada Geese and the more ubiquitous ducks on the water, Lapwing, Snipe and Dunlin on the mud flat, and Skylarks and Reed Buntings around the perimeter. Meadow Pipits, numbering up to 100 in winter, breed in much smaller numbers in summer. Gadwall have stayed on through the summer and one pair provided the county's first breeding record. Of the slightly more unusual species seen during most of the year, Shoveler and Oystercatcher are perhaps worthy of note. Shelduck are becoming more regular here too.

It is the ever-increasing list of regular, and less frequent, visitors however that has created Willen's enviable reputation. Of the more-or-less annual visitants, Wigeon, Pochard, Teal and additional Shovelers make up most of the numbers on the water's surface. Varying numbers, often up to 30, Goldeneye and good numbers of Goosander spend a goodly part of their time puncturing the water's surface whilst Pintail make a striking addition. Even this beautifully marked bird is eclipsed by the Bewick's Swan for those fortunate enough to be present on their regular but fleeting stay. Cormorants are usually around but in winter there is the chance of either Black or Red-throated Diver in some years and the three more scarce grebes, Slavonian, Black-necked and Red-necked, show up with similar irregularity. The same can be said of the Shag. Whooper Swans too are becoming a more reliable visitor but may remain happy enough with Hydelane Lake for the foreseeable future. Scaup and Common Scoter pop in from time-to-time but Smew seem difficult to tempt. During passage, Mandarin and Garganey have made bright additions to the scene on rare occasions. Meanwhile, the wader scrape provides another venue for other species. The more common varieties include Grey Plover, Black-tailed Godwit, Curlew and Turnstone whilst Knot, Sanderling and Little Stint are also frequently seen in small numbers. Passage waders such as Ruff, Greenshank and Green Sandpiper stop over briefly but Redshank, Ringed and Little Ringed Plover all breed on the island. The diminutive Jack Snipe and the even more dainty Curlew Sandpiper oblige every now and then.

Perhaps though one of the most spectacular sights at Willen in the wintertime is supplied courtesy of the local gull roost. It is symptomatic of Willen to do everything on a grand scale and the best time to view the returning mass of gulls is just before dark on an overcast evening with black clouds down to the horizon forming a backcloth against which flashing silver and white birds tumble out of the sky from all directions, twisting and turning erratically before alighting on the water. Thousands and thousands of Black-headed Gulls mix with varying numbers of Common, Herring, Lesser Black-back and Greater Black-back Gulls as they gradually blanket the water. Sometimes, most of the birds will rain down on the occupants of the northern pool, only to lift off again and filter down onto the southern water. An excellent place to observe this glittering ceremony is the raised embankment between the two lakes (where Snipe may well be discovered). These numbers reduce with the approach of spring which makes the task of picking out occasional passage Kittiwakes just a little easier. The spring passage invariably includes all five of the more common terns and the exceedingly scarce Roseate Tern has been recorded. Other infrequent species include the Spotted Redshank, and Wood Sandpiper in the autumn and Temmincks Stint in May.

Nor is all the action associated with the water. The lack of cover in the area generally curtails passerine numbers to some extent but the spring passage usually generates Wheatear, Whinchat and occasional Ring Ouzel and, in some years, the odd Redstart or Black Redstart. Rock Pipits occur almost annually and minor incursions of one or two Water Pipits are not unknown in some seasons. Most of the common warblers

153

pass through but only the Sedge Warbler seems certain to breed. Wagtails are prominent both in spring and autumn, the resident Pied Wagtail joined by anything up to 100 Yellow Wagtails, their numbers occasionally containing a representative of the Continental Blue-headed race. All the hirundines are found and Swifts may exist in a horde of up to 1,000 in dramatic migration movements. Hobbies call in every now and then but the only other two regular birds of prey are the Kestrel and the Sparrowhawk, although Tawny and Short-eared Owls are making more use of the site for hunting purposes in recent years.

The shortening days herald the coming of the winter spectaculars referred to above, but precursored by the autumn passage, bringing with it good numbers of Meadow Pipits and occasional Turtle Doves in most years. Winter thrushes pass over in sizeable flocks but do not often stop off. A harsh winter will lead to much icing, even on this expanse of water, and then the free water areas and the wader scrape will be taken over by large numbers of waders, gulls and waterfowl, including the local geese whose numbers will be swelled by visiting Canadas and roving feral Greylags. On rarer occasions, Brent, White-fronted and Pink-footed Geese have graced the island, but these should not be expected annually.

As can be seen, Willen Lake is a somewhat exceptional site for the birdwatcher and seems to go on making a habit of producing county firsts, such as the Kentish Plover and Sabines Gull in 1981, the Red-necked Phalarope in 1978 and even national rarities such as the 1979 record of a Ring-necked Duck. Other scarce species that have been seen at least once here include Raven, Purple Sandpiper and Lapland Bunting, whilst the improving national status of Avocets and Bearded Tits may explain their infrequent but gratifying appearances. It is difficult to pass on the intended impression of species-richness of this site in a compressed report of this nature without the chapter resembling a list from a spotter's guide but hopefully the contribution that Willen Lake has made to the avian scene over the years can be recognised, and enjoyed by a visit. Such a visit is unlikely to be unrewarding at any time but October to May is best.

Yellow Wagtail

Calendar

Resident Little Grebe, Great Crested Grebe, Cormorant, Heron (occasional), Mute Swan, Greylag Geese (feral), Canada Geese, Barnacle Goose (feral), Shelduck, Gadwall, Mallard, Shoveler, Tufted Duck, Moorhen, Coot, Oystercatcher (most months), Lapwing, Dunlin (most months), Black-headed Gull, Stock Dove, Woodpigeon, Collared Dove (occasional), Skylark, Meadow Pipit, Pied Wagtail, Dunnock, Reed Bunting, Corn Bunting, Yellowhammer.

December–February Large flocks of gulls and winter ducks, continuous movement of variety of waders and prospect of rare swans.

March–May Potentially most exciting period with numerous unusual visitors such as Garganey, Common Scoter, occasional Avocet and Jack Snipe. Most species of terns passing through with good numbers of Yellow Wagtails.

June–July Waterfowl, Redshank and Little Ringed Plover nesting. Swifts and hirundines plentiful.

August–November Strong passage in most autumns. Early arrival of Golden, and occasional Grey Plover. Little Stint fairly regular, Temmincks Stint less so. Ruff and Black-tailed Godwit, Greenshank and Green Sandpiper more numerous than in spring. Occasional Wood Sandpiper. Gradual build up of gull roosts. Winter ducks such as Pintail and occasional Long-tailed Duck. Chance of Rock and Water Pipit.

ADDITIONAL SITES

Boarstall Decoy (OS ref. SP 624 153)

This is a small BBONT reserve of some 17 acres (7 ha) which incorporates a small pool surrounded by woodland of a mixed deciduous nature. The site lies adjacent to Manor Farm along the B4011, north of Boarstall. Whilst a reasonable variety of woodland birds can be found on this compact area, the main function of the reserve is to demonstrate how the decoy is used to trap duck for ringing purposes (their legs nowadays, not their necks). Accordingly it is only open at weekends, Bank Holidays and Wednesday afternoons from Good Friday to the Summer Bank Holiday inclusively. A small charge is made to visitors who are not yet members of the National Trust or BBONT. Nearby is Muswell Hill, a stepped hill covered with closely grazed grass which has attracted Wheatear and occasionally Redstarts, on passage.

Brickhills (OS ref. SP 917 325)

Situated between Woburn Park and Milton Keynes is a large tract of mixed woodland, with some significant conifer compartments, 500 acres (200 ha) of which are within the county of Buckinghamshire. Access is from the A5(T) at Little Brickhill along the road to Pinfoldpond. The adjacent golf links at Back Wood in the north adds to the habitat variety of the site, and here, resident Sparrowhawks are seen regularly, although passage Hobbies can cause confusion. Wheatear and Redstart also on passage are likely near the links. In summer Grasshopper and Wood Warblers should be found though breeding is doubtful. In winter, Brambling are seen near the links and good numbers of Crossbills ply between Wavendon Wood and Stockgrove Country Park. Sizeable flocks of Redpolls are also in evidence. Resident birds include Green, Great Spotted and Lesser Spotted Woodpeckers, Tawny Owl and, most spectacular of all, the Lady Amherst's Pheasant which roams the woods in small parties.

Chess Valley (OS ref. SU 995 985)

Between Chesham and Chenies is a pleasant stream-side walk which takes in trout farms, cress beds, farmland and deciduous woods. At the Chesham trout farm, Water Rail and Grey Wagtails are always likely, together with Reed Bunting. The sewage works slightly to the east often has all three wagtails in summer, whilst the farmland around Blackwell Hall usually has Corn Bunting and Little Owl. The small pond west of Bois Mill has resident Little Grebe and Tufted Duck, which are joined by Gadwall and Pochard in winter. Frith Wood, in the centre of the walk, is privately owned but good for Tawny Owl and Jays. Woodcock are a prospect but regular shooting here may deter them. The fields to the north of the footpath usually have Grey Partridge and Skylark. The weir and wider waters at Latimer House are excellent for Grey Wagtails and breeding Dabchick and Spotted Flycatchers are present in summer. The fairly extensive woodland south of the road, Lane Wood, is a mixed deciduous wood with shrubbery containing the usual common woodland species, with passage Nightingale a good prospect.

Beyond Chenies, the footpath north of the river passes through boggy pastures which often contain Snipe in winter. In summertime, the dense bushes around these paddocks provide nesting sites for Whitethroat and Bullfinch. The small Bluebell wood beyond is most aromatic in summer and also hosts Great Spotted Woodpecker, Willow Tit and Treecreeper. Valley Farm has its own feral Guinea Fowl but the river attracts large numbers of House Martins and, occasionally Water Rail. The cress beds are again an area where all three wagtails can be found. Each end of this walk has mature woodland to explore. Mount Wood to the east is excellent for the three woodpeckers, Garden Warblers, Turtle Dove and Chiffchaffs whilst a similar wood at Chesham Bois is a regular haunt for Hawfinch.

Coombe Hill (OS ref. SP 847 066)

Situated south of the B4010 which runs between Wendover and Little Kimble, this significant pimple on the Buckinghamshire landscape rises some 850 ft (262 m) above the surrounding countryside to look down somewhat onto Wendover Woods 2.5 miles (4 km) away. It thus forms the highest point on the Chiltern escarpment and has been in the hands of the National Trust since 1918. Grazing has been introduced and Gorse that keeps appearing is mown off annually. An area of clear, grassed hilltop with heather has thus been formed, but adjacent is a natural mixed woodland of Oak, Hornbeam, Silver Birch, Rowan, Hazel and Hawthorn. Such a site in such a place is ideal for visiting during migration, and regular passage visitors here include Redstart, Buzzard and numerous hirundines. Ring Ouzel regularly pass through as do occasional Wood Warblers and there is always the prospect of Hawfinch. The spring passage is more prominent than the autumn migration. Access is via the lane to Dunsmore. At the top of the hill where the lane swings sharply to the right there is space for parking vehicles.

Dancers End (OS ref. SP 900 095)

This site is adjacent to Wendover Woods and comprises 80 acres (32 ha) of woodland and grassland with both public and BBONT members' access areas. Many of the conifers planted earlier have been replaced with Beech and Larch. The grassland is grazed by sheep. Another site high on the Chiltern ridge with a good variety of general woodland and meadow birds but with the chance of migrating raptors and passerines. Parking is on the verge along the road to St Leonard's and the site is 250 yds (230 m) along the bridleway.

Emberton Country Park (OS ref. SP 885 505)

Emberton is situated between Northampton, Bedford and Milton Keynes and is one of the four country parks in Buckinghamshire. Created from a total area of 175 acres (70 ha) of gravel workings, the Park includes four large lakes covering altogether 40 acres (16 ha) of water. There is parking for over 1,000 vehicles and facilities include toilets, camping and caravan sites. Unfortunately, there is no room specifically set aside for wildlife and all waters are used for angling, sailing, and model boats. Despite this, the site has a good range of birds including general woodland birds (woodpeckers, tits, Redpolls, Siskins), parkland species (Little Owl, Stock Dove, Jackdaw) and the more common waterfowl (grebes and dabbling ducks). However, the passage period and wintertime can attract good numbers of winter duck and occasional waders, particularly on non-sailing days. As a site, possibly under-watched and an opportunity for birdwatchers to contribute to local statistics by studying the species seen at the Park over a period of time.

Great Wood (OS ref. SU 765 867)

North of the Thames, between Henley and High Wycombe, there are many woodlands, mostly quite small and many privately owned, though with footpaths running through at least some of their area. Great Wood is such a site and, at 750 acres (300 ha) is one of the largest. Situated 1.2 miles (2 km) west of Hambledon, and accessed via a track travelling north from Greenlands on the A4155, the site occupies steep wooded slopes and an open grassland valley. It is a mixed woodland but has a more open aspect than nearby Homefield Wood. The approach track is worth checking for Brambling in winter, when Fieldfare are numerous. The woodland hosts Green and Great Spotted Woodpeckers. The open valley is a favourite hunting area for Sparrowhawk and large flocks of Woodpigeon gather there in autumn and winter. In summer the site is good for Spotted Flycatcher, Blackcap and Chiffchaff, and Wood Warblers on passage are a fair prospect. Recent clearing of a sizeable area of conifers at the top of the hill in the north-west sector may attract Tree Pipits in due course. Tawny and Little Owls are resident. Another wood of the same name, 1.25 miles (2 km) to the north, is almost entirely deciduous and possesses more Nuthatches and Treecreepers. The Lesser Spotted Woodpecker is also more prominent here. Watch out for Muntjac Deer and Roe Deer at both sites.

Golden Plover

Long Herdon Meadow (OS ref. SP 648 204)

An area of wet-meadows, remnants of unimproved ancient meadowland some 10 acres (4 ha) lying between Bicester and Aylesbury on the road to Marsh Gibbon, parking near Grange Farm. This is a BBONT reserve, open to members for whom much of the attraction is in the form of a wide range of sedge and grasses together with a selection of herbs. For birdwatchers, who can see over the meadows from the public footpath to the east, the main attraction will be over-wintering waders in the flooded areas, including Lapwing, Golden Plover, Snipe and possible Jack Snipe. Breeding species include Skylark, Reed Bunting, Yellow-hammer, Linnet. Passage birds may well include Greenshank and Redshank.

Philipshill Wood (OS ref. TQ 010 945)

Together with the adjacent Newland Park, the site represents some 250 acres (100 ha) of mixed woodland and open parkland. The scene is more deciduous to the west and the north. Access is off the B4442 road to Little Chalfont and parking is along the road to the Park, or the Park itself. An excellent site for general woodland birds with specialities including Hawfinch and Tree Pipit. Wood Warblers are regularly encountered and Firecrests have also discovered the location. Good numbers of winter thrushes in the Park during winter.

Pitstone Fen (OS ref. SU 941 142)

This is a a relatively tiny location which is perhaps of more interest to botanists than ornithologists but the extent of the flora and the protected nature of the reserve attracts a good number of birds and, in summer, there is a substantial community of breeding species. The 9 acre (3.5 ha) site consists of a strip of land adjacent to a railway line and possesses reedbeds, a copse of Scots Pine near the entrance (looking perhaps a little out of place), and the Fen itself at the face of the old chalk quarry workings. Access is strictly by permit only, details of which are available from BBONT. Best for summer warblers. Quiet at other times of the year. The reserve lies to the north of the B488 to the north-east of Tring and a visit to the museum and reservoirs of that town may encourage a short visit to the Fen whilst in the area.

Rushbeds Wood (OS ref. SP 670 158)

A 100 acre (40 ha) long-neglected woodland adjacent to a railway embankment beyond which is the private parkland and lake of Wotton House. The site is some 3 miles (5 km) south of the A41(T) Aylesbury to Bicester road and parking is available where the 'T' junction of the lanes abut the railway line. Another excellent site for woodland birds including all six tits, Nuthatch and Treecreeper. Great Spotted Wood-peckers are regularly seen but Lesser Spotted Woodpeckers less often, Tittershall Wood to the north being preferred. Passage birds seen are Tree Pipits and Nightingale. Tawny Owl is resident. Adjacent pastures host Lapwing, occasional Snipe and numerous winter thrushes. The lake, which can be viewed from the lane to the north-west, hosts Little Grebe and Great Crested Grebe, occasional Kingfisher and flocks of Canada Geese, with occasional feral Greylags. Sparrowhawk is a regular visitor in the general area and may breed in Tittershall Wood.

Salcey Forest (OS ref. SP 810 505)

The forests of Salcey, Whittlewood and Rockingham once provided hunting for monarchs but only part of the Salcey remains. Whilst it is the largest ancient forest in Northamptonshire, a goodly portion, containing a conservation area and a 35 acre (14 ha) BBONT reserve, lies on the Bucks side of the county border. It has been Forestry Commission land since 1924 and has been declared a SSSI. Many of the Oaks are 150 years old and there are many other deciduous species of tree including Ash and Hazel. Alas much conifer has been imposed but between the two types of woodland, scrub and shrubbery have developed and this has attracted Whitethroat, Garden Warbler, Chiffchaff and Willow Warbler to join the Nightingale, Grasshopper Warbler and occasional Wood Warblers that frequent the denser sectors. All three woodpeckers are present as are Woodcock, and occasional Tree Pipits.

Wendover Woods (OS ref. SP 890 085)

Wendover is one of the largest mixed woodlands on the Chiltern ridge and is managed by the Forestry Commission who have made excellent access arrangements for visitors. The only vehicular access is in the north at SU 887 105 just off the A4011 and the track is one way only through Aston Hill to ample car parking facilities just north of Halton Wood. Toilet and picnic facilities are also provided at this point. Much of Halton Wood is coniferous, but down the western slope to Halton Camp and Boddington Hill, a good deal of scrub has been left untouched. Down the eastern side are patches of Birch and Hawthorn thicket, and the vehicle exit is on this side along the lane leading to St Leonard's. The site is good for general woodland birds with Goldcrests and tits prominent in the centre and with finches and Jackdaws around the periphery. In summer, Blackcap, Chiffchaff, Garden Warblers and occasional Willow Warblers can be found in various locations. Tree Pipits and Spotted Flycatchers may also be encountered. Green and Great Spotted Woodpeckers are resident and Sparrowhawks are often seen. The main claims to fame for the site, however, are winter Crossbills on occasions and the regular sightings of Firecrest.

HERTFORDSHIRE

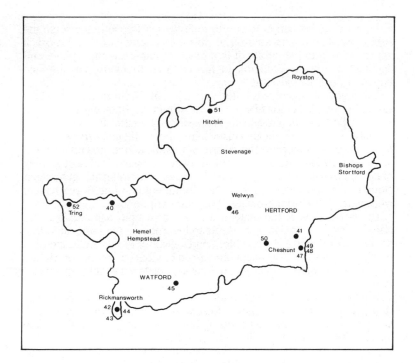

Royston

●51
Hitchin

Stevenage

Bishops
Stortford

Welwyn
●52   ●40   ●46   HERTFORD
Tring

Hemel
Hempstead   41
                                50 ●   ●
                                Cheshunt ●49
                                          ●48
                                        47

WATFORD
        ●45
Rickmansworth
42 ● 44
43

ASHRIDGE ESTATE Map 40/OS ref. SP 980 130

Habitat

From Ivinghoe Beacon in the north to Frithsden Copse in the south the Ashridge Estate covers an area of over 4,000 acres (1,600 ha) most of which is open to the public. It is a place of immense atmosphere and 'feeling', essentially Chilterns in flavour and, thankfully, in the safe hands of the National Trust.

Although the majority of the estate is in Hertfordshire the best examples of chalk downland can be found in Buckinghamshire at Ivinghoe Beacon, Incombe Hole, Steps Hill and on the slopes above The Coombe, with small remnants elsewhere. Sheep still graze these ancient pastures, close cropping the sward to ensure a rich downland flora. Scrub has invaded the escarpment in places, consisting almost entirely of Hawthorn with patches of Box and Juniper. Extending along the steep slope to the north and south of The Monument is a fine Beech hanger with many Whitebeam growing along the periphery.

The woodlands of the plateau are varied in both age and content. Native trees such as Oak, Ash, Birch and Hornbeam predominate with a scrub layer of mainly Hazel, Elder and Dogwood. Ponds are found here notably around The Monument and are an obvious attraction for wildlife during dry weather. Conifer plantations are scattered widely but are still in the minority.

The Commons are difficult to identify as many have been completely overgrown by trees. Northchurch Common is the most open with much bracken, Gorse and heather forming the semblance of a heath. Arable land is mercifully at a minimum but the meadow adjacent to the information centre can be good for watching deer early in the morning.

With such a mosaic of habitats, a wide range of wildlife takes safe refuge on the estate. Deer include a herd of 200 Fallow, many Muntjac and the occasional Chinese Water Deer. Badger inhabit the chalk slopes and Fox are common. The Squirrel-like Edible Dormouse is only found within a 15 mile (24 km) radius of Ashridge and is thought to have been introduced by Lord Rothschild around 1902. Some 37 species of butterfly and 300 species of moth have been recorded, many of the former attracted to the calcareous plants of the open downland.

Access

The estate is situated in the west of the county on the border with Buckinghamshire and Bedfordshire. The B4506 bisects Ashridge north to south between the A4146 at Dagnall and the A41 west of Berkhamsted. There are many lay-bys and car parks with even more bridleways and public footpaths, all well marked, giving access over most of the site. For further details of nature trails and general information, apply to the National Trust Shop and information centre at the end of Monument Drive.

For the downland sites drive to the car park at Steps Hill and explore along the ridge north and south. Avoid Sunday afternoons and Bank Holidays as disturbance from citizens band radio and model aircraft enthusiasts is chronic.

Coming south onto the Commons, Ivinghoe Common (popular with picnickers in the summer) is served with a car park making it ideal for exploring the surrounding mature deciduous woodland and conifer plantations. Aldbury and Pitstone Commons can be worked from Monument Drive as can the Beech hanger. Northchurch and Berkhamsted Commons both have roadside pull-ins along the B4506.

Species

The estate may seem quiet in the winter without the hustle and bustle of the summer visitors but several areas merit attention. The open chalk slopes around Beacon Hill attract good sized flocks of Yellowhammer and Corn Bunting. Noisy groups of Tree Sparrow can also be found here along with Greenfinch and Linnet, plus several pairs of Bullfinch working their way through the scrub. Occasionally the odd Hen Harrier or Buzzard drifts over driving the passerines into thick cover, although a hedge-hopping Sparrowhawk is more likely and far more dangerous. Winter thrushes feed out on the turf among the many anthills with the resident thrushes. Further south in the Beech hanger, Chaffinch and Brambling forage in the leaf-litter for mast, their numbers fluctuating annually according to the amount available. Roving flocks of tits can be seen almost anywhere most of them sporting shiny 'leg irons' applied by Chris Meads' ringing group. All three woodpeckers are resident with Green Woodpecker most likely on Northchurch Common, where sometimes a Great Grey Shrike spends the winter.

Wheatear are the first spring visitors on the downs with Chiffchaff paving the way in the woods. Very soon the Commons are alive with song as Willow Warbler and Blackcap pour onto the estate in large numbers. The other common Sylvia warblers arrive, as well as a few pairs of Grasshopper Warbler who prefer young conifer plantations or

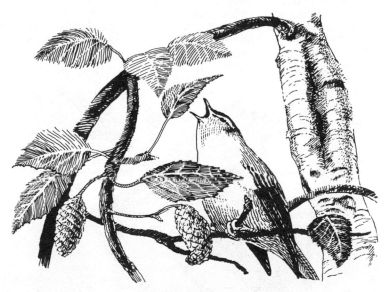

Wood Warbler

bramble patches. Each Common has at least a couple of pairs of Tree Pipit song-flighting around the glades, while Meadow Pipit haunt the more open scarp slope. Hovering overhead but for different reasons, are Skylark and Kestrel, the former still reasonably numerous. Hirundines filter along the slopes and a passage of Whinchat and less obviously Ring Ouzel occurs, although numbers are minimal. Cuckoo seem to like the scrub and call furiously with occasionally as many as ten within earshot at any one time. Spotted Flycatcher arrive in late spring breeding in abundance in the ancient woodland around The Monument.

Ashridge is the county stronghold for breeding Wood Warbler and Redstart, both birds requiring slightly different habitats. Listen for Wood Warbler where there is little undergrowth (usually beneath Beech or Birch) especially at Ivinghoe and Pitstone Commons. Redstart favour mature Oak in the same area but tend to be more elusive as they sing from the canopy. Probably under ten pairs of each have a tenuous hold in this most evocative of settings, therefore every effort should be made to keep disturbance to a bare minimum. Hawfinch occur erratically throughout the woodland usually in small parties and frequently come down to drink at the ponds.

Jay and Jackdaw are both abundant; the Jackdaw competing with Stock Dove and Tawny Owl for nest holes. Daylight sightings of the Owl are rare but the Beech hanger seems to be a good spot to see them, perched close to the bole of a tree.

Summer generally is a season to be avoided, due to human traffic, although an evening on Northchurch Common in June should yield 'roding' Woodcock and, in former years, Nightjar would have been 'churring' but now sadly are almost extinct as a breeding bird in Herts.

Autumn migration is usually evident on the downs with Steps Hill receiving a steady flow of warblers and hirundines with the occasional Whinchat and Ring Ouzel. Meadow Pipit and Skylark are on the move now as winter thrushes filter through. Migrating Goldcrest ceaselessly feed amongst the scrub with sometimes a Firecrest within their ranks.

Early morning birding is a must in Ashridge if the watcher is to sample the full flavour of ancient woodland birds without disturbance. Late April/early May is probably the best time when 50 species can be expected during a dawn chorus visit.

Hawfinch

164

Calendar

Resident Sparrowhawk, Kestrel, Red-legged and Grey Partridge, Woodcock (increase in winter), Stock Dove, Tawny Owl, Green, Great and Lesser Spotted Woodpeckers, Skylark, Mistle Thrush, Goldcrest, Marsh and Willow Tit, Nuthatch, Treecreeper, Jay, Jackdaw, Tree Sparrow, finches on downs, Redpoll, Hawfinch, Yellowhammer, Corn Bunting.

December–February Chance of 'ringtail' Harrier and Buzzard, possible Great Grey Shrike, winter thrushes, Brambling.

March–May Late March Lapwing, Chiffchaff, Blackcap, Wheatear, early April Willow Warbler, Meadow Pipit, Ring Ouzel, Mid-April Sylvia warblers, Grasshopper Warbler, Whinchat, Redstart, Wood Warbler, Tree Pipit, Turtle Dove, Cuckoo, hirundines. May, Spotted Flycatcher.

June–July Breeding passerines, possible Hobby.

August–November Passage on downs, warblers, chats, hirundines, Skylark, pipits.

BROXBOURNE WOODS   Map 41/OS ref. TL 340 080

Habitat

Broxbourne Woods is a collective name for a number of woods that form the largest block of mixed woodland in the county, stretching approximately 5 miles (8 km) from Box Wood in the north to Derry's Wood in the south.

Wormley Wood and Hoddesdonpark Wood, both now in the safe hands of the Woodland Trust, are the most interesting consisting mainly of Oak and Hornbeam; the former representing a classic piece of ancient woodland. Broxbourne, Cowheath and Highfield Woods are mainly blanketed with alien conifers but manage to support a few specialised species, particularly where the plantations are in their early stages of growth. Here the light encourages bramble and nettle patches to spring up allowing ideal conditions for scrub warblers to temporarily colonise during the summer. Streams dissect the entire complex making for interesting herbaceous growth and drinking sites even in the hottest summers.

Access

Situated west of Hoddesdon and south of Hertford, two lanes, Pembridge and White Stubbs, cross the centre of the woodland east to west. Two small car parks are located north of Pembridge Lane at Broxbourne Wood and two south off White Stubbs Lane at Bencroft Wood. Marked tracks lead into the woods giving access north and south. The Woodland Trust area at Wormley can be reached from the Bencroft Wood west car park while Hoddesdonpark Wood can be visited by careful and considerate parking along Lord Street. Alternatively park at either of the Broxbourne car parks and hike north and east until clear of the firs, entering Hoddesdonpark Wood from the west.

The Salisbury Estate owns the majority of the plantations around the centre of the complex and here birdwatchers should be particularly careful to keep strictly to the way-marked tracks. The pub at Brickendon is ideal for refreshments following a long morning's dawn chorus watch or prior to an evening conifer visit in the summer for crepuscular specialists.

Species

Winter is a fairly dull season with the usual roving tit flocks, visiting parties of Redpoll and Siskin and an influx of wintering Woodcock. Tawny Owl are resident and become increasingly more vocal towards the winter's end, especially in the deciduous woodland, while the elusive Long-eared Owl prefers the dense conifer stands around Cowheath Wood. The Hornbeam woods attract roving groups of the impressive Hawfinch seeking out the seeds of Hornbeam and Wild Cherry, while their distinctive 'tpik' contact call aids location.

In early spring Wormley Wood reverberates to the sound of numerous Great Spotted Woodpeckers drumming and Green 'laughing'. The tiny Lesser Spotted is also present but is much harder to find, keeping to the canopy most of the time. All six common species of tit breed in varying degrees of abundance with Long-tailed and Willow Tit the scarcest; the former preferring thickets, the latter woodland edges. Large hole nesting species, such as Jackdaw and Stock Dove, breed amongst the Oak on the

166

Woodland Trust holdings with the odd colonies of the declining Tree Sparrow around the periphery.

Warblers arrive throughout April with Chiffchaff, Blackcap and Willow Warbler first closely followed by Garden Warbler and a few pairs of Wood Warbler. The plantations attract Whitethroat and Grasshopper Warbler in small numbers; the latter best heard at dawn or dusk at Cowheath Wood, performing their monotonous 'reeling' song. Tree Pipit also exploit the clearings as a stage for song-flighting along with Reed Bunting who have recently colonised Birch plantations and seem totally out of place surrounded by dense woodland. Watch out for Cuckoo and Turtle Dove flying between stands and, in early spring, soaring Sparrowhawk. Nightingale and Redstart are both irregular breeders but can easily be overlooked when not singing although the chance of finding either is remote.

Late spring brings good numbers of Spotted Flycatcher to the broad-leaved woodland and two or three pairs of the county's last regular breeding Nightjar. Warm still summer evenings around the centre of the complex are the best areas to hear 'churring' and to occasionally glimpse this strange but sadly declining migrant. Beware of imitation 'cassette churring birds', usually discernible from the real thing by the diagnostic click of the rewind button! Some birders have developed the art of 'churring' (by blowing across the flap of skin between the base of the thumb and forefinger) to such an extent that they can even change the tone of the 'song'! Whilst out listening for Nightjar, 'roding' Woodcock are almost guaranteed and juvenile Long-eared Owls are at their most vocal emitting hunger cries similar to a rusty gate hinge in need of oil.

For a good cross-section in spring visit Wormley and Cowheath at dawn and dusk respectively when 40 to 50 species should be noted.

Calendar

Resident Sparrowhawk, Woodcock, Stock Dove, Tawny Owl, Long-eared Owl (scarce), three species woodpeckers, Mistle Thrush, Goldcrest, six species tits, Nuthatch, Treecreeper, Jay, Jackdaw, Tree Sparrow, Hawfinch, Redpoll.

December–February Small passerine flocks, Siskin and Redpoll.

March–May Common warblers, a few Grasshopper and Wood Warblers, Redstart and Nightingale scarce and irregular, Tree Pipit, Cuckoo, Reed Bunting, Turtle Dove.

June–July Nightjar, Spotted Flycatcher, breeding activity at its peak. Woodcock 'roding', possible Long-eared Owl calling.

August–November Quiet period with moulting taking place, finches flock in clearings.

COLNE VALLEY GRAVEL PITS   **Map 42**

The Hertfordshire section of the Colne Valley under discussion here consists of the river course from Oxhey to West Hyde, including Springwell and Stocker's Lake West, which, strictly speaking, are in Middlesex but form an integral part of the valley. In past years extensive gravel excavation has taken place leaving behind a chain of flooded pits, most of which are used for recreational purposes such as fishing and water sports. As most pits are exhausted, the banks become vegetated with mature willows and Alders and a typical lush summer undergrowth of water-loving plants. Most pits have fairly overgrown islands that are ideal for breeding wildfowl but less so for passage waders. Flowing water is provided by the River Colne with numerous small creeks and springs. The adjacent Grand Union Canal is also of interest having an accessible towpath alongside. Damp meadows are in short supply, the best being at Stocker's Farm, Batchworth and Croxley Moor.

An interesting feature of the Colne Valley in years past for the birdwatcher were its watercress beds, particularly around West Hyde and Springwell. Now mainly derelict these bird-rich habitats are still worth seeking out and continue to hold a few of the valley's 'special' bird in winter, the Water Pipit. Reed swamp and marsh can be found on the old sewage farm site at Maple Cross with other patches scattered along the valley. The open fields west of the A412 at West Hyde are worth checking in the winter for geese, Lapwings and gulls, with the occasional raptor passing through.

With this variety of habitats, it is not surprising that the area around Maple Cross proved to be the richest for breeding birds during the Atlas recording period in Hertfordshire. Encouragingly the main site, at Maple Lodge Sewage Works, is now an established nature reserve. Many similarities exist between the Colne and Lee Valleys including two active ringing groups and attempted colonisation by Cetti's Warbler, but the former is less urbanised and consequently more pleasant to birdwatch.

The scope of this book does not allow us to look at all of the Colne Valley sites. So, we shall select two only here, Maple Lodge and Stocker's Lake, for further investigation. (Three other sites, Batchworth, Croxley Moor and West Hyde are described in the Additional Sites at the end of this section of the book.)

MAPLE LODGE NATURE RESERVE (Map 43/OS ref. TQ 036 925)

Habitat

Owned by Thames Water, Maple Lodge Nature Reserve (formerly Maple Cross Sewage Farm) comprises an area of 40 acres (16 ha) of prime wetland habitat. The Maple Lodge Conservation Society was formed in 1982 and manage the site on a day-to-day basis under a licence granted by Thames Water.

The reserve is a relic of the old sewage farm days when sludge was disposed of into an old gravel pit, forming the main lake and some very unstable boggy areas! As pumping ceased, the shallow lake was in danger of drying out with subsequent colonisation by herbaceous growth, but manipulation of the water level and coppicing of willows have combined to create optimum feeding conditions for wading birds and wildfowl alike. Stoney islands still survive and are kept clear of vegetation to entice passage waders to pause and Common Terns hopefully to breed in the future. Scattered timber grows on the larger island and around the periphery of the lake with the recently felled Poplar plantation having been replanted with native hardwoods. The west and north sides are bordered by mature willows and Poplars respectively. Tangles of encroaching sallows grow vigorously around the western side and need to be constantly managed by the Society. An old predominantly Hawthorn hedgerow skirts the lake to the south with a particularly fine patch of spindle, discernible in autumn by its unusual pink fruit. A small reedbed, a stream and marshes combine to make this a near perfect wetland site.

The smaller tree-fringed lake to the north is of minimal interest but, being deeper, attracts the odd Great Crested Grebe. Other areas that can be viewed from the footpaths whilst on site are the fields towards the drying beds and arable land at Lynster's Farm.

Hides and seats are strategically positioned around the lake and food is supplied in the winter near the Shell Hide and in the south-eastern corner of the reserve, attracting flocks of passerines. Every conceivable type of next box has been tried and tested over the years and many are visible from the nature trail.

An abundance of invertebrate fauna proliferates with many types of aquatic insects, moths and butterflies. Over 125 different species of wildflowers occur, including Ragged Robin and Spotted Orchid. Also present are 20 species of tree and what must be the largest and most hostile Stinging Nettle beds anywhere. At dusk mammals as diverse as Fox and bats may be seen along with the less common Dormouse.

Access

Maple Lodge is to the east of the village of Maple Cross and can be reached along the A412 Rickmansworth to Denham road or from junction 17 of the M25. If approached from the motorway turn left at the traffic lights opposite The Cross public house. Drive down Maple Lodge Close, parking in the car park by the black barn.

Access onto the site is restricted to members of The Maple Lodge Conservation Society but visits by non-members and groups can be arranged by contacting the Society in advance. (For details of joining the Society or visiting the reserve contact the Amenity and Recreation Officer, Thames Water. See Useful Addresses.)

The entrance to the reserve is opposite the ringing hut and information centre, and keys are required for the gate and the Shell Hide. Toilet and washing facilities are also available. A circular footpath of about 1 mile (1.5 km) takes in all the screen hides, seats and the Shell Hide, although the western side of the lake may be out of bounds during the breeding season to reduce disturbance. Please keep to the footpaths as parts of the reserve are treacherously boggy! When returning the keys to the hut don't forget to fill in the log book on the latest sightings.

Species

Some degree of bias by the author for this county may prevail in the following paragraphs as over a period of 20 years he has accumulated 126 species at this site, many of them during the old sewage farm days.

Nevertheless over 100 species are still recorded annually with an average of 1,500 birds of some 50 species being ringed.

A good cross-section of wildfowl can be seen throughout the year with Mallard, Pochard, Gadwall, Shoveler, Teal and Tufted Duck present most months. Numbers increase in late autumn and winter when the occasional Goldeneye may appear on the clubhouse lake. Cormorants peak on the main lake and feral Greylag and Canada Geese can be seen in surrounding fields. Grey Herons stalk the shallows alongside small numbers of Snipe in the more overgrown patches. Water Rail are more visible now and can often be seen from the Shell Hide. A motley selection of gulls, mainly Black-headed, feed on the surface of the lake along with 50 or more Coot and Moorhen, Check the fields near Lynsters Farm for Lapwing and flocks of Meadow Pipit and Skylark. The feeding site attracts the usual common finches such as Greenfinch, Chaffinch and Linnet as well as Tree Sparrow and a few Brambling. Corn Bunting and Yellowhammer are often noted along the chain-link fence on the southern boundary. A small Siskin flock can usually be found in the vicinity of the Alder/Poplar wood. In winter, many passerines take advantage of the cover to roost, the most obvious being Starlings and thrushes including Redwing and Fieldfare. Buntings roost in the reedbed and Pied Wagtails form sub-roosts before finally settling for the night on the sewage works buildings. This is a good time of day to see a hunting Sparrowhawk taking any stragglers. Oddities have turned up in the past mostly by way of a mist net. Bearded Tits are most likely, along with Stonechat and the occasional Great Grey Shrike, the latter being extremely elusive.

Early spring Chiffchaffs may not be migrants at all as a few winter along the valley, surviving in all but the harshest conditions. Willow Warbler and the common scrub warblers soon move through the reserve in good numbers, with some individuals of each remaining to breed. Whitethroat usually haunt the brambles at the car park and along the southern footpath, while Garden Warbler and Blackcap prefer the more wooded parts of the site. Sedge and Reed Warbler both breed, the latter arriving latest. Yellow Wagtails sometimes alight on the playing field opposite the clubhouse as do the occasional Wheatears. Hirundines filter over the lake and small numbers of Cuckoo and Turtle Dove are noted. Wader passage is now only a shadow of its former self but a trickle of Common and Green Sandpipers still pause on the islands and along the muddier margins. Redshank and Little Ringed Plover occur intermittently as a few pairs still breed along the course of the river where conditions allow. A real gem in springtime is a sighting of the migrant Garganey, the drakes resplendent in their nuptial plumage. Unfortunately they seldom stay for long. Parties of Common Terns noisily pass through Maple Lodge, several pairs breeding in the south of the valley. The Black Tern is far scarcer, May being the most likely month to encounter this most delightful of terns. Resident passerines are well represented with all three species of woodpecker straying on site; the spotted species favour the dead timber in the middle of the lake. Black capped tits will almost certainly turn out to be Willow Tits, and Treecreeper can be heard among the larger trees. A couple of pairs of Spotted Flycatcher usually take up residence in the ivy-covered Alders by the entrance to the reserve.

A typical summer scene from the Shell Hide is of many duckling foraging beside their moulting parents; check thoroughly as Ruddy Duck have recently bred. A Kingfisher may appear on 'its' perch to fish and pose for the camera as warblers continually ferry insects to their nestlings. Swifts and hirundines hawk for winged insects over the lake and a Hobby may race overhead, sending them skywards.

Autumn passage commences in late July with the usual sandpipers and perhaps a Greenshank. A Garganey in eclipse plumage will be more difficult to identify, the 'striped' head markings being a valuable field mark. Many Sylvia warblers are extracted from mist nets hidden in the sallows as Goldfinch flocks muster on clumps of thistles. Grey Wagtails become evident with one or two wintering and a passage of Goldcrest is noted.

Although the main lake with its hides and continued activity is the chief attraction, two favourite areas in which to linger awhile are the feeding site during the winter and the Old Barge pool in summer. The latter spot seems somehow to highlight Nature's ability to correct and redress the balance, when given a fair chance. The crumbling concrete banks are adorned with plant growth and Moorhens rest on the rusting barge surrounded by Sedge and Willow Herb. Warblers sing from tree and bush whilst Kingfisher are regularly seen. Finches and tits pause to drink and a wealth of insect life is present with dragonflies over the water and perhaps a Speckled Wood butterfly patrolling a 'dappled' glade.

Oliver Pike in his book *Through Birdland Byeways* waxed lyrically about 'a corner of Hertfordshire'. His corner was probably in the Tring area; nowadays it is most definitely here, by the old barge.

Calendar

Resident Dabchick, Grey Heron, Canada and Greylag Geese, Mute Swan, Mallard, Gadwall, Shoveler, Pochard, Tufted Duck, Sparrowhawk and Kestrel, Water Rail, Moorhen, Coot, Tawny Owl, Kingfisher, three Woodpeckers, Pied Wagtail, Mistle Thrush, Willow and Long-tailed Tit, Treecreeper, Jay, corvids, common finches and buntings.

December–February Great Crested Grebe, Goldeneye (clubhouse lake), Cormorant, Teal, Lapwing, Meadow Pipit, and Skylark on farmland. Gulls, Stock Dove, Tree Sparrow, Siskin, Redpoll and Brambling, Corn Bunting, roosting birds.

March–May Garganey, Little Ringed Plover and Redshank irregular, Green Sandpiper and Common Tern April. Black Tern possible May, Yellow Wagtail and Wheatear on fields, hirundines, Chiffchaff, Willow Warbler, Blackcap, Garden Warbler, Whitethroat, Sedge and Reed Warbler, Turtle Dove, Cuckoo, Spotted Flycatcher May.

June–July Breeding riparian birds, Swift, possible Hobby and Ruddy Duck.

August–November Waders in August, sandpipers and Greenshank most likely, warbler passage, possible terns, Grey Wagtail, Snipe, ducks increase, winter thrushes arrive, Goldcrest, finch flocks.

STOCKER'S LAKE (Map 44/OS ref.TQ 048 935)

Habitat

Stocker's Lake is a large mature gravel pit with well vegetated islands, just south of Rickmansworth. The lake proper consists of deep water, with, in later summer, a few shallows around some of the stoney islands. Willows and Alders have colonised most of the islands and along the bank on the canal side, where a small damp wood has developed. A marshy patch has evolved nearby that becomes quickly overgrown during the summer with Willow Herb and sedge. The causeway and meadows between Stocker's and Bury Lake are heavily grazed and in the winter become quite boggy. The River Colne is of interest, along with the rank scrub-invaded fields towards the A412. The water cress beds at Springwell are best viewed from the bridge over the Colne. Although strictly speaking not a part of the reserve the wet meadow and fields near Stocker's Farm are always worthwhile checking. At 93 acres (38 ha) Stocker's Lake has Local Nature Reserve status and is also designated a SSSI.

Access

From Rickmansworth take the A412 south-west and turn left after 1 mile (1.5 km) down Springwell Lane at Drayton Ford. Just past the second bridge turn left again and park alongside the River Colne. Follow the circular footpath crossing the canal at Stocker's Lock for views over the meadow and farmland. Alternatively park in Stocker's Farm Road taking care not to block the farmer's driveway.

The lake is owned by the Rickmansworth and Uxbridge Valley Water Company and is leased to the Hertfordshire & Middlesex Trust for Nature Conservation (HTNC). A permit is required; for details apply to the Trust headquarters at Grebe House, St Albans. (See Useful Addresses.)

Species

Annually well over 100 species can be expected at Stocker's Lake, with some 50 species normally breeding. Along with Maple Lodge Nature Reserve it is one of the best sites in the Colne Valley and often turns up a local rarity. National rarities have occurred, such as Night Heron and more recently a Blue-winged Teal.

Winter is the best time of year to scour the collection of wildfowl scattered across the open water. Consisting predominantly of several hundred Coot, Tufted Duck and Mallard; lesser numbers of Pochard, Teal, Shoveler and Gadwall are always present. It is a particularly good site for Goldeneye although Wigeon are less frequently noted as are sawbills. A Stocker's Lake speciality is the Red-crested Pochard with one or two usually arriving in autumn or winter. Some doubt has been cast in the past over their genuineness, but the fact that they appear and disappear at the 'right' time of year suggests that the majority of records probably relate to truly wild migratory birds. Good numbers of the commoner two species of grebe mingle among the ducks with several pairs of each staying to breed. Large numbers of gulls rest on the islands while Cormorants perch in the bushes drying their plumage. Grey Heron are ever present as a small heronry has been established. The adults start nest building as early as February. The wet meadow near the farm attracts a motley array of feral Canada and Greylag Geese as well as small numbers of Teal and Snipe. Lapwing also pause here awhile and there is usually a flock of winter thrushes feeding on the drier parts. The small Alder wood holds a wintering Siskin/Redpoll flock and Treecreeper and Willow Tit are normally evident, perhaps within a flock of commoner tits. Check the nearby marsh for a Water Rail and the paddock at the rear for finches and Tree Sparrows. Sporadic visitors in this season are Bittern and Bearded Tits plus the chance of Water Pipit on the cress beds at Springwell.

The first signs of spring are heralded by Lapwing and Meadow Pipit moving overhead, with perhaps a couple of Shelduck on the open water. They are soon joined by the true summer migrants such as Chiffchaff and Sand Martin, although several of the former sometimes winter along the valley. The sheep-grazed slopes near the farm attract a few Wheatear as the main arrival of common warblers stream onto the reserve. Wagtails along the causeway, among the cattle, picking up insects, consist primarily of Pied and Yellow with the occasional continental White and Blue-headed Wagtail in their midst. A spring passage of waders is not obvious due to the lack of a suitable scrape, however Common Sandpiper do regularly occur on the main lake. The wet meadow, if still damp in spring, is the most likely spot to lure down Little Ringed Plover. They prefer the muddy patches in the middle therefore a telescope is essential to pick them out. It is a pity the meadow is not a part of the reserve because several other 'goodies' have occurred here in the past. Garganey is one and for this reason all small duck are worth scrutiny during passage periods. A steady stream of Common Terns are noted over the lake with occasionally small numbers of Arctic Tern moving through. Black Terns are only rarely noted in the Colne Valley, usually in small numbers at the end of the spring passage period. Displaying Goldeneye linger on sometimes into May, along with a pair or two each of Gadwall and Shoveler who probably breed most years. Resident species should not be ignored; indeed now is an ideal opportunity to hear Lesser and Great Spotted Woodpecker 'drumming' from dead timber out on the main island or along the canal. The Quarry wood across the cut harbours a pair of Sparrowhawk, while Kestrels prefer the more open quarry in which to breed. Kingfishers zip along the canal and across the lake performing their intricate breeding ritual at high speed. Tawny Owl haunt the old big ivy-covered willows and Little Owl can be found on the buildings at Stocker's Farm. A few pairs of late arriving Reed Warblers nest among the phragmites as similar numbers of Turtle Dove seek out the Hawthorn thickets. A pair or two of Spotted Flycatcher are especially noticeable near the reserve entrance, often hunting insects from the paddock fence.

Summer is a season best avoided when the fishing season commences as increased human traffic on Bury Lake and along the canal reduces the likelihood of seeing much. If a visit is planned during this period, early morning is by far the most productive time.

Early autumn brings a few more waders than does spring, with the chance of small numbers of Greenshank and Green Sandpiper attracted to the stoney islands. Wood Sandpiper have occurred in the past on the meadow, especially if it is damp. Whinchats are noted flicking along on open ground, their numbers made up mainly of drab immature birds. Grey Wagtails move in for the winter, calling along the river and canal as Goldcrest filter through the scrub. Meadow Pipit flocks are worthy of attention and could yield a larger dark-legged Water Pipit among them.

Wildfowl numbers increase on the open water with the likelihood of a Pintail for a day or two. The much rarer Ferruginous Duck put in an appearance once at this time of year so it really is worthwhile looking closely at every duck.

Calendar

Resident Dabchick, Great Crested Grebe, Grey Heron, feral geese, Mallard, Tufted Duck, Sparrowhawk, Kestrel, Moorhen, Coot, Tawny and Little Owl, Kingfisher, Great and Lesser Spotted Woodpecker, Willow and Long-tailed Tit, Treecreeper, Redpoll, Reed Bunting.

December–February Cormorant, Bittern possible, Water Rail, Wigeon, Gadwall, Teal, Shoveler, Pochard, Goldeneye, Lapwing, Snipe, gulls, winter thrushes, Siskin, Grey Wagtail, chance of Bearded Tit, Tree Sparrow.

March–May Shelduck, Sand Martin, Wheatear, Chiffchaff, Garganey possible, hirundines, Sylvia warblers, Sedge Warbler, pipits and wagtails, Little Ringed Plover, Common Sandpiper, Common Tern, Cuckoo, Turtle Dove, Reed Warbler.

June–July Breeding riparians, Swift, Spotted Flycatcher, waders in late July.

August–November Greenshank, sandpipers, Yellow Wagtail, Whinchat, possible Water Pipit in November sometimes wintering, ducks increase with chance of Red-crested Pochard and Pintail, finch and tit flocks.

HILFIELD PARK
RESERVOIR

Map 45/OS ref. TQ 155 960

Habitat

The whole site encompasses 195 acres (79 ha) of which 115 acres (46 ha) is open water. The reservoir, completed in 1955, has only one artificial bank on the western side. The other three margins are well vegetated during the summer with a variety of marshland plants including several small patches of reed. A mixture of deciduous and coniferous trees cover much of the adjacent land, along with some areas of long grass.

Although owned by the Colne Valley Water Company, an agreement was established with the Hertfordshire County Council for the creation of a Local Nature Reserve. The HMTNC perform the necessary management and have erected a hide on the southern bank.

The rank growth along the natural margins is ideal for aquatic insects, particularly dragonflies. Common butterflies abound in the long grass and Brown Hare are frequently noted.

Access

Hilfield Park Reservoir is situated just to the east of Watford, north of the A41 Watford by-pass and only 2 miles (3 km) from junction 4 of the M1 motorway. Limited viewing can be obtained from the A41, Dagger Lane to the east and a footpath running alongside nearby Elstree Aerodrome. Access into the site is by permit through the HMTNC and keys are needed for entry via the main gate. Once in, walk up the concrete steps and scan along the sloping bank for waders and wagtails. Keep checking the water for diving duck whilst heading for the hide. A full circuit should only take a couple of hours, eventually leading back to the pumping station.

Species

The reservoir was created a Local Nature Reserve because of its value as a wildfowl refuge in late autumn and winter. As it is a deep water, diving ducks predominate with Tufted Duck the most numerous, usually peaking at 200 in late winter. Pochard, being mainly nocturnal feeders, sleep through the daylight hours, allowing an accurate assessment of their numbers to be made; in this case up to 100. Small numbers of Goldeneye are present, their figures increasing towards spring with a maximum of ten. The most likely sawbill is the Goosander with one or two noted most winters. On the nearby London Reservoirs, Smew are a regular winter visitor but strangely enough are a gross rarity here and should not be expected. Coot number some 200 birds with a few pairs staying to breed amongst the reeds. Grebes include Great Crested whose numbers can reach 200 in late autumn and Dabchick at 30 to 40. The most regular of the 'rare' grebes in recent years has been the Red-necked, with infrequent visits from Slavonian and Black-necked; the latter more likely during autumn passage.

Dabbling ducks peak in late autumn with about 90 Shoveler and 30 Teal scattered along the shallow margins near the hide, where occasionally a Water Rail is noted picking its way through the dead vegetation. Mallard average around 50 with half as many Gadwall among them; the females being particularly difficult to identify at a distance. A gull roost of some 25,000 maximum features, predominantly Black-headed, although the size varies from winter to winter.

As spring approaches, duck numbers quickly decline although parties of Shelduck may be noted moving through. Attention is drawn to passage migrants from warmer climes, the concrete bank being the most likely spot to see the few waders that briefly stop off. Common Sandpiper are the commonest with up to ten on occasions 'teetering' at the water's edge. Little Ringed Plover arrive, some non-breeders remaining through the summer, and small numbers of Redshank and Dunlin appear. Although other waders do crop up, they are so few and far between as to be scarcely worth mentioning. A few Wheatear show along the bank and on the short turf with 20 to 30 Meadow Pipit. Yellow and Pied Wagtail are regular in spring with a couple of pairs of the latter breeding among the buildings; an odd White Wagtail is sometimes found in the flock.

About the middle of April, especially following strong winds, Kittiwake get blown inland with up to ten appearing most years. A more regular passage of Common Tern commences with flocks of 30 sometimes noted during May and the same in the autumn. Arctic Tern arrive, a few at a time, occasionally in flocks of over 50 but tending to be scarcer on the return passage. Black Tern are erratic but annual, being more numerous in autumn when flocks of 20 are not unusual.

Hirundines filter over the reservoir building up to several hundred by the summer, with once a Red-rumped Swallow seen in their midst. Large numbers of Swift 'wheel' and 'tumble' noisily, particularly on balmy evenings when flying insects mass over the water.

The patches of surrounding plantations contain the usual breeding tits, including Coal Tit, Treecreeper, a few Goldcrest and the predatory Jay. Willow Warbler and Blackcap breed, with Chiffchaff and the other Sylvia warblers only present on migration. The small reedbeds hold four to five pairs of Reed Warbler plus two to three couples of the quarrelsome Moorhen. Kestrel and Sparrowhawk are regular hunters with a pair of the former breeding nearby. Woodpeckers are scarce with Great Spotted the most likely. Stock Dove are resident with two to three pairs often breeding on nearby Hilfield Castle.

As summer wears on, a return wader passage is only of note if the water level has receded following a period of drought. A few Greenshank should be fairly obvious, delicately probing the exposed mud, along with several Green Sandpiper, Snipe and the occasional Ruff. Terns move through and duck numbers build up to complete the year's comings and goings.

Hilfield Park Reservoir is notoriously inconsistent for birds, with much of the year being quite dull. However it is worth a visit during April or January at best and, who knows, a White-winged Lark did appear once, in August 1955!

Calendar

Resident Dabchick, Heron, Mallard, Sparrowhawk, Kestrel, Coot, Stock Dove, Great Spotted Woodpecker, tits, Treecreeper, Jay, Pied Wagtail, Mistle Thrush, finches, Reed Bunting.

December–February Grebes, possible Red-necked, Cormorant, Mute Swan, Wigeon scarce, Gadwall, Pochard, Tufted Duck, Goldeneye, sawbills irregular, Goosander most likely, Water Rail, Coot, Lapwing, gull roost, winter thrushes.

March–May Shelduck, from end of March Chiffchaff, Wheatear, Blackcap, early April, Willow Warbler, Meadow Pipit, hirundines, Little Ringed Plover, Dunlin, Common Sandpiper; mid-April, Common and Arctic Tern, Kittiwake, Yellow Wagtail, White Wagtail occasionally with Pied; May, Black Tern, Reed Warbler, Swift.

June–July Breeding passerines, large Swift and hirundine flocks, returning waders end of July.

August–November Waders if water level low, tern passage, chance of Black-necked Grebe, duck and grebes peak, Grey Wagtail.

LEMSFORD SPRINGS   Map 46/OS ref. TL 223 123

Habitat

Lemsford Springs Nature Reserve was purchased in 1970 by the HMTNC when it was a derelict water cress bed. Covering only 9.27 acres (3.7 ha) it is perhaps a microscopic site in size but high in the quality of fauna and flora it supports. In fact it is a supreme example of how correct management can yield rich rewards for both wildlife and naturalist alike.

The River Lea runs south-east bisecting a series of lagoons and marshes, where once water cress was cultivated. The lagoons are fed by natural springs bubbling out of the chalk supporting some 50 species of Mollusca in the unpolluted waters. A rich flora proliferates in the marsh, sustaining such local rarities as the Star-of-Bethlehem and Golden Saxifrage. Trees include pollarded willows bordering the Lea, a small coppiced wood and peripheral hedgerows; one of which contains 17 species of tree and is of particular ecological value to the reserve. Patches of grassland and scrub complete the diversity of habitats.

The combination of water and wood encourages many insects including the rare Butterbur Moth. Mammals regularly noted are Water Vole and Stoat with the occasional Fox passing through.

Access

The Springs are situated west of Welwyn Garden City and the A1(M) just off the roundabout leading to Lemsford Village. Access is for members of the HMTNC and a key is required, obtainable from the Honorary Warden who lives nearby. Non-members can obtain entry via special arrangement with the Warden after initially contacting the HMTNC headquarters. (See Useful Addresses.)

Once inside, follow the track south, past the toilet and huts, to the hide for views across the main lagoon. Alternatively cross over Meadow Bridge to explore the marsh and Willow Wood. Most birds are best viewed from the hide (this causes less disturbance too), some approaching close enough to allow photography.

Species

Lemsford Springs play host to possibly the highest concentration of wintering Green Sandpiper in Britain and since 1982 has been the subject of a special study. At least 25 birds have been colour ringed and anyone seeing one of these birds is requested to fill in a form located in the hide. Present from late summer to spring, their numbers peak during hard winter weather and passage periods, when as many as 20 can be on show at once. Excellent views are obtainable from the hide as they feed completely at ease only a few yards away. Water Rail can also be seen from the hide, occasionally out in the open but retiring into thick cover when alarmed; five or six are on site most winters. The muddy edges attract up to 30 Snipe with perhaps half a dozen Jack Snipe amongst them. Both are extremely elusive birds when on the ground but here the opportunity exists for a detailed study of their cryptic plumage and secretive habits. A few Lapwing may probe the alluvial silt alongside a solitary Grey Heron with a scattering of Teal and Mallard dabbling in the shallows. The sharp piercing call of the Grey Wagtail is regularly

Green Sandpipers

heard, mixed in with the flatter note of Pied Wagtail. On occasions the former have bred but more usually is an autumn and winter visitor.

Breeding residents include a pair of Kingfisher which have a strategically-placed perch just outside the hide to entice them within camera range! Small numbers of Mallard, Moorhen and Reed Bunting are typical riparian breeders seen daily in all seasons. The scattered timber attracts Willow and Long-tailed Tit with sporadic roving flocks of the latter during the colder months. Woodpeckers sometimes stray from nearby Brocket Park, Great Spotted being the most likely. A pair of Stock Dove occasionally take up residence in a purpose built nest box in a pollarded poplar tree opposite the hide. Other parkland strays noted at times are Jay and Treecreeper.

Hirundines are the most obvious spring migrants passing low over the marsh to feed on flying insects. Most of the common warblers are recorded on passage with a few pairs of Sedge Warbler and Blackcap breeding.

Night Heron is the only national rarity to have appeared but more interesting is the recent occurrence of the European race of Dipper.

Lemsford Springs is a fascinating little site, as most derelict cress beds usually are, and well worth a visit in winter for riparian specialities with the added bonus of being ideal for photography.

Calendar

Resident Grey Heron, Mallard, Moorhen, Collared Dove, Kingfisher, Spotted Woodpeckers occasionally, Willow Tit, Long-tailed Tit, Pied Wagtail, Reed Bunting.

December–February Dabchick on river, Teal, Water Rail, Lapwing, Snipe, Jack Snipe, Green Sandpiper, Goldcrest, Grey Wagtail, chance of Dipper.

March–May Chiffchaff end March, Blackcap, Willow Warbler, Sedge Warbler, hirundines, occasional Common Sandpiper end April.

June–July Riparian breeders.

August–November Returning Green Sandpiper from August, Snipe, Water Rail, Grey Wagtail from September onwards.

LEE VALLEY GRAVEL PITS Map 47

Stretching from Ware in the north to Tottenham in the south, the Lee Valley Gravel Pits straddle the Hertfordshire and Essex county boundaries, before finishing in the London metropolitan area. The lower Lee Valley, south of Bowyer's Gravel Pit, is not included in this account as it lies completely outside the county. The main Hertfordshire sites are given full coverage with passing references to adjacent good sites in Essex.

The gravel deposits of the valley, which were left behind by retreating ice at the end of the last Ice Age, have been extensively exploited, drastically changing the landscape from one of predominantly wet meadows and marshes to many irregular-shaped lakes and large reservoirs nearer London. Small marshes and meadows do still exist, such as the RSPB reserve at Rye House and the meadows at Rye Meads, but are few and far between. The more barren pits still being worked (mainly in Essex around Nazeing) lure down some passage waders especially if a low spit or island is retained, but most simply pass overhead. Some workings have even been returned to arable farmland where they attract birds such as gulls, Canada Goose and Lapwing in the winter. Woodland is scarce although the more established pits do have patches of mature trees, typically willows and Alder, encouraging typical water-tolerant passerines. Peripheral scrub growth bordering the lakes harbours breeding warblers and, in winter, finches and buntings feed on weed seeds. The lagoons at Rye Meads Sewage Works are good for wintering duck and passage migrants and are extensively studied by a ringing group. Finally, the River Lee itself is of interest along with its Navigation, flood channels and streams giving rise to luxuriant plant growth and banks suitable for riparian breeders.

The Lee Valley Project Group was formed by local naturalists concerned with nature conservation in the Lee Valley and who considered that the wildlife should be recorded as an entity. It was envisaged that the recording would form a useful means to monitor the status of wildlife within the valley and the changes effected by development. This would allow the group to advise local authorities, including the Park Authority, on proposed developments likely to affect local wildlife. A report *Birds in the Lee Valley* is produced annually and is available at the RSPB Rye House Marsh Reserve or the Rye Meads Ringing Group hut.

The Lee Valley Regional Park Authority administers a number of pits and walks in the valley for general recreational purposes with much emphasis on wildlife conservation. For further information apply to the Park Authority. (See Useful Addresses.)

As we found earlier with the Colne Valley sites – with which there is much in common – the River Lee sites are too diverse to detail completely. So, we choose for further investigation, Cheshunt Gravel Pits and the Rye Meads area. (In Additional Sites, at the end of this section of the book, we also look at Amwell Gravel Pit and Broxbourne Gravel Pits.)

CHESHUNT GRAVEL PITS (Map 48/OS ref. TL 370 030)

Habitat
Cheshunt Gravel Pits consist of two areas of water known as North Met. and Seventy Acres, with the River Lee Navigation flowing between them. The North Met. is more open, attracting good numbers of winter wildfowl while Seventy Acres is dotted with small, mainly overgrown, islands and is a haven for breeding birds during the summer. A small Willow wood to the north is attractive with plenty more Willow and Alder scattered along the river and around the lakeside margins. Patches of scrub and briars grow on the drier parts with more luxuriant plant growth such as Willow Herb and nettle flourishing nearer water.

Access
Being a part of the Lee Valley Regional Park, access is fairly unrestricted with plenty of well signed tracks surrounding both lakes. For access to the car park at Seventy Acre pit turn off Holyfield Road at Fishers Green and drive down the lane and over the stream.

Alternatively, from Cheshunt High Street take Cadmore Lane, opposite the Woolpack public house, and park at the end of the road near the railway line. The nearest railway station is Cheshunt at the end of Windmill Lane, which is only five minutes walk away from the site via Turnford Marsh pit.

Common Tern

Species

Being one of the older pits in the valley the site has had time to develop and diversify, resulting in an area that is attractive to a great number of bird species. Spring passage is the best time of year as the summer migrants mingle with the last of the wintering wildfowl making a possible check list of 80 species for a morning's birdwatching.

Ducks are present in all seasons with the autumn/winter period witnessing a peak of Mallard, Tufted Duck, Pochard, Shoveler and Gadwall; the latter sometimes numbering over 100, making Cheshunt one of the region's strongholds for this species. The odd Goosander or Goldeneye dive for food alongside increasing numbers of Cormorant and many gulls, mainly Black-headed, rest on the surface. Seasonal visits from Bittern and Great Grey Shrike are logged most years while the more regular Water Rail can be found skulking around Seventy Acres or among the reeds bordering the wood. Up to ten may winter with the occasional pair staying to breed. Finches abound with variable numbers of Tree Sparrow and Brambling seeking out dead weed seeds or spilled grain alongside their more numerous cousins such as Chaffinch, Greenfinch and Linnet. The smaller and more arboreal Siskins and Redpolls haunt the lakeside Alders.

Early spring brings a few passage Shelduck mainly on North Met. pit with Sand Martin skimming the surface and Chiffchaff calling from the Willow tops. The farmland near the Electricity Station attracts small numbers of Wheatear, as well as Lapwing to pause a while beside the more sedentary Red-legged Partridge. Most waders pass high overhead although Little Ringed Plover and Common Sandpiper will settle on some of the more stoney islands on Seventy Acres.

The latter half of April is generally the peak migration period across the region and the Lee Valley is no exception. This is an exciting time at Cheshunt Gravel Pits as Common Terns stream up the river course along with the main arrival of hirundines and warblers. Yellow and Pied Wagtails and Meadow Pipits can be heard and seen on the more open areas west of the North Met. pit accompanied by a handful of Cuckoos whose repetitive call rings out across the entire site. Late spring migrants are Turtle Dove and Spotted Flycatcher with perhaps the chance of a Hobby dashing through. Now is an excellent time to study the warbler tribe as the combination of minimal plant growth and much territorial singing allows ideal and sometimes close viewing. The western side of Seventy Acres can at a pinch yield eight species of warbler to the patient observer. Reed and Sedge Warbler occur along the river with Willow Warbler and Chiffchaff in the mature stands of timber. Blackcap and Garden Warbler favour the salix scrub while Whitethroat prefer the drier bramble patches. Lesser Whitethroat are often noted 'rattling' from the more isolated thickets along the summit of the river bank. A possible ninth species could be a Grasshopper Warbler which is occasionally heard 'reeling' from thick cover, although that is stretching one's luck a little.

Summer is a time of high activity for adult birds but, due to the lushness of the plant growth, much goes on unseen. Common Terns are far more visible fishing over the North Met. pit among hordes of Swifts attracted to the legions of flying insects. The season drifts by as the return wader passage commences towards the end of July.

Autumn is a time of plenty with an abundant food supply for all. Wildfowl numbers increase and the odd Pintail puts in an appearance.

Grey Wagtails call along the stream and Kingfisher numbers are at their peak; the inexperienced juveniles having only a short while to perfect their hunting technique before the winter cruelly weeds out the weaklings. The now silent warblers exit south in contrast to the arrival of the first winter thrushes who noisily chatter overhead.

Calendar

Resident Dabchick, Great Crested Grebe, Mute Swan, Grey Heron, Mallard, Tufted Duck, Sparrowhawk, Kestrel, Moorhen, Coot, Kingfisher, Spotted Woodpeckers, Pied Wagtail, Willow and Long-tailed Tits, Treecreeper, finches and buntings, Cetti's Warbler possible.

December–February Wintering ducks including Gadwall, Goldeneye and odd Goosander, gulls, Cormorant, Tree Sparrow and Brambling. Siskin and Redpoll, occasional Great Grey Shrike and Bittern, Water Rail.

March–May End March Shelduck, Sand Martin, Chiffchaff, Wheatear. April for Little Ringed Plover, Common Sandpiper, warblers, wagtails, hirundines, Cuckoo, Meadow Pipit, Common Tern, large waders overhead. Swift, Turtle Dove, Spotted Flycatcher.

June–July Breeding riparian birds, chance of Hobby, returning waders end of July.

August–November Duck numbers increase, Pintail in November. Finch flocks, warblers depart, Whinchat, Grey Wagtail, winter thrushes from October, Goldcrest.

Rye Meads Area (Map 49/OS TL 388 100)

Habitat

Situated east of Hoddesdon the Rye Meads complex can be split into two administrative sites. At Rye House Marsh the RSPB has a small 15 acres (6 ha) reserve that comprises a number of wetland micro habitats. The south scrapes are both overlooked by hides where open shallows and mud are bordered by willow and Poplar scrub, Alder, and typical marshland vegetation such as sedge and reed. The creation of this area in front of the hide allows the maximum number of bird species to be seen with minimal disturbance to them. Further north are a small flood meadow, sections of glyceria marsh and reed fen and the North Hide that looks across a small shallow lagoon with willow scrub at the rear. A ditch separates the reserve from the sewage works' lagoons to the east and the River Lee passes down the western perimeter.

Rye Meads Sewage Treatment works owned by Thames Water comprises mainly the North Lagoons and the South Lagoons, either side of the Toll Road. The tree-fringed North Lagoons are provided with rafts for breeding Common Tern and two hides, supplied by the RSPB, that afford ample viewing over the two larger pools. The strictly private grazed meadows, further east, along with clumps of phragmites, bramble patches and scrub are attractive but can only be partially viewed from the road. South of the Toll Road are the South Lagoons, eight roughly symmetrical lagoons with surrounding drains and the ringing hut. The sewage works buildings are out of bounds.

Plant life includes the scarce Marsh Marigold, Comfrey, Bedstraw and the delicate pink Ragged Robin. Water Vole and Shrew are present and the dykes hold many species of coarse fish as well as Eels and Freshwater Crayfish.

Access

For Rye House Marsh take the Rye Road, east of Hoddesdon, towards the railway station, over the river bridge and turn left into the reserve car park. If it is full, parking is available on the opposite side of the road along with toilet facilities. British Rail's Eastern Region line at Rye House Station is within easy walking distance of the reserve. The Marsh is only open to the public at weekends between 10.00 a.m. and 4.00 p.m. as during the week field courses in environmental studies, and educational visits by schools, are in progress. The information centre incorporates a classroom and display area from which experienced staff conduct classes from primary to university level. The southern hides are accessible directly from the car park and one has a section for wheelchair users. For the northern and sewage lagoon hides a key is required from reception to gain entry via a gate along the Toll Road.

Access onto the remainder of the complex is severely restricted and is through the Rye Meads Ringing Group. Keen birdwatchers interested in joining should contact the secretary of the group whose address is in the annual ringing report, which is available at the RSPB information centre or the ringing hut. The hut is usually manned at the weekends, when permission must be sought to look round the South Lagoons.

Species

Rye Meads is perhaps best known ornithologically as the site of the county's first recorded nesting of Cetti's Warbler in 1978. Although young were not actually reared that year they were considered to be successful the following summer as juveniles were ringed in the autumn, after a season when three males held territories. They seemed to be establishing themselves fairly well in the ditches and willow scrub over the site until the intense cold spell in 1981 wiped out the entire population. They are now recorded only sporadically but no doubt their explosive song will be heard more regularly in future as this non-migratory warbler continues to expand its range northwards.

More typically however is the importance of the complex in offering safe sanctuary to migrant birds that pass along the valley during spring and autumn and a variety of habitats for the 50 or so species that regularly breed.

Winter is possibly the best season to visit the marsh at Rye House where close views of both species of snipe probing the mud for worms are almost guaranteed. Good numbers of Teal, 30 to 40, dabble the shallows while Water Rail slink around the margins alongside the more numerous Moorhen. A couple of Water Pipit are often present here or on the Meads but are often difficult to see. A slight spring passage is of note when the males exhibit a pinkish flush on the breast and are generally more active. Solitary Grey Herons are scattered over the site and most winters a Bittern takes up residence in the reedbeds. Parties of Bearded Tit are often associated with the Bittern's habitat but are mercifully easier to locate. Numbers vary with five to ten being about normal, most sporting silver leg rings as they are easy 'prey' for ringers and are much studied. Mixed flocks of Siskin and Redpoll seek out the waterlogged Alders as at dusk large numbers of Corn, Yellow and Reed Buntings swarm in to roost in the reedswamp and scrub. They are joined by winter thrushes, finches and Meadow Pipits on the meadows. A visit to the North Lagoon hides will be rewarded by 20 to 30 Cormorant loafing on the tern rafts and the inevitable Black-headed Gulls on the water. The deep water attracts many diving duck with several hundred Tufted the most abundant. Lesser numbers of Pochard, about 100, are joined by up to 500 Coot and single figures of the two common grebes. Sawbills are quite rare and even Goldeneye are unusual. Dabbling ducks are represented by 50 or so Shoveler, with the occasional pair staying to breed, alongside good numbers of Mallard and a sprinkling of Gadwall. Winter geese records normally refer to the Canada Goose 'honking' overhead in loose, noisy formation with the odd sightings of 'genuine' grey geese a rarity. The meadows sometimes entice a roving Short-eared Owl to hunt awhile in the short daylight hours but beware of falling into the trap that all diurnal hunting owls at this time of year are of this species; Long-eared do occasionally crop up.

Spring passage sees a variety of migrants moving north along the valley with a few Green Sandpiper stopping at Rye House Marsh and Common Sandpiper flitting over the lagoons.

Small numbers of Little Ringed Plover are noted every spring and throughout the summer as they breed on adjacent gravel pits. Sporadic visits of larger waders such as godwits and Curlew relate to birds moving overhead calling. Chiffchaff and Willow Warbler are soon filtering through the site searching for insects which are attracted to the sweet smelling 'Pussy Willow' catkins. Sedge Warbler also arrive early along with Blackcap. Out on the lagoons Common Tern start arriving, noisily wheeling overhead and plunge-diving for small fish. They spend many hours preening and resting after their long migration and as many as 40 pairs breed here raising young on the specially prepared rafts where they enjoy a high fledgling success rate. Other terns such as Black or Arctic are rarely noted at Rye Meads. Early Sand Martins are soon joined by other hirundines skimming over the surface of the water as small numbers of Yellow Wagtail and Wheatear move through the meadows. Stock Dove occur here along with one or two Whinchat flicking along the fence-posts. The main arrival of warblers takes place at the end of April with good numbers of Sylvia warblers spread throughout the site. Reed Warblers arrive late accompanied by a handful of Cuckoo and Grasshopper Warbler, the latter 'reeling' from the reedswamp or amongst brambles on the meads. Spotted Flycatchers nest in the ivy-covered trees at Rye House Marsh and increasing numbers of Turtle Dove summer, reflecting the improving habitat of willow scrub and mature bushes preferred by this species.

The summer scene is typified by hundreds of Swifts and hirundines swirling over the complex with the occasional appearance of a Hobby enough to scatter them skywards. Finches nesting in surrounding scrub include Bullfinch, Greenfinch, Chaffinch, Goldfinch, Linnet and Redpoll. The North Lagoons are busy, as adult Common Terns ferry in fish for their voracious youngsters in contrast to the ducklings of Mallard, Tufted Duck and Coot who obediently follow their parents around the margins, hurriedly scurrying for cover when danger threatens. Kingfisher young disperse in late summer and become more apparent often frequenting the area in front of the south hides. Returning waders seek out any muddy patches with the usual sandpipers and Greenshank most likely; calidrids such as Dunlin or Little Stint are irregular. Single Garganey and Pintail in eclipse plumage are almost annual autumn visitors to the lagoons as duck numbers build up for the winter. A passage of Sylvia warblers is noted by the ringers in the willow scrub as migrant Skylark and Meadow Pipits pass overhead, with a good sized flock of Yellow Wagtail congregating amongst the shorter sward. Finches and buntings seem to be everywhere, compensating somewhat for the warblers who surreptitiously depart south. The year turns full circle with the arrival of Grey Wagtail and Green Sandpiper to the marsh with the chance of a Stonechat on the meads.

With the intensive amount of watching and netting at the complex over the last 20 years many county, and a few national, rarities (e.g. Squacco Heron and Little Bunting) have occurred as a check list of over 200 species has been amassed. The most important point to bear in mind when visiting this site is timing. Only visit when Rye House Reserve is open as keys and permits are required at all times and viewing from the Toll Road is most unsatisfactory. The keen birders wishing to develop their skills and contribute to ornithology would do well to join the Rye Meads Ringing Group (see Useful Addresses) which operates one of the most dynamic inland ringing stations in the country.

Calendar

Resident Great Crested and Little Grebe, Mute Swan, Heron, Mallard, Tufted Duck, Kestrel, Moorhen, Coot, Kingfisher (increase in July and August), three woodpeckers sporadic, Pied Wagtail (increase in winter), Cetti's Warbler (in the future?), Tree Sparrow (declining), finches and buntings.

December–February Cormorant, Bittern irregular, Wigeon occasional, Pochard, Gadwall, Tufted Duck, Teal on marsh, Shoveler, sawbills rare, Water Rail from October, Lapwing, Snipe and Jack Snipe, Woodcock occasional, Green Sandpiper, gulls, Short-eared Owl irregular, Meadow Pipit, sometimes Water Pipit, Grey Wagtail, Stonechat irregular, winter thrushes, Chiffchaff a few, Bearded Tit regular, Siskin and Redpoll, bunting roost in reedbeds and scrub.

March–May End March Chiffchaff, Wheatear, Sand Martin. April for Willow Warbler, Sylvia warblers, hirundines, Stock Dove, Yellow Wagtail, Sedge Warbler, Common Tern, Grasshopper Warbler, Little-Ringed Plover, Common and Green Sandpiper, Cuckoo. From May, Whinchat, Reed Warbler, Turtle Dove, Spotted Flycatcher.

June–July Hobby, Swift, breeding in full swing.

August–November Some wader passage, sandpipers and Greenshank, Whinchat, Yellow Wagtail, Sylvia warbler passage August, Garganey and Pintail November occasional, duck numbers increase, Skylark, Goldcrest, thrushes, Grey Wagtail.

NORTHAW
GREAT WOOD

Map 50/OS ref. TL 285 045

Habitat

At 400 acres (162 ha) Northaw Great Wood is a remnant of the extensive forests that centuries ago covered much of Hertfordshire. Although most of the wood was clear-felled before the Second World War, much replanting and management has taken place, making The Great Wood one of the finest in the region for birds.

A good selection of deciduous trees are found with Oak, Beech, Hornbeam, Birch and Ash predominating. Each species produces a rich harvest of seeds and supports the vital diversity of insect life necessary to maintain a varied breeding bird population. There are open glades carpeted with Bluebells during the spring, 30 acres (12 ha) of coppiced Hornbeam and Chestnut, a Beech stand, Blackthorn thickets, a row of pollarded Lime, Ash alongside the brook and, above all, Oak. Amongst this feast of trees is a flora typically associated with an ancient woodland. Both Badger and Fox find safe refuge here along with Muntjac Deer.

Declared a SSSI in 1953 and a Country Park in 1968, Northaw Great Wood is managed by a committee composed of local councillors and specialists nominated by the NCC and the HMTNC.

Access

Situated to the north-west of Cuffley, The Great Wood is reached along The Ridgeway or B157 which runs east to west between Cuffley and Brookman's Park. The road runs alongside the southern perimeter of the wood with signposts to the car park towards the western end. A small parking fee is payable to the Warden either at the gate or near the cottage. Organisations wishing to visit as a party are requested to apply in advance to the Welwyn Hatfield District Council. (See Useful Addresses.)

An area of 290 acres (117 ha) is open to the public. Woodlands to the north of Cuffley Brook and to the west of Boundary Banks are private property. These, together with the school camp, are not open to the public.

Within the wood there are three way-marked paths of various lengths. These are: Yellow 2.5 miles (4 km), Blue 1.25 miles (2.1 km), Red 0.75 mile (1.1 km). Walks and paths are not rights of way and it is occasionally necessary to reroute them to prevent damage or disturbance to wildlife.

Species

In winter, woodland birdwatching is a case of finding a flock and staying with it. Tits make up the nucleus of these flocks along with Goldcrest, Treecreeper, Nuthatch and the odd Lesser Spotted Woodpecker. Their incessant contact calls aid their location throughout the wood. Great Spotted and Green Woodpecker range widely at this time of year, some leaving altogether to feed on bird tables in nearby suburban gardens. Goldfinches flock together with immigrant Siskin and Redpoll to feed on the plentiful supply of Birch seed. Chaffinch and Brambling hunt out the Beech, working their way through the litter in search of mast, the Brambling quite unobtrusive until they fly up into the branches flashing a white rump. Hawfinch are slightly easier to see in winter, especially in the vicinity of Hornbeam; check out Cuffley Brook as they often come down to drink using the same spot regularly.

On occasions, raptors rare to the region have strayed from their western strongholds with Buzzard being the most likely and once recently a Red Kite, although this is exceptional.

Due to a continuing planned management programme, The Great Wood is in a class of its own in the springtime, meeting the various habitat requirements for the specialised summer visitors. Small numbers of Redstart breed most years preferring the more mature Oak where suitable nesting holes can be found. The song of the male is distinctive enough, being similar to a Robin but richer, and is delivered from a concealed perch in the canopy. By late spring, with the foliage fully out, they become increasingly difficult to locate so an early visit is advisable for good views, towards the end of April to beginning of May being best.

The Birch usually hold a couple of pairs of Wood Warbler as they prefer woodland with little secondary growth. The males' song is a sheer delight, a series of far carrying 'pieu pieu' notes, not unlike that of a Willow Tit, followed by a shimmering trill. Wood Warbler are reasonably easy to see amongst the airy Birch, as they often sing from the lower branches. Tree Pipit can be seen singing from exposed song-posts in the numerous glades and later on in spring Spotted Flycatcher sally forth from similar perches in pursuit of insects.

Probably the most interesting part of the wood is The Coppice, with the Nightingale being the star performer. Their powerful song is delivered from within these man-made thickets, especially during the early morning. Nightingale numbers fluctuate annually as a consequence of being a long distance migrant and therefore they can never be guaranteed every year. The Coppice, being open and allowing good light, is an excellent spot to sit down and watch the common breeders going about their business. Nuthatch, Treecreeper, tits and warblers will all show eventually and a hunting Sparrowhawk is also likely. Keep a wary ear open for any flutey sounding Blackbirds as Golden Oriole are occasionally noted, probably on passage to their East Anglian breeding grounds. Tawny Owl abound in The Great Wood and about May their young are often found on the woodland floor by the many ramblers. The best thing to do is leave well alone as the parent birds will continue to feed their pitiful looking offspring for several months after fledging. Woodcock and Grasshopper Warbler, both active at dawn and dusk, are present in varying numbers, the former regularly seen 'roding' over the clearings; the latter, an occasional passage migrant, sometimes staying on to breed in small numbers.

The smaller passerines have to be very alert during the breeding season as Jackdaw and Jay prey heavily on any unguarded nest. Nevertheless, come the end of the summer there always seem to be large numbers of juveniles hunting the abundant supply of insects.

The Great Wood is most productive in April and May when a dawn visit should easily reward the patient observer with over 40 species. Indeed, an early morning trip is strongly advised, as later on disturbance from the dog-walking public shatters the tranquillity of the whole wood. Any birdwatcher with the slightest 'feel' for a wood will find themselves returning to this superb site time and time again and probably speculate why there are not many more like it left.

Calendar

Resident Kestrel, Sparrowhawk, Woodcock, Tawny Owl, Stock Dove, Green, Great Spotted and Lesser Spotted Woodpecker, Mistle Thrush, Goldcrest, Long-tailed Tit, Marsh and Willow Tit, Nuthatch, Treecreeper, Jay, Magpie, Jackdaw, Redpoll, Bullfinch, Hawfinch.

December–January Increase in Woodcock, Siskin, Brambling, tit flocks.

March–May Turtle Dove, Cuckoo, Tree Pipit, Nightingale, Redstart, Grasshopper Warbler (occasional), Lesser Whitethroat, Garden Warbler, Blackcap, Wood Warbler, Chiffchaff, Willow Warbler, Spotted Fly-catcher.

June–July A quiet period.

August–November Juveniles finding their way around, warblers leave, Starlings move in to roost at dusk.

OUGHTON HEAD
COMMON
Map 51/OS ref. TL 168 303

Habitat
Oughton Head Common is something of a misnomer as the word common usually conjures up images of a dry grassy area once used for grazing stock. Dry it most certainly is not, although cattle were once grazed here by the Hitchin 'commoners' from medieval times through to the First World War. At 15 acres (6 ha) Oughton Head Common is ideal for a morning's birdwatching, although with so much of interest to be found a full day could easily be spent here.

The Alder/Willow woodland to the north of the River Oughton is managed by the HMNTC as an Educational Nature Reserve. Keeping the Sycamore under control is one of the main management problems along with clearing some of the undergrowth to allow bog plants to flourish. The River Oughton bubbles out of the chalk to the West of the site and meanders across the Common creating its own unique habitat. The water is sparklingly clear and well oxygenated supporting a wealth of aquatic insect life and fish. Along the banks in the summer plant growth is thick and luxuriant. The Common proper, south of the river, is a mixture of marshy ground with small reedbeds and willows, rank Tussock Sedge, Hawthorn scrub, a Beech stand and thick hedgerows. The paddock and small wood near the mill are also of interest.

Conditions are ripe for a rich marsh flora and insect population, including many species of dragonfly and damselfly. Mammals to look out for along the river include both Water Shrew and Water Vole, with Muntjac Deer in the woodland.

Access
Take the A600 north out of Hitchin heading towards Ickleford. Turn left at the Angler's Reply Inn down Red Hill Lane. Park at the end of the lane and a narrow track will bring you out on the south side of the Common near the Beech stand.

Alternatively, from Ickleford head west along the old Icknield Way, or West Mill Lane. Turn off at West Mill Farm, where only limited parking is available, so care must be taken not to restrict access to the farm. Continue on foot down the lane, which is also a public footpath, through the Mill yard, over the river and turn right towards the Common.

Access to the woodland north of the river is by permit from the aforementioned HMNTC and is subject to seasonal variation. The Common proper has a footpath around the perimeter allowing good views across the whole site. A track also runs along the south side of the river to the Springs and then heads back east across farmland, eventually meeting Red Hill Lane.

Species
Early morning visits nearly always pay dividends. In the winter this is the best time of day to find a Grey Heron stalking the marsh or river's edge. Teal are present in small numbers, 'springing' out of the many boggy patches, along with Snipe who when flushed zig-zag and tower away out

190

of sight. A few of the smaller Jack Snipe are occasionally here, but often stay hidden until almost trodden on. They are usually silent, only flying a short distance before disappearing into thick cover making any plumage detail difficult to discern. Water Rail are sometimes seen crossing open mud between reed patches or amongst rank grass, although they are more likely to be heard. The marshy area to the north-east is the best spot to look for them. Winter thrushes invade the scrub at this time of year in search of berries of Hawthorn, Sloe, Guelder Rose and, later on, Ivy. The familiar resident thrushes also join in the harvest with the larger Mistle Thrush being particularly aggressive, sometimes defending a favourite bush against all comers. Both Long-eared and Short-eared Owl have been recorded in the winter, the latter easiest to see as they hunt in the daylight hours, but neither are regular. Tawny Owl are resident and are heard reasonably often, especially in late winter. Sometimes the odd bird can be found roosting in the woodland amongst the Ivy-covered willows. A large mixed flock containing Siskin, Redpoll and Goldfinch winters on the Common feeding on the riverside Alders, their flight notes a valuable locational aid. Redpoll numbers have steadily increased over recent years and consequently birds are present in all months with a few pairs breeding.

A feature of recent winters has been the presence of a Great Grey Shrike. They are quite difficult birds to find at the best of times but here on Oughton Head, with much human disturbance in evidence, they are even more so. Constant scanning of the scrub top is the only answer, plus a good deal of patience and luck. A bright, calm morning is best, particularly towards the end of the winter period when they become more active prior to migration.

Common passerines are plentiful on the Common, forming a staple part of the diet of the Shrike. Prey is impaled on thorns to form larders and they are worth looking out for. The other rarity at this time of year is the occasional visit of a Bittern; however, disturbance on a site of this size results in a disappearing act similar to that of Grey Heron, unless the weather is extreme in which case the unfrozen river will be an obvious attraction.

The Chiffchaff is the first spring visitor, calling frantically from the larger trees around the farm and along the river. Most are just passing through but several pairs stay on to breed in the wood. Blackcap and Willow Warbler move through in good numbers in early spring with many pairs of each staying to breed. In fact the Common is superb for warblers, with hordes of insects to feed upon and plenty of nesting sites amongst the rank growth. Sedge Warbler seem to be song-flighting everywhere and are probably the most numerous warbler. Anyone interested in photography will find them very obliging as they often sing close to the footpath near the reedbed. Here a few pairs of Reed Warbler linger on but tend to be difficult to find unless singing. Even scarcer is the Grasshopper Warbler, now only an occasional passage visitor whereas once breeding regularly. The scrub-loving Garden Warbler and Lesser Whitethroat generally inhabit the drier part of the Common and are quite plentiful, with Whitethroat frequenting the surrounding hedgerows.

Cuckoo and Turtle Dove both breed, the former being most vociferous on arrival, the latter 'purring' anxiously from thick cover. Hirundines migrate over the Common with Swallow breeding in the farm buildings. On arrival from Africa they spend long hours preening and dipping down

Willow Tit

to drink and bathe in the Oughton. Raptors that have survived the winter are indeed the fittest and ablest; Sparrowhawk hunt the cover and Kestrel hover over the grass searching for small mammals. Sometimes a Hobby makes an appearance, usually towards dusk, to hawk the larger flying insects or dash after a Swallow. Resident passerines breed everywhere, intricately marking out their territories and singing furiously to defend them. Reed Bunting breed in the marsh, Yellowhammer in the scrub, Corn Bunting sing from the hedgerows with Skylark overhead and finches nest in any available bush or thicket. The wood holds the commoner tits, Treecreeper and a high concentration of the latest arriving summer visitor, the Spotted Flycatcher. They are quite obvious along the wooded riverbank, and around the Mill yard paddock where Ivy-covered trees provide ideal nest sites. The two Spotted Woodpeckers also inhabit the wood with Great Spotted more numerous than Lesser Spotted.

As summer passes and the flycatcher returns south, Grey Wagtail can be seen along the river often staying through the winter with occasionally a pair breeding the following spring. Kingfisher are active in early autumn as the adults chase away their offspring to establish a winter territory. Listen out for the distinctive flight call along the Oughton. Masses of passerines are on the move now as large flocks of Meadow Pipit, Skylark and Starling stream overhead. Goldcrest start to reappear, warblers and hirundines leave and large numbers of Goldfinch flock together.

Oughton Head Common is a quality site at any time of the year but do visit early morning. To be realistic, there is only a remote chance of a rarity, but Little Bittern and Little Crake have been recorded in the past.

Calendar

Resident Mallard, Sparrowhawk, Kestrel, Pheasant, Moorhen, Little Owl on farmland, Tawny Owl, Kingfisher, Great and Lesser Spotted Wood-peckers, Skylark, Willow Tit, Treecreeper, Jay, Redpoll, buntings.

December–February Bittern occasional, Grey Heron, Teal, Water Rail, Jack Snipe a few, Snipe, Long-eared and Short-eared Owl irregular, winter thrushes, Great Grey Shrike, Brambling, Siskin, Redpoll increase.

March–May Late March Chiffchaff, Blackcap. Early April Willow Warbler, Sedge Warbler, hirundines. Yellow Wagtail overhead with Meadow Pipit. Sylvia warblers, Grasshopper Warbler occasionally, Cuckoo, Turtle Dove, Reed Warbler. Late May, Spotted Flycatcher.

June–July Peak fledging period for warblers. Hunting Hobby.

August–November Warblers depart early, Grey Wagtail, Goldcrest, finch and bunting flocks, tits in wood.

TRING RESERVOIRS   Map 52/OS ref. SP 920 135

Habitat

Situated in the Tring Gap in the Chilterns at about 330 ft (100 m) above sea level, Tring Reservoirs were created in the early-nineteenth century to provide a regular water supply for the Grand Union Canal. In 1955 the four reservoirs were declared a National Nature Reserve under the auspices of the NCC who manage 47 acres (19 ha) of banks and surrounding woodlands. A fifth independent water is being created as part of a purpose-built nature reserve at nearby Pitstone Quarry.

Wilstone is the largest of the reservoirs with open water and concrete banks in the north contrasting with natural well-vegetated margins either side of Drayton Bank. Fresh water from a nearby disused water cress bed feeds a small marsh and wet meadow, harbouring some interesting relics of a once prolific marsh flora. Exposed mud can be found in late summer around the hide and in front of the Poplar wood, attracting much attention from wading birds. Mature woodland, a reedbed, scrub thickets along the abandoned canal and arable farmland make for probably one of the best birdwatching sites in the region.

Tringford is much smaller and shallower, with at times an even more dramatically fluctuating water level. Two screen-hides are positioned strategically amongst natural cover, enabling close studies of wildfowl. A damp wood near the hides is of interest as are the peripheral meadows and paddocks.

Startop's End and Marsworth are bisected by a causeway affording good views over a reedbed at the latter. The former is more open with steep banks and mud in the southern corner by late summer. Adjacent to Marsworth is a sewage farm, the fortunes of which have varied over the years. Recently however conditions have been favourable with a large shallow lagoon attracting waders once more.

Tring Reservoirs is one of the region's premier sites and is rated a SSSI. It is also a pleasant location with views along the Chiltern Scarp, taking in the well-wooded slopes of the Three Hundreds of Aylesbury to the south.

Access

For Wilstone take the B489 off the A41 at Aston Clinton, heading towards Dunstable. Park alongside the reservoir in the car park just south of Wilstone Green.

A more central position for access to all reservoirs can be found along the Cemetary Lane, with ample parking even for coaches. Cross the lane following the track across the field to the stile, turning right for views across the water and reedbed. A circular walk is well marked out taking in the full range of habitats, including the Drayton Bank hide. The wood behind the reedbed is out of bounds to the birdwatcher.

For the other three reservoirs continue along the B489 to Startop's End using the car park by the canal. Once up on the bank, check out the meadows across the canal in spring for Wheatear and wagtails. Turn right towards a farm checking the water along the way. To reach Tringford cross the lane and follow the footpath through the wood to the hides. Once past the second hide turn sharp left by the pumping station where a path eventually leads back to the lane near the flour mill. Return to Marsworth checking the sewage farm on the way by the iron gate.

A point to bear in mind when visiting the reservoirs is that they are extensively fished during the season causing some disturbance, although Sundays are fishermen free. Wildfowling rights are still held by the Rothschild Estates but are rarely exercised and then only on weekdays. While on the reserve you may see one of the Honorary Wardens, recognisable by their NCC badges or armbands. They will be pleased to assist you whenever possible.

Species

Tring Reservoirs are steeped in ornithological history, commencing in the nineteenth century, at the time of the beleaguered Great Crested Grebe population, subsequently studied by Julian Huxley. Other milestones have included England's first record of breeding Black-necked Grebe in 1919 and, in 1938, the first pair of Little Ringed Plover to breed in Britain. Today, neither breed here but both are regular on passage. The reservoirs hold a good range of species the year round and being the only significant stretch of open water for miles about consistently attract migrant waders and seabirds.

The winter scene is dominated by wildfowl with between 100 and 200 Mallard, Shoveler, Pochard and Tufted Duck scattered over all four waters, the majority residing on Wilstone. Lesser numbers of Teal, Gadwall, Goldeneye and Wigeon are also present, along with an increasing Ruddy Duck population. Sawbills are erratic visitors in small numbers most winters. Rare grebes occasionally turn up among Great Crested and Dabchick, although Black-necked Grebe are more likely on Wilstone during autumn passage. The place to be in late afternoon is the causeway overlooking Marsworth reedbed. Wintering Bittern are often at their most active and can sometimes be seen commuting between here and Wilstone reedbed. A party of Bearded Tit may be feeding up till last light, their presence betrayed by sudden bouts of 'pinging'. Water Rail become reasonably visible as they occasionally stray from the safety of the reeds to feed along the margin. As dusk approaches many birds fly in to roost, in particular a sizeable Corn Bunting flock, at times numbering over 100 individuals. Other, much larger roosts are gulls (mainly Black-headed) on Startop's End and Wilstone plus hordes of Starling in surrounding scrub. In early winter the sewage farm, depending on the water level, normally holds a wisp of Snipe, a few solitary Jack Snipe (always difficult to see) and the odd Stonechat, sometimes obligingly perched atop dead vegetation.

Early spring Chiffchaff and Blackcap are usually wintering birds that have found their voices prior to the main arrival in early April. Warblers soon move into their respective habitats as migration peaks towards the end of the month. A Sand Martin hawking low across the water is the first harbinger of spring, usually by mid-March, with larger numbers of House Martin and Swallow arriving a little later. Parties of Yellow Wagtail and Meadow Pipit occur on the grassy tops of the concrete banks at Wilstone and Startop's End, while early waders such as Common Sandpiper and Little Ringed Plover flit around the edges. Any exposed mud could yield a passing Green Sandpiper, Redshank or Dunlin; Tringford or the sewage farm are likely locations. Be alert for larger waders such as Curlew or godwits calling overhead; unfortunately they rarely alight.

Out on the water, duck numbers diminish as the majority disperse to their breeding grounds; however a few Goldeneye often stay late frequently displaying. Small parties of Common Scoter move quickly through (sometimes within the hour) and Shelduck similarly appear. The superb Garganey (the only summer visiting duck) are just about annual, favouring the wooded edges of the smaller reservoirs in both spring and autumn. Startop's End and Wilstone attract varying numbers of Common, Arctic and Black Tern on both passages, with occasionally large flocks of the latter two. Visiting seabirds include a scattering of Little Gull and more recently a Kittiwake or two.

Reed Warbler and Spotted Flycatcher are the last to arrive with substantial colonies of the former at Marsworth and Wilstone reedbeds. Rarities sporadically stopping off in spring have included an exquisite Red-necked Phalarope or a spectacular Osprey, both en-route to Scottish tarns and lochs for the summer.

An early morning visit is vital during this season as most bird activity tends to peter out approaching mid-day. Riparian breeders abound from the abundant Reed Bunting to a small colony of Grey Heron. Unusually they use reedbed nesting sites at Tring with the Heronry at Marsworth containing under ten pairs. Kingfisher can be encountered almost anywhere with the old cress beds and the stream at Startop's End being particularly favourite haunts. Hobby hunt over the whole site hirundines and the larger flying insects, especially at dusk; in late summer several may be seen hunting together over Marsworth, spectacularly pursuing hirundines coming to roost in the reedbed.

Autumn is the time when every birdwatcher hopes the water level is low enough to lure down plenty of passage waders. A steady flow of the commoner sandpipers and plovers is regularly enlivened by parties of Greenshank and sometimes Whimbrel calling overhead. Small numbers of calidrids such as Curlew Sandpiper and Little Stint stop off, briefly, refuelling before continuing to West Africa and beyond. These magical little waders are true birders' birds, testing the watchers' identification skills to the limits, especially if a scarce Temmincks' Stint shows or, rarer still, a transatlantic Pectoral Sandpiper. Nationally rare waders have graced Tring Reservoirs at this time of year with such gems as Solitary Sandpiper and Long-billed Dowitcher, delighting wader enthusiasts.

Migrating Whinchat frequent suitably rusted barbed wire fences on adjoining farmland as a steady stream of wagtails, pipits and Skylark moves through. Check out the overflow corner at Startop's End for warblers in August and the open waters for returning terns.

Late autumn gales occasionally bring in storm-blown pelagics such as skuas and once a Grey Phalarope.

Calendar

Resident Dabchick, Great Crested Grebe, Grey Heron, Canada Goose, Mallard, Tufted Duck, Sparrowhawk, Kestrel, both partridges on farmland, Water Rail increase in winter, Moorhen, Coot, Tawny and Little Owls, Kingfisher, Great Spotted Woodpecker, Skylark, Pied Wagtail, Willow Tit, Treecreeper, finches and buntings including Corn Bunting.

December–February Chance of rare grebe, Cormorant, possible Bittern and Bearded Tit at Marsworth, Wigeon, Pintail and sawbills erratic,

Ruddy Duck

Gadwall, Teal, Pochard, Ruddy Duck, Goldeneye, Lapwing on fields, Snipe and Jack Snipe, Grey Wagtail from November, possible Stonechat, winter thrushes, Siskin and Redpoll, roosts – gulls, Pied Wagtail, Starling and Corn Bunting.

March–May From mid-March. Shelduck, Sand Martin, Wheatear, Chiff-chaff, Blackcap, April onwards chance of Garganey, small wader passage, e.g. Common Sandpiper, Little Ringed Plover, Little Gull, possible Kittiwake, tern passage into May, Cuckoo, hirundines, Meadow Pipit, Yellow/Blue-headed and White Wagtail, common warblers, May – Reed Warbler, Spotted Flycatcher.

June–July Riparian breeders, hunting Hobby, Swift over water, late July returning waders.

August–November Main wader passage, regular; Ringed and Little Ringed Plover, Snipe, Curlew and Whimbrel overhead, Green and Common Sandpiper. Redshank, parties of Greenshank, Dunlin and Ruff Wood Sandpiper, Spotted Redshank, Little Stint and Curlew Sandpiper, chance of inland rarity, e.g. Pectoral Sandpiper or Temmincks' Stint. Terns, warblers August to September, also Whinchat, ducks build up, rare chance of pelagics after October–November gales. Black-necked Grebe, terns and hirundines.

ADDITIONAL SITES

Aldenham Country Park (OS ref. TQ 170 955)

A Hertfordshire County Council site consisting of a reservoir with peripheral woodland and fields, close to junction 4 of the M1. It has typical country park facilities and is well-used by the public.

Some wintering wildfowl with a small passage of terns most years. Check the woodland for warblers during the summer.

Amwell Gravel Pit (OS ref. TL 378 130)

Situated in the north of the Lee Valley below Ware. A part of the Regional Park with views from a bridge over the Lee or along the towpath.

Typical cross section of the valley's avi-fauna with good conditions for waders. Osprey and Ring-necked Duck are among the impressive array of recently recorded species. A site of immense potential for the future.

Balls Wood (OS ref. TL 345 105)

A mixed woodland owned by the Forestry Commission with the HMNTC managing some 137 acres (55 ha); a permit is needed from the Trust. Nearby Hertford Heath is also of interest and both sites can be reached by parking along the B1197 Hertford to Hoddesdon road.

The wood supports a fine cross-section of woodland species including all three woodpeckers and Hawfinch. Check the Heath for warblers in summer and finches and buntings in winter.

Batchworth Area (OS ref. TQ 070 943)

An interesting wetland site at the confluence of the Rivers Colne, Chess and Gade. The rivers aside, there are several small gravel pits, the Grand Union Canal and one of the best remaining wet meadows in the valley to enjoy. Much of the complex can be viewed from the public footpath that runs atop an old railway embankment, starting by the roundabout at Batchworth. For views across the eastern end of the meadow, park considerately along Tolpits Lane at TQ 078 941 at the entrance to the gravel works. The pits are private but it is worthwhile applying to the Thames Water offices for a permit, as permission is seldom refused to bona fide birdwatchers. (See Useful Addresses.)

Although the pits have attracted Cetti's Warbler in the past, the main focus of attention must be the large cattle-grazed wet meadow that is traversed by ditches and small pools, ideal for a hunting Grey Heron. In spring the valley's few remaining breeding Redshank and Snipe display over what is a relatively safe sanctuary. Lapwing sometimes join them, tumbling overhead and stooping to mob any cattle that stray into their territory. Yellow Wagtails pause briefly while on migration, with the occasional pair summering. In autumn small passerines feed among the grass as well as the more obvious Redwings and Fieldfares.

Bramfield Forest (OS ref. TL 285 168)

A complex of mainly coniferous Forestry Commission woods, scattered around the village of Bramfield. Park along the lane north of the village and follow the track into the woods.

Not the best of woods but Woodcock, Redpoll and Goldcrest are resident. Check the clear-felled patches in summer for warblers and Tree Pipit.

Bricket Wood (OS ref. TL 130 010)

Most of the commonland is now overgrown but some areas have survived with open bracken and scattered Silver Birch. The majority of the wood consists of deciduous trees with the best Oak stand sandwiched between the M1 and the railway line. Access is good with parking along the lane from Bricket Wood Village.

The woodland holds the usual resident birds and is particularly good for Lesser Spotted Woodpecker. Wet meadows at nearby Mundon Ford are worthwhile checking for the odd wader or two.

Broad Colney Lakes (OS ref. TL 177 033)

A series of small flooded gravel pits with peripheral damp woodland near London Colney. The HMNTC manages a 13 acre (5 ha) reserve with an adjoining car park beside Shenley Lane. There is much disturbance from the public and the water is heavily fished.

Small numbers of wildfowl in all seasons with an increase in the winter. The wood supports Willow Tit and Treecreeper.

Brocket Park (OS ref. TL 215 125)

A country estate in the Lee Valley west of Welwyn Garden City comprising a landscaped lake with surrounding parklands and woods. Park in the lay-by along the A6129 and follow the track through the wood. The weir is a good spot to watch from for riparian birds, especially in early morning.

A particularly good site for seeing woodpeckers as opposed to just hearing them. Kingfisher and Grey Wagtail frequent the river. Check the fields west of the main road in the winter for Golden Plover.

Broxbourne Gravel Pits (OS ref. TL 378 080)

Ample car parking can be found at Dobb's Weir either side of Essex Road. Follow a footpath west towards Hoddesdon checking the meadow for passerines in summer, Snipe and possible Short-eared Owl in winter. The open water across the railway line attracts terns and the occasional Little Gull in spring and wildfowl in winter.

Cassiobury Park (OS ref. TQ 090 970)

A large municipal park close to Watford town centre with some attractive wetland habitat alongside the River Gade. The damp Alder/willow wood and cress beds harbour a wide range of species at all seasons. Parking is available in nearby side roads and at points around the park with Watford Metropolitan Underground station within easy walking distance.

Particularly good in summer for warblers and resident riparian breeders such as Kingfisher and Grey Wagtail. In winter Snipe, Heron and Water Rail are attracted to the cress beds and Bearded Tit have been noted.

Croxley Moor (OS ref. TQ 080 947)

An open mead south of the River Gade at Croxley Green. Approach via a footpath just south of the underground station. Scrub has invaded parts of the site attracting Sylvia warblers to breed alongside resident finches and buntings. Some wetter areas encourage the commoner riparian breeders such as Moorhen, Mallard and Sedge Warbler. In winter, large flocks of Meadow Pipit occur with the odd pair staying to breed. Due to total public access, Croxley Moor receives much disturbance making an early morning visit preferable.

Pryors Wood (OS ref. TL 266 265)

A 26 acre (11 ha) mixed woodland nature reserve managed by the County Trust on the outskirts of Stevenage. The best point of access is from Cartwright Road opposite the Sunblest factory. Open to HMNTC members only.

Resident species abound including all three woodpeckers, with Tree Pipit, Spotted Flycatcher and warblers in summer.

Sawbridgeworth Marsh (OS ref. TL 492 159)

A County Trust reserve of some 30 acres (12 ha) situated in the Stort Valley south of Bishops Stortford. A fine marsh consisting of small reed and sedge beds, open meads, salix scrub and pollarded willows. Accessible at any time from the Sawbridgeworth railway station to Little Hallingbury road; there is limited roadside parking.

In summer, breeding colonies of Reed and Sedge Warblers with the occasional Grasshopper Warbler. Water Rail, Grey Wagtail and Snipe winter, with the latter two species occasionally breeding. Wintering finches and thrushes feed on weed seeds and berries respectively and Jack Snipe are sometimes flushed from the marsh.

Sherrards Park Wood (OS ref. TL 230 137)

An ancient predominantly Oak wood, containing some particularly fine old specimens, west of Welwyn Garden City. Managed by Welwyn and Hatfield District Council, access is good with numerous footpaths throughout the wood.

A high breeding density of woodpeckers, tits, Treecreeper and especially Nuthatch. Summering warblers abound along with Spotted Flycatcher.

Stanborough Reed Marsh (OS ref. TL 231 105)

A small yet important 7 acre (3 ha) reed marsh managed by the HMNTC south of Welwyn. Park by the sailing lake and follow the track on the north bank of the River Lee towards the railway line.

The reserve supports a good population of Reed and Sedge Warblers as well as other typical wetland species. Bearded Tits have wintered in the past and on several occasions have even bred.

Therfield Heath (OS ref. TL 335 400)

A Local Nature Reserve and, at 417 acres (169 ha), the county's most important area of chalk downland, famous botanically for its Pasque flowers during April. A car park is available at the Royston end of the Heath along with access from the A505 and Therfield roads.

Typical downland birds such as Skylark, Meadow Pipit and Corn Bunting breed with a passage of Wheatear and possibly chats in spring and autumn. Winter brings the odd Short-eared Owl or Hen Harrier and Golden Plover frequent the surrounding arable land.

Ver-Colne Valley Walk

This is an 11 mile (18 km) long footpath between St Albans and Watford along the Ver and Colne river valleys. Special way-marked arrows take the walker through some pleasant countryside that is good for common birds.

A fair cross-section of waterside species can be expected, especially during spring when the warblers arrive. Some Snipe and Lapwing are noted in winter.

Although not part of the official walk, the watercourse north-west of St Albans between Redbourn and where the river meets the A5 is of interest. A public footpath follows the north bank of the Ver.

West Hyde Area (OS ref. TQ 036 910)

The northern Royal Oak and West Hyde Pits are completely private, the former being only partially visible from the entrance to Lynsters Farm.

The remaining four pits south of Coppermill Lane are accessible from public footpaths and regularly attract good numbers of wintering wildfowl. The more open Helycon and Troy Mill Pits are the best sites in the valley for terns in spring and autumn. Do seek out the delightful little water cress bed that forms a back garden to most of the houses in the hamlet. This is another birdwatchers' favourite haunt, and regularly harbours a wintering Water Pipit among the more common Meadow Pipits. Grey and Pied Wagtail feature here along with Kingfisher and Moorhen.

Whippendell Woods (OS ref. TQ 075 977)

A large block of mainly deciduous woodland west of Watford with good public access and two large car parks. To avoid disturbance, visit early morning.

The usual broadleaved woodland species occur, including Hawfinch. In winter, check the wide bridleways as Hawfinch often feed in loose flocks on fallen Beech mast or Hornbeam seeds.

OXFORDSHIRE

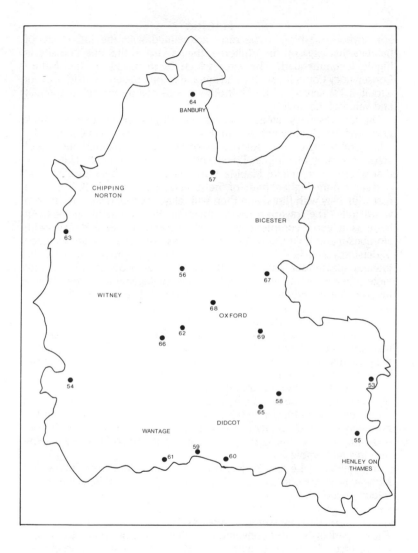

ASTON ROWANT NNR   Map 53/OS ref. SU 741 967

Habitat

For anybody wishing to become acquainted with the full range of habitats that exist on the Chilterns, then a visit to this one fine site is highly recommended. The site, which is managed by the Nature Conservancy Council (NCC) as a National Nature Reserve (NNR), covers a total of 331 acres (134 ha), but other woods nearby extend the interest and value of the area.

On the reserve's steep, west-facing slopes exists typical chalk grassland, it's short sward, rich in flowering plants, being maintained by rabbit and sheep grazing. Also on these slopes is a considerable area of scrub, primarily of Juniper, Privet and Dogwood, with Ash, Hawthorn, Blackthorn, Yew, Field Maple, Whitebeam and Wayfaring Tree all present. On the highest parts of the reserve, where the chalk is capped first with 'clay with flints' and then with clay, are found typical Chiltern woodlands. The towering Beech trees are the dominant species but there is a good complement of Ash, Rowan, Hazel and Oak with Hornbeam and Wild Cherry also seen. These woods give a very shaded understorey and floristically are at their best in spring, when shade-tolerant species such as Bluebell, Wood Sorrel, Wood Anemone, and violets make an attractive display. The management of the reserve involves the maintenance of this high level of diversity which does in fact represent typical Chiltern succession of grassland, followed by scrub and then woodland.

The site is in two parts, being separated by the M40, which cuts through this part of the Chilterns in a deep 70 ft (21 m) canyon. For the most part the presence of the motorway seems to worry the visiting naturalist more than the resident fauna and flora.

Adjacent to the reserve are two other areas of woodland both worthy of a visit. To the south is Cowleaze Wood, a plantation of conifer and mixed deciduous timber, owned by the Forestry Commission. To the north-east is the characteristic Beechwood landscape of Aston Wood, owned by the National Trust. Encompassing the whole area are grazing pastures and arable fields.

In addition to the fine flora and insect fauna of the area, Fallow and Muntjac Deer are common and Fox, Badger, Stoat and Weasel are also frequently noted.

Access

The car park is the most convenient starting point from which to explore the reserve. To reach it, leave the M40 at the Lewknor interchange (junction 6), proceed north-east for 660 yds (600 m) and turn right onto the A40. After 1.5 miles (2.5 km) and at the top of the hill, turn right, drive for a further 660 yds (600 m) and turn right once more into a narrow, metalled lane (care required) continuing to the far end where parking is available for up to 25 cars.

Just down the slope from the car park is an interpretive centre showing the features of interest upon the reserve and explaining aspects of its history and management.

Access on the reserve is limited to the nature trail and one other public right of way. As mentioned earlier the reserve has been split in two and although the section south of the motorway can be reached from the north using the Ridgeway path, it is probably best to park at Cowleaze Wood and to follow the footpaths onto the reserve from here. Cowleaze Wood itself is crossed by many paths and, as Forestry Commission land, has free access along these paths. It is however a favourite site for picnickers and is best avoided at likely peak times.

Aston Wood can be reached from the car park at the nature reserve but a lay-by on the A40 at the top of Aston Hill gives more immediate entry and a number of tracks lead one through the Beeches.

Facilities exist at the reserve for visits by parties but contact the NCC Warden beforehand to make the necessary arrangements. Dogs are not allowed.

Aston Rowant, diverse and interesting as it is, is not the only Chiltern site worthy of ornithological observation and the reader is urged to visit other sites in the area they cover.

Species

For the visiting birdwatcher, the areas of scrub on the scarp slope of the reserve probably provide the most interest. 70 acres (28 ha) of mixed scrub exist, this mixture providing many suitable nesting and feeding sites and, when interspersed with larger trees, convenient song-posts. Common Birds Census (CBC) studies have shown that, in any one season, over 45 species and a total of over 300 pairs of bird may breed here. Willow Warbler, Chiffchaff, Blackcap and Garden Warbler are all plentiful, nesting deep in the scrub, and Common and Lesser Whitethroat also nest. Wren and Dunnock are amongst the most numerous of the resident species, nesting alongside Long-tailed Tit, Robin, Blackbird, Song Thrush and Mistle Thrush. Several finches breed, Chaffinch and Greenfinch being the most obvious. The flash of a white rump and the quiet piping call will betray the presence of a Bullfinch, a good population of which can be found, while the cheery twittering of Linnet and Goldfinch complete the list of resident finches.

Turtle Dove and Tree Pipit are two more regular visitors in summer. The latter is the more conspicuous of the two, especially as it performs its splendid display flight, and whilst the former remains hidden from view, its purring calls do reveal its whereabouts. Cuckoos also haunt these scrublands.

As one moves from scrub into woodland there is a change in the complement of species encountered although some birds will be found in both habitat types. Species such as Nuthatch, Treecreeper and Great Spotted Woodpecker are common in the woodland but the Green Woodpecker, whilst nesting here, is more usually noted as it feeds on the ants on the open grassland. Marsh Tits tend to be found more in the woodland than the scrub but at this particular site, Willow Tits are rather infrequent. In some years, Wood Warblers join the list of species breeding at Aston Rowant; numbers are always low and the best chance of a sighting is early in the season when foliage cover is sparse. Another bird very occasionally encountered is the Hawfinch. This species seems to have a particular fondness for Hornbeam and can be seen, or more often heard, as it flies around the canopy. Sometimes the birds will move down to the woodland floor to forage for seeds and fruit or to find drinking water but, being very shy, will soon return to the shelter of the tree-tops when disturbed. Woodcock, beautifully camouflaged against

Wheatear

the leaf-litter, nest on the ground in the mature woodlands.

Of the birds of prey, Tawny Owls are to be found almost exclusively within the woodland, using it for both nesting and hunting. Sparrow-hawks nest in virtually any of the area's woods including the conifer plantations but hunt woodland edges and rides, and over scrub and hedgerow. Little Owl and Kestrel nest at the woodland edge but feed over the areas of grassland. In the winter time this grassland, which in summer is the breeding domain of Meadow Pipit and Skylark, occasionally becomes good hunting ground for Short-eared Owl and Buzzard.

Conifer woodland such as Cowleaze Wood does not show quite the same range of breeding species as elsewhere. There are though, good numbers of Robin and Chaffinch, Blue Tit, Chiffchaff and Willow Warbler and Goldcrest and Coal Tit are also abundant. Crossbills may sometimes be seen.

Winter time can be quiet but the diversity of habitat to be found in the area usually means that something of interest can be found. Redwing and Fieldfare gather in large flocks as they greedily devour berries of the scrub and hedgerow; Hawthorn and Whitebeam being particularly relished. Brambling may join the mixed flocks of foraging finches and small parties of Siskin and Redpoll can also be tracked down.

As at virtually any point along the Chiltern escarpment, Aston Rowant can be a great place to view migrating birds. In April, Wheatear feed boldly over the anthills of the grassland and Whinchat bob nervously on fence-posts. In April and May, every 'Blackbird' should be checked out as a potential Ring Ouzel. These same species appear, albeit with less regularity, in autumn. The vantage point that the escarpment presents enables active migration to be observed and during either passage period, particularly early in the day, birds can be watched as they move along or across the slope.

At any time of the year, if conditions are very windy, birds are less willing to show themselves and often move to more sheltered spots. It can mean therefore that a little more effort and patience, coupled with a certain amount of luck, may be necessary to create the best birdwatching days.

Calendar

Resident Sparrowhawk, Kestrel, Woodcock, Little Owl, Tawny Owl, Great Spotted and Green Woodpecker, Skylark, Meadow Pipit, Wren, Dunnock, Robin. Three thrush species, six tit species, Nuthatch, corvids, Chaffinch, Greenfinch, Bullfinch, Hawfinch.

December–February Buzzard, Short-eared Owl, winter thrushes, Siskin, Redpoll.

March–May Chiffchaff, Blackcap, Garden Warbler, Willow Warbler, possible Wood Warbler, Nightingale, Whitethroat, Lesser Whitethroat, Tree Pipit, Turtle Dove, Cuckoo. Passage migrants: Whinchat, Wheatear, Ring Ouzel.

June–July Breeding season in full swing.

August–November Winter thrushes and Brambling arrive later in period. Siskin and Redpoll usually evident, tits and finches flock together, Occasional Stonechat.

BADBURY FOREST & COXWELL WOOD

Map 54/OS ref. SU 960 260

Habitat

This site, lying to the west of Faringdon, comprises two areas of woodland situated on adjacent areas of rising ground separated and surrounded by open arable fields and improved grazing pasture. Badbury Forest, the larger area rising to 395 ft (120 m) is owned by the Forestry Commission and consists primarily of mixed conifer plantations, dense in parts but with blocks of mixed and deciduous woods, predominantly Oak, Birch and Hazel. Paths transect the area quite extensively, some forming quite wide rides.

The smaller area, Coxwell Wood, rises to 525 ft (160 m) and is also owned by the Forestry Commission. Here, despite a good number of conifers, there is a much more open character with a better shrub and ground layer and providing the better area for the visiting birdwatcher.

However a visit to the northernmost woods can be combined with a visit to Buscot Park Lake which, with the more varied treescape of its surrounds, increases further the selection of avifauna likely to be seen.

Adjacent to Coxwell Woods is Badbury Clump, an area of Beech plantation owned by the National Trust and renowned for its fine display of Bluebells and other springtime woodland flowers.

The woods as a whole have a rich flora and a good complement of butterflies and other insect life. Fox and Badger breed and Muntjac Deer are present in some numbers, often allowing good views as they feed along the grassy rides of Badbury Forest.

Access

To explore the woods in the southern part of the site, take the B4019 out of Faringdon and signposted to Highworth. After approximately 1.5 miles (2.5 km) there is a National Trust car park on the right hand side of the road with space for up to 50 cars. For views over Buscot Park Lake and the northern block of woodland, take the A417 Lechlade Road out of Faringdon. After 2.5 miles (4 km), on the left and just past a row of cottages, is a concealed gateway with large concrete posts providing access to a metalled road leading past the lake. Parking is possible on the roadside verge alongside the cricket pitch.

Within Badbury Forest and Coxwell Wood the Forestry Commission allow pedestrian access on all the paths, unless notices indicate otherwise. Similarly, Badbury Clump also has open access. A number of footpaths exist on the open land surrounding the woods.

Buscot Park, adjacent to the site described above, is strictly private and the only access, apart from the public path next to the lake, is on days when Buscot House and grounds are opened by the National Trust. A notice giving details of these is to be found at the main entrance to the park approximately 0.5 miles (1.25 km) further west on the A417.

Sundays and Bank Holidays can be quite busy at Badbury and, unless one visits early, are best avoided. Also, being at a higher elevation than the surrounding land, this site can be rather windy, especially in

Coxwell Wood and particularly if the wind is in the west, which can diminish bird activity.

In order to take in all aspects of the site's habitats, a typical visit would probably begin with a good exploration of Coxwell Wood and Badbury Clump before taking the short walk across open country to the larger forest. From here one would make one's way to view Buscot Park Lake returning on a similar route or using footpaths for further views over the fields and hedgerows. With the undulating ground often very wet and muddy this can be quite a trek and an alternative would be to explore the southern woods and to then drive around to the opposite end of the site to check out the lake and adjacent woods.

Species

As is noted elsewhere in this book, the woodlands of these five counties are at their best in spring and summer. To demonstrate this fully, pay a visit to Coxwell Wood early on a calm sunny spring morning in May to witness a truly fine dawn chorus. All of the breeding species will be apparently trying to out-sing each other with perhaps members of the thrush family being the star performers. Robin and Blackbird, Song Thrush and Mistle Thrush are all common here, and perch conspicuously, setting up their territories and attracting mates with their songs. Determined to make their presence felt, the Wren's explosive trill and the rather scratchy but nonetheless spirited song of the Dunnock will also be heard. Chaffinches, Greenfinches, Blue Tit and Great Tit are other residents that contribute whilst of the summer visitors Blackcap, Chiffchaff and Willow Warbler all play their parts. Garden Warblers are less common, and in some years the wonderful outpouring of the Nightingale may be heard. Other birds of the site, less tuneful but just as entertaining are the Green and Great Spotted Woodpeckers, both nesting in holes in mature or dying trees. Treecreepers are common throughout and a few pairs of Nuthatch nest, particulary in the older trees surrounding Badbury Clump. In the woods close to the lake and on the lower slopes of Coxwell Wood will be found Marsh and Long-tailed Tits, whilst in the conifers, Coal Tits nest. The large amount of coniferous woodland means that Coal Tit can be found in good numbers but probably not as common as the Goldcrest whose thin, shrill notes are often the only sound to be heard in the denser stands of conifer. Each year, records of Firecrest are made and with so much apparently suitable habitat available it would be very surprising if these birds were not breeding here.

Jay, Magpie, Woodpigeon and Carrion Crow are other common woodland residents with Tawny Owl and Sparrowhawk being the commonest birds of prey. Cuckoo and Turtle Dove complete the list of summer visitors.

By comparison, winter in the woods is rather dull with the usual scene of roving parties of mixed tit and finch flocks providing the main interest. Actually, these woods may have greater numbers of birds in winter than others since game-rearing takes place and the feed put out for Pheasants certainly attracts other species, helping them when natural food sources are scarce. In recent years, Crossbill and Redpoll have been seen in the woods and as both have been recorded well into March and April they could be breeding in the vicinity.

Buscot Park Lake adds another dimension to the site for the visiting birdwatcher. The main interest is in the breeding season and in particular the good sized heronry that exists, allowing good views. Up to 25 nests are occupied each spring, built mainly in the Oaks on the northern bank but with others scattered around the lake. The nests are huge, untidy affairs and very prone to damage by the winds which whip across the water surface. The birds therefore have to spend much time laboriously rebuilding and refurbishing at the start of each season, ready for the long period of incubation and rearing of their young. Herons may hunt for prey many miles away but a few can usually be found stalking the lakeside, or resting in some of the lower trees below the nest platform.

Other breeders on the lake include Coot, Moorhen and Mallard, Great Crested and Little Grebe. Pied Wagtails feed at the water's edge most of the year and hirundines hawk over the water in summer. The lake in winter is rather disappointing with only Teal, Tufted Duck and Black-headed Gulls joining the resident species.

Further interest is to be found in the open fields surrounding the woods. Most are arable and, except for Skylark and Red-legged Partridge, offer few nesting opportunities, but hedgerows and woodland edges do allow Whitethroat, Yellowhammer, Linnet and Bullfinch to breed. In winter the resident hedgerow birds are joined by Redwing and Fieldfare whilst in the now bare fields, flocks of Skylark, Lapwing and Black-headed Gull feed.

This site is not generally regarded as a local birdwatching hot-spot and as a consequence is probably under-watched. Such a large and relatively undisturbed area is always likely to produce something unusual, maybe breeding, maybe on passage, but even if only the regular species are present it is always worth a return visit.

Calendar

Resident Great Crested Grebe, Little Grebe, Grey Heron, Mallard, Sparrowhawk. Red-legged Partridge, Pheasant, Moorhen, Coot, Tawny Owl, Great Spotted and Green Woodpecker, Skylark, Pied Wagtail. Commoner thrushes, tits and finches, Goldcrest, possibly Firecrest, Nuthatch, Treecreeper, Jay, Magpie, Yellowhammer.

December–February Redwing, Fieldfare, Redpoll, Crossbill. Possible Teal on lake.

March–May Chiffchaff, Willow Warbler, Blackcap, Garden Warbler, Cuckoo, Turtle Dove, possible Nightingale.

June–July Height of breeding season.

August–November Arrival of winter thrushes, Skylark, Lapwing and finch flocks.

BIX, THE WARBURG
RESERVE   Map 55/OS ref. SU 720 880

Habitat

Owned and managed by BBONT, the Warburg Reserve is undoubtedly
the Trust's showpiece. Named after the eminent botanist and conserva-
tionist Dr E. F. Warburg, it was purchased in 1967 and is the only one of
the Trust's reserves to have a full-time Warden living on site.

The reserve nestles in the dry valley of Bix Bottom occupying 253
acres (102 ha) and lying totally on the upper and middle chalk between
300 and 500 ft (90 and 152 m). For the birdwatcher its prime importance
is as a woodland site with much of it having been so since before 1768.
A system of broad rides and open grassland totalling 20 acres (8 ha)
greatly adds to the interest.

The woodland itself has a very complex and diverse nature. The
steepest slopes of the valley comprise mainly Beech wood including a
good area of coppiced timber. There are blocks of conifer plantation the
rest being mixed woodland, predominantly Oak, Ash, Silver Birch and
Hornbeam, much with an extensive and well-developed understorey.
Areas of scrub are to be found, mainly of Hawthorn and Dogwood, Rose
and Elder which, when open and associated with areas of grassland,
supports a rich chalkland flora and fauna. Indeed, the whole reserve
with its degree of diversity boasts a wonderful flora (including 15
species of orchid) and this floristic richness is reflected in the overall
quality and range of animal life to be found on the reserve; from the
insects of all forms (including 37 butterfly species), to a fine collection
of vertebrates. Fallow and Muntjac Deer can be seen or heard on most
visits and Stoat and Weasel are common. On an evening visit Badgers
and Foxes can be expected. Adders, Grass Snakes and lizards, including
the Slow-worm, are also to be found in good numbers.

The reserve is actively managed in such a way that maximum diversity
is maintained with a continuous age structure within each habitat type.
In recent years, sheep-grazing has been used to maintain the grassland
habitat. Grazing keeps down scrub and rank vegetation and encourages
a wealth of flowering plants. Coppice management is undertaken in
selected areas of the reserve and many nest boxes have been provided
for birds.

A good account of the reserve is provided in *The Wildlife of the
Thames Counties* by Richard Fitter.

Access

The main point of access to the reserve is from the car park situated
opposite the information centre. This is at the northern end of the
unclassified road joining the B480 at Middle Assendon and the A423 at
Bix village. All roads are very narrow and care must be taken,
Additionally, footpaths lead to the reserve from Nettlebed and from
Maidensgrove Common. The latter route is well worth attempting since
panoramic views of the reserve and the surrounding countryside are to
be obtained as one descends to the valley bottom.

The reserve itself has good accessibility along a number of public footpaths and rides, and a nature trail (guide book available at the reserve) has also been laid out which takes visitors to all of the areas of interest on the reserve. Straying from these paths is unnecessary and potentially damaging to the flora and fauna.

To prevent too much disturbance upon the reserve, groups wishing to visit should telephone the Warden (0491-641727) to book beforehand. The narrow nature of the lanes leading to the reserve does however mean that access for coaches may prove difficult. Whilst visits from individuals and groups of all kinds are encourged (one of the main values of the reserve is its educational role), they would be expected to consider making some donation towards the upkeep of the reserve.

There is an information centre at the reserve explaining the work being undertaken, describing the plants and animals to be found and showing the valuable work of BBONT. Booklets listing the wildlife to be found are also available. Please note that the centre is closed on Thursdays and Fridays.

The presence of sheep on the reserve requires that dogs are kept on leads at all times.

Species

From the birdwatcher's point of view, the prime importance of a visit to Warburg lies in the large number and variety of woodland bird species likely to be encountered. As with most woods, the best time to visit is during spring and summer whilst the breeding season is in full swing and the birds are most active and vocal.

Probably the most widespread birds are the titmice. Six species can be seen here, all in good numbers with Blue and Great the most numerous. Long-tailed tits are also frequent, building their intimate, enclosed nests in areas of coppice and scrub, although occasionally at Warburg, nests will be built high up on the branches of mature trees. The reserve gives opportunity to identify and distinguish between the frequently confusing Marsh and Willow Tit. The less heavy looking Marsh Tit is by far the commoner of the two and is identified by its glossy black crown, smaller, neater bib and its habit of nesting in existing holes (including boxes) rather than excavating its own. Song and call of the two are however the easiest means of separation. The sixth, and smallest species, the Coal Tit is associated with the coniferous woodland and is accompanied by the tiny Goldcrest whose high-pitched call notes from the dense coniferous canopy betray its presence. It is quite likely that its rarer relative, the Firecrest, also nests on this reserve.

The three species of British woodpecker are all present with Green and Great Spotted being seen and heard on most visits. The Lesser Spotted Woodpecker is not found in such good numbers but Juniper Hill Wood, The Hanger or Big Ashes Plantation do offer a good chance of a glimpse of this, the most diminutive of woodpeckers. The other woodland specialists, Nuthatch and Treecreeper, thrive within the reserve.

Of the finches, Greenfinch and Chaffinch are very common whilst Goldfinch and Linnet will nest in areas of scrub such as is found within Freedom Wood. Yellowhammers also nest here. Scrub and coppice, particularly coppiced Beech provide nest sites for Bullfinch. Redpoll and Crossbill probably breed on the reserve and, although it has never been proven, both have been seen at all times of year the former being associated with Birch, the latter with Larch.

The mature woodland provides nest sites for up to ten pairs of Tawny Owl which often utilise nest boxes and are more often heard than seen. Long-eared Owls have also nested, whilst the Sparrowhawk is the most frequently encountered raptor on the reserve during the daytime. The boundary of the reserve provides nest sites for Kestrel and Little Owl both of which are more likely to be seen hunting over the adjacent open fields.

Woodcock are quite common at Bix although, because of their amazing camouflage, they are almost impossible to find when on the ground. Dusk, when birds 'rode' their territories uttering their curious croaking calls, makes them far more visible and often one does not have to go any further than the reserve car park to witness this behaviour.

Most of the common resident birds are to be found at Warburg and in good numbers. Songsters such as Robin, Blackbird and Song Thrush can make Warburg seem alive with song. Somewhat less tuneful but adding life with their colours, Magpie and Jay are also common. However, even more colour is provided by the pheasants of the reserve for as well as the familiar Common Pheasant, Golden and Lady Amherst's Pheasants are also present.

From April onwards the resident species are joined by a good number of summer visitors. Commonest are Chiffchaff and Willow Warbler whose spring-time songs can really make one believe that summer is just around the corner! Slightly after them come the Blackcap and Garden Warbler. There are small numbers of Turtle Dove, particularly in areas of younger woodland, and Spotted Flycatchers, confiding birds often allowing a close approach as they hawk for insects in the woodland glades or around the buildings, are very conspicuous.

Each spring, a number of species visit Warburg on passage to their breeding grounds elsewhere. Redstarts, Tree Pipits, Grasshopper Warblers and Wood Warblers are all species that have bred in the valley but which nowadays just make brief stop-overs. Perhaps one year some will decide to stay. Whilst Pied Flycatchers have not been recorded as a breeding species recently, their springtime appearance, as with any of the other four, can certainly give added interest to a day's birdwatching.

During the winter months woodlands can be very quiet with most activity concentrated within large mixed flocks of tits and finches, Goldcrests, Nuthatches and woodpeckers. They roam throughout the woods and scrub searching for insects and berries or quite commonly feeding upon the ground amongst the Beech mast crop. Many resident birds do move outside the reserve particularly since it lies in something of a frost hollow and, at times, the wood can be very quiet indeed. Some birds do appear on the reserve only during the winter months; Siskin and Redpoll feed amongst the Birch and conifer and Redwing and Fieldfare may forage in noisy mixed parties on the periphery of the reserve. Buzzards are regular winter visitors to the area patrolling the open areas of Bix Bottom in search of their small mammal prey.

In the not too distant past, Barn Owl, Stone Curlew and Nightjar all bred in the vicinity of the Warburg Reserve. For now, whilst we hope for their return, there is still much to offer the birdwatcher in what must be the most attractive woodland site in Oxfordshire.

Calendar

Resident Sparrowhawk, Kestrel, Woodcock, Tawny Owl, Little Owl,

Common, Golden and Lady Amherst's Pheasants, the six tit species, the three woodpecker species, Goldcrest, Nuthatch, Treecreeper, Chaffinch, Greenfinch, Bullfinch, Linnet, Jackdaw, Jay, Magpie.

December–February Buzzard, Siskin, Redpoll.

March–May Chiffchaff, Willow Warbler, Blackcap, Garden Warbler, Cuckoo, Possible Redstart, Tree Pipit and Pied Flycatcher on passage.

June–July Turtle Dove, Spotted Flycatcher.

August–November Mixed flocks of tits, finches and other woodland species congregate with the possibility of Brambling amongst them. Redwing, Fieldfare.

BLENHEIM PARK   Map 56/OS ref. SP 440 160

Habitat

Built in the early-eighteenth century at the behest of a nation grateful to the victorious Duke of Marlborough at the battle of Blenheim in 1704, Blenheim Park and Palace provides a wonderfully historic setting for one of Oxfordshire's finest birdwatching sites. With a total area of some 2,400 acres (960 ha) there are a number of distinct habitat types giving a very varied landscape and associated flora and fauna.

The focus of attention is supplied by the lakes and, until the relatively recent commencement in the county of gravel extraction and the building of reservoirs elsewhere, Blenheim held one of the few sizeable areas of permanent open water in Oxfordshire. The lakes were created in the 1760s by damming the River Glyme, their formation being the brainchild of Lancelot 'Capability' Brown who, at that time, attempted to naturalise the rather formal layout designed by John Vanbrugh (architect for the Palace) and Henry Wise. Brown was also responsible for planting most of the trees around the lakes and elsewhere, including the clumps of Beech and the impressive selection of cedars.

The water is in three parts. Queen Pool is the shallowest and takes water from the River Glyme. It covers some 40 acres (16 ha) and apart from the very shallow north end with its scrub and Glyceria beds, bankside vegetation is sparse. The largest area, the lake, covering some 79 acres (32 ha), is the deepest water. It is fringed with stands of Glyceria and has woodland running to its edge. Downstream, the long and narrow Bladon Water has an area of 20 acres (8 ha) and is well-blessed with bankside and emergent vegetation.

Perhaps the most attractive area of woodland and of greatest importance for breeding birds is to be seen in High Park. This is predominantly Oak, a relic of the ancient Wychwood Forest and, having quite an open nature, encouraging a rich ground flora. Oaks are also featured in Lower Park where they are scattered throughout the area of permanent pasture. In the north, the Great Park is a large open area of arable land and permanent grassland. Elsewhere there are further arable fields, blocks of conifer plantation, areas of shrubs, small thickets and woodland.

Much of the woodland is managed commercially but with landscape and natural history conservation in mind. Continuous, selective felling and replanting ensures that a mixed age structure is maintained. In addition, replanting has also been necessary since the Dutch Elm Disease of the 1970s led to a total loss of the species that was so very much a feature in the Park. Summer droughts have also killed off many of the Beech trees but it is hoped that the replanting policy will restore the Park to its former glory.

Access

The main access to Blenheim Park is at Woodstock, 6 miles (9.5 km) north of Oxford on the A34. Parking is possible in the grounds although a charge is made. Free parking is available in Woodstock (check the time limit) from where it is just a short walk to the main gate; a small admission fee is payable. Entering at this point gives immediate views over Queen Pool.

There are three other entry points for the pedestrian: at Bladon, the Ditchley Gate and at Combe Lodge. From Bladon there is an entrance adjacent to the White House pub in the village, 1 mile (1.5 km) west of Woodstock. For Ditchley Gate turn left off the A34 at the filling station 1.5 miles (2.5 km) north of Woodstock. Proceed along the B4437 for 660 yds (600 m) where the gate is to be seen on the left. The entrance at Combe Lodge is from the village of Long Hanborough, 3 miles (5 km) south-west of Woodstock on the A4095. Take the unclassified road to East End, Combe, turning right at the top of the hill.

Parking at these three entrances is rather restricted and not so convenient for viewing Queen Pool and the lake.

Many footpaths cross Blenheim Park and whilst large areas of Great and Lower Park are freely open to the public (unless notices indicate otherwise), access elsewhere is restricted to roads and footpaths, including the woodland of High Park. There is no access to the buildings and grounds in the immediate vicinity of Blenheim Palace. There is a garden centre, children's play area and butterfly house in the Park and refreshment and toilet facilities are available, both in the Park and in Woodstock. Since sheep are present most of the year and there is extensive Pheasant rearing, dogs must remain on leads.

The Palace and its grounds are a honey-pot for thousands of tourists and walkers. Whilst the Park is large enough to absorb these visitors without undue disturbance to wildlife, the birdwatcher who enjoys peace and quiet would be well advised to pay an early morning visit.

Species

Although in recent times Blenheim's value as a site for observing county rarities has decreased, the grounds are still of great value all year round for their ability to produce a very large number and variety of species. In recent times over 150 species have been recorded here – almost half of this figure being breeding birds.

As with any site, the areas of open water are probably the first that a birdwatcher should check out, with the shallower Queen Pool usually the most productive. Perhaps the most famous birds of the Blenheim pools are the Great Crested Grebes whose elaborate courtship displays can provide much fascinating and enjoyable watching. These displays are to be seen from early in the year when the courting birds indulge in much ritualised posturing and head shaking, continuing through to the impressive 'weed-dance'. Nests are built in the reedbeds and those built on Queen Pool afford good views. Other breeding species of the lakes include Coot and Moorhen, Little Grebe, Mallard, Tufted Duck and Mute Swan. The Canada Goose also breeds and there is usually a sizeable flock of non-breeding birds present, often including a few escapees from wild-fowl collections such as Pink-footed and Barnacle Geese. In 1975, the Gadwall was added to the list of Blenheim's breeding birds. It was also the county's first recorded breeding site for the species, and although the number of pairs nesting here have increased to eight, Blenheim remains the only regular Oxfordshire breeding site.

In autumn, the breeding birds are joined by individuals who use Blenheim as a wintertime feeding and roosting site. They are also joined by good numbers of Pochard, Teal, Wigeon and Shoveler, good views of all being possible. Gulls, mainly Black-headed, are always present.

Gadwall

Occasionally, winter visits will produce treats such as Black-necked Grebe or Smew, whilst during periods of passage, Garganey and Shelduck may put in an appearance.

Unless there is a significant drop in water level, the fringes of the pool generally provide little in the way of feeding opportunities for waders. Common Sandpiper do appear on passage and a number of non-breeders spend summer at the site. A few Snipe may occur, but apart from a few wintering Lapwing on the pastures, waders are not a regular feature of Blenheim's birds. An early morning visit may find Grey Heron stalking the shallows and in winter its close relative, the Bittern, may move onto the site during harsher weather, conditions which may also find Water Rail using the area. Kingfishers are regularly seen, particularly in winter when the rivers are in spate. Check all likely perches over the lakes, especially around the Queen Pool. A more than cursory glance is usually needed since, for such a brightly coloured bird, they can be remarkably well concealed. In the breeding season, birds of the water's edge will include Pied and Grey Wagtails with the area around the Grand Bridge a particular favourite. The Bridge itself has colonies of House Martin and Feral Pigeon. For anybody who has never had good views of Reed Warbler, Blenheim can be very useful; on a still evening in June, stand on New Bridge over-looking Bladon Water, scan the reedbeds nearby and watch as they feed or perform their courtship displays. Sedge Warbler and Reed Bunting also nest close to New Bridge, favouring the dense, bankside vegetation. When Sir William Chambers had the bridge built at the tail-end of the eighteenth century, one wonders if he could possibly have envisaged its future benefit to the birdwatching fraternity.

Blenheim Park presents plenty of opportunities for observing a good range of our woodland birds. Great Spotted and Green Woodpeckers, Nuthatch and Treecreeper are common wherever there are wooded areas. Often the more isolated clumps present the best view of these species with birds easy to detect as they fly from one stand to another. The conifer plantations are noted for Coal Tit, Goldcrest and Chaffinch with the majestic cedars having similar breeding species but are also frequented by Mistle Thrush whose nests, built early in the year, are found on the thick branches of these huge conifers. All of the usual tit species are present and in winter form mixed wandering flocks often in the company of Chaffinch and Greenfinch, foraging amongst the Beech mast. Check these flocks for Brambling, as the Blenheim Beeches are probably the most convenient place in the county to observe these wintering finches. For Long-tailed Tits, the area around Combe Lodge is ususally the most productive.

Warblers are more usually encountered in and around High Park. Here there is more ground and scrub cover providing nest sites and song-posts for Chiffchaff, Blackcap, Garden Warbler and Willow Warbler. Wood Warbler have nested in the past and occasionally appear in spring. Spotted Flycatchers hunt the more open areas, especially near to the pool, another place where Little Grebe, Moorhen and Mallard may nest. Other woodland species include Jackdaw (nesting in tree-holes all over the Park), Jay, Tawny Owl and Sparrowhawk. Hawfinches are regularly sighted at Blenheim, usually in the vicinity of the Garden Centre.

The large areas of open pastureland are probably the least exciting areas of the Park. The local resident Kestrels may hunt over it, coveys of both species of partridge are usually present and Rook and Jackdaw may feed here. At dusk a Barn Owl hunting over these fields is a regular, and very welcome, sight indeed.

Calendar

Resident Great Crested and Little Grebe, Mute Swan, Canada Goose, Gadwall, Mallard, Tufted Duck. Sparrowhawk, Kestrel, Pheasant, Moorhen, Coot, Stock Dove, Feral Pigeon. Barn, Little and Tawny Owls. Kingfisher, Great Spotted and Green Woodpeckers, Goldcrest, Nuthatch, Treecreeper, Jay, Jackdaw, Crow. Commoner finches, thrushes and tits. Reed Bunting.

December–February Increased numbers of winter duck, possible Smew or rare grebe, possible Bittern and Water Rail. Large corvid flocks, possible Lapwing flocks.

March–May Early in period; migrating Garganey and Shelduck, possible Wood Warbler. Reed Warbler, Sedge Warbler, Spotted Flycatcher, Blackcap, Garden Warbler, Chiffchaff, Willow Warbler, Grey Wagtail.

June–July Common Sandpiper. Breeding season at its height.

August–November Black-headed Gull, Pochard, Teal, Wigeon, Shoveler. Roaming tit and finch flocks including Brambling, numbers of Siskin and Redpoll rise steadily.

CHERWELL VALLEY   Map 57/OS ref. SP 490 300

Habitat

The River Cherwell rises just across the county boundary in Northamptonshire and flows almost due south to join the Thames at Oxford. The bed is mainly of clay and the water generally slow to moderate flowing with good emergent and bankside vegetation. For most of its course through Oxfordshire, the Cherwell runs parallel to the Oxford Canal and along a broad valley given over almost entirely to fields of arable crops and improved grazing pasture. In the summer, the level and flow of the river may be very much reduced but during the winter months it is very liable to flood, thus turning the adjacent fields into an area very attractive to a range of bird species. It must be stressed however that the number of birds likely to be seen depends very heavily upon the timing and duration of flood. Whilst flooding may occur anywhere within the valley, the most important area is the system of flood meadows covering 900 acres (360 ha) between Somerton and Nell Bridge. The importance of this area to wintering birds has, following much negotiation with the landowners involved, led to the area being designated a Local Nature Reserve. The species account in this chapter refers to observations made in this reserve but the same range of bird species may be encountered elsewhere along the valley.

Access

Access to the site is rather limited; one or two footpaths cross the meadows, but by far the best way to observe the birds of the area is from the towpath of the Oxford Canal which enjoys public right of way. The towpath is well above the level of the flood plain and so offers good views right across the valley. Venturing off the towpath is unnecessary and will disturb the wildlife and jeopardise the existing agreement.

Three roads cross the valley and roadside parking, albeit limited, is to be found close to where these roads cross the river and canal. From these points, access onto the canal towpath is possible.

Species

Having already described the Cherwell Valley as an area of ornithological interest primarily outside of the breeding season, its remoteness from major roads and conurbations does make it a pleasant enough site for a trip in spring and summer. The nearby air-force base, however, can be a little off-putting at times. At that time of year a look along the waterways will reveal nesting Mute Swan, Little Grebe, Moorhen, Mallard and Kingfisher. The areas of bankside scrub and vegetation, especially alongside the canal, can be excellent for Reed Bunting, tits, finches and warblers including Reed and Sedge Warbler, and if lucky, an occasional Grasshopper Warbler. Also in the scrub and hedgerows will be nesting Yellowhammer and where mature trees exist, Little Owl, Great Spotted and Green Woodpecker. On the meadows breed Skylark, Yellow Wagtail and Pied Wagtail, both species of partridge and, in undisturbed sites Curlew and Lapwing. These ground nesting habits are yet another valid reason for not wandering from permitted rights of way.

Whilst good views of all these breeding species can be obtained, winter, especially following prolonged heavy rain, is the best time for a visit. In such conditions, the valley has turned up a phenomenally high number of birds making the most of the feeding opportunities that the floodwaters present. If a very cold snap follows and the area freezes birds will move away rapidly so making the timing of a visit very important.

It is interesting to consider a typical winter's day; cold but not freezing and the area well covered by shallow floodwaters. Of the wildfowl likely to be present, three species make up the vast majority of numbers, namely Mallard, Teal and Wigeon, all dabbling and grazing duck, most likely at the water's edge. Up to 200 birds of each species may be found. Amongst them may be smaller numbers (never usually more than 20) of Gadwall, Shoveler and Pintail. In pools of deeper water Pochard, Tufted Duck and even Great Crested Grebe may be seen. Canada Geese are usually prominent in the area and in very wet conditions numbers may rise dramatically. This noisy goose flock will often attract some of the wild grey geese such as White-fronted or Pink-footed. Mute swans form loosely-knit herds over the floods and, with up to 40 present, can make quite an impressive sight as they wing their way along the valley. Small numbers of Bewick's Swans may join them, usually in the period from December to February, perhaps accompanied by White-fronted Geese. Virtually every year at least one family party of Whooper Swans will take up residence in the valley, whether it is flooded or not. These are truly wild birds, very wary and not tolerant of a close approach.

There are a number of bird species which in winter have the capability of forming huge flocks in the valley: Black-headed Gulls are usually present in reasonable numbers, whatever the weather but in some wetter periods have reached the 2,000 mark. On drier ground, mixed flocks of Woodpigeon and Stock Dove may congregate, occasionally totalling in excess of 1,000 birds. On similar terrain, or on the numerous Hawthorn hedges and bushes, large (up to 1,000), noisy flocks of Redwing and Fieldfare gather, usually accompanied by a few Mistle Thrush and Blackbird. The greatest avian accumulations are however created by Lapwing; flocks of 1,000 birds are common but twice this number may be seen, with maximum numbers reached towards the end of winter. During the winter the Lapwing range quite widely in the Cherwell Valley following the activities of the flood and the plough. They are often in the company of the well-marked, but rather less conspicuous, Golden Plover and up to 250 birds have been recorded in the early part of the year. Other waders are also found throughout the winter with Dunlin, Redshank, Ruff and Snipe being the most usual with counts of the latter reaching over 100. One or two Jack Snipe are also regularly recorded. Towards the end of winter and through into the period of the spring migration, other waders may, if there is suitable feeding ground available, use the location to make a brief stop-over visit with Ringed Plover, Grey Plover and Whimbrel all being good examples.

The winter floods also attract a number of passerine species in particular Pied Wagtail, Linnet and Meadow Pipit. Whinchat and Wheatear join them during the spring migration, frequently returning via the site in September.

The Cherwell Valley also has the potential to attract a few rarer species. In the past Avocets have appeared, usually in March and April as they return to their breeding grounds. Bittern have occasionally over-wintered in the area and, in autumn 1980, the appearance of Bluethroat caused much excitement.

Calendar

Resident Little Grebe, Mute Swan, Canada Goose, Mallard, Kestrel, partridge, Moorhen, Lapwing, Curlew (possible), Little Owl, Kingfisher, Great Spotted and Green Woodpecker, Pied Wagtail. Great Tit, Blue Tit, Long-tailed Tit, commoner finches and thrushes. Yellowhammer, Reed Bunting.

December–February Meadow Pipit, Woodpigeon, winter thrushes, Lapwing, Golden Plover, and Stock Dove flocks. Whooper Swan. Possible Bewick's Swan and White-fronted Goose. If wet; Teal, Wigeon, Gadwall, Shoveler, Pintail, with possible Tufted Duck, Pochard and Great Crested Grebe. Dunlin, Redshank, Snipe, Ruff, and possible Jack Snipe. Very occasional Bittern.

March–May Passage; Ringed Plover, Grey Plover, possible Whimbrel and Avocet. Wheatear, Whinchat, and possible Garganey and Shelduck. Reed and Sedge Warbler, Yellow Wagtail, Turtle Dove, possible Grasshopper Warbler.

June–July Occasional Hobby.

August–November Return movement of Whinchat, Wheatear and a few waders. If wet, build up of species as for December-February.

DORCHESTER GRAVEL PITS

Map 58/OS ref. SU 580 950

Habitat

Some 6.5 miles (10 km) to the south of Oxford in the area of countryside separating Dorchester-on-Thames and Berinsfield, and bounded by the Rivers Thame and Thames, is a group of water-filled, worked-out gravel pits. Although numbering only five, this small network of lakes has shown itself to be a fine site for birds during both summer and winter. Orchid Lake and Dorchester Lagoon have been well landscaped and provide leisure facilities, mainly angling and boating. Both have islands and a rich bank-side vegetation comprising reeds, scrub and overhanging willows. Along its southern edge, Orchid Lake has a small reedbed and area of fen vegetation with willows, Birch and Alder. Queenford Pit is the largest body of water and the prime site for waterfowl, gulls and terns. Its banks do not have such good cover as the other lakes but its eastern edge has an area of willow scrub and waste-ground. (To assist the reader in relating the text to the associated map, letter references are used in the following paragraphs.)

Further east is a medium-sized lake (A), surrounded by rank vegetation and with sprawling Bramble and hedgerows beyond. To the south of Queenford pit on the opposite side of the Dorchester bypass, A423, is a smaller and much older lake (B) much used by anglers. It has a thick hedgerow along its southern and eastern aspects and a bankside with dense cover and many mature trees, mainly willows.

Unless there is a drop in the water table following periods of drought, the Dorchester Gravel Pits provide little in the way of island and sand bars suitable for gatherings of waders or for nesting terns etc. Waders therefore tend to be found scattered along the shore-lines and terns only use the pits for feeding.

In addition to the features described, there are a number of hedgerows, mainly of Hawthorn, ringing the lakes, a small sewage treatment works just north of Orchid Lake and, to the north of Queenford Pit, a waste disposal site. The future of Queenford Pit itself is a little unclear but it is likely to be reclaimed over a long period, which may well alter the future status of the site.

Access

The pits are to be found just south of Berinsfield on the A423, some 6.5 miles (10 km) south of Oxford. For views over Queenford Pit and the lakes to its east and south, park in the lay-by on the left approximately 0.75 mile (1 km) beyond the Berinsfield roundabout and just before the footbridge. Queenford Pit can be viewed from the roads around its boundary and from the footpath along its western edge. The smaller pit to the east is privately owned and viewing is possible only from the road along its western shore. Cross over the bypass for the third, smaller pit around which there is a well worn path.

For Orchid Lake and Dorchester Lagoon turn right at the Berinsfield roundabout (signposted for Abingdon) and then left (for Dorchester) after 330 yds (300 m). There is a concealed entrance, 330 yds (300 m) from this junction, on the left leading into a car park. From here paths lead around both lakes.

Due to its popularity with the sailing fraternity, Dorchester Lagoon is best avoided on summer weekends and bank holidays unless a very early visit can be arranged.

Species

The main interest for the birdwatcher at these gravel pits undoubtedly lies with its wildfowl population and, at least among the local birders, it is thought that two species, the Goosander and the Ruddy Duck, are probably more representative of this site than any other.

During the winter, Dorchester Gravel Pits seems to be the favourite haunt in the county for the Goosander, that striking, handsome member of the sawbill family. Over 60 birds may be present and, provided there is no disturbance, small groups will be found on all of the pits with the majority remaining on Queenford. Goosander are large, elongated birds with long, down-turned bills. At a distance the drake stands out very clearly amongst other species present, appearing very white both in flight and on the water. Females and immature birds lack this conspicuousness being a more subdued tone of grey and with a characteristic red-brown head, although retaining the long body-shape of the male.

The second species particularly noted at this site is the Ruddy Duck. Whilst this bird can be found on any of the Oxfordshire waters during winter, Dorchester has always been a favoured haunt and in the first half of the 1980s the gravel pits became the first still-water breeding site in the county. Ruddy Duck are small, almost nondescript birds and easily overlooked, particularly in winter. In its breeding finery, the drake's blue bill and white facial patch will aid its detection whilst its dumpy body and erect, stiff-tail are diagnostic.

Duck species to be encountered all year include Mallard, Tufted Duck and Pochard, with maximum numbers being reached in the autumn. During the winter, Wigeon form the largest flocks on the pits when, depending upon the weather conditions, up to 500 birds may be present. Shoveler, Teal and Gadwall join them in smaller numbers with Goldeneye completing the list of regular winter visitors. Less regularly recorded but seen most winters are Pintail, Shelduck, Smew and exotic escapees such as Red-crested Pochard or Mandarin may also join the winter duck flocks.

Moorhen, Little Grebe and Great Crested Grebe are present all year on all of the lakes but in winter these birds (especially on Queenford Pit) may be joined by Black-necked and Slavonian Grebe or maybe even a Red-throated Diver. Coot take the prize for the most numerous water-bird on the complex, with winter counts over the area almost reaching 1,500. A local farmer uses Queenford Pit to dump his old potatoes and Coot and other birds are lured to the site by this free meal. Mute Swan and Canada Goose breed on any of the lakes but outside of the breeding season there is a dramatic increase in numbers so that as many as 60 Mute Swan and up to 700 Canada Geese may be present. With the Rivers Thame and Thames close by, Kingfishers would appear to be spoilt for choice of nesting and feeding ground. Ringing studies at the site confirm the observation that a sizeable population thrives in the area. The Grey Heron is another frequent visitor to the pits, quietly stalking the shallows, while at the water's edge Pied and Grey Wagtails can be watched as they flit busily along the margins.

Having stated that the area is not a prime site for waders, small numbers do use the site although visits tend to be brief. Most visit in the autumn, when the water level has dropped and Greenshank, Green Sandpiper, Ruff and Little Stint may be seen. Redshank, Lapwing and Common Sandpiper are present most of the summer, although in recent years nesting has become rather sporadic.

Early May is the time to look out for Black, Common and Arctic Terns. They may stop at the lakes for several hours working their way over the water surface in search of small fish. Before they move through, many of the summer migrants to Dorchester will already be on site. Earliest arrivals will be Sand Martin and Chiffchaff, joined later by Sedge Warbler, Reed Warbler and Whitethroat. In April, small numbers of Wheatear, Whinchat and Yellow Wagtail move through the site with some of the latter staying to breed in the area. The migrants which stay take their place alongside the resident Reed Bunting and Yellowhammer, tits, finches and Treecreeper. Where trees are to be found Great Spotted and Green Woodpecker nest with the latter being particularly evident around Orchid Lake. Small numbers of the Lesser Spotted Woodpecker also occur. Of the resident birds of prey Kestrel, Sparrowhawk and Little Owl all nest locally and remain active throughout the year, and are joined in winter by an occasional Merlin.

As well as a broad spectrum of wintering and breeding birds, the gravel pits do have the ability to provide a few rarities. On autumn passage Wryneck, Red-backed Shrike and Pied Flycatcher have all been recorded, usually in quieter areas of the scrub and hedgerow. In autumn Little Gull may feed over the water whilst the moderate gull roost that might form has included Glaucous Gull amongst its ranks.

Calendar

Resident Great Crested Grebe, Little Grebe, Mute Swan, Canada Goose, Mallard, Ruddy Duck, Sparrowhawk, Kestrel, Moorhen, Coot, Little Owl Kingfisher, all three woodpecker species, Pied Wagtail, common tits and finches.

December–February Rarer grebes, Pintail, Smew all possible. Large numbers of Canada Goose, Wigeon and Coot. Gull roost, mainly Black-headed and Lesser Black-backed but Glaucous possible. Goosander, Teal, Tufted Duck, Pochard, Shoveler, Gadwall, Merlin.

March–May Sand Martin, Chiffchaff, Wheatear, Cuckoo in first half of period followed by Swallow, Swift, Sedge Warbler, Reed Warbler, Sylvia Warblers, and Yellow Wagtail. Terns and a few waders on passage. Possible Redshank, Lapwing, Common Sandpiper.

June–July Most species at height of breeding season. Swift and hirundines over the lakes.

August–November Main wader passage with possible Little Stint, Ruff, Greenshank, Green Sandpiper. Much movement of finches and warblers and chance of Red-backed Shrike or Wryneck. Waterfowl numbers rise readily and gull numbers also increase.

DOWNLAND OXFORDSHIRE   Map 59

Habitat

The Downlands of Oxfordshire are formed as part of the large band of chalk that stretches in a huge, sweeping arc from Yorkshire south to Wiltshire. This chalkland manifests itself quite dramatically within the Oxfordshire landscape in two rather contrasting fashions. East of the River Thames it forms the elegant, wooded Chiltern Hills whilst on the opposite side of the river is the far more open countryside of the Wessex Downs. The Downs run westwards as far as Ashbury in Oxfordshire and thence on to Salisbury Plain.

From the Thames Valley, and the Vale of the White Horse at 200 ft (60 m), the hills rise in a steep, north-facing escarpment to an altitude of over 720 ft (220 m). Beyond the scarp they slope away gently southwards in a landscape dissected by an intricate system of mainly dry valleys.

The Downs themselves can be seen to possess a number of contrasting habitat types each having a bearing upon the wildlife likely to be encountered. Before the Second World War virtually the entire area would have been covered with short turf, grazed by sheep and rabbits but without the application of fertilisers or herbicides, and with areas of Hawthorn and Juniper scrub. This combination creates a particularly rich habitat for a wide range of wildlife. Today, whilst this traditional scene can still be witnessed in some localities, much of the landscape has been converted to intensive arable cultivation with its subsequent impoverishment of the wildlife. As some recompense for this loss of traditional grassland, the presence of a good number of horse-racing stables in the vicinity has created areas of permanent grassland (in places fringed with scrub) for use as training gallops. Whilst less rich floristically, they do add another dimension to the available habitat for birds, providing feeding areas for corvids, Starling and partridge.

The Downs are criss-crossed by a good many lanes and tracks. Many are ancient rights of way, wide, rich in flowers and insects and often with isolated bushes dotted along their length and sometimes lined by hedgerows. In places the open atmosphere of the Downs is further broken by stands of trees and shelter belts. Beech and conifers are the main species to be found but a few Oak woods can be seen. These wooded areas provide shelter for Fox and Badger, and Roe, Fallow and Muntjac Deer; the early morning observer will often see them feeding out on nearby fields.

The area is very dry, with few ponds or streams on the high ground. Whilst this restricts the species likely to be found, it does mean that the wet areas that do exist can act as something of a magnet for wildlife. In summer, a sizeable puddle can often be worth watching whilst small reservoirs and areas around farms (e.g. Churn Farm) are always worth checking.

Since the Downs are essentially a very open area, windy, stormy conditions can lead to an apparent dearth of birds. In these conditions they head for the shelter that is to be found in the valleys or around the villages at the foot of the escarpment. Here the greater amount of vegetation and man-made cover creates a less hostile environment for wildlife.

225

The hills straddle the Oxfordshire-Berkshire border and, but for a boundary change in the 1970s, would still be solely within Berkshire. Hence, even today, the whole upland area is still known traditionally as the Berkshire Downs.

Access

Throughout the year, but especially in winter and at periods of passage, the entire length of the Downs can be very rich in birds. However, because at these prime times birds can be rather localised, birdwatching can involve a fair amount of luck in order to find some of the most interesting species. It would therefore be rather artificial to describe individual downland sites alone since this may imply that the remainder has reduced ornithological value when this is far from true. Thus, this chapter will refer to sites across all of the Oxfordshire Downland and give details of access to two areas where a good range of birds and habitat types can be encountered. As they pass through Oxfordshire the Wessex Downs are well served by road, footpath and bridleways, making access relatively uncomplicated. However do not be tempted to stray from the beaten track into field or woodland; most are in private ownership and as well as the disturbance caused to wildlife, the action could jeopardise existing rights of public access.

CHURN AND THE FAIR MILE (Map 60/OS ref. SU 520 828)

This area, at the eastern end of the Downs is perhaps the area most favoured by Oxfordshire birdwatchers and, especially at times of passage, does turn up a good selection of migrating birds. Much of the area is arable fields but Moulsford and Aston Upthorpe Downs still retain typical chalk grassland. Racing gallops feature and the rights of way are wide with bushes and hedgerow. Further interest is added by the mixed woodland of Uphill and Ham Wood and also by the area of scrub and woodland at the eastern end of the Fair Mile. There are a number of points of access to the site.

From Kingstanding Hill on the A417 (SU 573 838) where car parking is available at the end of the Fair Mile. From Streatley, take the A417 north and after 4 miles (6.5 km), opposite the turning to Aston Upthorpe, turn left and follow the track south, parking at SU 550 843. From Blewbury, turn off the A417 south into Bohan's Road on the western edge of the village. Continue to the end of the lane, bearing left to Churn Farm and then following the straight, concreted road to the Field Studies Centre, where a car park will be found.

Of these, the final route is probably best for birdwatchers limited by the time they can spend at the site. For those wishing to explore the area at a more leisurely pace, any of the given points can be used as the start at some very interesting and not too taxing circular routes.

THE WARREN AND GINGE DOWN (Map 61/OS ref. SU 418 841)

Whilst lacking in the traditional grassland habitat this is another area much favoured by locals and in addition to the usual range of breeding birds is always likely to turn up a few of the less common species, e.g. Wood Warbler. Access is centred upon the Ridgeway but there are many footpaths creating circular routes and allowing views over the mixed woodland of the Warren, some extensive gallops and a good number of shelter belts. The most convenient point from which to gain access is from the B4494 2.5 miles (4 km) south of Wantage where it is crossed by the Ridgeway. Ample car parking is available here.

Species

The very open nature of most of Oxfordshire's chalk downland is reflected in the composition of its bird communities with ground and scrub nesting species being the most obvious and most frequently encountered. Of these, Chaffinch, Yellowhammer and Corn Bunting are typical and very common, using patches of scrub or any of the bushes that dot the landscape as convenient song-posts. The thick vegetation along the edges of tracks provide nest sites. Meadow Pipits too are common, indeed the Oxfordshire stronghold for the species is in this region. Whilst their feeble piping calls seem to be everywhere it is an even greater thrill to watch as they perform their display flights, rising high in the air and then descending, parachute-like uttering their rapid, shrill notes. All four of these species are abundant throughout the year, often forming quite large flocks in winter as they feed on fields of stubble or newly planted crops. Another bird present all year round, similarly forming larger winter flocks, is the Skylark. Their airborne songs throughout the spring and summer months fill the air helping to create the atmosphere that is so typically Downland.

Far less common is the Tree Pipit, a bird more usually associated with open woodland, but which uses the scattered trees and bushes of The Downs from which to perform its song-flight. Opportunities exist therefore, particularly in the Churn area to compare this bird with the very similar Meadow Pipit, with the Tree Pipit's slightly stockier build, upright stance and more musical song serving to separate the two.

Red-legged and Grey Partridge are common downland residents, nesting along field edges and frequently seen feeding on the gallops, lanes and arable fields. Game-rearing, especially in the vicinity of the Warren, ensures that the Pheasant is very abundant. In summer the list of gamebirds is added to by the arrival of the Quail. It is a bird more often heard than seen and from May onwards its deceptively ventrilo-quial calling, especially at dusk, is always worth listening out for. Quail seem to have good years and bad. In a good year they may be encountered anywhere. If they are more thinly distributed, the area of Nutwood Down, south of Letcombe Bassett is perhaps a good area to visit (SU 365 825).

The ground nesting species are completed by the waders. The Lapwing, whilst having declined in numbers over the years is still to be found in areas of sheep-grazed grassland, where arable fields have been left fallow for a season or two, or on fields of late-sown corn. Springtime, when the birds are displaying and holding territory can provide some very memorable birdwatching. Outside of the breeding season, Lapwing form huge flocks of up to several thousand birds, often accompanied by Golden Plover. These flocks roam extensively, and in harsher weather may move to areas below the scarp, such as Aldfield Common (SU 465 877). The lack of water precludes visits by other wader species, but some of the waterways at the foot of the hills do provide sites for Snipe, whilst the woodlands (e.g. Unhill Wood or the Warren) may harbour Woodcock. These Downs were once the place for Stone Curlew in good numbers.

Sadly their numbers have declined to almost zero with perhaps just one pair being found each year. It is though, still worth keeping eyes and ears open during the summer, particularly over fallow ground or ground which has been sown late in the season, since it is always possible that they may appear at new sites.

Where the open ground changes to areas of denser scrub and hedgerow, so the associated bird community also alters. Chaffinch and Greenfinch, Goldfinch and Linnet now become common, along with Dunnock, Wren, Magpie and Blackbird. Also present, and perhaps something of a surprise in the absence of water, are Reed Bunting, often found in the scrub along the gallops. Little Owl are also seen. In summer, Chiffchaff, Willow Warbler, Blackcap and Whitethroat also occupy the hedgerows and scrub, while Spotted Flycatchers are regular. A similar range of species is found within the Downland woods, added to by Great, Blue and Coal Tits, Great Spotted and Green Woodpeckers, Jay, Nuthatch and Treecreeper. Tawny Owl and Sparrowhawk are also found here, the latter more often seen as it hunts over scrub and hedgerow for unsuspecting passerines, or soars high overhead on summertime thermals.

Hen Harrier

It is probably the birds of prey of the Downs which receive most attention from the birdwatcher, particularly in winter. Typical birds of the area are now Short-eared Owl and Hen Harrier, providing some exciting watching as they hunt over any rough grassland. Again, Churn is perhaps the most consistent site for both species with Hen Harrier often seen at dusk hunting along the disused railway line. Both can however turn up almost anywhere, probably moved around by factors such as weather and disturbance over the feeding and roosting sites. Wintertime can also turn up the occasional Merlin, preying upon the flocks of pipits or mixed finches (including Brambling) which wander the area in winter. Kestrel and Sparrowhawk are found all year, nesting within woodlands on both high and low ground. Also seen throughout the year, but not proven to be nesting, are Buzzards. These magnificent raptors can be observed hunting over grassland for their small mammal prey or, during the summer, soaring majestically overhead riding the thermals. Summertime will also find Hobbies in the area particularly in late summer when hirundines gather along the escarpment prior to migration.

Passage periods, either spring or autumn can be some of the best times to pay a visit to the Downs. The north-facing escarpment seems to act as a line of travel for birds allowing them to be observed either during flight or on the ground as they make a brief stop-over. As emphasised elsewhere, the point of stop-over can be almost anywhere, but the Churn area can be the most productive. During the springtime Wheatears are the first visitors to drop in, beginning to arrive from March onwards. Later, Whinchat and Ring Ouzel also visit and with the chance of Dotterel or Nightjar, this can be quite a lively time of year. Autumn passage can see the return movement of these birds, in particular Whinchat and Wheatear, as well as the first of the incoming winter visitors such as Redwing and Fieldfare. Meadow Pipit, gulls and waders can also be seen 'on the move' during September and October.

Birdwatching on the Downs can be rather frustrating, and one should not be put off if a blank is drawn on the first visit. Periods of passage, both spring and autumn undoubtedly provide the best birdwatching days and if there has been a clear night, followed by cloud, areas of scrub can be alive with migrants forced down in the course of their long-distance travels.

Wintertime too can give many memorable moments and so, whilst timing is all important, there is a certain amount of luck involved; but with a little patience, The Downs will eventually reveal just why they are one of Oxfordshire's most exciting birdwatching areas.

Calendar

Resident Sparrowhawk, Kestrel, partridges, Lapwing, Little Owl, Meadow Pipit, Skylark, Corn Bunting, Yellowhammer, Reed Bunting. Scrub and woodlands; usual tits, woodpeckers and finches, Nuthatch, Tree-creeper, Goldcrest, Woodcock, Jay and possible Buzzard.

December–February Short-eared Owl, Hen Harrier. Large Golden Plover and Lapwing flocks. Possible Merlin.

March–May Migrating species especially during April; Wheatear, Whin-chat, Ring Ouzel and Meadow Pipit, possible Nightjar and Dotterel. Tree

Pipit, commoner warblers, Cuckoo, Turtle Dove, Spotted Flycatcher. Possible Nightingale.

June–July Quail, possible Stone Curlew, Hobby.

August–November Early in period: Whinchat and Wheatear on passage. Build up of hirundine numbers. Finches and tits flock together, possible Brambling.

FARMOOR RESERVOIRS   Map 62/OS ref. SP 450 064

Habitat

The two reservoirs at Farmoor, just to the west of Oxford, are owned by Thames Water and used for river regulation and water supply purposes. Since their completion in 1976, they have also been extensively used by countless thousands of birds and appreciated by a rather large number of birdwatchers. The reservoirs' importance to birds is in two areas: firstly, during the winter period (October–April) as a feeding, resting and roosting site for very large numbers of waterfowl and gulls, and secondly as a site for those birds resting and feeding on migration.

The vast open areas of water incorporating both Farmoor I and Farmoor II cover a total of 378 acres (153 ha) and, from the air, they are clearly visible for many miles around – an ideal landmark for interested species. However, upon arrival at the site some of those passage birds may be a little disappointed since the reservoirs are essentially two huge concrete bowls, devoid of bankside vegetation and muddy feeding areas. Large numbers of small fish, together with air and water borne invertebrates do provide ample opportunities for a hungry bird. The rather sterile nature also means that bankside nesting opportunities are nil, but the area just beyond the perimeter of the works does provide some recompense. Some tree planting of the grassed areas beyond the embankment has been undertaken and in future years similar methods may be used to further 'soften' the environment. The River Thames (to the west of the reservoirs) and its associated flood meadows, shrubs and bankside trees is widely used by breeding birds, as too is the area of open fields and mixed woodland to the south.

Access

The reservoir complex is situated just south of Farmoor village. From Oxford proceed west along the B4044 turning left onto the B4017 immediately upon reaching the village. The main entrance and car park is on the right, approximately 800 yds (750 m) from this junction.

Access to the reservoir embankments is by permit only, available from the gatehouse, or by writing to the Senior Warden. (See Useful Addresses.) The current price is £1.50 which is valid for one year and entitles the holder to take a guest. Day tickets are also issued and a leaflet describing the birds of Farmoor is available. The gates are open from sunrise until half an hour after sunset although they may be subject to change. Due to a limit set on the number of birdwatchers using the reservoir, any parties wishing to visit should inform the Warden in advance. Toilet facilities are available and there is a birdwatchers' log book kept in the last building on the right overlooking Farmoor II, and just past the sailing-club. Here one can preview the birds likely to be encountered and, at the end of the visit note down one's own observations. The permit allows access only to the embankment, it does not allow the holder to wander around the works or the sludge tanks at the north of the site.

With 3.5 miles (5.6 km) of embankment one could easily spend half a day birdwatching around the reservoirs. If however, there is a time limit to your visit, a jaunt along the causeway will provide adequate views of most of the species present. A telescope is invaluable at this site. In the winter warm clothing is essential since a bitter wind can blow across the water and ruin a visit if unprepared. Dogs are not permitted.

The reservoir complex is used for other recreational activities such as windsurfing, sailing and angling. The first two pursuits are mainly confined to Farmoor II where they do cause a certain amount of disturbance to the birdlife but Farmoor I is seldom disturbed to the same extent. Angling, primarily fly-fishing, takes place along most of the embankment and though disturbance to birds on the open water is minimal, bankside feeders such as waders, wagtails and pipits may be more mobile. Anglers may actually pose greater problems to birdwatchers – more than one local birder has found himself impaled by a fishing hook and in need of some first-aid, victim of an angler's back-cast!

The land beyond the reservoir compound has access permitted along footpaths and the river towpath providing an enjoyable, rather more rural circular route. Some views of the reservoir, if rather limited, can be obtained along this route. For the information of the less energetic visitor, most of the surrounding landscape can be observed from the reservoir embankment.

Species

When, in the early 1960s plans to build these reservoirs were first put forward, local birdwatchers were worried. The gravel pits which were to be destroyed had provided some of the finest bird records imaginable for such a land-locked county as Oxfordshire. However, apart from the obvious and regrettable loss of nesting habitat (and a new gravel pit complex was being created at nearby Stanton Harcourt) the quality and variety of birds visiting the site has remained at least as good as before, if not better! Some exciting and spectacular species, as well as very high numbers of birds, have been, and still can be, enjoyed at Farmoor.

Gulls may not be everybody's favourite group of birds, either to identify, or because of their anti-social behaviour, but the sight and sound of the Farmoor gull roost is well worth experiencing. Numbers start to build up on the site from early September onwards, at first perhaps no more than a few hundred birds – mainly Black-headed but accompanied by Lesser Black-backed and a few Herring Gulls. By December and January numbers have swollen to be in excess of 10,000 birds. Well over half will be Black-headed with up to 2,500 Lesser Black-backed and 2,000 Herring Gull, and since birds of all ages and plumages will be among them, one has plenty of opportunity to polish up one's gull identification techniques. Birds start to arrive up to two hours before dark, approaching the reservoirs from their feeding grounds in all directions. They are a little restless at first, refusing to remain in one place for long but eventually settling to form huge rafts in the middle of the water. Overhead, the air is full of crying, screaming gulls, arguing and fighting their way to roost. Even as darkness falls, formations of gulls are still arriving, their calls still filling the air as one departs. Probably the best time to pick out some of the less common species is while the gulls are on the water. Common Gulls are not very common, maybe only 100 birds, with even smaller numbers of Great Black-backed. With so many gulls present, it is always advisable to double-check in the hope of a Glaucous or Mediterranean Gull – not an easy task but sometimes very worthwhile.

Whilst rarely featuring in the great roosts, the Little Gull is a regular visitor, particularly on spring passage. Usually, only small numbers occur but it is readily identified by its agility, small size and most notably by the way in which it feeds tern-like over the water. Indeed, it may well be found in the company of terns, most usually Black and Common, but occasionally Arctic, as they pause to feed at Farmoor. The terns occur at both ends of the breeding season but are in their best plumage and hence most identifiable in late April and early May, when numbers reach a peak.

Terns and gulls are regarded by the majority of people as birds of the sea. Whilst most birdwatchers are aware of their appearance inland, it nonetheless comes as a surprise to know that Farmoor, despite being so far inland has produced some truly maritime species. Gannet, Arctic Skua, Manx Shearwater, Kittiwake and even a Leach's Petrel have all been recorded, usually as a result of violent gales, blowing birds off course. A visit therefore after one of these storms can be most rewarding.

Despite the reservoirs being essentially concrete bowls, it is remarkable just how many waders are still to be seen at Farmoor. April and May provide the greatest variety and number of birds with Grey Plover, Knot, Whimbrel, Greenshank, Sanderling and both godwit species making stop-over visits most years. Ruff, Turnstone, Oystercatcher and Spotted Redshank may also drop in, these also making regular visits on the return migration in August and September. Purple Sandpiper and Little Stint are most likely to be seen during the autumn passage. Common Sandpiper and Little Ringed Plover can often be seen through the summer, although individuals of the former do remain at the site in winter. Dunlin, Redshank and Ringed Plover are recorded at all times of the year and represent Farmoor's commonest waders. Very occasionally, birdwatchers will be rewarded with real gems; an Avocet perhaps, elegantly wading the water's edge and deftly sweeping the water surface for invertebrates, or maybe a Grey Phalarope – a confiding little bird apparently undisturbed by the onlooking birdwatcher as it swims rather than wades the shallows, picking insects and other morsels from the water's surface.

Passage birds also include a number of passerine species. Wheatear are common during March to May and again in August and September, to be seen darting along the causeway. They are often accompanied by Whinchat, although the bushes and fences between reservoir and river can often be the better site for this typically moorland bird. Less colourful, but more numerous, at least in spring, is the Meadow Pipit with as many as 100 birds passing through. Some Meadow Pipits over-winter at the site and flocks occasionally include Rock/Water Pipits among their ranks. Wagtails are abundant at Farmoor, feeding along the water's edge, the causeway and around the treatment works. Pied Wagtail, which nest on the works' buildings, form quite large flocks in winter; at migration periods check for White Wagtails, as one or two appear most years. In spring, Yellow Wagtails arrive in good numbers, but in August large post-breeding flocks with many young birds amongst them congregate at the reservoir, creating a bright and lively scene. In spring, look out for individuals of the handsome Blue-headed race of Yellow Wagtail.

For sheer numbers of birds, the Swifts, Swallows and martins create quite a spectacle as they feed on the hordes of flies rising from the water. Large numbers of Swift congregate here soon after arrival in Britain and from the tail-end of April, up to 3,000 birds scream and wheel over the waters. Ahead of them a steady stream of Swallows and martins use Farmoor to replenish food reserves utilised on migration, while local birds of all these species use the reservoir as a feeding area throughout the summer. A few House Martins actually nest on site, using the buildings of the treatment works. Numbers of all these birds reach a peak in August and September after the young have fledged with, on one occasion, an estimated 15,000 House Martins using the site. When large numbers are feeding like this it is common to find Hobbies, sometimes as many as four (and probably not long off the nest themselves) attempting to cash in on this abundance of prey.

There is a rapid turnover of birds at the site and no sooner have the summer visitors left than the winter ones begin to arrive and at Farmoor this primarily involves the waterfowl. Late September and early October will see the first Goldeneye return; small numbers at first but rising to as many as 60 by January. Tufted Duck, Pochard and Mallard numbers also rise steadily, birds flying in to join the flocks of non-breeders that have summered at Farmoor, with each species peaking at around 400 birds. As the year progresses smaller numbers of Teal, Gadwall and Shoveler also join the flocks, but by far the most numerous species is the Wigeon, with up to 1,000 birds present. The exact numbers depend on the weather conditions, particularly the amount of flood water available elsewhere in the county. Of the other regular duck species, the Goosander is probably the most conspicuous, the bold, predominantly white plumage of the Drake being instantly recognisable even at some distance, while the elegant, upright posture of the Pintail is another frequent sight.

Total numbers of waterbirds present vary according to the weather with maxima being reached in very cold weather; Farmoor usually being the last of the local waters to become ice-bound. Birdwatching can then be most memorable as birds are often concentrated into small areas of open water. At these times, and also during migration periods, one can expect species such as Scaup, Common and Velvet Scoter, Smew and Long-tailed Duck; birds that are more likely to be seen off the coast during the winter. There seems to have been a trend in recent years for these birds to remain at Farmoor for several days or weeks rather than just a fleeting visit as used to happen.

The stocking of the reservoirs with fish has created feeding opportunities for a number of other birds – some being rather unwelcome. Great Crested Grebe are numerous for most of the year and generally a few Little Grebe are present. Red-necked, Black-necked and Slavonian Grebe are all regular winter visitors. Divers also appear, most commonly Red-throated, during the autumn passage but increasingly noted during wintertime is the Great Northern Diver. Grey Heron may occasionally stalk the reservoir while Kingfishers make regular visits, particularly when the River Thames becomes turbid, to fish in the shallows at the western end of the causeway. Probably the most unwelcome fish-eater is the Cormorant. Despite attempts to move them on, winter numbers have steadily risen at Farmoor so that there are often as many as 70 birds present. They roost on the limnological towers of Farmoor II but feed in both pools. When disturbed they disperse to nearby gravel pits, feeding and resting there until a safe return to the reservoirs is possible.

Apart from the birds found on the water, Farmoor reservoirs are relatively quiet in winter. Some passerines such as Meadow Pipits, Pied Wagtails, Linnets and Goldfinches are usually present and may be joined by 'goodies' such as Snow Bunting and Black Redstart. In such a large area though, thorough searching may be necessary in order to locate them.

In the area surrounding the reservoirs, particularly along the river, breeding species of the open field, hedgerows and woodland can be found. In winter when there is flooding of the meadows, flocks of Canada Geese gather to graze, often in the company of some of the local feral Greylag. Lapwing also use the area and, if it is very wet, Curlew may feed. Species such as Wigeon and Teal commute between the meadows and the reservoirs, while Grey Heron hunt the pools and ditches. Therefore, at any time of year, this particular area is well worth investigating.

Farmoor's rise to become the county's top birdwatching haunt is thus not without good reason. The large number and variety of bird species, and the reservoirs' close proximity to Oxford, certainly make it the most watched site, with every visit likely to bring the possibility of something else to add to the extensive and spectacular bird list. A visit is thoroughly recommended.

Calendar

Resident On and around reservoir, Pied Wagtail, Tufted Duck, Mallard, Coot, Mute Swan and Little Grebe. On surrounding area, partridges, Moorhen, Kingfisher, Reed Bunting, Yellowhammer.

December–February Gull roost at peak (Good time for Glaucous), occasional Snow Bunting, Black Redstart; possible Great Northern Diver or rarer grebes, winter duck numbers at peak with Goosander, possible Scaup, Common Scoter, Smew, Long-tailed Duck.

March–May During March and April Wheatear, Whinchat, Yellow Wagtail, Sand Martin, Meadow Pipit. April–May is the main passage period with tern and Little Gull. Possible Kittiwake, Knot, Grey Plover, Whimbrel, Ringed Plover, Little Ringed Plover. Swallow, House Martin, Swift.

June–July Swift and hirundines over water, a few non-breeding duck, swans and grebe, Common Sandpiper.

August–November Early in period, build up of Yellow Wagtail, hirundines and Swift numbers, possible Hobby. Migrating waders – Little Stint, Ruff, Oystercatcher, Turnstone. Build up of Cormorant and gull numbers. Return of winter duck e.g. Wigeon, Teal, Shoveler, Goldeneye; possible Red-throated Diver, Red-breasted Merganser; Redshank, Common Sandpiper.

FOXHOLES

Map 63/OS ref. SP 254 206

Habitat

Close to Oxfordshire's boundary with Gloucestershire and tucked away rather inconspicuously, Foxholes is a quiet reserve of some 160 acres (64 ha) lying on the west bank of the River Evenlode. The site is managed by BBONT and is part-owned, part-leased by them. Its tranquil charm stems from it being part of a sizeable estate, much of which is undisturbed. Another reason for its undoubted attractiveness is the variety of habitat found in and around the reserve boundaries. At the lowest altitude, 330 ft (100 m), is the River Evenlode. Its course follows a quite intensively arable valley but at Foxholes the reserve includes an attractive, unimproved base-rich wet meadow. From the river, the reserve slopes quite gently through woodland and open grazing meadow to reach a plateau at 460 ft (140 m). The site is a remnant of the once vast Wychwood Forest and is generally quite wet. On the lower limestone slopes the woodland comprises Oak, Ash and Beech with a good shrub layer of Hawthorn, Bramble and Hazel, some of which is coppiced. On higher ground, the soils become more acid, encouraging Bracken, some heather, and a more open woodland with Oak and Birch dominant. Part of the plateau is given over to a sizeable Larch plantation.

The quietness of the reserve makes it a superb site for mammal watching, even in daylight. Look out for Fox, Stoat and Weasel, Fallow, Muntjac and the occasional Roe Deer. The reserve is noted for its flora (it is rather picturesque at Bluebell-time) and is particularly renowned for its fungi.

Access

Foxholes lies close to Bruern Abbey between Milton-under-Wychwood and Bledington. To reach it, proceed north out of Burford on the A424 towards Stow-on-the-Wold and take the third turning on the right. Proceed north-east along the unclassified road to Bruern for 2 miles (3.5 km). Just before Bruern, turn off left along the track which follows the edge of Cocksmoor Copse. After 820 yds (750 m), and just before reaching the farm buildings, there is a small car park on the right.

A number of bridleways and footpaths cut across the reserve giving good access to all areas of interest; BBONT members though, do have access along a number of other tracks and rides including access to the wet meadow, allowing an even greater appreciation of the reserve.

The woodland can become very wet underfoot in the winter months and wellingtons are advisable.

Species

Whilst not noted for any rarities, Foxholes is a site where a good number and variety of typical woodland bird species can be seen. In addition, the presence of river and wet meadow increases this variety particularly in spring and summer.

Since it is conveniently close to the car park, the river is probably the best point from which to begin a tour of the reserve. The wet meadow provides nest sites for a number of pairs of Mallard and Moorhen as well as Reed Bunting; species that are present all year. Snipe often over-winter in the meadow and in some years one or two pairs may breed. Mute Swan and Canada Goose are seen throughout the year and whilst they may not actually nest here, preferring sites elsewhere in the valley, they may both be seen either on the river in summer or grazing the fields adjacent to the reserve in winter. Along the river itself, Little Grebe breed – very wary birds quickly diving below the water if one approaches incautiously, surfacing silently beneath overhanging vegetation. The high, steep river banks allow Kingfisher to nest and at any time, there may be a couple of pairs in the area.

Adjacent to the wood but outside of the reserve, are several grazing meadows, the largest being Fifield Heath. Whilst these are usually too disturbed to provide nest sites, except for Skylark or the occasional Lapwing, they are used as regular feeding areas by birds such as Rook, Mistle Thrush, Green Woodpecker, Kestrel and Little Owl, all of which nest in the reserve and are found all year round. In winter, Lapwing may gather in small flocks in these fields. Scattered across the fields and along their boundaries are Oak trees, always worth checking for Lesser Spotted and Great Spotted Woodpeckers. Whilst present in good numbers over most of the reserve, the two species are often easier to see around these meadowland Oaks. They betray their presence by the familiar calling and display in springtime and their characteristic undulating flight as they move from tree to tree. More at home in the woodland are Treecreeper and Nuthatch, with views of the latter more likely within the Beech woods. The dampness of the reserve and the presence of so much dead timber means that hole-nesting species in general do quite well. Willow Tit for instance is ever present but probably outnumbered by its close relative the Marsh Tit. Great and Blue Tits are very common, with Jackdaw, Starling and Tawny Owl adding to the list of hole-nesters. Of the other members of the tit family, Long-tailed Tit is more likely in the Hawthorn scrub at the north-west of the reserve, and the Coal Tit, most numerous within the conifers, often associates with Goldcrests. The wet conditions of the site also create ideal conditions for that secretive woodland bird, the Woodcock.

All over the reserve, typical breeding finches are Chaffinch and Greenfinch, with Goldfinch and Bullfinch nesting in areas of scrub. Wintertime may find a few Siskin and Redpoll using the reserve, particularly around Birch trees, and while foliage cover is reduced, this may be a good time to look for the few resident Hawfinch.

Significant numbers of avian summer visitors provide good watching and listening on the reserve. Chiffchaff, Willow Warbler, Blackcap and Garden Warbler are the most common in the woods whilst Whitethroat is to be found along the woodland edge and in nearby hedgerows. A small number of Nightingale breed each year and the area on the northern edge of the Blackberry Field, known as 'Wet Foot Corner', is the most regular haunt of this melodic migrant. Foxholes House and its outbuildings provide good habitat for nesting Spotted Flycatchers, Swallows and House Martins. Each spring, hopes rise that species such as Redstart and Wood Warbler may decide to take up summer residence at Foxholes. Nesting conditions in the woods seem right and, as both species make short visits on passage each spring, there is the feeling that it could be just a matter of time before they decide to make a longer stay.

The good numbers of passerine species, coupled with the general open nature of the area provide ideal hunting conditions for Sparrow-hawks. Nests are high in the canopy and each year a few pairs build at Foxholes, particularly in Bould Wood or in the plantation upon Herberts Heath. June and July are probably the best times to watch them since, with chicks on the nest, adult birds will be kept very busy in order to provide enough food for their rapidly growing young.

Being situated on high ground, the woods, especially in winter, can be a little on the quiet side. Many of the resident species will move to more sheltered sites, with the remainder forming feeding flocks, consisting of a number of species. In winter therefore, it pays to be patient and to try and seek out these flocks, following them for a while as they roam noisily through the wood. Winter also sees the influx of visiting thrushes, Redwing and Fieldfare. Both may be present in large mixed flocks (including some Blackbird and Song Thrush) feeding on Hawthorn and other berries, at the periphery of, and inside, the wood.

Even in the absence of any rarities, Foxholes can give some very pleasurable birdwatching moments: Sparrowhawks feeding recently fledged young, a Willow Tit noisily and industriously chiselling away its nest-hole, a displaying Lesser Spotted Woodpecker or a glimpse of a spring visiting Redstart.

Calendar

Resident Woodcock, Kestrel, Sparrowhawk, Little Owl, Tawny Owl, Great Spotted, Lesser Spotted and Green Woodpeckers, Goldcrest, all six tit species, Nuthatch, Treecreeper, Jackdaw, Rook, Crow. Common thrushes, Bullfinch, Chaffinch, Goldfinch, Greenfinch, Linnet, Hawfinch (possible).

On wet meadow and river: Little Grebe, Mute Swan, Canada Goose, Mallard, Moorhen, Kingfisher, Skylark, Reed Bunting. Possible Lapwing and Snipe.

December–February Redwing, Fieldfare, Siskin, Redpoll, increased numbers of Woodcock.

March–May Yellow Wagtail, Nightingale, Blackcap, Garden Warbler, Chiffchaff, Willow Warbler, possible Redstart and Wood Warbler, Spotted-Flycatcher, House Martin, Swallow.

June–July Breeding activity at peak.

August–November Summer migrants in large parties before departure. Resident tits and finches form flocks.

GRIMSBURY RESERVOIR   Map 64/OS ref. SP 458 417

Habitat

While its small size 16 acres (6.5 ha), prevents it from joining the ranks of the inland reservoirs of national importance for birds, Grimsbury Reservoir and the surrounding area does provide sufficient diversity of habitat to be of importance at the county level.

Owned by Thames Water, the reservoir itself has a concreted -shore-line lacking in vegetation and so is of limited use to nesting birds. A great deal of sailing also takes place, further restricting the opportunities for breeding species. Above the shoreline, the banks have a covering of dense herbage and, if they remain unmown, offer shelter to nesting passerines. To the east of the reservoir runs the River Cherwell, its banks generously lined by coarse vegetation and reeds, with scattered Alder, Birch and Hawthorn trees. Other, more recent tree-planting has taken place. To the east and north-west and bounded by the Oxford Canal are areas of permanent pasture composed of rough grasses and rushes. A stream, lined by willow and Hawthorn crosses this area and, as a consequence, these fields can be very wet in winter. Just beyond the reservoir's northern tip is a small plantation. The dominant species are Alder and Corsican Pine and there is a dense ground layer.

The site is held in high esteem by members of the Banbury Ornithological Society who, as well as collecting much data about the wildlife of the site, have collaborated with Thames Water to help conserve and improve the site's flora and fauna. Plans are in hand to improve the plantation involving the creation of more open areas and a pond, and to improve the flow of the stream that runs through it. Eventually it is hoped to create a full nature trail around the site.

Access

The reservoir lies on Banbury's northern edge and is reached from the link road joining the A423 with the A361. Turn off at the roundabout situated approximately 600 yds (500 m) east of the junction with the A423. The reservoir and water treatment works are signposted from here with car parking available on the left hand side of the lane almost opposite the main gates.

From the main entrance, a footpath takes one around the reservoir along the River Cherwell and through the plantation. Good views over the adjacent meadows are also obtained from the path but no rights of way exist over these pastures. The public are permitted along the canal towpath although for most of the way tall, thick hedgerows prevent good viewing.

Species

The site is definitely at its best in winter and during periods of bird migration. Disturbance and the general nature of the reservoir means that the reservoir has little scope for breeding birds but an evening or early morning visit during the nesting season can be profitable. Along the river, Moorhen and Mallard are common and Little Grebe and Kingfisher may breed, with Wren, Reed Bunting and Sedge Warbler making the most of the dense bankside vegetation. In the plantation, and in other trees and shrubs, nest the resident finches and thrushes as well as the more usual warblers. Goldcrest, Treecreeper and a number of tit species breed within the plantation. Pied Wagtails are present on site all year, nesting on the buildings of the treatment works. During the breeding season, birds to be found upon the open fields will depend on the level of grazing disturbance and upon how wet it is. Lapwing may breed and partridge (both species) and Skylark are usually to be seen or heard. In the pollarded willows, Little Owl nest and at any time of the year a Barn Owl may be watched as it hunts silently for small rodents. In the daytime Kestrels may be encountered over these fields, whilst a Sparrowhawk can often be watched hunting the hedgerow by the canal or through the plantation. In late summer these fields, and the reservoir, may draw hirundines to feed which in their turn may attract the attention of a hungry Hobby or two.

A visit in early spring may be rewarded by the presence of one of a number of species who utilise the reservoir as a stopping off point on their migration. Wheatear are the most frequently seen, feeding boldly on the open grassy banks around the reservoir or in the nearby meadows. Whinchat and Redstart are also regular – look for them as they perch on a convenient fence-post. Though the reservoir is small, and perhaps lacking in typical wader feeding grounds, a number of species are seen during passage, notably Ringed Plover, Dunlin and Common Sandpiper. Less commonly encountered are Oystercatcher, Turnstone and Sanderling. Garganey are also recorded and during May the waters of the reservoir may also attract terns; Black, Common and Arctic appear most years, sometimes moving through in the company of Little Gull. Many of these birds on spring passage can also be seen at the tail end of summer when, typically, the flocks comprise family parties and many young individuals. During August and September some species form large congregations as local birds flock together. Swallows, for example, chatter noisily over the site, roosting with Yellow Wagtails, Reed Bunting and Pied Wagtail. Of course two of these move on to over-winter in continental Africa but the latter two remain all winter and in recent years Pied Wagtails have formed significant roosts with numbers reaching a peak during December. As autumn progresses, Meadow Pipits arrive in good numbers, feeding across the site in the company of Pied Wagtail and Linnet. A few Grey Wagtail and occasionally a Stonechat may also over-winter.

With Alder trees in abundance, it is hardly surprising that, in winter, the Siskin is one of the most conspicuous birds of the location. They probe the cones acrobatically for seeds and are often joined by Redpoll. In winter, resident birds show more social tendencies forming mixed flocks: Tits, Treecreepers and Goldcrest group together and Chaffinch and Greenfinch, accompanied by wintering Brambling, forage widely in search of food. On areas of rough ground, and especially where thistle and teasel heads still stand, Linnet, Goldfinch and Redpoll may be found.

Provided the water remains undisturbed and does not become ice-bound, a good selection of wildfowl take up winter residence on the site, using both the reservoir and the fields if flooded. Mallard, Pochard and Tufted Duck are the commonest but numbers of any one of these seldom reach above 150. Wigeon may also be seen in small numbers. Shoveler and Teal make up the list of ducks regularly seen and Great

Crested Grebe are usually present. Although too small a site to regularly attract many of the less common duck, Goldeneye and Pintail, Scaup, Shelduck, Common Scoter and Red-breasted Merganser have all been recorded, thus making a thorough check of all the birds present most important.

In common with the majority of English reservoirs, gull roosts are a feature of Grimsbury, although the congregations here are more likely to be pre-roosting flocks which move off to join larger, overnight roosts elsewhere. Forming at dusk, numbers are never huge and Black-headed Gulls make up the majority with Lesser Black-backed and Herring Gulls also present. Small groups of Great Black-backed and Common Gulls may join the flocks and one year a Glaucous Gull was a very notable visitor. If it is decided to make an evening visit for the gulls then use the occasion to check over the neighbouring fields for owls. During winter, in addition to the resident species, Short-eared Owls may well take up residence and, although a diurnal species, are most active at dusk. The sight of this superb bird makes an exciting end to any day's birdwatching.

Calendar

Resident Moorhen, Mallard, Little Grebe, Kestrel, Sparrowhawk, Little Owl, Kingfisher, Pied Wagtail, Goldcrest, Blue Tit, Great Tit, Coal Tit, Treecreeper, Chaffinch, Linnet, Skylark, Reed Bunting. Possible Barn Owl.

December–February Best time for winter duck especially Pochard, Tufted Duck and Mallard, Wigeon, Teal and Shoveler. Occasional Goldeneye, Common Scoter and Scaup. Peak time for gulls, occasional Glaucous Gull. Grey Heron, Short-eared Owl.

March–May Passage: Whinchat, Wheatear, possible Redstart, hirundines. Occasional Ringed Plover, Little Ringed Plover, Dunlin, Common Sandpiper, Sanderling, Oystercatcher, and Turnstone, Little Gull, Black Tern, Common and Arctic Tern, Yellow Wagtail.

June–July Riparian breeders.

August–November Build-up in hirundine and wagtail flocks. Occasional Hobby, Stonechat, Siskin, Redpoll. Large finch and tit congregations. Build-up of duck, Great Crested Grebe and gull numbers.

LITTLE WITTENHAM
NATURE RESERVE
Map 65/OS ref. SU 570 930

Habitat

Although only acquired by the Northmoor Trust in the first half of the 1980s, this 250 acre (100 ha) site bordering the River Thames is rapidly becoming a favourite among the county's naturalists. From the ornithological viewpoint, a year-long survey of the reserve has been carried out and much of Roger Wiggins' findings are noted in this chapter.

With a number of distinct facets to its structure Little Wittenham supports a good range of wildlife and of foremost importance, particularly so far as breeding birds are concerned, is Little Wittenham Wood. Sloping down to the river's edge this is an ancient woodland site of some 130 acres (53 ha) with some fine old Oak trees and areas of coppice. Unfortunately much has been replanted with dense conifer stands and mixed timber plantations. Significant areas of scrub are found and there are two woodland ponds. To the west of the wood, and on the same steep slope is an area of open chalk grassland, towered over by the group of ancient Beech trees stop Round Hill and from where panoramic views over the Oxfordshire countryside can be obtained. Just to the south-east of Round Hill is Castle Hill, the site of an Iron Age hill fort dating back 2,500 years. These two neighbouring hills are known locally as the Wittenham Clumps.

The third facet of importance to the naturalist is the River Thames and the adjacent flood meadows. Worthy of special mention is the length of bank where the woodland runs down to the river's edge and which remains relatively undisturbed, thus offering quiet nesting sites for the typical riverside birds and other forms of wildlife.

Whilst a relative newcomer to the nature reserves of Oxfordshire, the site has enormous potential and much active work is being undertaken by the Northmoor Trust to create and maintain the widest diversity of habitat. This management includes the removal of conifers, the opening of broad rides and the coppicing of timber within the wood and also the improvement of the chalk grassland by a regime of sheep-grazing and wildflower planting. Many of the magnificent Beech trees on Round Hill are unfortunately dying and so a replanting scheme has been initiated.

Much survey work has been done to assess the status of the site's flora and fauna, and to look at changes as management plans are put into operation. Additionally, a very active ringing group operates on the site.

Access

The reserve is situated to the east of Little Wittenham Village and a large car park is provided, close to Castle Hill, and reached from the unclassified road between Little Wittenham and Brightwell-cum-Sotwell.

The grassland of Round Hill stretching down to the river and including Castle Hill is designated a Country Park and, apart from fenced-off experimental and replanted areas, the public has free access over it. Through and around the woodland is a public footpath and bridleway, offering some access. The Trust has also opened up a number of other 'permitted-paths', along which the public may walk. Please note that there is no public access to the woodland ponds, primarily in an attempt to prevent disturbance to breeding wildlife.

The river can be viewed from the towpath running along its north bank, and a footpath from Day's Lock leads across the fields to Dorchester-on-Thames. Groups wishing to visit the reserve should telephone the Warden beforehand (086730-7374). This is to prevent excessive disturbance and also, if necessary, to arrange for one of the Warden's staff to act as a guide.

Species

Whilst a good range of species has been recorded, the birds to be seen in this locality depend very much upon the time of year and, according to the time of the visit, the birdwatcher's attention is best directed at one particular part of the reserve. Winter for instance sees the main avian activity centred upon the river and adjoining flood meadows. Snipe and Redshank feed on the edges of pools, and flocks of Starling and Lapwing haunt the drier areas. Black-headed Gulls also move in, noisily harrying the Lapwing. Small groups of Herring Gulls and Lesser Black-backed Gulls will also be seen. Meadow Pipit and Pied Wagtails also frequent these fields and the lucky observer may be rewarded with the sight of a hunting Short-eared Owl. Of the duck, Teal and Wigeon are the most numerous, feeding around the flood waters, sometimes in the company of a few Shoveler. On the river, small parties of Tufted Duck and Pochard may congregate. As is common elsewhere in the county, Canada Geese form large flocks in the fields around Day's Lock. These flocks are always worth a second glance since they are sometimes joined by small numbers of Pink-footed and White-fronted Goose. If very cold weather conditions ensue, and still waters freeze, then as well as an increase in the birds present, other species of wildfowl may move on to the Thames with Goldeneye, Goosander and Red-breasted Merganser all being possible.

Present all year and breeding on the river will be Mallard, Moorhen and Coot. Mute Swan and Great Crested Grebe are regularly seen but do not appear to breed on site. Grey Heron feed all along the river and that most colourful of fishermen, the Kingfisher, is also around most of the year, nesting close to Day's Lock, and sometimes raising two broods. Pied Wagtail also nest near the lock while Yellow Wagtail join Corn Bunting, Reed Bunting and Yellowhammer nesting on some of the surrounding fields. Throughout the summer, Swifts, Swallows and House Martins feed on the insects rising from the river and wet meadows. All breed in the nearby villages but nests of the latter are clearly visible on the lock keeper's house just below the weir. During periods of passage, the weir pool may prove attractive to Common or Arctic Terns gracefully dipping and diving into the waters. Due to disturbance by boats on the river during summer, an early visit to this part of the site is usually the most profitable.

However, in summer the main interest of the site shifts to Little Wittenham Wood and the good variety of woodland species that it supports. The Nuthatch does not breed but its absence is more than made up for by a good woodpecker population. Great Spotted are certainly the most obvious and as many as nine pairs may be present, their noisy drumming and loud calls allowing birdwatchers to locate them with relative ease. The ringing, laughing call of the Green

243

Woodpecker is another common sound and the opening of broad grassy rides in the wood will certainly improve the chances of sighting this bird. One or two pairs of the smallest native woodpecker, the Lesser Spotted, nest in the wood but are also occasionally seen in the vicinity of the orchard which abuts the reserve next to the village. The woodpeckers are, of course, all residents and visible at most times of the year. Other residents include good numbers of Treecreeper, Wren, Jay, Magpie, Robin and Blackbird, a good population of Goldcrest (in the conifer plantations) and the usual titmice with almost equal numbers of Marsh and Willow Tit. Of the finches the Chaffinch is very prolific and the Bullfinch regularly seen. In the more open areas of the wood, Mistle Thrush and Dunnock thrive. Up to five pairs of Tawny Owl and one or two pairs of Sparrowhawk nest. Summer visiting warblers are dominated by Chiffchaff, Blackcap, and Willow Warbler with lower numbers of Garden Warbler. Small numbers of Common Whitethroat breed, particularly around cleared areas of woodland but more frequently in the local hedgerows. A few Lesser Whitethroat nest in the locality while around the village Spotted Flycatcher may be seen. The Cuckoo, widespread and common in the area, and the Turtle Dove concludes the list of summer visitors. The area in the vicinity of the woodland ponds often acts as a focus for passerine birds providing feeding and drinking opportunities as well as some nest sites. Species such as Moorhen, Mallard and Little Grebe nest on the ponds, Tufted Duck are often seen but are not known to breed and Grey Heron may feed. At periods of passage, Green and Common Sandpiper have been noted on the ponds, also occurring along the river.

Corn Bunting   GC··

The area of open chalk grassland is rather less well-blessed for birds. Both species of partridge can be found, nesting on the tops of the hills or along hedgerows with Little Owls noted in similar areas. In the summer, Swallows and martins feed energetically over the fields and Swifts tumble and scream overhead. A Kestrel can often be seen, hovering gracefully, ever watchful for potential prey below. Later in the year, Rook and Jackdaw feed on these grasslands where in winter flocks of Meadow Pipits take up residence. The informed and careful observer may like to take the opportunity to check for Rock Pipits since one or two are recorded each year. Various finch flocks may move into the area in winter and parties of Linnet, Goldfinch and Greenfinch may be present particularly around patches of rougher grassland towards the foot of the hill.

This reserve is one that is still undergoing active development in order to create the best selection of habitat for all forms of wildlife and which will certainly continue to improve in the years to come.

Calendar

Resident Woodcock, Sparrowhawk, Tawny Owl, Little Owl, Pheasant and partridge. Three woodpecker species, Skylark, Treecreeper, typical woodland corvids, thrushes etc. Common tits and finches, Goldcrest, Corn Bunting, Yellowhammer.

On and around River: Great Crested Grebe, Mallard, Canada Goose, Mute Swan, Moorhen, Coot, Kingfisher, Pied Wagtail, Reed Bunting.

December–February Snipe, Redshank, mixed gull flocks, Starling, Short-eared Owl, Meadow Pipit, winter thrushes. If flood water present, Teal, Shoveler, Wigeon, Tufted Duck, Pochard, possible wild swan and geese, occasional Goldeneye, Goosander.

March–May Passage: possible Wheatear. Blackcap, Garden Warbler, Chiffchaff, Willow Warbler, Yellow Wagtail, House Martin, Swallow, Swift, Cuckoo, Common and Lesser Whitethroat, Turtle Dove.

June–July Spotted Flycatcher. Much breeding bird activity.

August–November On passage: Green and Common Sandpiper, possible terns. Flocking of many resident species. Influx of wintering species as outlined for December–February.

LOWER WINDRUSH VALLEY GRAVEL PITS

Map 66/OS ref. SP 405 045

Habitat

Spread over the general area of Stanton Harcourt, Hardwick and Standlake, and straddling the River Windrush, is a sprawling complex of pits created by gravel and sand extraction. Something in the order of 35 pits, most of them water-filled lakes, are found in this complex, making it the largest in the county and of great importance to wildlife. Nor is it just the bodies of water that are of interest, as the lands around create a very varied landscape being a mixture of open fields, 'waste-ground', scrub and hedgerows with mature trees. The pits themselves show considerable heterogeneity ranging from shallow dry scrapes, some still undergoing extraction, through to deep, established lakes with well-developed bankside vegetation. Many of the worked pits have been landscaped and given over to recreational pursuits such as sailing, power-boating and angling. Unfortunately the disturbance created by some of these activities does rather limit the breeding birds. However, in winter when disturbance is reduced, most pits are worth a visit, for during this time of year the entire complex becomes very important for wintering wildfowl.

The area is likely to be worked for gravel for many years to come. New pits will be dug; worked out ones reclaimed or landscaped for leisure activities. As long as a diversity of form exists among the pits with some remaining undisturbed then the wildlife interest will be retained.

Access

With many of the pits still being actively worked or held in the hands of private groups using the lakes for recreation, full access to the site is not possible. However, virtually all the waters can be seen from one of the roads or footpaths which traverse the area. Additionally, many of the landowners (if approached tactfully) will grant access to individuals or groups, but check before entering.

To visit all of the pits and study them properly would be a huge undertaking. Hence, in order for visiting birdwatchers to be a little more selective in their choice of pit to watch, the ornithologically most important and the ones with easiest access are now given.

Vicarage Pit A 23 acre (9.2 ha) pit lying alongside the road between Hardwick and Stanton Harcourt and in the safe hands of BBONT. Park at the side of the road from where adequate views can be obtained.

Linch Hill Complex Three lakes managed by Amey Roadstone Corporation (ARC) for leisure activities such as fishing and sailboarding. All day visitors wishing to use the site will have to pay an admission charge but birdwatchers wishing to make regular visits can write to the Area Manager of ARC (see Useful Addresses) for a permit. Entrance to the lakes is approximately 1.25 miles (2 km) south of Stanton Harcourt on the B4449.

Dix (or Devil's Quoits) Pit A large deep water pit with two islands and good bankside vegetation. Thankfully, recreational disturbance is very limited since this water is probably the single most important of the complex for winter wildfowl. Limited views are obtainable from the road leading to the refuse disposal site (gate is locked when site not in use) but bankside viewing is only permitted upon application to the Local Manager of ARC. (See Useful Addresses.) Outside of working hours, parking is possible in front of the offices near the Dix Pit gravel workings.

'The Scrape' A dry shallow pit (maintained by pumping) adjacent to Dix Pit and traditionally the prime site for waders. Part of the area is now a tip for household waste but extensive excavations are still in progress. A footpath along the north-east edge allows good views. Park on the roadside verge on the southern edge of Stanton Harcourt village. A permit available from the address given above will be needed if one intends to watch the pit from along the other banks.

The pits of the area are constantly changing, their status altered and birds may need to move from one to another. Footpaths over the area are often re-routed but if in doubt, check with the owners first.

Species

Probably the most striking feature of the birdlife on this gravel pit complex is the astonishing number and variety of wildfowl to be encountered. Mallard are common all year, found on virtually every pit. Tufted Duck and Pochard remain all year, a few pairs of Tufted breeding on the deeper waters (e.g. Dix Pit) but groups of non-breeders are also usually present. From September onwards, the numbers of these species rise dramatically so that by the end of the year, a combined total in excess of 2,000 birds is to be seen. Wigeon, Teal, Shoveler and Goldeneye are winter visitors to the pits where the careful observer may also be able to pick out small numbers of Pintail, Gadwall, Goosander and even Shelduck. Of the larger species of wildfowl, the most obvious is the Canada Goose. Their unparalleled success in Britain is due to the increased number of gravel workings and almost every one of the waters of this particular complex will have a number of breeding pairs with flocks of wandering, non-breeding birds also evident. From June onwards the goslings form large creches, shepherded by a group of ever-watchful adults. By the autumn the birds gather in even larger congregations, noisily roaming the pits, and 'honking' their way up and down the Thames Valley. Mute Swans are also present all year with pairs nesting on any of the less disturbed waters and herds of non-breeders doing their best to avoid water-skiers, sailors and the aggressively territorial breeding birds. Most winters, a few Bewick's or Whooper Swan will make a (usually brief) stay on one of the waters, often in the close company of White-fronted Geese. Tagging on to parties of any of these waterfowl may be quite an array of feral birds, and individuals that have escaped from wildfowl collections. At times, Dix Pit can look like a mini-Slimbridge with Bar-headed, Snow, Greylag and Barnacle Geese joining up with other geese, whilst amongst the duck flocks, Mandarin and Wood Duck, and Red-crested Pochard will be present during the winter period. Coot and Moorhen are very common breeding birds and on some waters Great Crested and Little Grebe nest. In winter, numbers of all these birds increase as individuals move into the area to find shelter and food during the colder periods of the year. A close scrutiny of the birds on the deeper waters may also reveal regular winter visiting species such as Black-necked or Slavonian Grebe.

Towards dusk, sizeable gull roosts build up on the large waters although the presence of a rubbish tip on site means that gull-watchers can now be kept happy all day long. With Farmoor Reservoir close by, birds have a choice of roost site depending upon the degree of disturbance and, just before dark, may move en masse from the gravel pits across to Farmoor. Black-headed, Lesser Black-backed and Herring Gulls are the most numerous with fewer Great Black-backed and Common Gull. As with any roost a close check should be made for other species since Mediterranean, Iceland and Glaucous Gulls have been noted in the past. In recent years more and more gulls have been found in the area in the summer months and Black-headed Gulls now breed in small numbers. The Cormorant is another species that is constantly commuting between pit and reservoir depending upon disturbance with numbers at Dix Pit rising to over 60 birds.

While wildfowl and gulls make up the bulk of the birds present on the pits, most birdwatchers probably visit them for the waders. Representatives are to be found all year round but the main interest is during times of migration. In either passage period check the edges of any water but pay particular attention to dry and shallow pits such as 'The Scrape' for Ruff, Dunlin and godwit, Knot, Sanderling and Whimbrel. A visit at any time of day can be worthwhile but early morning offers the best opportunities of catching those birds that have made an overnight stay. The autumn passage is probably better for Wood Sandpiper, Curlew, Sandpiper, Greenshank and Little Stint. Redshank are present all year, nesting in the shelter of good bankside vegetation. Lapwing also breed, particularly in the dry pits and, in winter, form large flocks accompanied by a few Golden Plover at similar sites or on nearby fields. Common Sandpiper, probably failed and non-breeding birds, are present in summer, bobbing characteristically along the wave-washed shoreline. Some Common Sandpiper over-winter joining other regular winter visitors such as Snipe and Green Sandpiper. Checking out all the waterlines and scrapes for waders can be quite a laborious task as birds have a knack of remaining hidden amongst stands of vegetation and in gullies. However, patience (and perhaps a telescope) can work wonders, and with 'gems' such as Turnstone, Avocet, Grey Phalarope or Pectoral Sandpiper always possible, the exercise can be well worth the effort.

Passage times do not just mean waders. Any of the terns are likely, particularly at the end of April and in early May. Osprey and Garganey are likely, and passerines such as Meadow Pipit, Pied Flycatcher, Whinchat, Wheatear and Yellow Wagtail (check for individuals of the Blue-headed race) all visit.

Resident breeding birds of the area include virtually all of the commoner species associated with open fields, hedgerows, scrub and waterways. The commoner tits, thrushes and finches, Skylark, Yellowhammer, Corn Bunting, Reed Bunting, Stock Dove, Kingfisher, Great Spotted and Green Woodpeckers are all likely with the list further extended by Kestrel and Sparrowhawk, Little Owl and Barn Owl.

Among the first wave of summer visitors is the Sand Martin. In the past, large colonies have built up along open sand faces on some of the pits near to Stanton Harcourt, but due to problems encountered in their winter quarters the breeding population has diminished considerably. Hopefully numbers will one day recover. Large numbers of hirundines and Swift feed on insects over any of the waters with the largest gatherings noted in late April and early May and again in early September.

Other summer visitors make use of the hedgerows and scrub in the area. The common Sylvia and Phylloscopus warblers are very numerous whilst, amongst the dense vegetation bordering pit and river, the chattering, rattling song of the Sedge Warbler can be heard. A few Nightingales frequent the area, often close to the leisure parks and industrial sites and can occasionally be heard at mid-day. Maybe the noise of power-boat and heavy equipment stimulates them into song? The Cuckoo is widespread in the area and the gentle purring of Turtle Doves is a regular summertime sound of the site.

As the summer visitors are still preparing to depart, wintering birds start to move in. The bulk are of course the wildfowl but the adjoining countryside attracts Brambling and Meadow Pipit, Fieldfare and Redwing and often increased numbers of the resident species. With always a very good chance of a wintering Short-eared Owl or Merlin using the area, there is never a lull in the avian activity of this very varied gravel pit complex.

Calendar

Resident Great Crested Grebe, Little Grebe, Mute Swan, Canada Goose, feral Greylag, a variety of exotic escaped wildfowl, Mallard, Tufted Duck, Coot, Moorhen, Sparrowhawk, Kestrel, Barn Owl, Little Owl, Redshank, Lapwing, Kingfisher, Skylark.

December–February Occasional Bewick's Swan, possible Black-necked and Slavonian Grebe, large flocks of Lapwing and Golden Plover. Short-eared Owl and Merlin.

March–May Passage: Dunlin, Ruff, godwit, Knot. Possible Whimbrel, Garganey, and Osprey, Wheatear, Whinchat, Meadow Pipit, Yellow Wagtail. Sand Martin, Turtle Dove, Nightingale, Cuckoo, common warblers.

June–July Non-breeding birds on water; feeding hirundines, occasional Hobby. Common Sandpiper present.

August–November Passage waders: Little Stint, Curlew Sandpiper, Wood Sandpiper, Greenshank, Ringed Plover. Gradual rise in wintering duck: Pochard, Teal, Wigeon, Shoveler, Tufted Duck, Goldeneye; possible Mandarin Duck, Wood Duck and Red-crested Pochard. Snipe, Green Sandpiper, Brambling, Meadow Pipit, Fieldfare, Redwing.

OTMOOR

Map 67/OS ref. SP 575 140

Habitat

Situated approximately 7 miles (11 km) north and east of Oxford, Otmoor is a flat plain lying approximately 195 ft (60 m) above sea-level, drained by the River Ray and its tributaries. The plain overlies a surface layer of either alluvium or Oxford clay, beneath which is a further 450 ft (140 m) of clay. These features combined to produce an area with immense water-retaining qualities and contributing significantly to the nature of Otmoor. Indeed, had this account been written some 150 years previously the whole area would have been a vast expanse of moorland and open pools, probably of national importance for wildfowl and waders. However the improved drainage technology of the mid-twentieth century has transformed the area so that much is now agricultural land. Today, the only permanently wet area is that known as Fowls Pill which, in wet seasons, can become quite a sizeable pool with marshy surrounds. In addition, some of the large well-established drainage ditches bordering the arable fields do retain water and are attractive to a number of birds and other animals as feeding and nesting sites.

Although dry, much of the centre of Otmoor still remains unimproved with large fields (e.g. '100-acre field') of coarse grasses, sedges and rushes, some of which have areas of invading scrub. The fields, particularly those in the north, have extensive hedgerows, primarily Blackthorn and Hawthorn with occasional mature standards of Oak and willow. On higher ground and running down to the plain are the remnants of the forest which once surrounded the moor and is now represented by Noke Wood. Although small, a good variety of wildlife is supported beneath the mainly Oak canopy. The Spinney, and the adjacent rifle range which is regularly used by the Territorial Army Volunteer Reserve (TAVR), is managed by BBONT as a nature reserve.

The area as a whole is very rich in all forms of plant and animal life and part of Otmoor is a designated SSSI. Dragonflies are well represented wherever there is water and a good range of butterflies, including Marsh Fritillary, is to be found. Muntjac Deer frequent the slopes above Otmoor and Hare and Fox are often seen on the grasslands. Grass Snakes are common; look for them along any of the water-ways or whilst they bask on sheltered banks during periods of sunshine.

Access

The area is well served by footpaths from which much of Otmoor's wildlife can be viewed. Access can be gained at various points, with paths leading onto the moor from each of the villages that ring the site. The most convenient are:

Oddington Park at the village green and proceed eastwards along Oddington Lane. Once over the bridge one can continue straight on or bear right and follow the river.

Charlton-on-Otmoor Park in the village and walk south-east along

Otmoor Lane which runs alongside the Crown Public House.

Beckley Two routes are possible. Park in the village and walk past the church to follow the footpath north then north-west along the path through Noke Wood. Alternatively from Beckley, walk or drive along the lane which runs north-south from the rifle range to the village. If one drives, limited parking is possible at the far end. Walking the lane can be more interesting, allowing one to savour more fully the atmosphere and wildlife of Otmoor.

There are two very important features to be borne in mind when visiting Otmoor. Firstly, the rifle range and spinney as a BBONT reserve is accessible to permit holders only. Secondly, on all days except Tuesday and Thursday, the rifle range may be in use. This means that access to the range is *forbidden* and also that when in use the area in front of it becomes a Danger Area and attempting to cross these meadows would be *extremely foolhardy*. When in use a red flag flies from the Stop Butts and warning notices are to be found. Whilst it can shatter the peace of Otmoor, the resident birds seem to have become accustomed to the noise and so one need not be put off walking the safe areas on such days.

Despite the drainage schemes employed in the area, many of the lanes and fields do become very wet, hence, particularly in winter, wellingtons are advisable.

Species

Whilst Otmoor is well past the halcyon days of the nineteenth century when Bittern and Black Tern nested, it can still be one of the most exciting places in the county for the birdwatcher. During the winter, particularly if rainfall has been high, the area around Fowls Pill becomes waterlogged and thence very attractive to wildfowl. Mallard and Teal are most common although rarely do numbers reach above 100. Wandering parties of Wigeon may also make an appearance, with up to 80 birds feeding across the shallow waters, occasionally joined by a few Shoveler, Pintail and Tufted Duck. Small parties of any of these duck are just as likely to be found feeding along the network of rivers and channels. As colder weather arrives, so too may the wild geese and swans. Small flocks of White-fronted Geese appear very occasionally during winter, perhaps storm driven or else one of the groups that roam Oxfordshire following the floods. Bewick's and Whooper Swan make brief visits in most years. All of these wildfowl are wary birds and will not stay for long if shooting is in progress. Even on quiet days the birdwatcher will need a cautious approach to obtain the best views. Observation from the southern edge of the field is probably the best strategy aided by telescope and a little patience since many of the duck may remain concealed from view by the clumps of rush and sedge.

If duck are 'well concealed', then the Snipe is almost impossible to pick out as it busily probes the muddy edges for food. Very often the fast erratic flight of the bird as it is flushed almost from underfoot is usually all one sees. Snipe will feed along all ditches and pools and these should be checked out before one ventures too close. In winter all Snipe-like birds should be carefully scrutinised. The dumpier Woodcock often leaves its woodland retreat to feed along streams and ditches and the smaller, secretive Jack Snipe may also be present. The commonest winter wader of Otmoor is the Lapwing. Flocks of over 1,000 birds may form on the damp, recently-ploughed fields, often in the company of Golden Plover. Scan all flocks of Lapwing very carefully since 'Goldies' can be almost invisible to the naked eye when static, and often it is only their rapid running movements that betray their presence.

Every winter a number of Short-eared Owls take up temporary residence on Otmoor and may be found almost anywhere in the area, hunting over grassland and arable fields alike. In most winters, Hen Harrier make intermittent visits and Merlin also have short stays on Otmoor. These raptors join the Sparrowhawk and Kestrel, both of which are active all year round. Of the nocturnal birds of prey, the Little Owl is the species most frequently encountered and is particularly at home in the pollarded willows along the River Ray. Often seen in daylight hours, they are vocal throughout much of the year and on a clear, still evening can be heard calling right across the plain.

In winter perhaps the noisiest birds of Otmoor are the large parties of Fieldfare and Redwing. The harsh chatter of the Fieldfare and the thinner, high-pitched calls of the Redwing are to be heard constantly. They will be encountered feeding on hedgerows, where the abundant haws are particularly favoured and also on higher ground in fields of shorter grassland near the villages. The flocks are often joined by some of the resident thrush species, some parties having representatives of all five species among them.

The hedgerows in winter provide food and shelter for many small birds: mixed flocks of titmice, accompanied by Treecreeper and Goldcrest are a common sight as too are mixed finch and bunting flocks. For the latter, look in fields where food has been put out for cattle, sites where grain has been put down for game birds and around farm buildings.

As winter ends, resident birds begin to set up territories prior to breeding and winter visitors make preparations for departure. At this time (March to May) Otmoor is a good place to search for migrating species using it as a stop-over site for feeding and resting. A good variety of waders has been recorded at this time, including Whimbrel and Wood Sandpiper. Hen and Marsh Harriers are regular as too is the Garganey, a duck which has in the past bred on Otmoor and may one day return.

In most years Snipe breed on the open fields. If the spring has been wet, then up to eight birds may be seen performing the territorial display flights and heard 'drumming' over and around the marshier areas. Lapwing also breed here although a few pairs nest on the spring-sown arable fields. Contributing to the feeling of remoteness that is so much part of Otmoor's character will be the bubbling, liquid trilling of the Curlew. Two or three pairs may nest, although unless one visits early in the day or at dusk, the birds can remain rather elusive. A fourth wader, the Redshank, is another bird which has nested on Otmoor. Although appearing most years during the winter or on passage it has not been recorded as a breeding species for some years but one day it may return to nest.

Nesting amongst the reeds and coarse grasses of the unimproved fields are Meadow Pipit and Skylark. Both of these birds are found throughout the year. Their numbers during winter become swollen by birds probably having bred further north, with the latter species forming large flocks from November onwards, feeding on the arable fields. The wet ditches provide good nesting habitat for the Reed Bunting and the

Snipe

strikingly-marked male is often seen and heard as it proclaims territory from atop bushes and hedges. All over the area, nesting low down in vegetation close to hedgerows, its brightly coloured relative the Yellowhammer is very common, while a third member of that family, the Corn Bunting, can also be found, usually around the fields of barley.

Hedgerows and scrub provide ample nesting opportunities for good numbers of warblers. Willow Warbler, Chiffchaff, Blackcap and Whitethroat are all widely distributed and quite common. Lesser Whitethroat are also present but, being rather more skulking in habit, are easily missed unless one is familiar with the rather monotonous rattling song. Sedge Warblers, while not numerous, frequent the river banks wherever dense bankside vegetation will permit. Similarly, the Grasshopper Warbler is not widespread over the area and is most usually found in the hedgerows along the lane down to the moor from Beckley and more particularly in the scrub, hedges and rank vegetation in the vicinity of the rifle range. A warm, still evening in May is the best occasion to listen to its curious 'reeling' song and perhaps to get a glimpse of this most retiring of birds. In close attendance to the Grasshopper Warbler and at its most active around the same time is the Nightingale. Good numbers breed close to The Spinney and the rifle range, and in dense hedgerows elsewhere over Otmoor – on a warm May evening as many as eight birds can be heard. Other summer visitors to Otmoor worthy of mention include Tree Pipit – regular on the rifle range; Spotted Flycatcher – common in the villages and usually seen feeding in the lanes leading to Otmoor; Turtle Dove – nesting deep in hedges but often seen resting on trees and telegraph wires; Yellow Wagtail and Hobby – these two are most evident late in the season when young birds are off the nest.

In addition to this influx of summer visitors, Otmoor boasts a good variety of resident species. Dunnock, Wren, Robin and the three thrushes are common as are most of the tit family. The woodlands hold Nuthatch, Treecreeper and all the woodpeckers. The Great Spotted Woodpecker though, is just as often seen in the mature Oaks along the field boundaries while the Green Woodpecker is frequently seen feeding on the ground, particularly around the rifle range. Most finches are numerous, with Otmoor being one of the best places to see Bullfinch.

With so many small birds nesting in the area it is not surprising that the Cuckoo is also common. In May and June, as many as a dozen birds may be seen or heard, patrolling open fields and hedgerows for nests of Dunnock and Whitethroat or, more commonly, Meadow Pipit.

Throughout the year, all five crow species are present. Horton Spinney has a sizeable rookery and is also used as a winter roost by hundreds of Rook and Jackdaw. Along any of the drainage channels and waterways the resident Moorhen breed, while Coot favour the river and Fowls Pill. The Water Rail, the third member of this family, has bred on Otmoor in recent times in some of the overgrown ditches. It is however more usually seen as a winter visitor. Mallard nest at sites all over Otmoor and at least one pair of Mute Swan breed and a number of non-breeding birds of this species are usually present. Little Grebe by and large remain on the River Ray for most of the year, nesting under the shelter of a well vegetated bank. Also along the river, Kingfishers are frequently found.

Late July and August is a relatively quiet period with very little song and little activity as birds are undergoing moult. From mid-August one starts to see a movement of birds away from their breeding grounds with parties of Whinchat and Wheatear moving through in discrete family parties. If there is open water still available, a few waders may make a brief visit and, with a steady flow of groups of the more usual summer migrants through the site, there is always the possibility that a Golden Oriole or Red-backed Shrike has joined up with them, a sight to gladden the heart of any birdwatcher!

As autumn arrives birds show tendencies to flock together in feeding parties. Tits and finches are particularly noted but maybe the most noteworthy is the Woodpigeon. Huge flocks of these birds numbering several thousand make quite a sight as they mass together on the wing before roosting or before homing in on a recently-harvested, or recently-sown field. Among the flocks will be a good number of the smaller, more compact Stock Dove, easily recognised by its lack of a white collar. Both species do nest locally but these massive flocks probably include birds from many miles around. However, whilst the sight of so many birds gathered together is impressive to the birdwatcher, it will do little to impress the unfortunate landowner upon whose fields these birds descend!

Calendar

Resident Little Grebe, Mute Swan, Mallard, Sparrowhawk, Kestrel, partridges, Pheasant, Moorhen, Coot, Water Rail (possible), Snipe, Lapwing, Stock Dove, Woodpigeon, Collared Dove, Little Owl, Tawny Owl, possible Barn Owl, Kingfisher, Great Spotted and Green Wood-peckers, Skylark, Meadow Pipit. Commoner tits, corvids, finches and thrushes, Tree Sparrow. Corn Bunting, Yellowhammer.

December–February On pools: Mallard, Teal and Wigeon and possible Shoveler, Pintail, wild geese and swans, Snipe, Lapwing, Golden Plover, possible Jack Snipe. Mixed flocks of finches and buntings, mixed tit,

Treecreeper and Goldcrest flocks, winter thrushes, Short-eared Owl, possible Hen Harrier, occasional Merlin, possible Water Rail, occasional Great Grey Shrike.

March–May On passage: Wheatear, Whinchat, waders including occasional Whimbrel, Garganey, Hen Harrier, Marsh Harrier. Meadow Pipit, Chiffchaff, Willow Warbler, Blackcap, Garden Warbler, Common and Lesser Whitethroat, Grasshopper Warbler, Nightingale, Cuckoo, Turtle Dove, Sedge Warbler, Tree Pipit, Spotted Flycatcher, Yellow Wagtail, Curlew.

June–July Much breeding activity, occasional Hobby.

August–November From August to September: return passage of Wheatear and Whinchat, possible Red-backed Shrike. Build up of dove and pigeon flocks. Resident species become more wide-ranging in their movements and flock together more. Influx of Redwing and Fieldfare.

PORT MEADOW Map 68/OS ref. SP 495 095

Habitat

Wedged between the River Thames and the Oxford Canal, close to the heart of Oxford, Port Meadow is a flat, low-lying urban common owned by Oxford City Council. Its 418 acres (167 ha) have a long and rich history and for the most part have remained as they are today, that is, as unimproved grazing meadows. The area is subject to much disturbance and ground nesting species such as Redshank and Lapwing no longer breed. These species are though amongst a host of waders and other birds which appear at times of flood, the time when the meadow is at its best and most worthy of a visit.

The meadow is not the sole feature of importance in the area. To the west is the River Thames; broad, slow moving, and although lacking in bankside vegetation and potential nest sites, its gravelled and muddy shores make attractive feeding places. Beyond the Thames is a patchwork of permanent grazing land dissected by hedgerows and ditches. East of Port Meadow is the Oxford Canal flanked at its northern end by allotments, reeds, small unimproved meadows and hedgerows. As the canal ventures closer to the City, so these features give way to houses, factories and railways. Although these are of generally limited interest, the strips of land alongside the railway are wet and relatively undisturbed, allowing growth of reeds, thick herbage and, in places, good areas of scrub.

The southern edge of Port Meadow is bounded by the Castle Mill Stream, a tree-lined sidestream of the Thames with good bankside vegetation of reeds, Meadowsweet and Willowherb. This channel also forms the northern edge of Fiddler's Island, a particularly interesting area of lush vegetation and scrub. Alder, Osier and pollarded willow are found here, tree species which are found bordering much of Port Meadow and the towpath of the River Thames.

Between the meadow and canal is a disused and reclaimed refuse tip, currently used as grazing land. It is however, possible that the area will be transformed into an amenity area with provision for wildlife appearing high on the list of priorities.

There can be few places where one can be so close yet feel so far away from a city as at Port Meadow. Conveniently close to Oxford to provide opportunities for a quick, pre-breakfast visit, there is enough variety of habitat to spend a much longer time in the area.

Access

Port Meadow can be approached from a number of points. For anybody in a car the most convenient are: from the centre of Oxford, proceed north along Walton Street turning left after approximately 0.5 mile (1 km) into Walton Well Road and proceed to the far end where a car park will be found, or drive north out of Oxford on the Woodstock Road until the roundabout is reached. Turn left for Wolvercote and drive for 1 mile (1.75 km) where, just before a river bridge, there is a car park on the left. Toilets are available here. One can walk out onto the meadow from this point or walk further along the

Godstow Road, passing The Trout public house to join the towpath along the river.

At times of flood the first route is best, for, whilst access to Port Meadow is unrestricted, it is impossible to negotiate its southern part when very wet. Also, in approaching the flood water from the north, one is more likely to disturb the birdlife. It is generally far better to view either from the towpath along the west bank of the Thames or from the vicinity of the metalled road joining Walton Well Road with Aristotle Lane. A telescope can be a great help at this site.

Towpaths exist along the River Thames and Oxford Canal with access to both being possible from either car park. Do not attempt to gain access to the railway properties; views over the area can be obtained from either of the bridges that cross it or from Willow Walk in the meadow's south-east corner.

The meadow is best visited, summer or winter, early in the day before birds disperse and fly off to feeding grounds elsewhere. Provided that it is not too hot, the areas around the meadow can be visited most times of day. If one is able to spend perhaps a morning exploring the site then a final stop at one of the riverside inns (The Perch at Binsey or The Trout at Godstow) can round off a trip nicely and of course allows a check of one's notebook, and the results of the morning's activities.

Species

Bird activity on Port Meadow itself is at a peak during wintertime. The flooded river creates a large shallow pool towards the southern end and renders part of the remainder a marshland. Even if flooding has not occurred, heavy rains may create enough wet areas to attract birds. The dabbling ducks are the most conspicuous; Mallard are very common and as winter progresses Wigeon and Teal can be found in rapidly increasing numbers. These two small duck species form large flocks, often up to 700 birds. This creates a magnificent sight as they wheel over the meadow, whistling and calling in an excited flurry. The larger and colourful Shoveler can be found and a careful scan across the flocks can usually reveal the presence of one or two Gadwall. As an added bonus, the elegant Pintail is a regular visitor later in the year albeit in small numbers. Resident species such as Mute Swan, Coot and Moorhen are attracted to feed on the flood waters and one can occasionally find them joined by parties of White-fronted Goose and Bewick's Swan. Flocks of gulls are usually in the area, Black-headed the most numerous, with a few Lesser Black-backed and Herring Gulls. Actually, in recent years less common species such as Little and Mediterranean Gulls have been noted, so it is always worth checking the flocks carefully.

If it is sheer numbers of birds that gives delight, then Port Meadow will not disappoint. First there are the Canada Geese, common birds in the county but winter flocks in excess of 1,000 birds may form on the meadow, spread along its length, often avoiding the wettest parts. There are also Lapwing; the number often reaches 500 but flocks of over 1,000 birds are regular. Large, mixed flocks of corvids add to the numbers. Should a passing Grey Heron or Sparrowhawk disturb the flocks, the ensuing panic created among all these birds is an impressive sight.

Perhaps not as conspicuous as the species mentioned so far, is the Snipe, feeding across the wet, marshy meadow beautifully camouflaged from predator and birdwatcher alike. By very carefully scanning the meadow, several hundred, and often approaching 1,000 birds can be

Grey Heron

located – when one at first thought the meadow was bare! Other waders, including Redshank, Ruff and Dunlin, are also present in winter. These often feed betwixt river and flood such that viewing from the west bank of the Thames can afford the better views. Golden Plover, Bar-tailed and Black-tailed Godwits may join the other waders, whilst along sheltered margins, a wintering Water Rail can sometimes be seen feeding. A number of passerine species will also exploit the feeding opportunities created by the floods with Pied Wagtails, Linnets and Meadow Pipits being common and Grey Wagtails occasional visitors.

During winter, especially if hard weather has frozen the still waters, the River Thames is always worth investigating. Many of the surface feeding ducks (Teal, Mallard etc.) will congregate here but diving species such as Tufted Duck, Goldeneye and Goosander or perhaps a Common Scoter or Scaup may also be attracted.

As winter turns to spring and birds begin moving towards their breeding grounds there is always the prospect of a good many of them paying Port Meadow a visit. Waders such as Ruff, Spotted Redshank, Whimbrel, Curlew and Sanderling occur most years and Shelduck and Garganey are also likely if the meadows remain wet. By the time they make their return journey in autumn, the meadow will be dry and more disturbed, holding little interest for them. Whinchat and Wheatear though are regularly sighted at either period of passage.

As summer progresses and the meadow loses its surface water and muddy feeding grounds, the birdwatcher's binoculars are best trained on the surrounding areas. Mallard, Moorhen, Coot and Mute Swan breed along all of the waterways, finding nest sites on secluded backwaters, but since the main river itself is subject to so much disturbance it tends to be rather quiet for birds. Grey Heron will feed here early in the day and Pied Wagtails are always present, flitting for insects amongst the vegetation, gravel and litter at the waterline. Later in the summer Common Sandpiper will appear, either non-breeding birds, or individuals that have bred early and are now en route for their wintering grounds. Black-headed Gulls feed over the water all summer, fighting for whatever scraps they can find and Common Tern may move along the river in search of prey. Kingfishers are occasionally seen but are probably more regular along the quieter backwaters than the main river.

In the thick bankside vegetation of the Castle Mill Stream and on Fiddler's Island there is cover for resident nesters such as Reed Bunting and Dunnock, and summer visitors such as Chiffchaff, Whitethroat and Sedge Warbler. A visit in May or June can find these species actively setting up and maintaining their territories and, with much song and display, giving good views to the birdwatcher. Cuckoos too will be watching closely, searching for suitable nests in which to deposit their eggs. Good vegetation cover exists along the Oxford Canal. The patchwork of gardens, allotments, scrub and waste ground allows Goldfinch, Linnet and Bullfinch to thrive alongside the common Greenfinch and Chaffinch. In winter when these birds group together more, Redpoll and Yellowhammer may also be found. Tree Sparrows may join these flocks at this time, but often remain as separate groups. These delightful birds are slightly smaller than the more familiar House Sparrow, and are distinguished by a chestnut crown and black blotch on the side of the head. They form small breeding colonies, particularly in some of the pollarded willows (a site also favoured by Treecreepers), and in winter frequent the car park at the end of Walton Well Road.

To the west of the Thames, the thick hedges provide nest sites for Magpie, Yellowhammer and a number of finches and warblers. In and around the fields, Skylark and Red-legged Partridge nest.

Of the birds of prey, Sparrowhawk and Kestrel are the most likely to be encountered, but in summer the birdwatcher may be pleasantly surprised to find Hobby being added to the day's tally of species. This smart, compact falcon is usually seen as it hunts for insects over the waterways or attempts to take feeding hirundines; a successful catch by this most agile of raptors is indeed a spectacular sight.

Calendar

Resident Grey Heron (feeding), Mute Swan, Canada Goose, Mallard, Sparrowhawk, Kestrel, partridge, Moorhen, Coot, Little Owl, Linnet, Goldfinch, Bullfinch, Treecreeper, Tree Sparrow, Reed Bunting and Yellowhammer.

December–February When wet: Wigeon, Teal, Shoveler, Gadwall, possible Pintail, occasional Bewick's Swan, Dunlin, Redshank, possible Golden Plover, large congregation of Snipe, Lapwing, Canada Goose. Meadow Pipit, possible Grey Wagtail; occasional Goosander, Goldeneye, Water Rail.

March–May Passage: Garganey, Common Sandpiper, Ruff, Whimbrel, Spotted Redshank, Sanderling, Yellow Wagtail, Whinchat, Wheatear. Breeding: Chiffchaff, Whitethroat, Sedge Warbler, Cuckoo.

June–July Feeding hirundines.

August–November Occasional Hobby, possible terns and Common Sandpiper on river. As meadow becomes wet, duck and wader numbers rise.

SHOTOVER
COUNTRY PARK
Map 69/OS ref. SP 565 055

Habitat

Owned and managed by Oxford City Council, Shotover Country Park is situated just outside the City Ring Road and occupies some 410 acres (164 ha) of Shotover Hill's south facing slopes. The park represents one of the remnants of the Shotover Royal Forest which, prior to its disafforestation in the mid-seventeenth century, covered some 5,750 acres (2,300 ha). Despite this size reduction, today's park remains immensely diverse and, with the wealth of wildlife that flourishes, is a designated SSSI.

The slopes of the hill are predominantly a mixture of grassland, scrub, bracken and open woodland. Horseshoe Field is a good example of how scrub will invade when grassland is left unmanaged for, up until the Second World War, this area was in agricultural use. There are few trees, being mainly Hawthorn and Gorse scrub, separated by grassland. Adjacent to this area is Johnson's Piece, an interesting open woodland. It is edged with very old pollarded Oaks with the wood itself dominated by Ash, Birch and Pedunculate Oak. Species such as Whitebeam, Wild Cherry and Wild Service also feature. There are areas of bracken and in places, scrub has entered. The Sandpit Field comprises mainly scrub and open grassland, a scene also noted in Mary Sadler's Field. The scrub here is mostly Hawthorn and Oak with smaller amounts of Elder and Sycamore. The western edge of the slope is a conifer plantation, mostly Larch. At the foot of the hill are two areas of woodland. Brasenose Wood is a fine example of Hazel coppice with an over-canopy of Oak standards – a traditional style of woodland management dating back to medieval times. The wood is still specifically managed in this way, selected areas being coppiced in rotation such that a wide range of age classes of Hazel are present at any one time. With an extensive system of grassy rides, the wood has quite an open feel, resulting in a diverse wildlife and offering good viewing of the woodland birds found here. Magdalen Wood is a much smaller area and because it is younger and more enclosed it does not exhibit the same diversity as Brasenose.

Between the two areas of woodland and to the west of Brasenose, is an area of grassland and scrub known as Slade Camp Fields which, until well after the Second World War, was used for army dwellings. There is a wide range of bushes and shrubs here (mainly Blackthorn and Rose) encouraging much invertebrate activity.

Other features of the site include small areas of heathland (though now rather overrun with Bracken) and areas of marsh and wetland created by springs emerging in Johnson's Piece and Holme Ground. Adjoining the Country Park to the north and east, are open pastures and arable fields, bounded by hedgerows and giving the whole area a very rural feel, despite being so close to the city. The well-established and well-wooded gardens which also exist on Shotover Hill means that the area available to wildlife is increased still further.

In recent years, Oxford City Council has adopted a more positive conservation policy at Shotover so that, while catering for a wide range of recreational activities, the intent is to maintain, and if possible to increase, the diversity of habitat available for wildlife.

Access

Shotover Country Park is a designated open space and the public have unrestricted access on foot along all paths. The park therefore is greatly favoured by dog-owners, runners, orienteers, picnickers and casual walkers, all out to enjoy the countryside and the marvellous views that can be had from the vantage point the hill offers. For anybody wishing to avoid the multitudes, a weekday visit, or a visit at either end of the day is recommended.

Ample car parking is available on Shotover Plain. Approach either from Wheatley or from Old Road, Headington. Note however that there is no direct vehicular access from the Ring Road (A4142). Toilets are available at the car park.

The City Council has a number of marked nature trails within the park, a descriptive booklet being available from the park's Rangers. Dr David Steel's *The Natural History of a Royal Forest* makes further interesting reading for anybody wishing to acquaint themselves fully with the site.

Species

Whilst unable to boast any rarities amongst its avifauna, anybody wishing to observe and to familiarise themselves with the majority of woodland and farmland birds common to this part of the country, will be well rewarded. Throughout the year there is much to see but it is perhaps during spring and early summer that bird activity reaches a peak, especially just after the summer visitors have arrived. The descending musical song of the Willow Warbler and the repetitive bisyllabic tones of the Chiffchaff fill the park. At this time of year, with leaf cover scanty, good views of both species can be obtained although, even with the very best of views, one will have trouble distinguishing between them except by their song. A little later arriving are Blackcap and then Garden Warbler. Whilst easy to separate if seen well, it is the song of these two species that can be so similar, but by visiting the park early in the season both are easy to find and one should have ample opportunity to directly contrast and compare their song. Also very vocal early in the season will be the Cuckoo and, whilst likely to be encountered anywhere, some of the best views are to be obtained on the Slade Camp Fields. Here there is dense cover, in which potential hosts such as Dunnock and Whitethroat nest, and plenty of bushes and fences to use as song-posts or vantage points. Other summer visitors to note include Turtle Dove and Lesser Whitethroat, nesting in areas of scrub, and Spotted Flycatcher – particularly obvious in the open areas of Brasenose Wood.

The song and calls of these summer birds will be heard alongside the many resident species. The highly melodious Blackbird and Robin are plentiful around the site although the range and musical quality of the Song Thrush puts this bird amongst the very best of songsters. Actually, its habit of singing well into the night does lead some people to believe they are listening to a Nightingale. The Nightingale however, is only an occasional breeder at Shotover and is of course only a visitor during summer. The Wren, another noisy if rather less tuneful bird, is common all over Shotover, its loud explosive song apparently out of all proportion to its size. The raucous calls of Jay and Magpie are common as is the call and song of Chaffinch.

Of all of Shotover's compartments, Brasenose Woods is probably best for birds particularly in the breeding season. In this relatively small tract of woodland 45 acres (18 ha) some 34 species have been shown to breed and in good numbers. This is the place in which to find Nuthatch and the woodpecker species including the often elusive Lesser Spotted Woodpecker. Views of this small woodpecker are best early in the year when birds are 'drumming' and the Oaks not yet in full leaf. There are ample nest sites available in the wood for all the woodpeckers and larger holes (natural and excavated) are readily taken by Stock Dove, Jackdaw and Tawny Owl. Treecreepers nest in Brasenose but are likely to be found wherever medium and large trees exist in the park.

The tit family is well represented on Shotover. Most can be found nesting throughout the areas of scrub and woodland although Coal Tits are more usual in the Larches along with Goldcrest.

Of the birds of prey on Shotover, the Kestrel is frequently seen, hovering over areas of grassland whilst Sparrowhawks haunt the woods and hedges for small birds. On most evenings, Tawny Owls can be heard calling from the woods and from some of the large wooded gardens on the hill, whilst on the periphery of the park and along the nearby hedgerows, Little Owls may be seen.

It is always well worth checking some of the surrounding fields for species not normally present in the park itself. Skylark and Red-legged Partridge are common and the rattling song of the Corn Bunting may be heard. Yellowhammers are very common although they do nest in areas of good scrub cover within Shotover's boundary (e.g. Horseshoe Field) often in the close company of Linnet, Chaffinch and Whitethroat.

The elevation of the site provides a convenient stop-over point for birds to rest. In spring, Wheatear, Redstart, Tree Pipit, Woodlark, Pied Flycatcher and Wood Warbler all make brief visits and sometimes stay around for a number of days, perhaps exploring the park for nesting opportunities. In September or October, it is an exciting place to stage a 'migration-watch'. Birds such as waders, pipits and finches move past on their way to winter quarters on the coast. Late Swallows move through on their way to Africa and early arrivals of Redwing and Fieldfare fly over. Many of these latter species will remain for the winter, making the most of the plentiful food and shelter in the park and nearby gardens. Also present in winter will be Redpoll and Siskin hanging upside down to feed on the Birch and Larch seeds, or maybe on a convenient bag of nuts! In recent years large numbers of Crossbill have frequented the Park's hillside. The result of large scale movements from the Continent when food becomes short (irruptions), these birds are seen from July onwards and small flocks remain in the general area until the following spring. Whether they will ever stay to breed at Shotover remains to be seen!

Calendar

Resident Sparrowhawk, Kestrel, Red-legged Partridge, Pheasant, Stock Dove, Magpie, Jay, Jackdaw, Wren, Skylark, common tits, finches, thrushes and woodpeckers, Nuthatch, Treecreeper, Yellowhammer, Corn Bunting.

December–February Increasing number of Siskin, Fieldfare, Redwing, Redpoll.

March–May Willow Warbler, Chiffchaff, Blackcap, Garden Warbler, Spotted Flycatcher, Turtle Dove, Whitethroat, Lesser Whitethroat, Cuckoo, possible Nightingale. Passage: possible Wheatear, Wood Warbler, Pied Flycatcher, Woodlark, Redstart, Tree Pipit, and Meadow Pipit.

June–July Height of breeding season, occasional Hobby.

August–November Crossbill, Redpoll, Siskin, winter thrushes. Passage: waders and hirundines overhead, Meadow Pipits. Tits and finches in typical aggregation.

ADDITIONAL SITES

Banbury Sewage Farm (SP 473 408)

This 68 acre (27 ha) site consists of four large meadows onto which effluent from the nearby Sewage Treatment Works is pumped. The meadows are flooded in rotation and, while wet, are most attractive to birds. Surrounding meadows, hedgerows, 'waste-ground' and permanent grazing pasture add to the interest of the area.

Whilst many birds typical of open meadows, wetland and hedgerow breed here, the main interest to the birdwatcher is during the winter months when good numbers of duck and waders move into the area. Wigeon, Teal and Mallard, Curlew, Lapwing, Redshank and Snipe are the usual birds to be seen, with Shoveler, Pintail and Jack Snipe also regularly recorded. In most winters small numbers of Water Rail, Stonechat, Grey Wagtail and Meadow Pipit take up residence and, at the onset of harsher weather, wild swans and geese may visit. A visit during the spring or autumn migration period can also be worthwhile for species such as Greenshank, Ringed Plover and Garganey. The site has also been known to produce the occasional rarity and in the winter of 1983, a Lesser Yellowlegs was a very special visitor.

The site, which is managed as a nature reserve by BBONT (in conjunction with Thames Water), can be found approximately 0.5 mile (0.75km) east of Banbury on the Kings Sutton Road. Park at the roadside and follow the footpath that leads along the western edge and then across the meadows. However, if the meadows are flooded, the last section of the footpath may be impassable. A number of information boards mark the reserve and visitors are urged to stay well away from the deep and dangerous sludge pits present on the site.

Jarn Mound and Matthew Arnold Field (SP 485 022)

Situated at the top of Boars Hill, south-west of Oxford, this location consists of two adjacent areas owned by the Oxford Preservation Trust. Matthew Arnold Field is a small site managed by BBONT as an educational reserve and comprises areas of woodland and scrub with a small, stream-fed pond. Jarn Mound and its immediate environs includes further areas of scrub, an orchard and other mature trees. Open paddocks and large, well-wooded gardens encompass the site.

A good range of the common woodland birds can be seen here including Nuthatch and Treecreeper, Great Spotted and Green Woodpecker and with most tits, warblers and finches represented. Cuckoo and Spotted Flycatcher are regular and Kestrel and Sparrowhawk can both be seen. During the winter Fieldfare and Redwing move into the area as do Siskin, Redpoll and the occasional Crossbill. However the main value of the site is for the good views of Hawfinch which are to be obtained. Whilst they roam the gardens of Boars Hill quite widely, the cherries of Jarn Mound are a favourite and birds can be observed quite readily as they feed in the canopy. Access to the area is along a number of public footpaths.

Oxfordshire Chilterns

Extending for some 50 miles (80 km) from the River Thames at Goring, running across the south-east corner of Oxfordshire, on through Buckinghamshire, Hertfordshire and Bedfordshire, is the ridge of chalk which forms the Chiltern Hills. They rise in a steep, west-facing scarp, reaching up to 870 ft (265 m) and slope away gently eastwards. Overall, they give a general impression of a long string of rounded hills with grassy downs, wooded escarpments and ridges and many valleys beyond the scarp. Most valleys are dry but on the western slope where clay meets chalk, a spring line emerges, often providing man-made ponds, cress beds etc, attractive to birds.

Access to the area is very good with many miles of well marked footpaths and including the Ickneld Way/Ridgeway path, all of which, thanks to the commendable efforts of the Chiltern Society and various landowners, allow a greater appreciation to this designated Area of Outstanding Natural Beauty (AONB).

Two Chiltern sites have already been described in this book. However, these are not the only sites within the Oxfordshire Chilterns where a birdwatcher may gainfully spend many hours, particularly in the spring, summer and during periods of migration when the species found are much the same as at Aston Rowant and Warburg. Hence, a brief account of each additional site is now given, commencing in the north and moving south-west.

Chinnor Hill (SP 766 002) This 70 acre (28 ha) site is owned by BBONT and exhibits each typical Chiltern habitat. Oak and Ash woodland exists at the south-west of the reserve where the chalk is capped by clay, while on the chalk escarpment, Beech woodland dominates. Except for a small area of grassland, the remainder is scrub, dense in parts, and mainly of Hazel coppice, Cherry, Whitebeam and Hawthorn, but Juniper, Yew, Silver Birch, Field Maple and Wayfaring Tree also feature.

Good views are to be obtained over the escarpment making it particularly worth watching during passage. The Hill was the county's last known breeding site of the Cirl Bunting.

To reach the reserve leave Chinnor on the unclassified road up the escarpment following the signs for Bledlow Ridge. Approximately 1.25 miles (2 km) from Chinnor, turn left into Hill Top Road. Car parking is available at the end of the lane. Access to the reserve is by way of a number of established footpaths allowing views over all types of habitat and the birds within.

Ewelme and Swyncombe Downs (SU 680 910) These rather open areas of the Chiltern escarpment mostly include some areas of chalk grassland and scrub but sadly, most have been converted into arable fields. This was once a stronghold of the Stone Curlew, now unfortunately very rare in the district, but still worth watching out for. The rolling landscape may attract occasional Buzzards and harriers in winter, roosting in the nearby woods.

Interesting walks, following the Ridgeway and other public footpaths, begin at Park Corner on the B481 Watlington to Nettlebed Road, or from the unclassified road leading west from Cookley Green further along the same road.

Queen, Fire and College Woods (SU 715 932) Park on the roadside just east of Christmas Common and follow the broad Hollandridge Lane south-east. From the lane, one is free to explore these Forestry

Commission owned woods using any of the rides and way-marked paths. Primarily of interest in the breeding season, these woods support a good variety of species, particularly where areas of more open scrub prevail.

Shotridge and Blackmoor Woods (SU 713 935) Park on the right hand side of the road leading north from Christmas Common and in the vicinity of the radio mast. From here, footpaths lead eastwards, down through a superbly wooded valley. One first negotiates an area of Oak wood with a good scrub layer and then on into an area of Chiltern Beech woodland. Following the track down the valley one then comes into a wetter area, with Salix and Birch scrub – ideal habitat for warblers and titmice. After 1.5 miles (2.5 km) from the starting point, one bears south-west, climbing the steep escarpment through Blackmoor wood to Northend. Here, there is an area of well-drained acid soil with thickets primarily of Gorse, just right for Yellowhammers and warblers, Linnets and other breeding finches. By rejoining the road and turning right, the route returns to the starting point.

Watlington Hill (SU 711 936) In the safe hands of the National Trust, this 96 acre (38 ha) site on the west-facing scarp, with superb views of Oxfordshire (and migrating birds), is a favourite with walkers and picknickers. Visits should therefore be timed to avoid the usual busy periods. Much of the Hill is chalk grassland and scrub, providing nesting and feeding sites for many bird species. Some Beech woods exist but the bulk of the wooded area is the Great Yew Wood, very dense and believed to date back to the time of the Napoleonic wars. The dense cover prevents a good ground or shrub flora but breeding species, including Coal Tit, Goldcrest, Robin and Mistle Thrush thrive.

Ample car parking is available at the top of Watlington Hill approximately 1.5 miles (2 km) from Watlington village. There is open access to most of the grassland areas and numerous paths run through the areas of scrub and woodland.

Oxford University Parks (SP 513 071)

Despite the close proximity to the city centre the University Parks offer excellent birdwatching opportunities throughout the year. They are laid out in a rich mixture of native and ornamental trees surrounded by areas of herb-rich, rough grassland as well as more formal flower beds and lawns. There is also the added attraction of the River Cherwell, tree-lined and providing further opportunities for birds.

Most of the typical woodland species breed here, including the commoner warblers, the six common tit species, Spotted Flycatcher and Cuckoo. It is, in fact, one of the best sites in Oxfordshire for observing all three species of woodpecker. Pied Wagtails and the resident thrushes feed out on the open grassed areas and the commoner finches can also be seen. On the river, Mallard, Mute Swan, Coot, Moorhen and Little Grebe all breed. In winter, the sheltered nature of the Parks means that most of the aforementioned resident birds remain, being joined by good numbers of Redwing, Fieldfare, Redpoll and Siskin. When in flood, the river and adjacent meadows attract gulls, waders (such as Snipe and Redshank) and an increased number of duck.

The Parks, which are locked each night, are also attractive to a large number of human visitors and an early morning visit is desirable. The main gates are in Parks Road, Oxford and the public is free to use the various paths and open areas. By crossing over the river and making use of the footpaths on the opposite bank, the University Parks also serve as a starting point for exploring other parts of the River Cherwell, its banks and adjacent meadows.

River Windrush

Rising on the Cotswolds, the River Windrush flows eastwards through Oxfordshire to join the Thames at Newbridge. Particularly to the west of Witney, it is a clean, fast-flowing stream (much favoured by trout anglers), with good emergent and submerged vegetation. Along much of the valley the adjacent meadows are of permanent pasture, much of it unimproved, and having good hedgerows and many small copses along their boundaries. Many footpaths traverse the valley making it quite an accessible tract of countryside.

Most of the usual birds of hedgerow, open countryside and woodland may be encountered, including Barn, Little and Tawny Owl, Kestrel, Sparrowhawk, Yellow Wagtail, Cuckoo and Spotted Flycatcher. In winter Redwing and Fieldfare forage widely, and Siskin and the occasional Buzzard may take up residence.

Along the river, its adjacent meadows and close to the many ponds that exist (for example, at Widford), one can find Pied Wagtail, Grey Wagtail and Sedge Warbler, Kingfisher, Moorhen, Mallard and Mute Swan. Dippers have bred in the past and still sometimes visit in winter. At undisturbed, grassland sites, Snipe, Lapwing, Curlew and, more rarely, Redshank may breed. During the winter, when the valley floods, wader numbers, particularly Lapwing, rise and large flocks, often including Golden Plover may be noted. Various wildfowl may also be attracted to the floods.

It is worth noting that all of Oxfordshire's waterways can be regarded as linear havens for wildlife and therefore potential birdwatching sites. All still have their undisturbed reaches with lush bankside vegetation and adjacent woods and meadows offering ample opportunities to birds. Most of the waterways have good access along towpath or public footpath allowing views of a similar range of species as outlined for the River Windrush.

Ryecote Park (SP 670 050)

Ryecote Park comprises areas of mixed woodland, open fields (arable and pasture) and a small reed-fringed lake. Whilst it is in private ownership, a number of footpaths do cross the area, allowing views over all aspects of the site.

The lake supports the usual breeding duck and grebe and is a regular haunt for the Grey Heron. Small colonies of Reed and Sedge Warbler thrive along its edge and Kingfishers are frequently seen. Skylark and Lapwing nest on the open fields whilst the hedgerows hold both species of whitethroat, Yellowhammer, Linnet and Little Owl. Yellow Wagtail, Stock Dove and Cuckoo may also be seen. The woodland is home for the three woodpeckers, Treecreeper, Spotted Flycatcher and the common tits, thrushes and warblers. There is a sizeable rookery. Winter may be quite quiet but gulls and a few wintering duck may be found on the lake whilst Redwing and Fieldfare forage over the surrounding fields and hedgerows.

Stonesfield Common (SP 390 165)

Lying on the west bank of the River Evenlode, this area of limestone grassland, damp meadow, scrub and hedgerow provides nesting and feeding opportunities for a wide variety of species including Tree Pipit, Lapwing and Reed Bunting. In the recent past, Grasshopper Warblers have bred. Little Owl, Barn Owl and Kestrel use the area as a hunting ground throughout the year, whilst foraging parties of Redwing and Fieldfare are regularly seen in winter.

Access is along footpaths either from Stonesfield village or from the unclassified road between Stonesfield and North Leigh.

Whitecross Green Wood (SP 600 150)

This is a 156 acre (62 ha) ancient woodland site owned by BBONT lying on Otmoor's north-eastern edge. Much of the wood has been replanted with conifers but a substantial area of Oak and mixed woodland remain. It is bursting with wildlife. The typical breeding birds of the English woodland occur in good numbers including Nightingale, Grasshopper Warbler, Turtle Dove and Sparrowhawk. The presence of a large, open pond enriches the habitat still further. The reserve is situated approx imately 1 mile (1.5 km) on the right-hand side of the unclassified road east of Murcot. Park on the roadside verge close to, but not obstructing, the access gate which is opposite a small cottage on the other side of the road. A track leads from the gate into the wood. There is public access along all rides but dogs are not admitted.

Wytham Wood (SP 460 080)

Owned by Oxford University, Wytham Wood serves as a field study area for a wide spectrum of biological research. Species such as Sparrowhawk and Tawny Owl as well as members of the tit family have been the subject of much detailed research and probably more is known about the birds of this tract of woodland than any other in the region. It is rich in birdlife with most of the typical woodland species represented, including Nightingale, Tree Pipit and Grasshopper Warbler.

Access is however, strictly by permit only and by applying in writing to The University Land Agent. (See Useful Addresses.)

Skylark

BIBLIOGRAPHY

Easterbrook, T.G. (ed.) *Birds of the Banbury Area 1972–1981* (B.O.S., 1983)

Fitter, R.S. (ed.) *The Wildlife of the Thames Counties* (Dugdale, Oxford, 1985)

Frankum, M. & R.G. *The Birds & Plants of Freemen's Marsh* (Private, 1970–1974)

—— *The Birds & Plants of Freemen's Marsh 1975–1979* (Private)

—— *The Birds & Plants of Hungerford Common* (Private)

Harding, B.D. *Bedfordshire Bird Atlas* (Private, 1977)

Hobson, M.G. & Price, K.L.H. *Otmoor and Its Seven Towns* (Private, 1967)

Kennedy, A.W.M.C. *The Birds of Berkshire & Buckinghamshire* (Private, 1868)

Mead, C. & Smith, K. *The Hertfordshire Breeding Bird Atlas* (Private, 1982)

Montgomery-Massingbird, H. *Blenheim Revisited* (Bodley Head, London, 1985)

Radford, M.C. *The Birds of Berkshire & Oxfordshire* (Longman, London, 1966)

Sage, B. *The Birds of Hertfordshire* (Private, 1959)

Steel, D. *The Natural History of a Royal Forest* (Pisces, Oxford, 1984)

Wiggins, R.H. *The Birds of Little Wittenham* (Northmoor Trust, 1985)

Youngman, R.E. & Fraser, A.C. *The Birds of Buckinghamshire and East Berkshire* (Middle Thames Natural History Society, 1976)

In addition to the works listed above, the annual reports of any of the bird clubs in the region make fascinating reading and provide an up-to-date assessment of the local birds. These reports may be obtained by writing to the secretary of the relevant bird club or organisation. (See Useful Addresses.)

MAPS

Key to Symbols

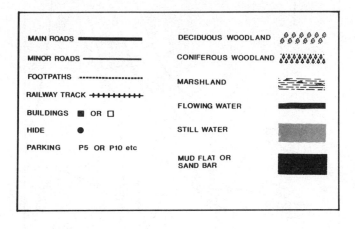

MAIN ROADS	DECIDUOUS WOODLAND
MINOR ROADS	CONIFEROUS WOODLAND
FOOTPATHS	MARSHLAND
RAILWAY TRACK	FLOWING WATER
BUILDINGS ■ OR □	
HIDE ●	STILL WATER
PARKING P5 OR P10 etc	MUD FLAT OR SAND BAR

Map 1: Stewartby Lake

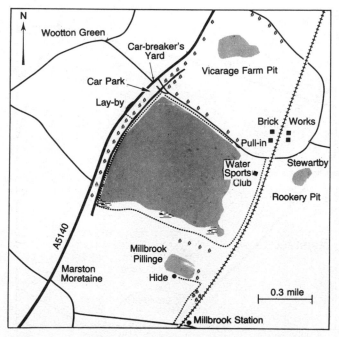

N

Wootton Green

Car-breaker's Yard

Car Park

Lay-by

Vicarage Farm Pit

Brick Works

Pull-in

Water Sports Club

Stewartby

Rookery Pit

A5140

Millbrook Pillinge

Marston Moretaine

Hide

0.3 mile

Millbrook Station

Map 2: Bedford Clay Pits

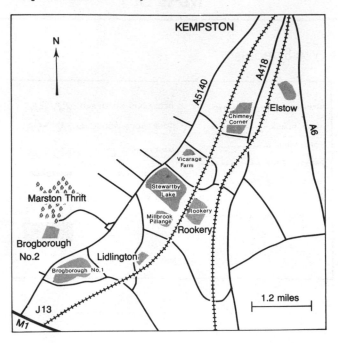

Map 3: Blows Downs

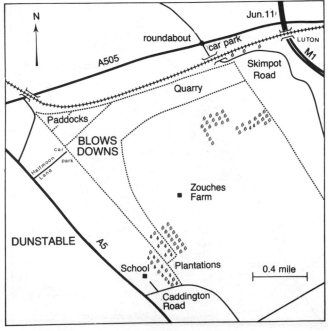

Map 4: Flitwick Moor

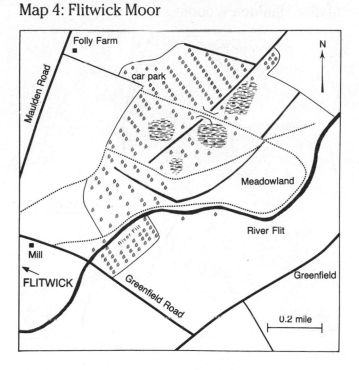

Map 5: Harrold & Odell Country Park

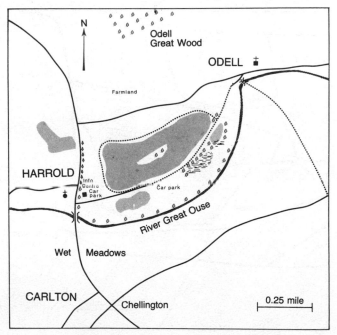

Map 6: Maulden Woods .

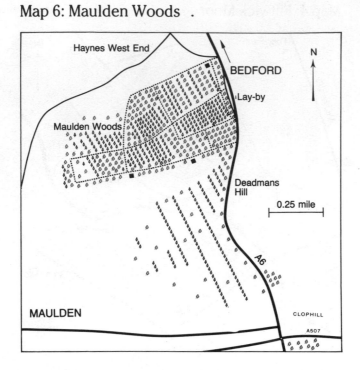

Map 7: Priory Country Park

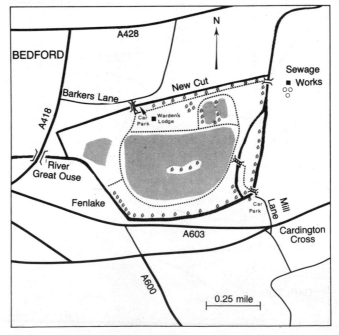

Map 8: The Lodge

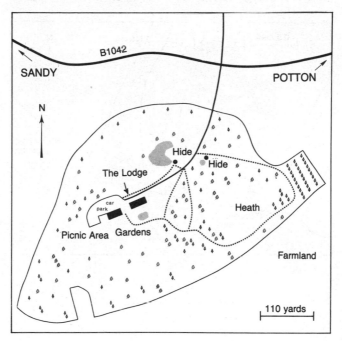

Map 9: Warden & Galley Hills

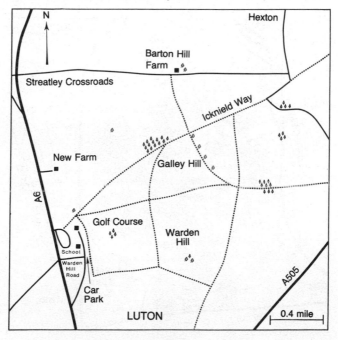

Map 10: Burghfield & Padworth Commons

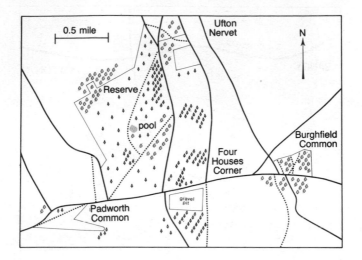

Map 11: Dinton Pastures & Lavell's Lake

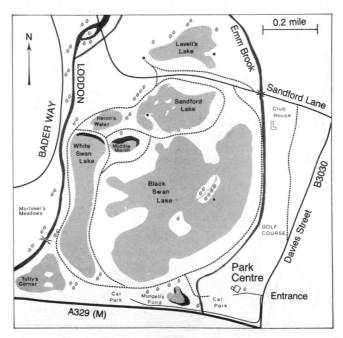

Map 12: Englemere Pond

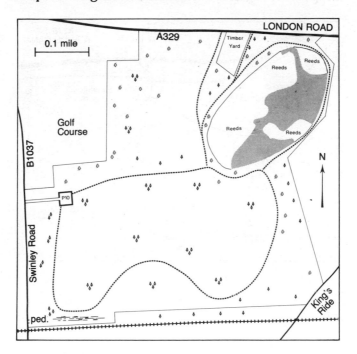

Map 13: Freemen's Marsh

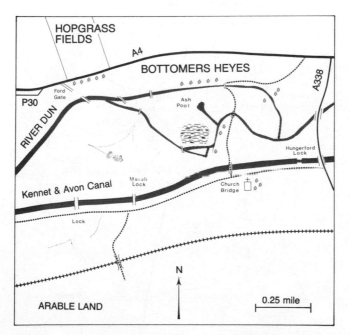

Map 14: Hungerford Common

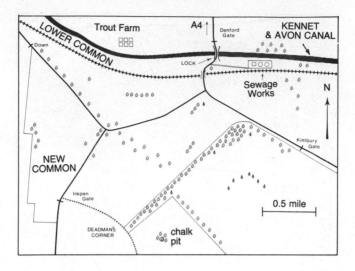

Map 15: Inkpen & Walbury Hills

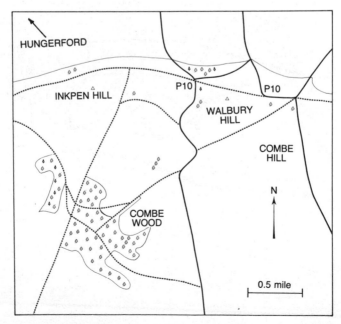

Map 16: North Cookham

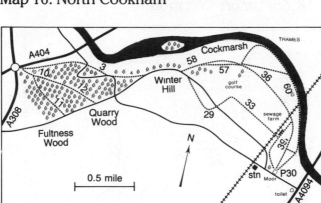

Map 17: Queen Mother Reservoir

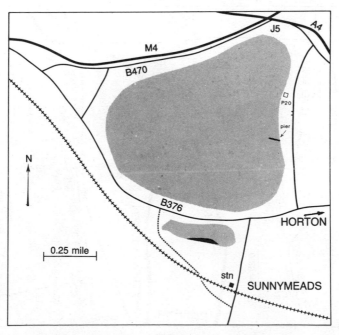

Map 18: Snelsmore Common

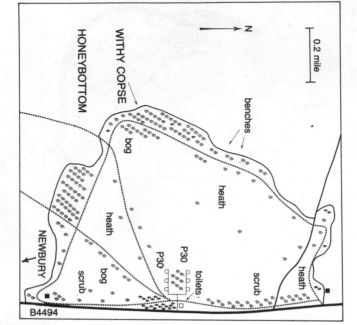

Map 19: Thatcham Moor

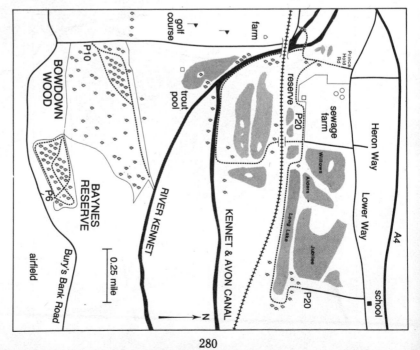

Map 20: Theale Gravel Pits

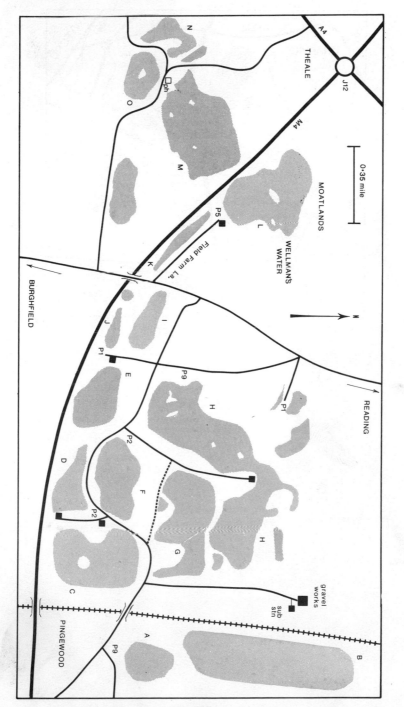

Map 21: Twyford Gravel Pits

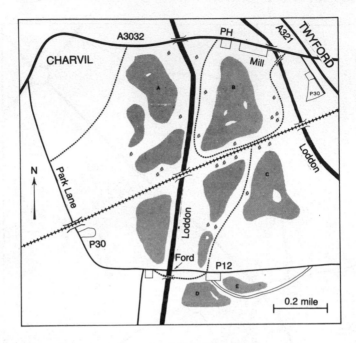

Map 22: Wraysbury Gravel Pits

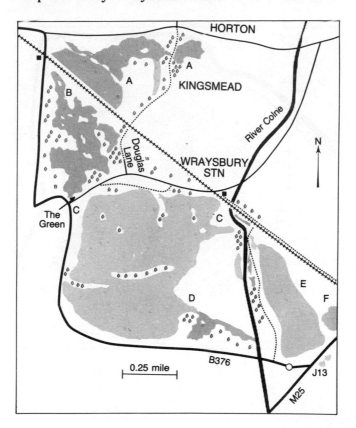

Map 23: ARC Wildfowl Centre

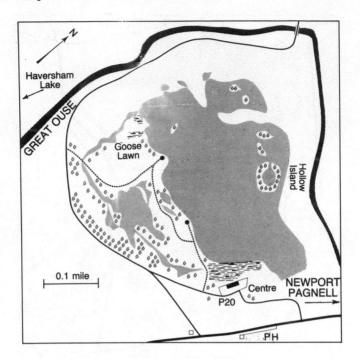

Map 24: Black Park

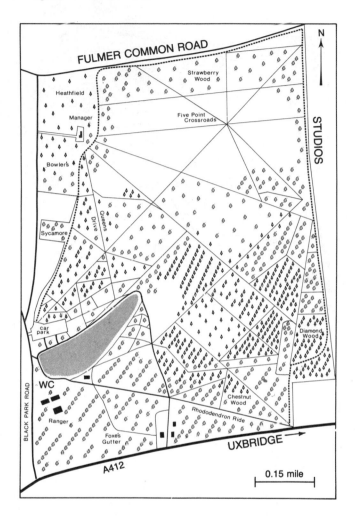

Map 25: Langley Park

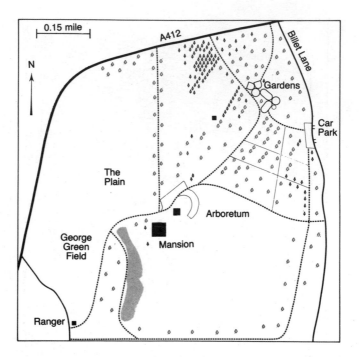

Map 26: Burnham Beeches

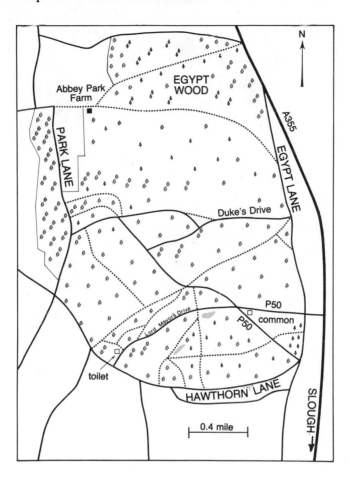

Map 27: Caldecotte Lakes

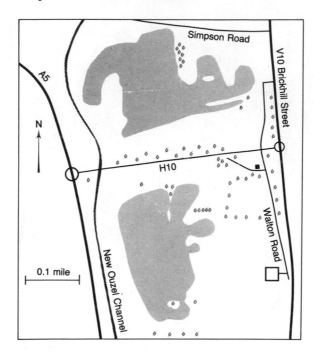

Map 28: Calvert Jubilee

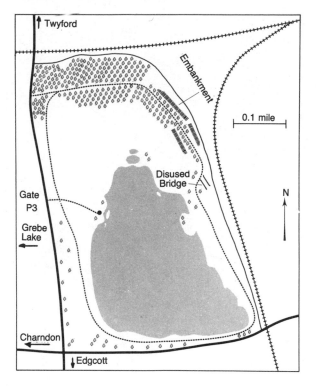

Map 29: Church Wood

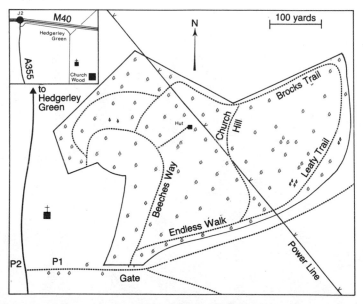

Map 30: Foxcote & Hydelane Waters

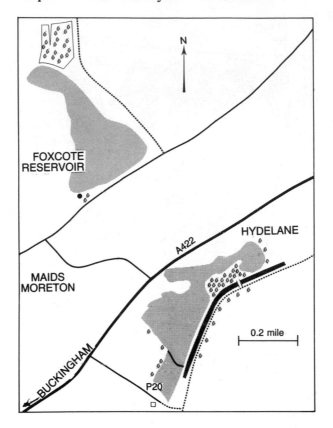

Map 31: Grangelands & Pulpit Hill

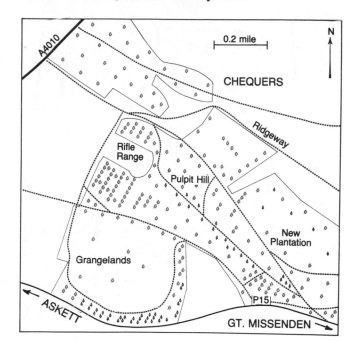

Map 32: Homefield Wood

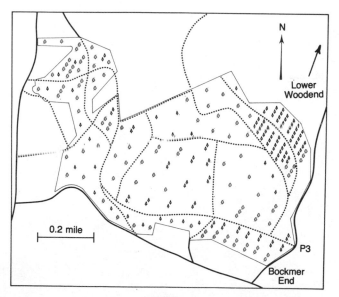

Map 33: Little Britain Country Park

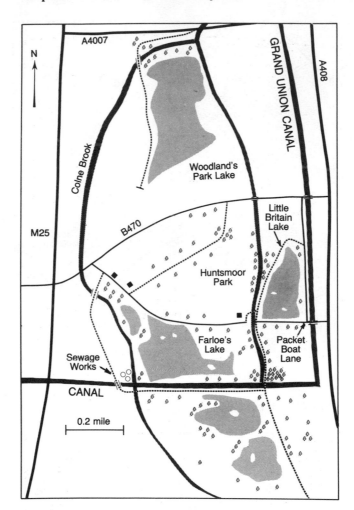

Map 34: Little Marlow Gravel Pit

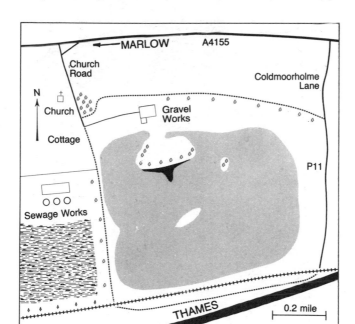

Map 35: Shabbington & Waterperry Woods

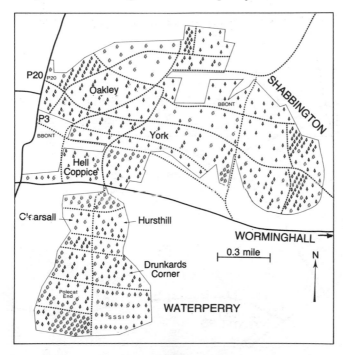

Map 36: Shardeloes

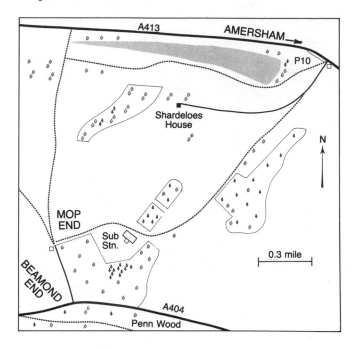

Map 37: Stony Stratford Nature Reserve

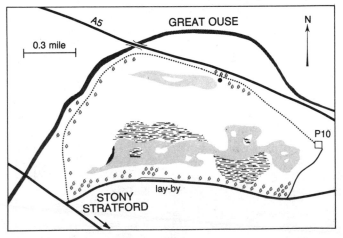

Map 38: Weston Turville

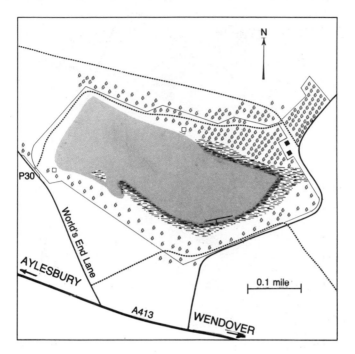

Map 39: Willen Lake

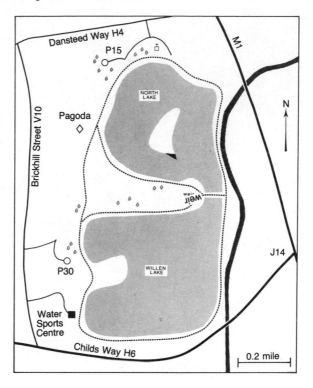

Map 40: Ashridge Estate

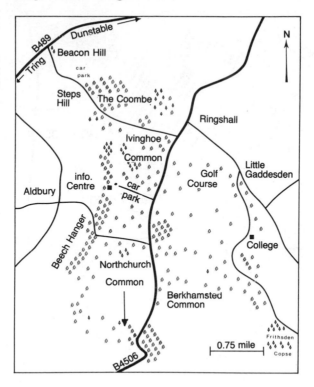

Map 41: Broxbourne Woods

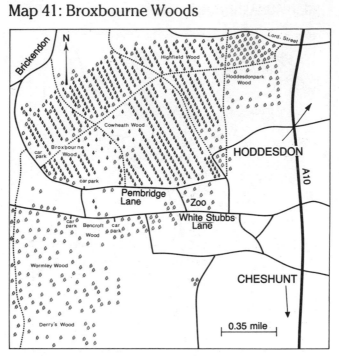

Map 42: Colne Valley Gravel Pits

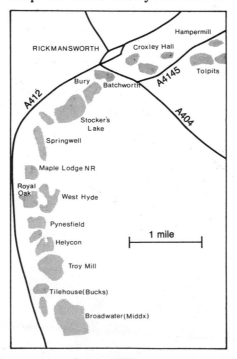

Map 43: Maple Lodge Nature Reserve

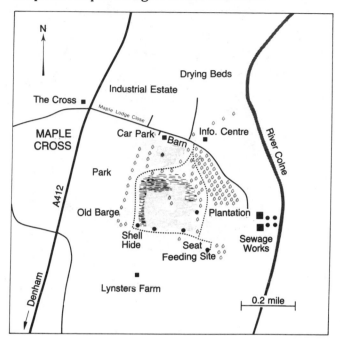

Map 44: Stocker's Lake

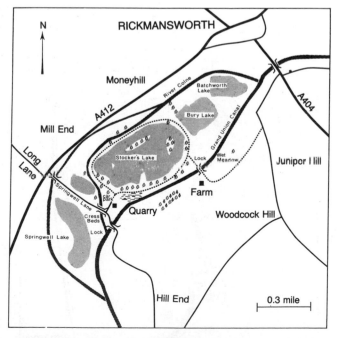

Map 45: Hilfield Park Reservoir

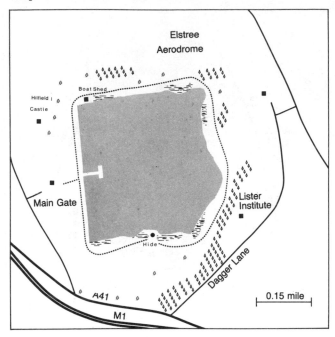

Map 46: Lemsford Springs

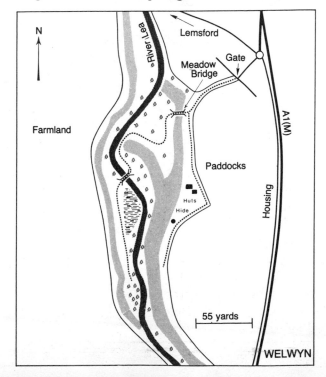

Map 47: Lec Valley Gravel Pits

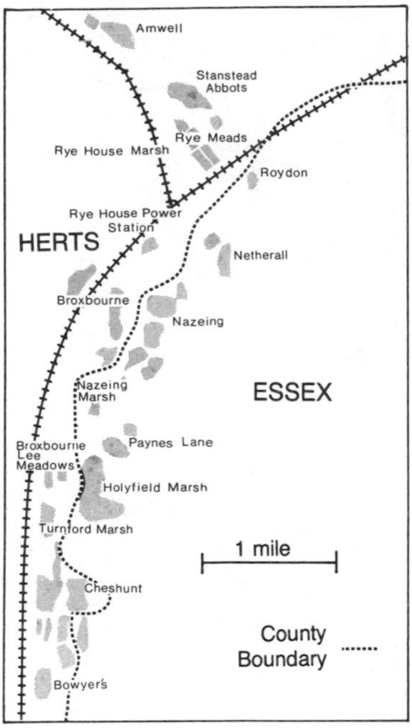

Amwell

Stanstead
Abbots

Rye Meads

Rye House Marsh

Roydon

Rye House Power
Station

HERTS

Netherall

Broxbourne

Nazeing

ESSEX

Nazeing
Marsh

Broxbourne
Lee
Meadows

Paynes Lane

Holyfield Marsh

Turnford Marsh

1 mile

Cheshunt

County
Boundary

Bowyers

Map 48: Cheshunt Gravel Pits

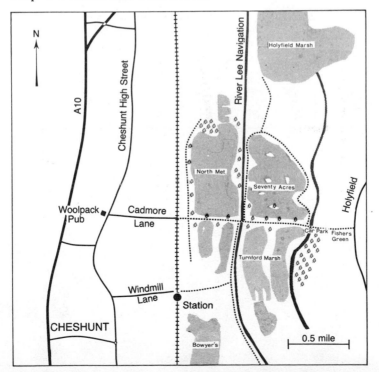

N

A10

Cheshunt High Street

River Lee Navigation

Holyfield Marsh

North Met.

Seventy Acres

Holyfield

Woolpack
Pub

Cadmore
Lane

Car Park Fishers
Green

Turnford Marsh

Windmill
Lane

Station

CHESHUNT

Bowyer's

0.5 mile

Map 49: Rye Mead Area

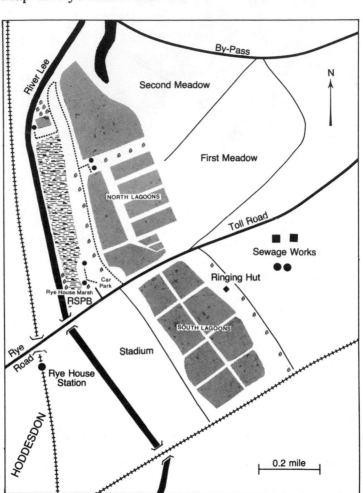

Map 50: Northaw Great Wood

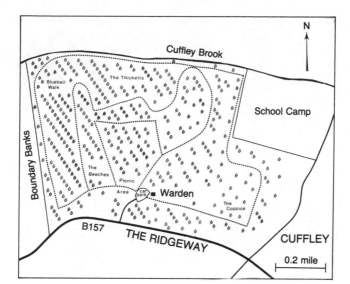

Map 51: Oughton Head Common

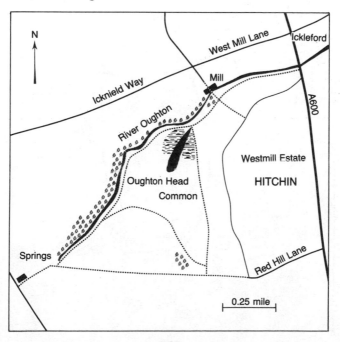

Map 52: Tring Reservoirs

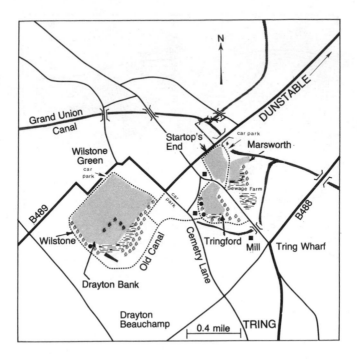

Map 53: Aston Rowant NNR

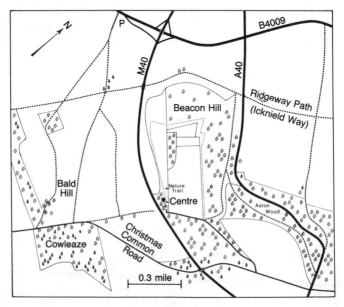

Map 54: Badbury Forest & Coxwell Wood

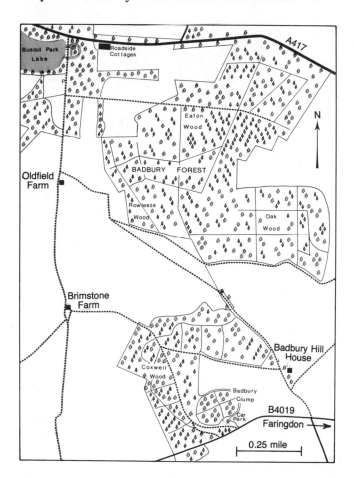

Map 55: Bix, The Warburg Reserve

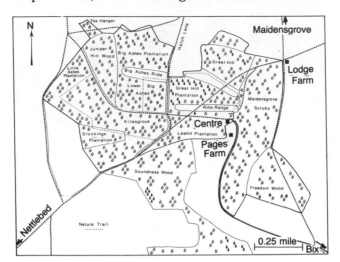

Map 56: Blenheim Park

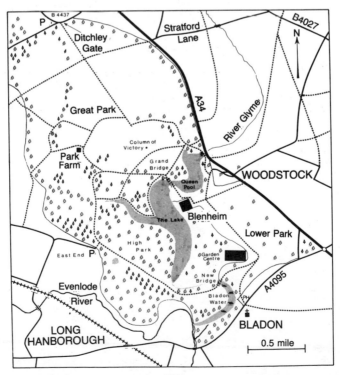

Map 57: Cherwell Valley

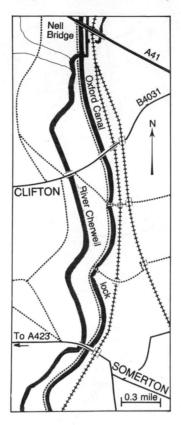

Map 58: Dorchester Gravel Pits

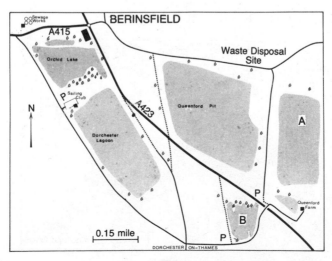

Map 59: Downland Oxfordshire

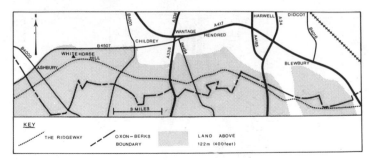

Map 60: Churn & the Fair Mile

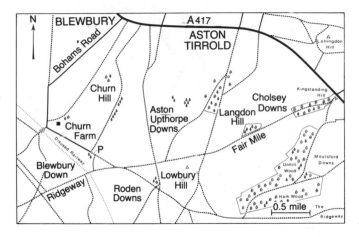

Map 61: The Warren & Ginge Down

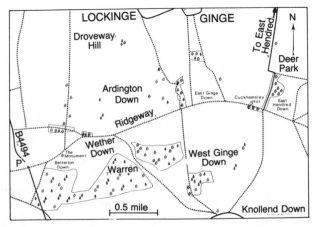

Map 62: Farmoor Reservoirs

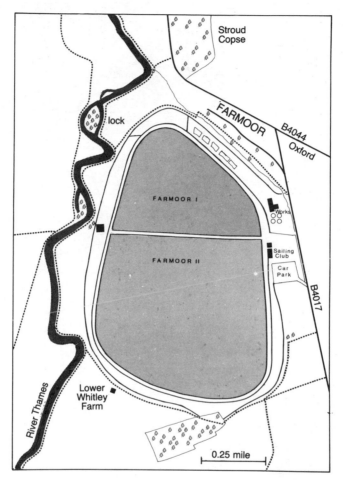

Map 63: Foxholes

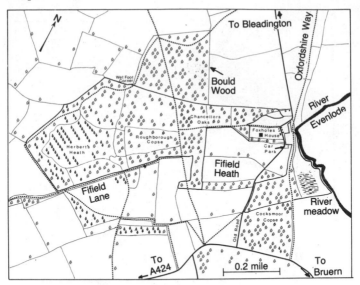

Map 64: Grimsbury Reservoir

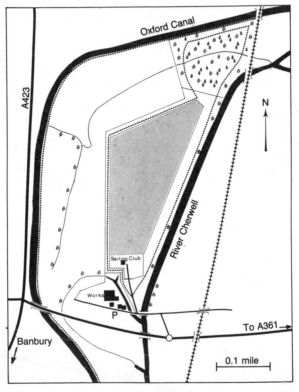

Map 65: Little Wittenham Nature Reserve

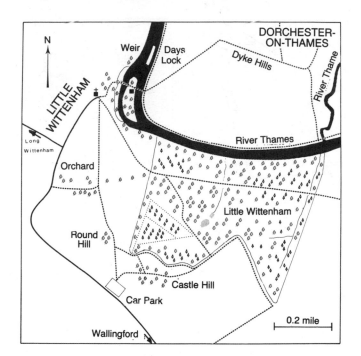

Map 66: Lower Windrush Valley Gravel Pits

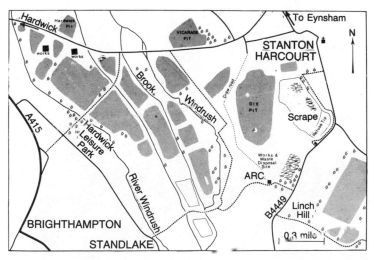

Map 67: Otmoor

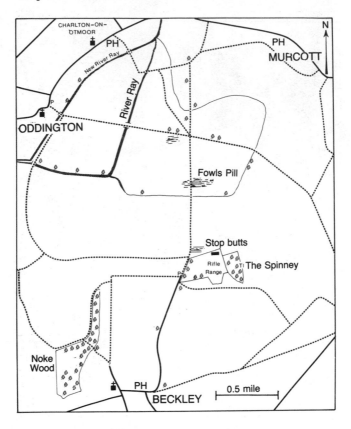

Map 68: Port Meadow

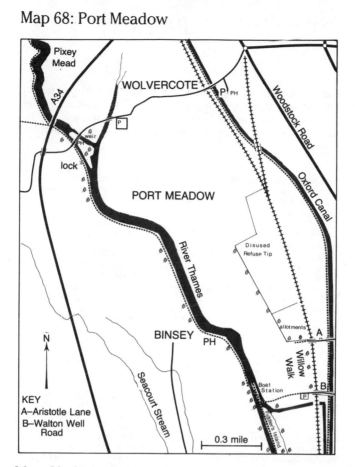

KEY
A—Aristotle Lane
B—Walton Well Road

0.3 mile

Map 69: Shotover Country Park

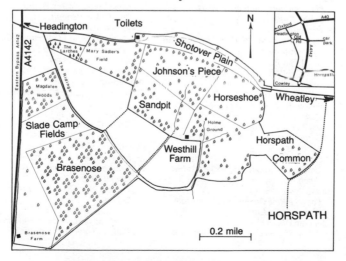

0.2 mile

INDEX

The index takes the form of a list of all sites referred to in this book, together with the page number concerned. In addition, a brief summary of the more notable birds that may be seen at each site is included, although of course it cannot be guaranteed that they will be found on each visit.

314

INDEX